Machine-Aided Linguistic Discovery

Machine-Aided Linguistic Discovery

An Introduction and Some Examples

Vladimir Pericliev

Equinox Publishing Ltd

LONDON • OAKVILLE

Published by

UK: Equinox Publishing Ltd., Unit 6, The Village, 101 Amies St., London SW11 2JW

USA: DBBC, 28 Main Street, Oakville, CT 06779

www.equinoxpub.com

First published 2010

British Library Cataloguing-in-Publication Data

A catalogue record for this book is available from the British Library.

ISBN-13   978 1 84553 660 2   (hardback)

Library of Congress Cataloging-in-Publication Data

Pericliev, Vladimir.
 Machine-aided linguistic discovery : an introduction and some examples
/ Vladimir Pericliev.
    p. cm.
 Includes bibliographical references and index.
 ISBN 978-1-84553-660-2 (hb)
 1. Computational linguistics. I. Title. P98.P473 2010
 410.285--dc22
                        2009025102

Typeset by Vladimir Pericliev
Printed and bound in Great Britain by Lightning Source UK Ltd, Milton Keynes

Contents

Introduction

Linguistics may be viewed from two perspectives, as a result or as a process. From the first perspective, linguistics is the body of knowledge accumulated throughout the ages, while from the second, it is the problem solving processes, or methods, that (may) have led to the accumulation of this knowledge. The book is devoted to the latter aspect, to "linguistics in the making", or linguistic discovery.

Linguistic discovery is a multi-faceted phenomenon, inviting two essentially different approaches, having their close parallels in linguistics in the discrimination between descriptive and normative grammars. One of them, the descriptive approach, usually adopted by historians of linguistics, studies, in a broad context, how specific discoveries of outstanding linguists have taken place. The normative approach to linguistic discovery, adopted by linguistic methodology and philosophy of linguistics, in contrast, addresses the "logic of discovery", or the methods and processes that can increase our chances of making a discovery, with little or no attention at all on whether and how this logic has been applied to make specific discoveries in specific historical environments. Machine, or machine-aided, linguistic discovery, which is the topic of this book, is the discipline concerned with automating research methods and with how computer programs can act as collaborators to linguists in their investigation process. I thus basically adopt a normative approach to discovery in searching for new linguistic knowledge, although it should be noted that machine discovery is not in principle limited to this approach, and in the early stages of the development of the field computer programs were almost exclusively focused on replicating great scientific discoveries, given as initial information that available to the original discoverers. In order to avoid this indefiniteness, in the book I prefer the term "machine-aided discovery" to "machine discovery", as the former term makes my goals more explicit.

Machine-aided linguistic discovery is a novel area, generally unfamiliar to the vast majority of practising linguists. Indeed, computational linguists are predominantly concerned with Natural Language Processing (NLP), while the computationally uninitiated linguists either do not suspect the need for automation of part of their work, or limit themselves to mere computational storage of large bulks of data or to the use of programs for routine, uncreative tasks. Intelligent programs for doing linguistics on the other hand are in principle rare, as a rule difficult to comprehend by a general audience, and mostly published in disparate computationally specialized and/or not widely known journals/proceedings. Also, current work in the area is almost exclusively limited to historical linguistics and not always has led to impressive linguistic results. This book is intended as a further contribution to the development of the field by presenting in a more accessible manner, and in one place, a general view and several intelligent programs automating different tasks, and by showing their applicability to a wide variety of problems whose solutions are considered both creative and important.

I propose to view linguistic discovery as a process in which the original problems linguists encounter are reduced to "tasks", or well-defined problems, recurrent across linguistic disciplines (and indeed outside of linguistics), which linguists need to perform in order to find a solution. One problem usually dissolves into a sequence of general-scientific tasks (such as concept formation and revision, taxonomy/classification formation and revision, pattern/law inference, multiple-concept discrimination, etc.) and meta-scientific tasks, imposing some further constraints on these solutions (such as their being the simplest and/or plausible). It is argued that insofar as many of these tasks may be computationally complex and generally beyond human reach, they require automation. In such situations, the difference between having and not having computational tools to handle them not infrequently amounts to the difference between finding and not finding a solution at all. The basic goals of the book are to introduce the basic conceptual apparatus of this theory of machine-aided linguistic discovery, to isolate and automate some computationally complex tasks, and to apply the resultant systems to substantial problems from diverse linguistic fields. Thus, the book may serve as an introduction to machine-aided linguistic discovery, arguing for the fruitfulness of the computational approach by presenting a theory and illustrating it with a number of credible examples.

Chapter 1 introduces the basic notional apparatus: a definition of linguistic discovery is given, and the objects and types of linguistic discovery are discussed, illustrating them with four path-breaking discoveries from the history of linguistics. The chapter also briefly reviews some more important work in the field of (linguistic) machine discovery, as well as introduces the idea of task of linguistic discovery.

Chapters 2 to 7 are devoted to examples. They present several computational systems, integrating mechanisms for handling two (or more) computationally complex tasks, usually a general scientific and a meta-scientific one.

Chapter 2 describes the KINSHIP program, performing componential analysis of kinship terminologies. The KINSHIP system incorporates multiple-concept discrimination and a simplicity check, thus accomplishing a guaranteed-simplest discrimination of kin terms. The system models the fundamental Saussurian notion of "linguistic system", and thus, for the first time, after almost a century after the introduction of this concept and structuralism in general, linguists are capable to handle adequately this recurring difficult task.

Chapter 3 describes the Maximally Parsimonious Discrimination (MPD) program, which extends the functional capabilities of KINSHIP (e.g. with partial, or statistical, discrimination). It shows the generality of the task of parsimonious discrimination by illustrating its application to a variety of linguistic problems like distinctive feature analysis, and the profiling of the world languages in terms of their segment inventories.

Chapter 4 introduces the UNIVAUTO (UNIVersals AUthoring TOol) system, which incorporates pattern/law inference and a simplicity and plausibility (significance) check. This is another recurring linguistic task, modelling e.g. the problem of searching for Greenbergian language universals. Importantly, the program states its discoveries in an intelligible form, viz. a comprehensive English language text, thus constituting the first computer program to generate a whole scientific article.

Chapter 5 describes the application of UNIVAUTO to phonological universals. The system was applied to the UPSID-451 database and discovered and verbalized in English 146 plausible implicational universals, holding between a pair of segments. A meta-universal is derived, nicely describing the recurrent patterns in the found list of universals in terms of feature values.

Chapter 6 describes the MINTYP (Minimum TYPological description) program, which combines the task of pattern/law discovery and that of ensuring the simplicity of the found patterns. Given a typology as input, the system computes a minimal set of implicational universals that describe all and only the attested types in the typology.

Chapter 7 deals with the RECLASS system, which implements the task of classification revision by checking whether a member of some class does not bear greater-than-chance similarities to members of a different class, and therefore there exists an eventual misclassification, necessitating classification revision. This program models the common problem of searching for anomalies/errors in language genetic classification.

The systems presented in the book are applied to diverse linguistic problems from the domains of phonology, lexical semantics, typology, historical linguistics, etc. Some notable discoveries of the systems include: the first componential analyses of the kinship terminological system of English conforming to all generally accepted criteria for adequateness, which is furthermore the simplest one known so far (KINSHIP); the simplest distinctive feature analysis of Russian phonemes (MPD); the discovery and verbalization in English of a sizable number of novel phonological universals (UNIVAUTO); the discovery of minimal accounts of the word order typologies proposed by Greenberg and Hawkins (MINTYP). The RECLASS program made the most unexpected discovery that the Kaingang language family on the Atlantic coast of Brazil (currently classified as Macro-Ge) bears greater-than-chance similarities to the Austronesian family spoken in the Pacific in both kinship patterns and in 100-item basic vocabulary lists, suggesting some historical relationship between these families. This computer-generated hypothesis was subsequently supported by manual detection of regular sound correspondences between these families and diagnostic similarities in their phonological and grammatical structure, as well as by evidence from population genetics. The hypothesis has far-reaching linguistic and general scientific implications (e.g. probable trans-Pacific migrations for the peopling of the Americas). Also, beside the discovery of novel knowledge, the application of the programs consistently showed errors in the human solutions, including in such proposed by authoritative linguists like Jakobson and Halle, Greenberg, Hawkins, Maddieson, etc., thus providing further support for our computational approach.

To the best of my knowledge, this monograph is the first book-length treatment of the field of machine-aided linguistic discovery, so I hope its appearance would fill a gap and would seem timely in the context of the recent increased general scientific and linguistic interest in "machine thinking", as witnessed e.g. by the 2006 Special Issue '2020 Computing' of the *Nature* magazine or the US National Science Foundation multi-disciplinary, multi-year initiative "Cyber-Enabled Discovery and Innovation", launched in 2007 and announced on the Linguist List.

The book summarizes some results from my research on linguistic and machine discovery over the last twenty years. The KINSHIP and MPD programs were designed in collaboration with computer scientist Raúl E. Valdés-Pérez from Carnegie Mellon University, and co-founder of Vivisimo, Inc., though each of us implemented a separate program in a different programming language (Lisp or Prolog). These programs owe a great deal to Raúl's knowledge and ingenuity. I am also much indebted to other friends from disciplines as diverse as physics and biology, theoretical mathematics, linguistics, and computer science for their expert aid and support. I also gratefully acknowledge financial support for my investigations during the years from the US National Science Foundation, a Marie Curie grant from the European Commission and grants from the Bulgarian Ministry of Education and Science. Grateful acknowledgement is due to the Institute for Mathematics and Informatics of the Bulgarian Academy of Sciences, where I have had the freedom to pursue my research interests and conducted most of the reported work.

Material from the following journal articles is included in the book with the kind permission of the publishers:

1. Implicational phonological universals, published by *Folia Linguistica* (2008).

2. There is no correlation between the size of a community speaking a language and the size of the phonological inventory of that language, published by *Linguistic Typology* (2004).

3. Economy in formulating typological generalizations, published by *Linguistic Typology* (2002).

4. The Kaingang (Brazil) seem linguistically related to Oceanic populations, published by *Journal of Universal Language* (2007).

5. Universals, their violation and the notion of phonologically peculiar languages, published by *Journal of Universal Language* (2004).

6. Automatic componential analysis of kinship semantics with a proposed structural solution to the problem of multiple models, published by *Anthropological Linguistics* (1998) [with Raúl E. Valdés-Pérez].

7. Computer enumeration of significant implicational universals of kinship terminology, published by *Cross-Cultural Research* (1999) [with Raúl E. Valdés-Pérez].

8. More statistical implicational universals in Greenberg's data (another computer-generated article), published by *Contrastive Linguistics* (2000).

Sofia,
April 2009

Chapter 1. Introducing the Basic Notions

Machine, or machine-aided, linguistic discovery is a discipline concerned with the automated solving of (substantial parts) of important linguistic problems. In this chapter, I introduce some preliminary notions, using as illustrations four famous discoveries from the history of linguistics, viz. Saussure's discovery of the concept of "linguistic system", Jones's discovery of Indo-European, Greenberg's implicational universals, and Verner's law. I define linguistic discovery and look at objects and types of linguistic discovery, then discuss the major factors for discovery: intuition, chance, and problem solving. Previous attempts at automating the (linguistic) discovery process are briefly reviewed, and the central notion of "task of linguistic discovery" is introduced.

1.1 What is a linguistic discovery?

From a pragmatic point of view, a "linguistic discovery" (and more generally, scientific discovery) can be defined as a finding which is publishable. Such a definition is common in the literature on machine scientific discovery, as it reflects a human assessment of the merits of the results obtained by computer systems. Acceptance by reviewers and editors in specialized journals is a good sign of machine success. However, though useful in machine scientific discovery contexts, such a purely pragmatic definition does not specify the features that demarcate a finding which is publishable from one which is not. When do we say that a finding is a discovery? Or, put differently, what criteria do reviewers and editors employ in assessing a result as a substantial advance in knowledge, and hence publishable? There are several defining features which we normally use in order to label a finding a discovery. Apart from the self-evident requirement of its *truthfulness*, the finding additionally also needs to possess *novelty*, *unexpectedness* and *importance*.

These characteristic features of a discovery (and their combinations) are logically independent of one another, i.e. neither feature implies logically another feature. Thus, e.g. the claim that none of the languages known today are genetically related would be novel, unexpected and most important, as it would change our whole present conception of language growth and change, but apparently false. As another example of logical independence, to find that a previously insufficiently studied language — known to be a member of some language family, which typically possesses some property — also possesses this very property, would be true, novel and relatively important, yet a quite expected finding, as all or most of the languages of the family also have the property, and one expects features of the parent language to be inherited by descendent languages. Despite their logical independence, however, the characteristic features of a discovery are not wholly unrelated, and the presence of one feature may enhance or undermine another feature. For example, we tend to consider unexpected findings as more important and expected ones as less important, insofar as only in the former case they not only cumulatively enlarge, but also challenge, our previous knowledge; also, we are apt to consider a finding with more chances of being true as more important than one that seems to have less chances of being valid.

1.1.1 Some prototypical examples

There are small and big linguistic discoveries and in any one of them one can trace the essential features of a discovery, though perhaps present to a different degree. For illustrative purposes, however, it is better to look at some groundbreaking rather than smaller linguistic achievements, and below I turn to several such peaks from the history of linguistic thought.

1.1.1.1 Saussure and the notion "linguistic system"

Ferdinand de Saussure (1857–1913) is generally considered the founding father of "structural linguistics" with his posthumously published *Course in General Linguistics* (*Cours de linguistique générale*, 1916), written by his students Charles Bally and Albert Sechehaye on the basis of their lecture notes at the University of Geneva during 1907–1911. Saussure created a sophisticated and coherent linguistic theory, which we do not need to discuss here, at the heart of which lay the notion of "linguistic system". Language (*langue*), Saussure taught, is a system in the sense that the meaning or value (*valeur*) of all linguistic entities can only be determined by their *contrasts, distinctions* from all other entities in the same system. "*In the language itself, there are only differences*", wrote Saussure (Saussure 1996[1916]: 118; italics in original), "A linguistic system is a series of phonetic differences matched with a series of conceptual differences" (op. cit., p. 118). A central task of linguistics, according to Saussure, is to reveal the structure of linguistic systems by applying the *structural method* of contrasts and oppositions.

Saussure's idea of language as a system was new in that it broke a long tradition in Western thought dominant from Plato on of viewing language as just an inventory of names (whatever they stood for, ideas or things in the external world), and the goal of language science as relating these names (whether derived from the true nature of things or by convention) to ready made ideas and things given in advance of language. Saussure, in contrast to this view, writes:

> In all these cases [illustrations] what we find, instead of *ideas* given in advance, are *values* emanating from the linguistic system. If we say that these values correspond to certain concepts, it must be understood that the concepts in question are purely differential. That is to say they are concepts defined not positively, in terms of their content, but negatively by contrast with other items in the same system. What characterises each most exactly is being whatever the others are not. (Saussure 1996[1916]: 115; italics in original)

The extent of novelty in these ideas was emphasized for instance by Louis Hjelmslev who attributed some infelicity in Saussure's exposition of his theory in his lectures to the fact that Saussure's observations opened before linguists paths so completely new, that it came as no surprise that Saussure himself had to struggle with traditional views.

Saussure's structuralism was also quite unexpected in the context of late 19th and early 20th century linguistic thought. Nothing in the atomistic approach to language, characteristic of the then prevalent Neogrammarian school, led or even suggested such a radical turn of approach. Saussure himself was of course fully aware of the unexpected nature of his idea of system and its consequences, and at various places in the *Cours* characterizes his idea or its consequences as "surprising", "striking", etc.

The importance of the idea of language as a system, and structuralism in general, cannot be overstated. It influenced both researchers in linguistics and outside of linguistics. Within linguistics, the structural method came to be recognized as an indispensable tool at all levels of linguistic analysis: phonology ("distinctive feature analysis"), semantics ("structural semantics"), morphology, etc. Transformationalists (esp. Chomsky) emphasized that formal, generative grammar as a whole is a "systemic notion" in that a simplification in some component led to more complexities in another component. Also, the idea gave rise to different linguistic trends like the Praguean school (Trubetzkoy, Jakobson), the Copenhagen school (Hjelmslev) and American structuralism (Bloomfield, Bloch, Harris, etc.). Outside of linguistics, the principles and methods of structuralism were adopted by scholars of such diverse areas as anthropology (Claude Lévi-Strauss), psychoanalysis (Lacan) and literary criticism (Barthes) and implemented in their respective areas of study. According to Assiter (1984), there are four common ideas regarding structuralism that form an "intellectual trend". First, the structure is what determines the position of each element of a whole. Secondly, structuralists believe that every system has a structure. Thirdly, structuralists are interested in "structural" laws that deal with coexistence rather than changes. And, finally, structures are the "real things" that lie beneath the surface or the appearance of meaning.

1.1.1.2 Sir William Jones and the discovery of Indo-European

Sir William Jones (1746–1794) was an English philologist and student of ancient India, particularly known for his suggestion of the existence of a relationship among Indo-European languages. On February 2 1786, in *The Third Anniversary Discourse, On the Hindus*, he made his famous and widely cited pronouncement to this effect:

> The *Sanscrit* language, whatever be its antiquity, is of a wonderful structure; more perfect than the *Greek*, more copious than the *Latin*, and more exquisitely refined than either, yet bearing to both of them a stronger affinity, both in the roots of verbs and in the forms of grammar, than could possibly have been produced by accident; so strong indeed, that no philologer could examine them all three, without believing them to have sprung from some common source, which, perhaps, no longer exists: there is a similar reason, though not quite so forcible, for supposing that both the *Gothick* and the *Celtick*, though blended with a very different idiom, had the same origin with the *Sanscrit*; and the old *Persian* might be added to the same family, if this were the place for discussing any question concerning the antiquities of *Persia*. (*Works 3*: 34–35)

This family is today known as Indo-European.

The idea of affinity between the old European languages and Sanskrit was novel in the context of the views prevalent at the time. Genetic language classification before Jones was to a great extent based on the Babel story and the dispersion of the descendants of Noah: Shem, Ham, and Japheth. It was assumed that the number of world languages was seventy two, following the Bible tradition, and these languages were assigned a specific lineage in accordance with Noah's descendents. The belief in this theory was so strong indeed that if languages unknown to the Bible story were encountered, they could be included in the list of world languages only at the expense of others.

Jones's suggestion was most unexpected. First, it posited a genetic relatedness between languages that were geographically very distant, Sanskrit being many thousands of miles away from the classic European languages. Secondly, who would like to admit, at that time, kinship between the civilized Western races and a supposedly "savage" race like the Indians? It required both a penetrating and an unbiased mind in order to recognize such a relationship.

The importance of Jones's discovery cannot be overestimated. It is generally considered as the beginning of 19th century historical and comparative linguistics. Thus, in a standard history of linguistics, it is written that "If any single year can, albeit artificially, be taken to mark of the contemporary world of linguistic science, it is the year 1786." (Robins 1967: 134). Hockett (1965: 53) characterizes this discovery as the first of the only four really important breakthroughs in linguistics as a whole. From a purely linguistic perspective, this discovery not only was a decisive step in the shaping of the ideas as to what languages constituted the Indo-European family, but significantly, brought to the attention of linguists the previously unstudied Sanskrit, which happened to be both in some respects older, and thus nearer to the original prototype, and structurally quite transparent, and thus allowing linguists to gain a much better understanding of the family as a whole and to more easily work out reconstructions. But this discovery was also a major advance in humanistic studies as a whole, in the study of human prehistory and migrations, Indian and eastern culture, mythology, etc., the primary targets of Jones, who only viewed linguistics as a subsidiary science serving to throw light on these fundamental problems of the history of mankind.

1.1.1.3 Greenberg and word order universals

Joseph Greenberg (1915–2001) made significant contributions to various fields of linguistics including the study of African languages, language classification, and typology. His famous paper *Some universals of grammar with particular reference to the order of meaningful elements* from 1966 marks the beginning of modern word order typology and the quest for "empirical" universals, based on an explicit and representative sample of the world languages. Greenberg compiled two samples of wide genetic and areal coverage, introduced the notion of "implicational universal", as a statement of the form "If a language has the property X, it will also have the property Y", which could be "non-statistical" (i.e.

valid with no exceptions) or "statistical" (i.e. valid with some minor exceptions). He then proposed an ordering typology, based on the relative position of Verb (V), Subject (S) and Object (O). He noted that three of the logically possible relative orders are actually attested in the world languages: SVO (e.g. English), SOV (e.g. Japanese), and VSO (e.g. Welsh), while the remaining three possibilities, VOS, OVS and OSV, were excessively rare. The three isolated and attested types, viz. SVO and VSO on the one hand, and SOV on the other, naturally grouped in two, VO–languages and OV–languages (a step explicitly made by Lehmann and Vennemann, following Greenberg). This allowed a bipartite typology with high predictive power. Thus, being a VO–language implied — possibly with some exceptions — the orderings Verb – Object, Auxiliary – Main Verb, Preposition – Noun, etc. (cf. left-hand column below), while being an OV–language implied, possibly with some exceptions, the mirror image of these orderings (cf. right-hand column):

VO–languages imply	OV–languages imply
Verb – Object	Object – Verb
Auxiliary – Main Verb	Main Verb – Auxiliary
Preposition – Noun	Noun – Preposition
Noun – Relative Clause	Relative Clause – Noun
Noun – Possessive	Possessive – Noun
Noun – Adjective	Adjective – Noun
Noun – Demonstrative	Demonstrative – Noun
Noun – Number	Number – Noun

Despite the fact that the correlation between the position of verb and object and other word order characteristics had been noted at least as far back as 19th century linguistics, as Greenberg himself acknowledged (Greenberg 1966a: 105; fn. 4), the orderliness of his findings and their breadth, as well as the form of their statement as implications was novel to the general linguistic public. The proposal of a word order typology, based on these universals, was also quite unexpected in the context of current linguistics at the time, all previous typologies employing morphological criteria, and classifying languages into isolating, agglutinative and inflectional (later adding a fourth type, incorporating).

Greenberg's work on universals had great impact upon typology, and linguistics in general. First, it initiated a number of works intended to provide a unitary explanation of the empirically observed universals in word order. Secondly, the quest for universals was extended from word order to other areas of linguistics like phonology, semantics, etc. Thirdly, Greenberg's paper set a more rigorous standard for the work in the area, obligatorily comprising the archiving of data, or explicitly stating the database used to make the observations, and an explicit listing (numeration) of the universals, thus allowing both the test of the proposed universals against the data and further research on the same data.

1.1.1.4 Verner's law

Karl Verner (1846–1896) is remembered today for what is known as "Verner's law", an amendment to Grimm's law, which he discovered in 1875. According to Grimm, the Indo-European consonants [*p, t, k, s*] developed correspondingly into Germanic [*f, þ, x, s*] in word-initial, medial, or final position. Grimm was not bothered by a number of exceptions to his formulation, in which the original Indo-European consonants developed, contrary to prediction, into the voiced counterparts [*b, d, g, z*], respectively. A striking example occurs in Germanic kinship terms: whereas Germanic *brôþar* 'brother' regularly shifts from Indo-European *bhrâtar*, following Grimm's rule IE *t* = Gmc *þ*, the Germanic terms *môdar* 'mother' and *fadar* 'father', correlative to the Indo-European relationship terms *mâtar*, *patar*, do not follow the rule and exhibit the shift IE *t* = Gmc *d*. Verner showed that the Indo-European placement of stress was the cause for this development, as follows: if the immediately preceding syllable did not bear primary stress, then the alternate forms (the voiced versions) were produced; otherwise, the forms complying with Grimm's rule resulted. Thus, the enigma *brôþar*, *môdar*, *fadar* was resolved. The Sanskrit (and Indo-European) accentuation is *bhrâtar–*, but *mâtár–*, *pitár–*, and according to Verner's law, in Germanic we must have *brôþar* in contrast to *môdar*, *fadar*. It is worth noting that, chronologically, Verner's law describes a development that must have occurred after Grimm's law (because Grimm's Law provides most of its input) and before the Germanic shift of stress to the initial syllable (because the voicing is conditioned by the older location of stress).

Verner's explanation of the exceptions to Grimm's law was original. While Grimm was aware of the existence of exceptions to his rule, but did not seem to bother about this fact, others have not been able to find an adequate explanation. Actually, the only person who had sought an answer to this question was Scherer who proposed that the shift to voiced stops occurred "in frequently used words (like *fadar*, *môdar*)", consequently the regular shift occurred in less frequently used words.

Verner undermined this explanation by noting the implausibility of the claim that *fadar* and *môdar* were used more frequently than *brôþar*. Besides, he remarked, in Ulfila's writings *môdar* does not even appear, the word *aiþei* always being used instead; and he uses *fadar* only once, otherwise however *atta*, while his *broþar* has no parallel synonym at all. Thus, it was Verner who offered a new and compelling account, and it was immediately accepted by his contemporaries on the strength of his argumentation.

Verner's finding furthermore was quite unexpected. He found the crucial evidence where few people would dream of looking for, viz. in Greek and Sanskrit, while everyone else had tacitly assumed that Germanic changes can be explained in Germanic terms without recourse to external comparison. Verner's discovery was also most unexpected in that no researcher before him had attempted to explain the sound shift by the location of the accent in older forms (a circumstance, which might have been triggered by Verner's study at the time of accentuation in Danish and Slavic languages, but which in no way undermines the unexpectedness of the finding).

Verner's paper is labelled by Winfred Lehmann (1967) "the single most influential publication in linguistics". First, Verner's article was important because it made an essential amendment to Grimm's law, which was itself important. Secondly, attention was drawn to suprasegmentals, and publications after Verner are full of articles proposing explanations of linguistic phenomena by means of accent. And, thirdly, and perhaps most importantly, the article had tremendous methodological impact. While Grimm noted only in passing problems like the –d– in Gothic *fadar* and the like, and Lottner and Grassmann clarified only some of the exceptions, while other exceptions still remained unaccounted for, Verner managed to explain all residues, and from then on it became the methodological standard that sound change is mechanical and goes without exception, and therefore the linguist must explain all the data. Actually, Verner had phrased this more mildly, in the following memorable words:

> Comparative linguistics cannot, to be sure, completely deny the element of chance; but chance occurrence en masse as here, where the instances of irregular shifting are nearly as frequent as those of regular shifting, it cannot and may not admit. That is to say, in such a case there must be a rule for the irregularity; it only remains to discover this. (Verner 1875, quote from translation by Lehmann 1967)

* * *

It is worth noting that the defining features of a discovery are not categorical (yes/no), but are rather graded, degree notions, and any one finding possesses them to a different degree. Besides, in some cases they are less than uncontroversial and unambiguous, and their predication of a finding may cause some complexities. This, of course, may have wider implications, but a detailed discussion of similar matters is beyond the scope of the present book. The goal of the following remarks is simply to give some illustrations to this effect from the discoveries we have so far considered.

At the start, we may note that even the feature of truthfulness, which seems an indispensable characteristic of any discovery, does not seem to be appropriate in the cases of a discovery of a "hypothesis", which is by definition a proposition with an unknown truth value, or of a "principle", which, under some understandings, is a proposition without truth value (i.e. it is neither true nor false, but only convenient). Even more importantly, in every science as linguistics, which is fundamentally based on inductive generalizations (in contrast to mathematics, based on deductive inferences), universal inductive generalizations may be plausible or probable, but, strictly speaking, cannot be proven to be true insofar as any further observation may eventually falsify them.

The feature of a finding's importance may also cause complexities. For example, some observations which we consider as a trifle today may eventually turn out to be crucial evidence in a solution to a problem which we conceive as important, in which case we could hardly deny the importance of the observations themselves. Conversely, many ideas that were considered important at some time in linguistics are long forgotten. Language is much too complex a phenomenon for us to be able to predict precisely the "usefulness" of any finding we make.

One of the greatest difficulties, however, is presented by the question of whether an idea is novel or not, a circumstance well known to philosophers and historians of linguistics investigating priority, to which I turn below.

Thus, Saussure's idea of language as a system is essentially holistic in that language's constituent parts cannot exist independently of the whole, and in Saussure's time such holistic ideas were not uncommon in neighbouring disciplines such as sociology and psychology. In sociology, Durkheim held that there exists an order of facts that are the properties of collectivities, not individuals, and cannot be reduced to facts about individuals. Before him, Spencer and Darwin conceived societies as "organisms" whose parts cannot exist independently of the whole. In Gestalt psychology at the end of the 19th and the beginning of the 20th century, holistic theories of different aspects of human behaviour (from perception to problem solving) were widely popular. Even in linguistics itself, the notion of "system", often used interchangeably with "organism", was not unknown, as seen for instance from the review by Koerner (1973: 357–60). However, the extent to which Saussure borrowed, or was indeed influenced by any of these sources, is a matter of debate. The depth and insightfulness with which he developed this idea and its applicability to linguistics in the *Cours* make it safe to grant the originality of his contribution.

Far more controversial seems Sir William Jones' discovery. In actual fact, he was not the first to note the link of Sanskrit with the Old World languages. Thus, first, Jesuit missionaries to India as far back as the 16th century were commenting on the similarity of Greek or other European languages to Sanskrit. The first known reference is the Italian Filippo Sasseti, noting a number of similarities in words between Italian and Sanskrit. The German B. Schultze and the Frenchman Coeurdoux noticed resemblances between Sanskrit and some European languages (cf. Robins 1967: 135). Some of these missionaries made the leap to families of language, and some did not, but what is important is that the observation of similarity was common.

Secondly, as Cloyd (1969) notes, James Burnett, Lord Monboddo (1714–1799), mentions a possible affinity between Greek and Sanskrit in the second volume of his *Origin and Progress of Language* (pp. 530–531), a work that first appeared in Edinburgh on February 23, 1774, that is 12 years before Sir William Jones's Address. Monboddo argued that the languages are so similar in their fundamental systems that one must assume not that one language is derived from the other, but rather that "both Indians and Greeks got their language, and all their other arts, from the same parent-country". In establishing a link between Greek and Sanskrit, Monboddo was implicitly relating Sanskrit to other Indo-European languages, for he had already linked Greek to other languages of Europe.

Finally, Jones at the time was not the best informed linguist to make this pronouncement. It is known that Jones began his serious study of Sanskrit in September, 1785, which, importantly, was less than four months before Jones made his famous pronouncement. Four months were apparently a period of time insufficient for mastering the language. In his first mention of affinity between Greek and Sanskrit, Monboddo indeed also did not have personal knowledge of Sanskrit, but had based his assessment, from what he understood of the structure of roots and elements, on similar "remote analogies and distant relations of things", using as information on Sanskrit a letter dated November 22, 1740, from a Jesuit missionary in India Père Pons. Lord Monboddo, however, also made a second mention of the relationship between Greek and Sanskrit in the fourth volume of his *Origin and Progress of Language* reaching London in 1878, in which he better supported his claim by comparing a series of verbs in both languages, now having improved his knowledge of Sanskrit from Nathaniel Brassey Halhed's *Code of Gentoo Laws* (London, 1776), in whose introduction a more detailed description of the inflection and etymology of the language is presented. Besides, Monboddo had also studied Sanskrit in London under Charles Wilkins.

Summing up, Jones was neither the first to surmise the affinity of Sanskrit with the Old World languages nor was he the most well-informed linguist on Sanskrit at the time (taking for granted the then common knowledge of the classic European languages, which was the other indispensable information for making the comparison). In response to a paper by Cannon (1968), which seems to suggest that Jones influenced Monboddo, Cloyd (1969), who holds that it is rather Monboddo who influenced Jones, assesses the facts in the following manner:

> There is no point whatever, at this date in history, in trying to deprive Sir William Jones of the credit he has, and, in a sense, deserves for leading philologists in the right direction. <...> What must be said is simply this: if Sir William Jones was not the first or the best informed to speak, at least he spoke at the right moment to the right audience, and perhaps, in the end, this is what really matters. (Cloyd 1969: 1135)

One could hardly disagree with these words in the sense that what is of primary importance for linguistics is the ultimate result and not so much who obtained this result. At the same time, however, in the historical assessment of scientific contribution in this particular case it seems that linguistic authority and other social factors have won over real originality.

Finally, let us turn to Joseph Greenberg and the idea of implicational universals, which has dominated linguistic typology from the 60s on. To the general linguistic public, we owe this idea to Greenberg, and this is indeed true to the extent that it became *popular* via his seminal paper on the ordering of meaningful elements in 1966. In actual fact, however, as we learn from Greenberg himself, who has always been scrupulous to acknowledge debt to other linguists, he borrowed the idea of implicational universal and related notions and *discovered for himself* its implications. Greenberg actually borrowed it from the Prague school of structuralism via Roman Jakobson whom Greenberg met at the New York Linguistic Circle. In his paper *The influence of Word and the Linguistic Circle of New York on my intellectual development* (Greenberg 1994), he acknowledges his interest to universal aspects of languages to be due on the one hand to the psychologist Osgood, noting that what would interest a psychologist would be what is common to all languages, and to "the influence of Jakobson, who talked about universal implicational relationships" (p. 23). The story, told by Greenberg himself, is the following:

> By 1953–1954 then, I had clearly been influenced by the Prague structuralism that I encountered at Columbia and in the Linguistic Circle. In a sense, it was still a blooming, buzzing confusion like that of the infant as described in a famous passage by Henry James the psychologist. Somehow, typology, linguistic change, marking and universals must be connected. However, it was not until I did my paper on word order, first given at the Behavioral Sciences Center at Stanford in 1959, where also during the same academic year the memorandum on Language Universals was written by Jenkins, Osgood and me in preparation for the Dobbs Ferry Conference on Language Universals held in 1961, that the interconnection between marking, typology and universals began to take form. Put briefly, we can state them as follows. In the relation between the marked and the unmarked, whenever there is a universal implication, the unmarked is the implied. In a typological scheme, the non-existence of a particular type is logically equivalent to a universal, usually an implicational one. For example, the non-existence of languages which were VSO and post-positional could be stated in the following fashion. If a language is VSO, this implies that it is prepositional. Although these conditions are easy to state, they required a number of years to gradually mature in my mind. I recall that at one point, as the key role of implicational universals became clear to me, I had what German psychologists called *Aha-Erlebnis*. So this was what Jakobson was driving at all these years! (Greenberg 1994: 24)

1.1.2 Objects of linguistic discovery

Broadly speaking, linguistics is the study of specific languages, language in general, and the relation of language to the world, to the culture of society, and to the psychology of man. However, what epistemological kinds of objects do linguists discover, or what is the structure of the pieces of knowledge that constitute the body of the acquired linguistic knowledge? Traditional philosophy of science has equipped us with the conceptual apparatus of dealing with the structure of units of scientific knowledge (for a more detailed linguistic discussion, placed in a broader philosophical context, cf. e.g. Botha 1981).

The simplest and fundamental linguistic knowledge structure is the *concept*, used to describe linguistic phenomena. Thus, early linguistics arrived at the concepts of "sentence" and "words", which are the component parts of the sentence. Within the concept of words, some words were found to designate an object or a person ("nouns"), while others an action or a state ("verbs"), etc.

Some of the discovered concepts may be found to be organizable into a hierarchy, or *taxonomy*. For example, the words in the sentence have been found to form a hierarchy, or a taxonomy, as they group into phrases, which themselves form increasingly higher-order phrases, and ultimately the sentence. A more "usual" type of taxonomy would be the morphological division into "parts of speech", in which all words are split into categories like "verb", "noun", "adjective", "adverb", etc., these categories split into sub-categories (e.g. the verb into transitive, intransitive), the latter into sub-sub-categories, etc. Throughout the history of linguistics, a lot of effort has been invested into building this taxonomy. A typical taxonomy from the field of historical linguistics would be the grouping of the languages of the world into language families, and one great such discovery is the postulation of the Indo-European language family we have already talked about.

Another object of linguistic discovery are *inductive generalizations* (or *empirical laws*), expressed as relations between concepts. The role of inductive generalizations in linguistics cannot be overstated and e.g. has found expression in the well-known dictum of Bloomfield (1933) that the only valid generalizations about language are empirical generalizations. We have already mentioned the famous Greenberg's universals of word order, which are generalizations of this form.

Linguistic *theories* are more complex linguistic knowledge structures, usually comprising a set of concepts and empirical laws that are explained by these theories. A common example of a theory is Phrase Structure Grammar. Such a grammar comprises a non-terminal vocabulary (NP, VP, etc.), a terminal vocabulary (word strings), and an initial symbol S(entence), which are the concepts of the language theory. The re-write rules (S $\rightarrow$ NP+VP, etc.) represent the "is-a" relation holding between concepts (S is-a NP and VP), and any well-formed string of words in some language can be said to be "explained" by reference to the set of grammar, or re-write rules, for that language that generate it; e.g. the string *John laughs* is a well-formed sentence because *John* is-a NP, *laughs* is-a VP, and their concatenation, NP+VP, is-a S.

An *n*-ways ambiguous word string can be explained by the presence of *n* different sequences of re-write rules that are used for its derivation. It may be noted that most linguistic (and scientific) theories have a much more complex and heterogeneous nature. Thus, theories not infrequently involve the postulation of unobservable objects or processes, as e.g. the postulation of "deep structure" in Chomskyan transformational generative grammar, which is an extension of Phrase Structure Grammar.

Other familiar objects of discovery in linguistics (and science generally) are *explanations*, which narrate the reasons (the "explanans") why whatever needs to be explained (the "explanandum") is the way it is. Thus, Verner has found the reason for violation of Grimm's law in the older Gothic accent. There are shallower and deeper explanations of the same facts, and Verner found also a deeper explanation, this explanation pertaining to articulatory reasons. Broadly, it amounts to the effect that stress requires greater articulation and thus produced a fortis (voiceless) consonant, while no stress produced the lenis (voiced) variant. In Verner's own words:

> The fact that the voiceless fricatives did not follow the general tendency and become voiced in accented syllables, is easy to explain physiologically. For the older period of Germanic we have to start with an accent which was not purely chromatic like the accent in Sanskrit and the Classical languages, but which, like modern accentuation, had something expiratory about it, that is, was based on greater activity of the muscles of expiration and to the subsequently stronger exhalation of air. The essential distinction between the voiceless and voiced consonants is dependent on the position of the vocal cords <...>. For voiceless consonants, the vocal cords are wide open; the air stream from the chest cavity has free passage: it is therefore more forceful than for voiced consonants, and this stronger expiration of air manifests itself in the stops by a more rigid muscular occlusion and a more powerful explosion. For voiced consonants on the other hand, the vocal cords are brought together almost until they touch; the narrow glottis hinders the free expiration of air; the air-stream is therefore weaker, the occlusion in the oral cavity accompanying the voiced stops and the explosion itself are not as energetic as those of the voiceless stops. Therefore, the stronger expiration of air is an element which the expiratory accent has in common with the voiceless consonants. Accordingly the intensified air-stream in the accented syllable could keep the voiceless fricative voiceless; that is, it could hinder the vocal cords from becoming narrowed for voicing, as happened with the normal expiration of air in the unaccented syllable. (Verner 1875, quote from translation by Lehmann 1967)

There exist also other linguistic discovery-objects, which we will only mention here, as *predictions* (deriving logical consequences from laws and theories), *anomalies* (facts disagreeing with currently accepted laws and theories), as well as *methods* and *problems*. All of the knowledge structures reviewed may be *revised*, as our knowledge increases in the respective aspects.

The analysis of great linguistic achievements often reveals a number of diverse discovery-objects. A nice example is furnished by Verner's contributions. Thus, he may fairly be said to have discovered:

- an anomaly in seeing a frustrating circumstance in the existence of exceptions to Grimm's law, wherever Grimm himself seemed not to bother about that fact;
- a new problem arising from this anomaly, viz. the problem to resolve the anomaly, or to find the conditioning of this sound shift;
- a revision of Grimm's law;
- an explanation of his formulation: a more shallow one, attributing Germanic exceptional forms like *fadar*, *môdar* to the older accent in Gothic, and a deeper articulatory explanation, saying why this placing of the accent results in the voicing; and
- a methodological standard for accounting for all data, and the heuristic of looking for accent and suprasegmentals in describing sound shifts.

1.1.3 Types of linguistic discovery

Some linguistic discoveries essentially involve data, and inferences from these data, while other discoveries, in contrast, involve theoretical knowledge, and logical deductions from these theoretical premises. The first type of discoveries can be falsified or supported by adducing (further) data, while the second cannot, in a similar manner, be either additionally confirmed or be falsified (the latter with the provision that the theoretical premises are true and the logical deductions sound). I shall refer to the first type of discoveries as *empirical* (or *data-driven*), and to the second as *theoretical* (or *theory-driven*) linguistic discoveries.

A typical example of empirical discovery is the set of ordering universals proposed by Greenberg. Greenberg starts his investigation with an explicit database, the 30–language sample, in which each language is described in terms of 15 features. He then, based on these data, uncovers implicational relations holding between some of these features such that are valid for all (or most) of the languages in the database (and hopefully for all languages). The universals thus found can be tested, and falsified, by his own data, or by adducing further data from other languages not in his database, as indeed some of these universals have been. In contrast to these empirical universals, sometimes called "non-definitional", there have been proposed so-called "definitional" universals, which are logically derived from theoretical linguistic knowledge, not low-level observation, and which do not depend on observation to this extent. For example, Hockett (1966: 21) has proposed, among others, the universal "Every human language has proper names". One does not conceive such a proposition from observations of relevant data from a set of diverse languages, and for testing it one does not need to recourse to such observations. Thus, the universal can be both derived and tested by the purely logical inference that, for a communication system to be deservedly called a human language, it must be capable of naming classes of objects as well as individual objects, including of course of naming of humans, animals, etc., which, ultimately, means that the language must have proper names. Not surprisingly, while Greenberg states the language sources for his universals, and the more numerous and varied in structure his sources were, the more truthful his proposals would have seemed, Hockett does not mention such sources, for they could neither increase nor decrease the credibility of his proposals; one immediately grasps that this must be the case.

As another example, if we imagine Sir William Jones's discovery as being made by juxtaposing "both ... the roots of verbs and ... the forms of grammar" of Latin, Greek and Sanskrit and by making some (intuitive) assessment that these coincidences could not possibly have been produced by accident, then this finding is also empirical, as it is essentially based on data. The finding could have been challenged by adducing further data, but later data provided more support; in any case, empirical data is indispensable to the conception and the testing of a proposition like this.

A classical example of empirical, or data-driven, discovery is provided by Verner's explanation of the exceptions to Grimm's law, which I discuss later in this chapter. Suffice it to say here that he starts with data and analyses these data with the familiar induction methods of Francis Bacon and John Stuart Mill.

Finally, consider Saussure's discovery of the concept of linguistic system. This is a theoretical discovery. Any linguistic system comprises a set of linguistic entities, or is a classification, and if each such entity is to have existence at all, it *must* be different from all other entities. All the objects of a classification must a priori be distinct from one another. Saussure was well aware of the epistemological status of the notion, and justifies the idea of system at the material level, or sounds, by saying that it is not the sound of the word that is important but the phonetic contrasts with other sounds. Then he continues:

> *But how could it possibly be otherwise?* No particular configuration of sound is more aptly suited to express a given message than any other such configuration. *So it is clearly the case – indeed it must be the case* – that no linguistic item can be based, ultimately, upon anything other than its non-coincidences with the rest. (Saussure 1996[1916]: 116; italics mine)

Neither the origin nor the subsequent linguistic fate of this notion were, or could be, dependent on examination of empirical data. On the other hand, the *application* of the notion of system, the revealing of a specific system's structure, is an empirical matter; e.g. the determination of the sound system of a language can be correctly or incorrectly accomplished according to whether each phoneme is correctly or incorrectly demarcated from all other phonemes.

In the next chapters of the book, I will describe computational systems which are data-driven: they take as their primary input a body of data which they try to describe parsimoniously and intelligibly. Needless to say, such an approach is one-sided and should be supplemented in the future with work on theory-driven discovery and better with systems combining both approaches, which would fit to a greater extent good scientific practice. As Francis Bacon (1960)[1620] wrote in the *Novum Organum*:

> Those who have treated the sciences were either empirics or rationalists. The empirics, like ants, lay up stores, and use them; the rationalists, like spiders, spin webs out of themselves; but the bee takes a middle course, gathering up her matter from the flowers of the field and garden, and digesting and preparing it by her native powers. (cited in Langley *et al.* 1987: 25)

1.2 Ways to scientific discovery: intuition, chance, or problem solving?

It is generally agreed that scientific discoveries belong to the greatest achievements of human productive thinking. There is however much less agreement among scientists on the processes leading to such discoveries. Some of the most brilliant scholars in the history of science have expressed opinions on the matter. These can be classed under several basic views, to which I turn below.

1.2.1 The intuitionist view

In the first, so-called "intuitionist view", a sharp distinction is made between the "context of discovery" (i.e. the way we arrive at a novel idea or problem solution) and the "context of justification" (i.e. the way we confirm or justify this idea or solution), and the context of discovery is proclaimed to be in the realm of "intuition", "insight", etc., and hence to lie outside logical analysis.

Biographers and historians of science, who are proponents of this view, give instances of inventions where the novel ideas occur all of a sudden and seemingly unrelated to previous conscious thoughts, often citing in support the experiences related by the discoverers themselves. Here are some of the most popular instances, which often ring somewhat anecdotally.

The German chemist Kekulé discovered the benzene ring in a dream; he relates the story as follows:

> [I] sank into a half sleep. The atoms flitted before my eyes. Long rows, variously, more closely, united; all in movements wriggling and turning like snakes. And see, what was that? One of the snakes seized its own tail and the image whirled scornfully before my eyes. As though from a flash of lightning I woke; I occupied the rest of the night in working out the consequences of the hypothesis ... Let us learn to dream, gentlemen. (cited in Beveridge 1961: 56)

The American psychologist William James also dreamt things which seemed important, but forgot them awakening. The happy ideas may suddenly befall the discoverers on other circumstances as well. This usually happened to the mathematician Littlewood while he was shaving, and Poincaré invented the Fuchsian functions while walking:

> Just at this time I left Caen, where I was then living, to go on a geological excursion under the auspices of the school of mines. The changes of travel made me forget my mathematical work. Having reached Coutances, we entered an omnibous to go some place or other. At the moment when I put my foot on the step the idea came to me, without anything in my former thoughts seeming to have paved the way for it, that the transformations I had used to define the Fuchsian functions were identical with those of non-Euclidean geometry. (Poincaré 1956)

In an excellent essay on mathematical discovery (Hadamard 1949) also stresses the role of intuition, citing the experience of the great mathematician Gauss who was for years incapable of solving a problem, and then:

> finally two days ago I succeeded [...] like a sudden flash of lightning the riddle happened to be solved. I cannot myself say what was the conducting thread which connected what I previously knew with what made my success possible.

In the philosophy of science, this mystical view of discovery is most strongly upheld by the philosopher Karl Popper who is also known by having denied the subject of his classical book *The Logic of Discovery* (German original *Logik der Forschung* from 1935) in a famous passage that deserves to be cited at length:

> [...]the work of the scientist consists in putting forward and testing theories.
>
> The initial stage, the act of conceiving or inventing a theory, seems to me neither to call for logical analysis nor to be susceptible of it. The question of how it happens that a new idea occurs to a man — whether it is a musical theme, a dramatic conflict, or a scientific theory — may be of great interest to empirical psychology; but it is irrelevant to the logical analysis of scientific knowledge. The latter is concerned not with questions of fact (Kant's quid facti?), but only with questions of justification or validity (Kant's quid juris?) ...
>
> My view of the matter, for what it is worth, is that there is no such thing as a logical method of having new ideas, or a logical reconstruction of this process. My view may be expressed by saying that every discovery contains "an irrational element", or "a creative intuition", in Bergson's sense. In a similar way, Einstein speaks of the "search by pure deduction. There is no logical path", he says, "leading to these ... laws. They can only be reached by intuition, based upon something like an intellectual love ("Einfuehlung") of the objects of experience". (citation from the English translation Popper (1961: 31–32); italics in original)

Popper's influential work banned the study of the so-called "context of discovery" (i.e. how we arrive at novel hypotheses or ideas) from the realm of philosophy of science for many years to come. Only the "context of justification" (i.e. the problem of how we confirm, or in his terminology "corroborate", the ideas already conceived) was subsequently considered a legitimate philosophical goal.

More than 20 years later, a no less influential figure, in linguistics, stated that "the fundamental concern [of linguistic theory] is the problem of *justification* of grammars" (Chomsky 1957: 49; italics mine), and "we shall never consider the question of how one might have arrived at the grammar", whether this be "by intuition, guess-work, all sorts of partial methodological hints, reliance on past experience, etc." (op. cit. p. 56). In the familiar chapter "On the Goals of Linguistic Theory" from *Syntactic Structures*, from which the above are citations, Chomsky was in fact criticising the view, attributed by many to the school of descriptive linguistics, according to which the aim of linguistic theory is to provide analytic procedures, or "discovery procedures" of the type segmentation-and-classification, for the derivation of grammars of languages from corpuses of these languages. In particular, Chomsky expressed his doubt *in principle* as to the attainability of the discovery task by descriptivist techniques:

> I think that it is very questionable that this goal is attainable in any interesting way, and I suspect that any attempt to meet it will lead into a maze of more and more elaborate and complex analytic procedures that will fail to provide answers for many important questions about the nature of linguistic structure. (pp. 52–53; cf. also p. 56)

He also notes that some *concrete* attempts in this direction, despite their proclaimed goal, are not in fact discovery, but rather "evaluation procedures", helpful for choosing from among alternative grammars, already discovered in some way or another (p. 52, fn. 3). To the structuralist conception, judged as much too ambitious and premature, Chomsky contrasts his own view — in his evaluation more modest but more realistic and sufficiently interesting at the same time — amounting to the requirement that linguistic theory should only provide a means for evaluation, or choosing a particular grammar from a set of *given* alternatives.

Chomsky's discussion had an effect in linguistics very similar to that of Popper's view in philosophy. Thus, the very term "discovery procedures" has ever since acquired a largely negative connotation for some. Dougherty (1973) for instance is sharply critical of such methodology, believing it to have been overturned by *Syntactic Structures*. He follows Chomsky closely, claiming:

> I have nothing to say about the creative process by which a linguist develops a new grammar, I am only concerned with the method of selecting the superior grammar from a given field of proposed grammars. (Dougherty 1973: 435)

and Teeter (1964) comments on the question in an article with the indicative title *Descriptive linguistics in America: triviality vs. irrelevance*, to mention but a few published reactions.

Still worse, this negative bias to descriptive methods has illegitimately extended its scope and has led to a marked tendency to refrain from discussions of *any* type of discovery issues as well. Some linguists with continuing methodological interests accordingly have taken much care to divert an eventual suspicion that their concerns have anything to do with discovery (in the sense of novel ideas generation), claiming their work to fall entirely into the line of justification (i.e. with how an idea, already conceived, is checked or confirmed) (cf. e.g. Leech 1970, Labov 1971: 413–14 and elsewhere); others have gone so far as to claim that the very advocates of discovery, the American descriptivists, in their greater and most "theoretically-minded" part at least (Bloomfield, Harris, etc.), have not actually been concerned with discovery but with justificational matters, as if the former enterprise were sinful:

> [...]it is undeniable that the leading theorists [Bloomfield, Harris, Hockett, Wells] (with the exception of Pike) were not concerned with the development of discovery procedures.

> [...]in the work of these linguists a distinction is carefully drawn between the actual process of discovering the structure of a language and the business of describing a structure which has already been discovered. (Miller 1973: 123)

Assuming this to be the case, only the less significant figures could be charged of being friends of discovery:

> Whereas the four linguists cited in the preceding paragraph were the leading theoreticians of the "structuralist school", there were many linguists, less theoretically minded, who did interpret these techniques of segmenttion as discovery techniques for use in the field. (op. cit. p. 125)

A similar interpretation, intending to rehabilitate the work of American descriptivists in the eyes of Chomsky's followers, is also upheld by such linguists as Lyons and Sampson (Lyons 1970: 40–42; Sampson 1979: 373–75).

Aside from the above purely methodological linguistic debate, linguistic history does not abound in descriptions of how happy ideas befell suddenly their discoverers, so I will confine re-citing Greenberg's "aha-experience" in the realization the link between typology, linguistic change, marking and universals:

In a sense, it was still a blooming, buzzing confusion like that of the infant as described in a famous passage by Henry James the psychologist. Somehow, typology, linguistic change, marking and universals must be connected.... Although these conditions are easy to state, they required a number of years to gradually mature in my mind. I recall that at one point, as the key role of implicational universals became clear to me, I had what German psychologists called *Aha-Erlebnis*.

Verner also seemed to have a similar experience which triggered his efforts in an attempt to explain the exceptions to Grimm's law. According to his own account, upon getting up one morning, he was puzzled by the question why the Gothic words *fadar* and *broþar* have different consonants after the root vowel.

1.2.2 The chance view

Another conception of discovery, the "chance view", lays the emphasis on luck and chance in scientific work. All of us know the anecdote according to which the apple falling on Newton's head was responsible for his discovery of gravitation. Among the classic examples cited to more seriously support this view are the discoveries of Röntgen, Fleming, and Pasteur.

Thus, Röntgen discovered X-rays when he was in search actually of invisible rays, and quite by chance noted that rays could penetrate black paper. He himself afterwards comments that his discovery of this fact was purely accidental. Fleming worked with cultures of staphylococci, which left open several times, got contaminated. He observed that the colonies of staphylococci around one colony died. Thus, he discovered penicillin. The chance element in this story is further increased by the fact the he worked under unfavourable conditions in an old house with a lot of dust; happily, these conditions facilitated the occurrence of contamination. Pasteur's discovery of immunization has a similar ring. After an interruption of his work on fowl cholera for a vacation he found almost all cultures had become sterile. After an unsuccessful attempt to revive them, he was about to discard everything and start anew, when it suddenly occurred to him to re-inoculate the same fowls with fresh culture. The result was that almost all those fowls survived, unlike the fresh fowls which had no "immunization". As later commented, this was a surprise not only to his collaborates, but to Pasteur himself.

Practising scientists — especially those in the natural sciences — seem to be great proponents of this view; Beveridge (1961) for example mentions more than a dozen of such cases.

Chance may be a noticeable factor in linguistic discovery as well, as the discovery of Indo-European mother language attributed to Sir William Jones might have been, in case he independently arrived at the idea. It required a polyglot to compare a number of languages and Jones was indeed a hyperpolyglot with thorough knowledge of 13 and basic knowledge of 28 other languages, but it required a lucky polyglot to compare the *needed* set of languages, viz. Latin, Greek and Sanskrit. Thus, while Jones's knowledge of Greek and Latin could be taken for granted in an era of admiration for classical culture, his turning to the study of the "exotic" Sanskrit language was accidental and due to the more or less happy circumstances of his being appointed as a judge in the Bengal Supreme Court and, specifically, due to his related desire to have law translations from Sanskrit, which he could not acquire otherwise but with making the translations himself. Another happy historical circumstance was that Jones was appointed a judge in India, and did not migrate to America, as he contemplated to do because of his opposition to the British military and political oppression of the American colonies.

Hitting upon the *relevant data* in similar comparisons can also be due to chance. Here is the account of the origin of the idea of a possible relationship between Ket and Na-Dene, conceived by Ruhlen (1998) in an indeed somewhat less impressive finding (the first person to claim a genetic link specifically between Yeniseian and Athabaskan-Tlingit (Eyak was then unrecognized as a Na-Dene language) was the Italian linguist Alfredo Trombetti in 1923). The story is told by Lysek (2000) in *Mammoth Trumpet*:

> As so often occurs in science, Ruhlen happened by chance upon the link between Ket and Na-Dene while he was doing research on another problem, in this case the origins of the Basque language. He was looking at the six language families that are related to Basque, and in the process he began comparing Na-Dene to Yeniseian (Ket). The word for birch bark is so similar in both families that it caught his attention and caused him to take a closer look at the relationship between the two families.
>
> Both Na-Dene (Athabaskan) and Yeniseian (Ket) have one word for birch bark. This is significant, says Ruhlen, because most languages combine two words to delineate birch bark as does English. Furthermore, Yeniseian uses a completely different word for birch tree. One can infer from this that for Na-Dene and Yeniseian language speakers birch bark was a very important part of their culture. (Lysek 2000)

It seems that the origin of ideas regarding unknown genetic relationships between languages, aside from being triggered by rational consideration, pertaining to geographical proximity, known historical contacts, archaeological or genetic evidence, etc., not infrequently reside in pure chance. Below is a recent case that will serve as my final example. Blevins (2007) argues that Proto-Ongan, comprising two related languages of the southern Andaman Islands, Jarawa and Onge, may be related to Proto-Austronesian. She describes how the idea befell her:

> This paper has a very unlikely origin that may interest those whose days are full of teaching and student advising. Several months ago, Mr. Pramod Kumar, a PhD student at the Max Planck Institute of Evolutionary Anthropology, passed along a draft of his phonology chapter on Jarawa for comment. I took the document home, and gave it a careful read, during which time I noticed resemblances between Jarawa words and words with similar sounds/meanings in Austronesian languages, or Proto-Austronesian itself. To convince myself that this was a figment of my imagination, I spent the next two days combing Jarawa wordlists. After this proved surprisingly fruitful, Mr. Kumar was kind enough to lend me his copy of Dasgupta and Sharma (1982) on Onge. When I saw that the Onge word for 'rain' was *ujeŋe* and 'communal house' *berei, berai*, I realized that the matter was serious enough to deserve more time and attention. (Blevins 2007: 155, fn. 1)

1.2.3 The problem solving view

A third conception of discovery, the "problem solving view", looks upon productive processes as essentially a rule-governed activity. A discovery is seen as an application of systematic, scientific methods, directing the problem solver in the solution process.

The latter view also has its great advocates.

The idea of logic of scientific inquiry flourished in 17th and 18th centuries, and scholars like Descartes and Francis Bacon believed the use of rules, or methods, to be indispensable to any discovery. Descartes, for instance, insisted that the use of "methods" is the only way of making an invention; "A method is necessary for investigating the truth of things", says Rule IV of his famous *Regulae ad directionem ingenii* (*Rules for the Direction of the Natural Intelligence*) (1619–1628). In the same essay, Descartes compares scholars who use no method to one obsessed with such an insane desire to find a treasure that he would "perpetually roam the streets seeking whether he might perhaps find any lost by a passerby".

Both Descartes and Bacon were convinced that, with the appropriate methods at our disposal, the most difficult problems will be within the reach of even the most mediocre of men.

Leibnitz was known to value the ways to make an invention much more than the inventions themselves. No wonder that he included discovery rules (*ars inveniendi*) as an indispensable component of his project for a Universal Science.

Failing to make a clear distinction between what many years later came to be known (due to the philosopher Hans Reichenbach) as the context of discovery and the context of justification, these earlier writers conceived discovery rules as *infallible methods* serving both purposes. To uncover something by the right method, they believed, guarantees the truth of what has been thus found, hence there is no place for testing. Koertge (1980: 140) e.g. writes in this context:

> scientists-philosophers of this period [17th and 18th century] would have found our present distinction between the logic of discovery/conjecturing and the logic of testing/justification quite unintelligible. After all, isn't Bacons's method of Tables and Prerogative Instances claimed to be a means of arriving at true Interpretations of Nature? And doesn't Descartes's method of systematic doubt simultaneously lead to and establish the First Principles of science?"

This point is also convincingly elaborated in Laudan (1980), in the same volume.

More recently, discovery viewed as a rule-governed activity — but cleared from the infallibilism of Renaissance scientists — has been revived in the now classic works on mathematical heuristics by G. Polya (Polya 1957, 1965). Polya was far from the overly optimistic stands of earlier writers on the subject regarding the infallibility of discovery rules:

> Infallible rules of discovery leading to the solution of all possible mathematical problems would be more desirable than the philosophers' stone, vainly sought by alchemists. Such rules would rule magic; but there is no such thing as magic. To find unfailing rules applicable to all sorts of problems is an old philosophical dream; but this dream will never be more than a dream. (Polya 1957: 172)

At the same time, Polya clearly and convincingly shows the role of heuristic procedures in triggering mathematical thinking. His work, however, has wider import and applies to discovery in general. So are most of his heuristic procedures (Polya 1957), e.g.: Understand the problem (asking questions like What is given? What is the unknown?

What condition must the unknown satisfy? Can the condition be divided into parts?); If you cannot solve the problem as it stands, find a more general or a more specific one; Try an analogous problem, or solve only part of the problem, satisfying just a part of the conditions, etc. Such recommendations are clearly relevant to solving any kind of scientific, or even everyday, problem.

Another important defender of the problem solving view was the philosopher and physicist Hanson (1958). Reviving the ideas of Pierce on a reasoning method, known as "abduction", he meticulously described the abductive reasoning path leading Kepler to the discovery that the orbits of planets are elliptical. Hanson, opposing to the view of Popper, which has had the unfortunate effect of banning the study of discovery from contemporary philosophy for many years, has a major credit for rehabilitating a logic of discovery:

> H-D [Hypothetico-Deductive] accounts all agree that physical laws explain data, but they obscure the initial connexion between data and laws; indeed, they suggest that the fundamental inference is from higher-order hypotheses to observation statements. This may be a way of setting out one's reasons for accepting an hypothesis after it is got, or for making a prediction, but it is not a way of setting out reasons for proposing or for trying an hypothesis in the first place. Yet the initial suggestion of an hypothesis is very often a reasonable affair. It is not so often affected by intuition, insight, hunches, or other imponderables as biographers or scientists suggest. Desciples of the H-D account often dismiss the dawning of an hypothesis as being of psychological interest only, or else claim it to be the province solely of genius and not of logic. They are wrong. If establishing an hypothesis through its predictions has a logic, so has the conceiving of an hypothesis. (p. 71)

Still another influential work, in psychology, was Wertheimer (1959). In a gestalt framework, Wertheimer shows the reasoning paths, without appealing to subconscious processes or mere chance, of Einstein's discovery of the theory of relativity and Galileo's discovery of the law of inertia.

Finally, we need to mention work in cognitive science and artificial intelligence, which, taken together with the previous advances, revolutionized the field. To testify to the problem solving approach to discovery we now have impressive cognitive models of human problem solving (e.g. Newell and Simon 1972) and computer programs rediscovering, among others, great scientific achievements such as Robert Boyle's law, Galileo's law of uniform acceleration, Ohm's law, etc. (Langley *et al.* 1987).

The friends of "logic of discovery", though their work significantly differs in scope, emphasis, and even conceptualization of the process of discovery, seem to share a number of basic tenets, the most important of which may be summarized as follows:

(1) Science is essentially a problem solving enterprise. The methods scientists use to solve their problems are *natural* in the sense that they spring from common sense and describe what we usually do in solving a problem. Anyone engaged in problem solving (whether consciously or not) has to pass through more or less similar states of mind if he/she is to successfully resolve a task (cf. e.g. Polya's rules mentioned above).[1]

An important consequence from this assumption is that people, solving everyday problems, as well as scientists of different magnitude, share basically the same repertoire of methods. Werthheimer found out underlying identity in the thought processes going on in pupils solving elementary mathematical problems and discoverers like Galileo and Einstein. Herbert Simon, one of the founders (with G. Polya) of Artificial Intelligence, and a Nobel Prize winner in economics, writes in this connection:

> I have encountered no evidence that there exist significant differences between the processes that great scientists use in achieving their discoveries and the processes used by those men we regard merely as "good" scientists.

> The theory of scientific discovery ... rests on the hypothesis that there are no qualitative differences between the *processes* of revolutionary science and of normal science, between work of high creativity and journeyman work. (Simon 1977: 288)

---

[1] In passing, it is interesting to note that, being a natural way of thinking, heuristic reasoning is reflected also in language itself. Thus, language bears clear traces of heuristic thinking (in the sense in which language uses like "the *rising/falling* of the Sun" bear undoubtful traces of human knowledge at some period of time concerning the relative rotation of Sun and Earth). To give just one example, heuristic reasoning by analogy reveals itself at different levels of language. Cf. the following dialogue from L. Carroll's *Alice in Wonderland*: "I have never heard of 'Uglification,' Alice ventured to say. What is it? The Gryphon lifted up both its paws in surprise. Never heard of uglifying? it exclaimed. You know what to beautify is, I suppose. Don't you? Yes, said Alice doubtfully. It means to-make-anything-prettier. Well then, the Gryphon went on, if you don't know what to uglify is, you are a simpleton.")

(2) Scientific methods are *general* in character in that they are applicable to diverse problems, being domain-independent, rather than task-specific, methods, strongly tied to a particular subject matter.

Descartes, for instance, wrote:

> This discipline should contain the primary rudiments of human reason and it should extend to truths to be elicited in any subject whatsoever. (*Regulae*, p. 89).

And further on:

> [...]there must be some general science which could explain all that which can be investigated concerning order and measure irrespective of any particular subject matter. (*Regulae*, p. 97)

(3) Methods are usually classified into *algorithms*, which are methods guaranteed to lead to a solution, and *heuristics*, which are only methodological guides or directives, suggesting more plausible directions for search. Using algorithms in solving scientific problems, of course, does not resolve the "induction problem", i.e. the impossibility to prove true assertions about infinite sets by a finite set of observations; as a rule, the guaranteed solutions found by algorithms hold over the finite set of observations made.

A brief illustration of the use of heuristics is given in the Appendix to this chapter. Verner's discovery provides a beautiful example of the use of algorithmic methods of experimental science, viz. the methods of induction, or of detecting causality, having their roots in Francis Bacon's (1620) *Novum Organum* and later fully developed by John Stuart Mill (1879). Very rarely does a linguistic exposition bear the sign of logic reasoning to the extent Verner's paper does. This article may serve as an illustration of the inductive (causal) rules of inference, so deserves to be cited at length, with only minor comments on my part.[2]

First, Verner finds a very interesting class of exceptions to Grimm's law, occurring in the conjugation of Germanic verbs:

> When, for example, we have for OE liðe 'navigo, proficiscor' a participal form lidan, then here there is apparently the same differentiation as in lið 'limb' as against lid 'vehicle'. That Germanic philology has until now so readily ignored this fact, which is very interesting in itself and demands reflection — for a modification of the root consonant for the purpose of conjugation does not belong to the realm of the commonplace — may have its basis in the fact that Gothic,

---

[2] In passing it may be noted that Mill's Method of Difference came to be known in linguistics as "minimal pair" or "commutation" test.

from which one usually proceeds in a comparison, does not even know this differentiation in the conjugation. It can, however, be established through compilation of the relevant materials that this differentiation in the conjugation originally belonged to all the Germanic languages, and consequently that it must also at one time have been present in Gothic. The Germanic voiceless fricatives and voiced stops which arose from the Indo-European voiceless stops are so distributed in the conjugation, that all present tense verb forms (inf., pres. ind., subj., imper., and part.) as well as the singular forms of the preterite indicative show voiceless fricatives and all remaining verb forms show voiced stops.

Secondly, Verner isolates *all* potential causes that might have led to the occurrence of the exceptional forms:

From the regular occurrence of differentiation in the conjugation of these verbs, the important conclusion may now be drawn that the differentiating force must be sought in a certain phonetic relationship which varyingly accompanied the conjugation. Through this conclusion the investigation is confined to rather narrow limits. The differentiation took place after the sound-shift had begun; therefore it is peculiar to Germanic. The differentiating impetus, on the other hand, must be older and may very well have already belonged to the Indo-European language. Consequently, this impetus must be sought in that language stage which has its end members in the underlying Indo-European forms on the one hand and on the other, in the forms to which one can attain through a compilation of the Germanic languages. Fortunately, the principal forms of the Germanic strong verbs are transparently clear back to Indo-European. The Indo-European conjugation is based on the following four means of formation:

1) varying ending
2) varying root vowel
3) the use or non-use of augment and reduplication
4) varying accent
These and no others.

Thirdly, having identified all possible reasons, Verner turns to the Method of Residues, in an attempt to eliminate all but one possibility (the method also used by Sherlock Holmes, who tells his friend Watson "How often have I said to you that when you have eliminated the impossible, whatever remains, *however improbable*, must be the truth", *The Sign of the Four*):

If one now looks at a series of Germanic basic forms, for example:

kveþana–,   slahana–,   lîþana–,
kvarþ,   slôh,   laiþ,
kvâdum,   slô,   lidum
kvedana–,   slagana–,   lidana,

it is readily apparent that the phonetic basis for the differentiation
cannot lie in the phonological material of the endings: the endings of
the infinitive stem (kveþ–ana–, slah–ana–, liþ–ana–) is the same as that
of the participle stem (kved–ana–, slag–ana–, lid–ana–) and yet
differentiation is present. Secondly, the basis cannot be sought in the
quantitative aspects of the roots, for the voiceless fricative appears with
long as well as short root vowels (lîþana–, slôh; kveþana–, kvaþ,
slahana–); the same is true of the voiced stop (slôgum; kvedana–,
slagana–). And these same quantitative conditions were already present
in Indo-European. Thirdly, and finally the use or non-use of
reduplication — the augmented verb forms have been lost in Germanic
— could not have caused the differentiation, since then we would have
to have for some forms the same root consonants in the entire preterite
indicative, which is not the case; for others outside the conjugation, a
special explanation would have to be given for the differentiation, since
reduplication is essentially a purely verbal process.

Finally, the single explanation (the varying accent is the real cause),
arrived at by the Method of Residues, is additionally specified and
supported by the Method of Agreement ("If two or more instances of the
phenomenon under investigation have only one circumstance in
common, the circumstance in which alone all the instances agree, is the
cause (or the effect) of the given phenomenon"):

Consequently, only one explanation remains and it is no desperate
hypothesis, to which I must take recourse because all other attempts at
explanation have failed, but rather a decision which has of necessity
thrust itself upon me by sober argumentation: The differentiation must
be based on the fourth means of formation of the conjugation, on the
varying Indo-European accent. This assumption is confirmed in the
highest degree by a confrontation of the Germanic verb forms with the
corresponding forms of the Sanskrit verbs. When the accent in Sanskrit
rests on the root syllable, we have the voiceless fricative for the root
final in Germanic; on the other hand, when the accent in Sanskrit falls
on the ending, the Germanic forms show a voiced stop for the root final.
In the following compilation, I am juxtaposing to the Sanskrit forms
first the etymologically corresponding Germanic paradigm and then a
paradigm with the differentiation. In the following compilation, I am

juxtaposing to the Sanskrit forms first the etymologically corresponding Germanic paradigm and then a paradigm with the differentiation. Since we are concerned here only with the root final, I am citing the Germanic forms with Gothic endings.

A. The accent rests in Sanskrit on the root; the root final is a voiceless fricative in Germanic.

<table>
<tr><td colspan="2">a. Skt pres. ind.</td><td>= Gmc pres. ind.</td><td></td></tr>
<tr><td>sg. 1.</td><td>bhédâmi</td><td>= bîta</td><td>lîþa</td></tr>
<tr><td>2.</td><td>bhédasi</td><td>= bîtis</td><td>liþîs</td></tr>
<tr><td>3.</td><td>bhédati</td><td>= bîtiþ</td><td>lîþiþ</td></tr>
<tr><td>pl. 1.</td><td>bhédâmas</td><td>= bîtam</td><td>lîþam</td></tr>
<tr><td>2.</td><td>bhédatha</td><td>= bîtiþ</td><td>lîþiþ</td></tr>
<tr><td>3.</td><td>bhédanti</td><td>= bîtand</td><td>lîþand</td></tr>
</table>

B. The accent in Sanskrit rests on the ending; the root final is a voiced stop in Germanic.

<table>
<tr><td colspan="2">a. Skt perf. ind. pl.</td><td>= Gmc pret. ind. pl.</td><td></td></tr>
<tr><td>1.</td><td>bibhidimá</td><td>= bitum</td><td>lidum</td></tr>
<tr><td>2.</td><td>bibhidá</td><td>= bituþ</td><td>lituþ</td></tr>
<tr><td>3.</td><td>bibhidús</td><td>= bitun</td><td>lidun</td></tr>
</table>

Verner knows what he is doing and the effect his logic reasoning must have on the reader. So he concludes:

If my conclusions, however, are found to be remarkable, then I hope that they will not to the same degree be found improbable. Remember the course of the investigation. Proceeding from a seemingly irregular point in the conjugation by apagogic reasoning — a means of proof which is not despised even by exact mathematics — I have arrived at an explanation which was not only completely satisfactory for that point; but at the same time a series of language phenomena also viewed previously as irregularities were proved in this way to be completely organic products of the development of the language. Precisely in the harmonic interrelationship of various language phenomena with one another and with the total development of language as discovered through this explanation, I find the best confirmation for the correctness of my demonstration.

Summing up Verner's powerful argumentation, he starts with the observation of the anomaly of the Germanic verbal conjugation, and isolates all potential causes for this anomaly. Note that Verner is careful to emphasize that these are all potential causes, and there are no others (the failure to do this, would have made his argument vulnerable, since the "real" cause could have resided in reasons other than those listed, which is, in principle, one of the major objections against Bacon/Mill's rules). He then turns to the algorithmic methods familiar from these authors. Applying the Method of Residues to data from the Germanic conjugation allows him to exclude all but "varying accent", as a potential cause of the anomaly. Applying the Method of Agreement to further data reveals the exact role of accent in older (Sanskrit) forms.

1.2.4 Reconciling the views

There is a grain of truth in either of the briefly reviewed views. Scientific discovery is a complex phenomenon in which intuition, luck and logic reasoning all play a part. However, the magnitude of these parts is different and therefore the cases that can be made for each of these components of scientific creativity do not have equal weight.

The chance view, for instance, seems to exaggerate the role of chance since, besides citing a number of examples, there is no empirical evidence available that in a significant number of scientific attainments chance has played any part at all. Another point is that there is certainly much more than luck in any act of creation, even in an "accidental" one, or as Pasteur himself put it, "accident favours the prepared mind". Our linguistic examples in which chance played a part also attest to the indispensable role of accompanying linguistic knowledge to make the discovery possible. Finally, accepting chance as a primary factor is a destructive stand in that it eliminates the need to subject discovery to objective, scientific investigation.

The final point of objection can be equally rightly made against the intuitionist view, where usually no concrete processes are postulated to explain the mysterious *i*-words (intuition, insight, illumination, imagination, etc.) and they merely serve as accordion words which stretch to cover mental states we do not understand, and do not try to explain.

The problem solving view, in contrast, attempts to subject discovery to scientific investigation. Not in the least denying the role of intuition, or even luck, in scientific discovery, it only stresses that science is a rational enterprise in some important sense, and not totally, or even predominantly, subconscious and accidental.

For obvious reasons, I could do no more than give a rather black and white account here. Nevertheless I need to emphasize that I do not mean to suggest that the great scientists, proponents of either view, literally subscribe to its extreme tenets. Thus, Popper, for instance, does not claim that creativity is totally irrational and beyond the realm of *scientific* study; as the quote given above indicates, he leaves this ground to empirical psychology. Einstein, who at various places in his writings mentions unconscious processes in discovery, has provided most insightful rational analysis of inquiry (for an excellent discussion, cf. Holton 1979). Poincaré (1956) also posits a rational, as he calls it "preparation phase", in which the problem solver consciously struggles with the problem; he also tries to give an account of intuition (in terms of associanist psychology), claiming that the conscious efforts trigger an innumerable number of combinations of ideas in our subconsciousness, our intuitive feeling of beauty filtering these combinations, and letting go into our conscious mind only those that satisfy the criteria of beauty. This account is still quite popular in mathematical quarters. The adherents of the problem solving view, in their turn, readily admit essential aspects of chance in discovery. Simon (1977) e.g. argues that since science is built upon previous advances, achieved in a routine way, it is mere chance for big discoverers to be born exactly at a time which is ripe for making their discoveries, etc.

In linguistics, we seem to have a similar situation. The most ardent critic of discovery procedures, Chomsky (1957), does not totally deny the usefulness of even partially adequate discovery procedures as valuable hints to the practising linguist (p. 55, fn. 6; p. 106). He only insists that *linguistic theory* should not be identified with a manual of such procedures, thus shifting the focus of interest from the process of linguistic discovery — conceived as the generation of novel ideas or solutions — to justification.

To date, this is the predominant view on discovery. There is a large body of literature on discovery in the sciences. Besides some of the classic works already cited, I may mention only some further important books and collections of general interest, containing further references. The philosophical perspective on discovery is most comprehensively discussed in the two-volume collection Nickles (1980a, b) containing papers from the "International Congress on Discovery and Creativity". A wider view, including also computational approaches, is the selection of papers from the same congress published in the journal *Foundations of Science* (1999: 4 (3-4). The standard references on the cognitive modelling of productive thinking and machine discovery still seem to be Newell and Simon (1972), and Langley *et al.* (1987), respectively; but cf. also Thagard (1988), Shrager and Langley (1990). Giere (1992) is a collection of papers looking at discovery from different perspectives.

Popular work of serious scientists includes e.g. Medawar (1967) and
Selye (1964).

1.3 The computational approach: tasks of linguistic discovery

A natural outgrowth of the problem solving view of discovery is the
computational approach. If discovery is essentially rule-governed and
involves the application of systematic methods, then some of these
methods may be (at least partly) automated. The degree of success of
computational discovery systems will depend on the extent to which
such systems are capable of generating truthful, novel, unexpected and
important knowledge, i.e. their ability to produce discoveries. A
successful system should also represent its results in a form that is easy
to understand by its users, and preferably should be general enough to be
portable to other problems than those it is originally designed to solve.

I start the discussion by a brief review of research in mainstream
machine scientific discovery and the attempts in similar direction that
have been made in linguistics.

1.3.1 A brief history of research in machine scientific discovery

With the advent of Artificial Intelligence in the 60s and 70s of 20th
century, computer scientists tried to extend the scope of computing to the
automation of aspects of scientific discovery. A classical example of
these early efforts is the Logic Theorist, designed by Newell and Simon
in 1955. The system proved 38 of the first 52 theorems in Russell and
Whitehead's *Principia Mathematica*, and found new and more elegant
proofs for some, these results being submitted to the *Journal of Symbolic
Logic*. Another instance of modelling mathematical reasoning was
Gelernter's (1983)[1959] Geometry Theorem Prover. DENDRAL, the
first expert-system, discovered hypotheses about chemical compounds,
given mass-spectrographic data (Lindsay *et al*. 1980, 1993) and was
followed by Meta-DENDRAL, which constructed new rules in mass
spectrographic analysis, so as to by-pass the problem of getting rules
from experts (Buchanan and Feigenbaum 1978). Although the original
algorithm of the programs mimicked in an efficient way Nobel Prize
winner in physiology and medicine Lederberg's original systematic scan
strategy for generating molecular structures (Lederberg 1965),
DENDRAL did not have as its focus the modelling of the cognitive
aspects of human discovery, but was built with the intention of carrying
out a difficult scientific task.

A more historical-cognitive approach was adopted by work of the 80s at Carnegie Mellon University, culminating in the book *Scientific Discovery* by Langley *et al.* (1987). The different versions of their BACON program (named after Francis Bacon, some of whose methods it implemented) replicated a number of first class discoveries from various fields in early science by finding patterns in numerical data. Some of these discoveries are Boyle's law, Kepler's third law, Galileo's law, and Ohm's law. A notable feature of BACON was its capacity to decompose relational data in order to hypothesize intrinsic properties in one or more of the objects engaging in the relations. This feature went beyond curve-fitting and was based on the metaphysical assumption that an entity's relational properties are caused by its intrinsic properties. In addition to the data-driven tasks modelled in BACON, the group also investigated theory-driven discovery in the STAHL system (after the German chemist Georg Ernst Stahl, who invented the phlogiston theory). These programs were designed to model actual cognitive processes of famous scientists, and they were given as input the same initial conditions as those of the original discoverer. Further advance in the cognitive-historical approach was the KEKADA system (Kulkarni and Simon 1988), which was based on notebook evidence. The program modelled reasoning patterns in some discoveries of the biochemist Hans Krebs and focused on responses to surprising experimental results, helping to dispel the mystery of serendipity in discovery.

Two seminal conferences on computational methods for scientific discovery took place in Stanford. The first one in 1989 led to the collection *Computational Methods of Scientific Discovery and Theory Formation* (Shrager and Langley (eds) 1990). The second conference, in 1995, was a part of the AAAI Spring Symposium and was published as *Systematic Methods of Scientific Discovery*. They are useful sources for the state-of-the-art at that time. If the emphasis of the first collection were programs that acted as "computational models", the second emphasized systems that were "computational actors" in scientific discovery, i.e. programs that were designed to aid actual scientific practice (a distinction also known as "cognitive" vs. "expert system" approaches).

More recent research explicitly focuses on building systems that aid the investigator in current scientific practice rather than only replicate old discoveries. A notable example is Valdés-Pérez (1994), whose program MECHEM is able to discover reaction path-ways in chemical reactions. Data-mining in scientific databases is also an active area of research, as are other computational approaches applied to individual sciences, e.g., intelligent systems in molecular biology. It is becoming more difficult to locate computational discovery work because much of it is published in scientific journals — a good sign that the methods are producing results of interest to practising scientists. The conference "Discovery Science" for more than a decade includes papers from variety of fields.

What is the situation in linguistics regarding machine discovery?

Linguists were never a part of mainstream machine discovery research, one important consequence of which was that within the (computational) linguistic community the distinction between the historical-cognitive approach and the expert-system approach was never recognized, and no one in linguistics ever tried, to my knowledge, to computationally (cognitively) reconstruct historically important discoveries in our science. To be sure, the purely historical, non-computational, investigations of such discoveries, exemplified in good historical analyses such as e.g. those of Koerner and others, do not contain the details needed for a computational reconstruction. The second consequence is that, unlike mainstream machine discovery research, works concerned with linguistics did not focus on automating general scientific inferences, and the linking of these into coherent and powerful systems with wide applicability, but rather modelled *specific*, even if important problems in linguistics, with no explicit concern for their further application to other problems in linguistics or outside of linguistics.

In this brief review, I cannot do justice to all, or even most, work in a similar vein that has appeared during the last decades, and it is beyond the scope of this book to make a detailed review (for some good reviews of the state of the art during the years, cf. e.g. Hewson (1989), Embleton (1991), Atkinson and Gray (2005); for the current state of the art, cf. also *Proceedings of the Ninth Meeting of the ACL Special Interest Group in Computational Morphology and Phonology*, Prague, June 2007). I will only sketch the basic trends, mentioning some typical work for this trend. By far the most active area of research during the years was computation in historical/comparative linguistics (including also dialectology). Other areas included authorship attribution and computer-assisted reconstruction of texts, but this work, as well as other minor applications, as toolkits for field work or concordances addressed more routine and uncreative tasks, and will be outside this review. The most impressive results thus were undoubtedly achieved in the field of historical/comparative linguistics, and below I sketch the basic directions of this research.

By far the most widely known application of computational techniques is to solving historical linguistic problems, and especially the *reconstruction of language family trees*. One of the basic branches of research is known as "lexicostatistics", which simply reconstructs a family tree, given a set of related languages, described in terms of features and/or wordlists of these languages.

The other branch, "glottochronology", usually associated with Morris Swadesh, is concerned with reconstructing family trees, and additionally provides dates for the branching points, or nodes, in the trees. Glottochronology assumes that some meanings are universal and occur in all cultures, and they are less prone to diachronic change and borrowing. These comprise so-called "basic core vocabulary" and include words for kinship, body parts, basic actions, lower numerals, etc. Assuming further that the replacement rate is constant for words from the basic core vocabulary, we can compute the "time depth", or the time since any pair of languages have split from their common ancestor language.

Mathematical methods for building trees borrowed from ethnology and physical anthropology were transferred to linguistics and were used before the introduction of computers, one of the earliest attempts being Kroeber and Chrétien (1937), who employ 74 features to reconstruct Indo-European. Other early work includes e.g. Ross (1950), Gleason (1959), and Dobson (1969). A major problem with manual approaches to tree building is the immense number of logically possible trees which can be constructed from a set of languages. Thus, if for three languages there are 3 possible trees, for six languages there are 945, and for seven as many as 10 395, a number which quickly grows with the increase in the number of classified languages. The introduction of computers in the 1970s allowed a clustering technique from numerical taxonomy, viz. "hierarchical cluster analysis", to be used to handle the costliness of the problem. An early work using cluster analysis is Henrici (1973), applying the method to Bantu languages. Further work in this direction is Kruskal, Dyen, and Black (1973), Dyen, Kruskal, and Black (1992), Ringe *et al.* (1997), Ringe, Warnow, and Taylor (2002). More recently, McMahon and McMahon (2005) present a general introduction to the field, Dunn *et al.* (2005) apply biological cladisic methods to grammatical structure (rather than to lexicon) to study prehistory and early human dispersals, and Holman *et al.* (2008) attempt to improve the input to classification programs by varying the size of inspected wordlists, as well as combining wordlists with grammatical features.

Another important application within historical linguistics is the modelling of the historical method, including the *identification of proto-forms, cognates and sound correspondences*, given wordlists in related languages. Work in this direction include Hewson (1974), Lowe and Mazaudon (1994), Guy (1994), Covington (1996, 1998), Oakes (2000), Kondrak (2001), and cover different aspects of the historical method and implement the method to a different degree.

A further application is the determination of *distant relationships* between languages. For example, Dolgopolski (1986) compiles a list of 15 words, believed to have most stable meanings, and computes the most probable phonetic correspondences in diachronic change. This allows the probability of random coincidences of the words, standing for these stable meanings, to be computed for any languages. If the probability is much smaller than could be expected to occur by chance, then we have evidence for the existence of a relationship. Oswalt (1970, 1991), Guy (1994), and Kessler (2001) use larger, Swadesh 100– or 200–word lists, in pairs of languages. Some of these works compare the number of word matches (according to predefined phonetic similarity criteria) between the original wordlists and the number of word matches in randomized wordlists, obtained by permutations. If the number of matches in the original wordlists is significantly larger than the number in the randomized wordlists, showing what would be the expected number of chance word coincidences, the result indicates a possible relationship.

If we summarize the linguistic efforts in using computers in the conduct of linguistic research, the following may be said. First, computational linguistic tools have been thematically limited predominantly to historical/comparative linguistics.

Secondly, only a small number of original and general computational machinery was developed to solve the limited tasks linguists set before them. The reason was basically that the impetus as a rule came from computational scientists and AI specialists, who were only interested in extending the scope of computation, or alternatively, from computational biologists transferring their tool by analogy to linguistics, rather than from computationally literate and active practising linguists interested in actual results. Not infrequently, advices were given to use available computer programs from fields like AI, biology, genetics, statistics, which is commendable in itself, but still is not all we linguists should do. For example, in an interesting paper, clustering languages into language families, given wordlists of these languages, Batajelj, Pisanski and Keržič (1992: 339) summarize their goal in the following manner:

The purpose of this paper is to show that current mathematics and computer science can offer expertise to various "soft" sciences, e.g. linguistics. [...] The authors regard the results presented in this paper merely as an example of a possible application of cluster analysis to linguistics. The results should not be regarded as conclusive but rather as suggestions to linguists that similar projects can be carried out on a much greater scale, hopefully yielding similar results and better understanding of language families.

Finally, not infrequently the intended audience was non-linguistic or computational linguistic, which made this work not fully understandable to linguists without considerable formal background and thus the work remained outside mainstream linguistics.

What we need therefore is an impetus within linguistics, and a broader perspective, that will both make possible the extension of the scope of linguistic computation beyond its "traditional" applications to historical and comparative linguistics, and further make linguists recognize the need for computational tools in their everyday work.

1.3.2 Tasks of linguistic discovery

In studying the multi-faceted phenomenon of language, linguists face innumerable variety of problems. By a *problem*, we understand a situation which presents perplexity or difficulty to the problem solver. A problem may be viewed from different perspectives, but three binary dimensions seem essential, as follows:

I. Definiteness/indefiniteness of the problem;

II. Presence/absence of method for solving the problem;

III. Well-formedness/ill-formedness of the problem.

The definiteness/indefiniteness dimension relates to the formulation, or statement, of the problem. A problem has two component parts: the *unknown* (or what is required to be found) and the *given* (or the information that can be used in the solution of the problem). A problem in which both components, the unknown and the given, are explicitly stated in the problem's formulation is called *definite*; otherwise, the problem is called *indefinite*.

The second dimension relates to the existence or absence of a method to solve the problem, given the information in the problem's formulation.

The third dimension relates to the question of whether or not the solution, once found, can be recognized as the valid solution to the problem. Problems in which the valid solution can be recognized are called *well-formed*, and problems in which one cannot say whether a found object is a true solution or not are called *ill-formed*.

The three binary dimensions define a typology of linguistic problems having eight theoretically possible types.

In Table 1.1, the types of linguistic problems are ordered in an ascending order of information completeness regarding the three dimensions. Thus, type 1 is fully informationally incomplete, as the problem solver neither disposes of a definite formulation of his/her problem, nor does he/she know of a method for its solution or can recognize a given object as the valid solution. In type 8, in contrast, we have the reverse situation and information completeness: the problem solver is informed on all three dimensions, and therefore has all the necessary information to be capable (at least in principle) to solve the problem. Cases 2 through 7 are intermediate, and the problem solver is informed on one dimension (types 2, 3, 4) or two dimensions (types 5, 6, 7). I shall call the first seven types *classical research problems* insofar as, usually, scientists start their investigations at a point at which at least something is unknown. The informationally complete type 8, I shall call a *task*.

Table 1.1. Typology of Linguistic Problems

No.	Definite	Method	Well-formed	
1	no	no	no	
2	yes	no	no	
3	no	yes	no	"Classical
4	no	no	yes	Research
5	yes	yes	no	Problems"
6	no	yes	yes	
7	yes	no	yes	
8	yes	yes	yes	"Task"

The notion of task seems central in a theory of machine-aided linguistic discovery, for the following reasons. (A related idea of a task of scientific discovery has been developed by computer scientist Valdés-Pérez 1995.)

The first reason is that the task is apparently the only type of *immediately* solvable linguistic problem: one has only to apply the known method to the known information in the problem's formulation to find a solution that can be readily recognized as the valid one; all necessary conditions are available. However, note that these conditions may *not* be sufficient to successfully resolve the task (e.g. I have a full understanding of what it means and how to lift a one hundred kilos weight, but this does not make me capable of doing this). All the other types, or all the classical research problems, miss some necessary information for their solution: regarding what exactly is to be found, regarding the method to use or regarding how to verify the correctness of the solution, and therefore require the missing information to be further acquired. An important corollary follows from the above circumstance, viz. that if we face a classical research problem and if this problem is to be solved at all, it must be transformed — at some stage in the solution process — to one task or a sequence of several tasks. Put differently, to solve a problem means to reduce something which is unknown to something that is known.

Secondly, the task is apparently the only type of linguistic problem that is automatable since it alone contains at the outset all necessary conditions for its solution; classical research problems lack some of this information and cannot be automated, for computer programs cannot by themselves, without being previously taught, acquire the missing information.

Thirdly, *original problems*, i.e. the problems linguists start with, are not infrequently complex and therefore can be reduced, or decomposed into, a sequence of more elementary problems (classical research problems or tasks).

Thus, the problem's principled solvability, automatability and elementarity guarantee the central role of the notion of task in machine-aided linguistic discovery.

It will be misleading to think that tasks are trivial and uninteresting problems, because everything one needs to know for finding a solution is known, while what I called "classical research problems" are the only problems worthy of the attention of good scientists, because there is some, possibly crucial, missing information. As we shall see in the course of this book, some tasks can be both interesting and very difficult to carry out. However, how do we handle the usual classical research problems that are the most common in linguistic (and more generally, scientific) practice? The answer is that they need to be decomposed and recast in terms of manageable tasks that solve them completely, or at least partially. This seems to me to be one of the most imaginative and productive stages of linguistic research, even if aided by machines. And this is one of the reasons why linguists cannot be "replaced" by machines irrespectively of how far we go in developing intelligent computer programs.

Now, from a set of possibly sizable number of linguistic tasks, what makes a task a good candidate for automation? Two characteristics of a task seem essential in this respect, viz.:

(i) the task must be *computationally complex* (and therefore of appreciative help to the linguist if mechanized);

(ii) the task must be *general* (and therefore applicable not only to the specific problem at issue, but to other problems as well).

Our final remark relates to the epistemological nature of the *types of tasks*. From this perspective, tasks fall into *general-scientific tasks*, which reflect usual scientific inferences (such as e.g. concept formation and revision; classification formation and revision; multiple concept discrimination; inferring laws/patterns from data, discovery of causal relations; reconstructing evolutionary trees; generating research problems, etc.), and *meta-scientific tasks*, which reflect inferences about the reliability or quality of the solutions already found (such as finding the simplest, plausible (significant), sound, exhaustive solutions, etc.).

The major *goal* of the discipline of machine-aided linguistic discovery is to uncover appropriate tasks, implement them into running computational systems, and use them for the generation of truthful, novel, unexpected and important knowledge, i.e. use them for making linguistic discoveries.

In order to put some flesh on this skeleton of a discovery theory, let us turn to some examples.

Let us first look at a problem that has already been successfully automated, viz. the problem of reconstruction of family trees, and use as an illustration (adapted from Embleton 1991) the tree building of the Romance languages French (Fr), Spanish (Sp), Portuguese (Po), Rumanian (Ru), Catalan (Ca), Italian (It). Different attempts at tree building may employ comparisons between different aspects of languages (features or wordlists); in this case, 215–word lists are compared from the Romance cognate data given in Rea (1973). The original problem is to find a family tree, given the cognate 215–word lists. The original problem reduces to two tasks:

TASK 1 (assessment of (dis)similarities)

Given the cognate 215–word lists, find, for each pair of languages L1 and L2, the number of items for which L1 and L2 do *not* have cognate forms and register the result into a *dissimilarity matrix*. This dissimilarity matrix, which obviously would always be symmetric, is:

Table 1.2. Dissimilarity matrix

	Fr	Sp	Po	Ru	Ca	It
Fr	0	64	66	97	61	49
Sp	64	0	32	99	60	63
Po	66	32	0	101	62	57
Ru	97	99	101	0	97	84
Ca	61	60	62	97	0	56
It	49	63	57	84	56	0

The problem of assessment of (dis)similarities apparently belongs to the type we call task, as it is informationally complete: we know what to find (a dissimilarity matrix), what information we dispose with to this end (cognate 215–word lists), the method for finding the solution (counting non-cognate forms in the given wordlists), and how to verify the solution (the correctness of the counting operation by itself ensures the correctness of the solution). The task is also a reasonably good one to automate: repetitive counting is costly (note that the pairs of languages we may need to compare may become immense when we classify larger sets of languages); besides, counting of this type is apparently general enough and recurs practically in every task.

TASK 2 (tree, or taxonomy, formation)

Given Table 1.2, build a tree employing to this end the following clustering method. First, find the smallest dissimilarity in the matrix (in our case, the number 32 for Sp and Po) and form the lowest tree node, which is the bifurcation of Sp and Po. Secondly, merge the two rows for the clustered languages into one row (Sp–Po) including the smaller number of the two entries and do the same for the Sp and Po columns. At this step, the dissimilarity matrix is:

Table 1.3. Dissimilarity matrix after first step in clustering

	Fr	(Sp–Po)	Ru	Ca	It
Fr	0	64	97	61	49
(Sp–Po)	64	0	99	60	57
Ru	97	99	0	97	84
Ca	61	60	97	0	56
It	49	57	84	56	0

Thirdly, repeat the same procedure with the new dissimilarity matrix until all languages are clustered. The resultant tree, in bracket representation, is ((Sp–Po)–((Fr–It))–Ca)–Ru).

The problem of tree, or taxonomy formation, is a task in our sense: it is definite (with unknown = tree, and given = dissimilarity matrix); there exists a method for its solution (described above); and, finally, it is well-formed (since the execution of the method guarantees the correctness of the result). Additionally, the task is a good option for automation, for apparently it is both computationally complex and generally beyond the reach of a human, as well as general (building taxonomies recurs in various linguistic problems, and in science generally).

The original problem of historical linguistics of family tree reconstruction has been shown above to be decomposable into two general-scientific tasks, similarity assessment and taxonomy formation. Frequently, however, linguistic problems reduce to general-scientific and meta-scientific tasks, the latter putting further constraints on the solution-object, such as simplicity, significance, etc. Thus, a natural further requirement to the building of family trees would be to find the most parsimonious tree, but we need not be concerned with this problem here. Rather, below I shall briefly present some examples which will be discussed in detail in the next chapters of the book.

Let us first look at the Saussurian idea of linguistic system. According to this idea, the meaning (or value) of a linguistic entity is the conjunction of contrasts this entity bears to all other entities in the system. The discovery of the structure of the system thus apparently can be reduced to the task of *multiple concept discrimination*: given all the concepts of a system, alongside with their descriptions, say in terms of features, for each concept the linguist must find the features that distinguish this concept from all remaining concepts in the system. Beside this general-scientific task of concept discrimination, linguists would often face another task and require that the structure so revealed conforms to the further, meta-scientific, requirement that the structure be the *simplest* (e.g. in the sense that the discrimination uses the minimum number of overall features and/or minimum features for the profiling of each concept). These two tasks make an excellent choice for automation, since, besides the importance of automating the structural method, the tasks are both computationally complex and general. Thus, discriminating concepts is difficult as it is difficult to uncover the exact set of necessary and sufficient demarcating features needed globally and for each concept individually; choosing the simplest set of discriminating features is also computationally costly insofar as it presupposes that *all* such demarcating sets are first of all found. Concept discrimination is general because it recurs at various linguistic levels and in diverse problems within and outside of linguistics; the same applies to the meta-scientific task of ensuring simplicity of the found solution.

As another example, let us look at the search for Greenbergian universals. An analysis of this problem shows that the problem of discovery of universals actually reduces to the general-scientific task of *finding laws/patterns* from data: given a set of languages, described in terms of some features, the linguist needs to discover patterns of various kinds (implicational, or non-implicational) holding universally or with some exceptions. Generally, the patterns so found would be required to conform also to the meta-scientific constraint of being *plausible*, or statistically significant, in order to minimize the possibility that they arise from the investigated sample of languages simply by chance. In solving other related problems, e.g. in describing a given typology in terms of universals, it is natural to require that the set of universals describing all and only the attested types in the typology, be the simplest (i.e. comprises the minimum number of universals). Thus, the solution to a linguistic problem may reduce to resolving several tasks of general-scientific and meta-scientific nature.

Table 1.4. Some tasks of linguistic discovery

General-Scientific Tasks
assessment of (dis)similarity
concept formation (and revision)
multiple concept discrimination
tree/taxonomy formation (and revision)
law/pattern inference
detecting causality
finding explanations
generating research problems
Meta-Scientific Tasks
ensuring simplicity of solution
ensuring plausibility/significance of solution
ensuring soundness and completeness of solution

Again, we note that the tasks of law/pattern inference and guaranteeing their plausibility/simplicity are general and recur across all linguistic levels, and indeed outside of linguistics (all scientists try to infer plausible and simplest laws from data). Also, the tasks are computationally complex, even when samples with a small number of languages, described with small number of features, are explored.

This short survey of tasks of linguistic discovery may be complemented with other potential tasks, known to be implementable from other disciplines like Artificial Intelligence and machine learning. Table 1.4 summarizes the tasks.

An important goal of machine-aided linguistic discovery and linguistics generally, is to attempt to recast important and difficult linguistic problems in terms of tasks, and build intelligent computational systems for carrying out these tasks. The success of the discipline of machine-aided linguistic discovery may be measured by the extent to which this goal is achieved.

1.4 Conclusion

In this chapter, some basic notions of linguistic discovery were introduced, using as illustrations four famous discoveries from the history of linguistics. Findings which we are apt to call discoveries usually possess the features truthfulness, novelty, unexpectedness, and importance, and these properties may be present in a discovery to a different degree. Linguistic discovery-objects may be different (concepts, empirical laws, theories, etc.) and they may either be of an empirical type (or the result of data-driven processes) or of a theoretical type (or theory-driven). Intuition, chance and the use of systematic methods may all accompany a linguistic discovery, but the use of methods in general seems to be an indispensable component of noteworthy achievements.

The computational approach to discovery focuses on automating methods. The review of linguistic work shows that, apart from some definite successes, previous efforts suffer a number of limitations: research is thematically limited basically to historical and comparative linguistics; most often it addresses specific, if important, problems, however with no attention on the generality of the implemented computational mechanisms and how they can be ported to other analogous problems across linguistic disciplines; not infrequently this research is conducted by non-linguists, whose primary aim is the illustration of the usefulness of some computational techniques (from Artificial Intelligence, computer science or computational biology) for the solution of linguistic problems rather than making linguistic discoveries, and whose much too technical expositions usually addressed to a non-linguistic audience have made this research remain outside mainstream linguistics. Contemporary linguistics therefore needs a broader perspective, allowing us both to extend the scope of linguistic computation beyond its "traditional" applications, and to make linguists recognize the need for computational tools in their everyday work.

I suggest as one possible approach in this direction the analysis of linguistic problems in terms of "tasks", which are computationally costly (and therefore cannot be properly handled by a human analyst) and recur in a variety of problems across linguistic disciplines (and therefore can be ported to diverse problems). Tasks relate either to general-scientific or to meta-scientific aspects. The solution to a linguistic problem may reduce to the carrying out of one task, but usually it involves both general-scientific and a meta-scientific tasks. I briefly reviewed several such tasks. Linguists concerned with machine-aided discovery should isolate such tasks, computationally implement and link them into sophisticated systems, having variety of capabilities, and then apply them to substantial problems. The next chapters of the book are examples of attempts in this direction. The described computational systems fall into the realm of empirical, or data-driven, discovery. Further problems of empirical linguistic discovery and a computer program modelling J. S. Mill's canons of induction is sketched elsewhere (cf. Pericliev 1995).

Appendix. An exercise in linguistic heuristics

Problem solving in general, and in linguistics in particular, is usually guided by rules of the thumb, or heuristic procedures, most insightfully described by Polya (1957, 1965) in applications to mathematical problems. General heuristic rules are e.g.: *Formulate the problem*; *Understand the problem* (asking questions like *What is given? What is the unknown? What condition must the unknown satisfy? Can the condition be divided into parts?*); *If you cannot solve the problem as it stands, find an equivalent problem or modify the problem; Try an analogous problem, or solve only part of the problem, satisfying just a part of the conditions*, etc. Such recommendations are clearly relevant to solving any kind of scientific, or even everyday, problem.

To my knowledge, linguistics has not paid attention to and explicitly described such rules and how they can be applied to the solution of linguistic problems. This appendix is a brief illustration of heuristics to a real research problem: the testing of a hypothesis (the next paragraphs are taken from Pericliev 1987; more details can be found in Pericliev 1990).

The Hypothesis. It is almost universally taken for granted that if a sentence is constructionally homonymous (i.e. has more than one syntactic representation), then it is ambiguous (i.e. has more than one understanding). In the literature, numerous examples have been given at various times urging this point. As an illustration, consider a favourite example of descriptive linguists, *old men and women.* The phrase is constructionally homonymous (with analyses *[[old men] and women]* or *[old [men and women]]*) and ambiguous, meaning 'old men and also women' (under the first analysis) or 'old men and old women' (under the second analysis). This hypothesis was later promoted to the status of a linguistic law and was incorporated into a well-known criterion for testing the adequacy of grammars, proposed by N. Chomsky (1957):

> We can test the adequacy of a given grammar by asking whether or not each case of constructional homonymity is a real case of ambiguity. More generally, if a certain conception of grammar leads to a grammar of a given language that fails this test, we may question the adequacy of this conception and the linguistic theory that underlies it. (p. 86)

Formulating the problem. Clearly, we have to test the hypothesis in question, but what does that mean? A popular answer, originating from the philosopher K. Popper, is to scrupulously try to falsify the hypothesis. If this attempt fails, the hypothesis can be counted as additionally supported. We thus reduce our problem to the problem of finding a falsifier to the hypothesis investigated.

Understanding the problem. Our problem has the following constituents, an unknown (a sentence), which has to satisfy the following two conditions: a. the sentence must be homonymous; b. the sentence must be unambiguous.

An analogical problem. Now that we know what we have to find, the question is how to proceed searching for it. One thing is to find and solve an analogical problem, and then to see how this can help solve the original problem. An obvious candidate for analogical problem is to find a word (rather than a sentence) which is homonymous but unambiguous. It is trivial to find such words, known as "syntactic derivatives", as e.g. *Chinese, aged* (nouns or adjs), *fast* (adj or adv), etc. From here, there is just one step realizing that the homonymity of a sentence with respect just to these words will not lead to ambiguity. Two examples are:

(1) *They are Chinese* (N/Adj)
(2) *The young people are happy, the aged* (N/Adj) *are not.*

An equivalent problem. Alternatively, we can rephrase equivalently our problem, requiring e.g. that we find difference in the syntactic structure of a sentence which does not lead to a semantic difference. For example, if we have the following difference in the syntactic structure of the string ABC, B goes either with A or with C, can this be immaterial to the meaning of ABC? It is not difficult to realize that we can obtain this situation in case B is semantically redundant, in which case it will be immaterial semantically whether B goes with A or with B. An example from Bulgarian is:

(3) *Vaznamerjava–sh* (A) *li ti* (B) *da otide–sh* (C) *tam*?
　　　　Intend–you 　　do you 　to go–you 　　　there
　　　　Do you intend to go there?

where the pers. pron. *ti* 'you', which can go with either of the two verbs, 'intend' or 'go', makes no contribution to their meaning since their endings, *–sh* mean (among other things) 'you'.

A modified problem. We can also address a problem with a modified unknown and/or conditions. For example, we may modify the unknown, requiring several sentences (rather than one sentence) with different syntactic structures and the same meaning. These are in fact the so-called "syntactic synonyms" as e.g. *Mary expects John to arrive, John is expected by Mary to arrive, John's arrival is expected by Mary*, etc. If we can "merge" a pair of such strings into just one string, we will ensure the objects we require. To do such a "merging" these strings must be maximally close to one another (which the given examples are not). On some search, we can come across pairs such as *He isn't happy — He is unhappy* (in fact such constructions will be found in any paper on syntactic synonymy). Their almost complete overlapping is seen in the frame *He is — happy.* Now we can ask: Is there a word that can fill the slot with the desired effect? Clearly, this is the word *not:*

(4) *He is not happy,*

where the particle *not* can negate either the verb or the adjective, the meaning being preserved under both analyses.

We can summarize the merits and basic idea underlying heuristics as follows: the original problem is reduced to a number of quite diverse, and, on the whole, easier other problems (analogical, equivalent, etc), which further belong to a quite distant body of linguistic knowledge: lexico-grammatical problems (finding syntactic derivatives), semantic problems (finding redundant words), syntactico-semantic problems (finding syntactic synonyms), etc. Naturally, this reduction of the original problem into several other, and easier, problems, in opening new and diverse fields of investigation, substantially increases our chances to unearth the solution to our original problem. In any case, it is better to have many, and easier, targets rather than only one difficult one.

Chapter 2. Parsimonious Discrimination I: KINSHIP and the Problem of Componential Analysis

The KINSHIP program is designed to handle two tasks: the general-scientific task of multiple concept discrimination and the meta-scientific task of finding the simplest solution(s). KINSHIP models the Saussurian notion of linguistic system by discriminating in a concise manner a set of concepts forming a system. More precisely, KINSHIP performs componential analysis of kinship terminologies. Given the kin terms of a language with their attendant kin types, KINSHIP can produce the guaranteed-simplest analyses, employing a minimum number of features (dimensions) and components in kin term definitions. In this chapter, some of the discoveries of the system are discussed and a structural solution to the familiar problem of the multiplicity of solutions of kinship systems is proposed.

KINSHIP's computational architecture comprises a feature-value extraction module, which is specific to the kinship domain, and a multiple concept discrimination module, which is domain-independent. In the next chapter, this domain-independent module is isolated under the name of Maximally Parsimonious Discrimination (MPD) program, its functional capabilities are extended and further applications are described.

2.1 The problem of componential analysis as parsimonious discrimination

Componential analysis is a method of structural semantics for describing the meaning of a set of words in terms of smaller meaning components, discriminating each word from all others in the set. It is an application to semantics of the Saussurian structural method, whose idea is to reveal the structure of a system of meanings in terms of contrasts or oppositions, in perfect analogy to the discovery of the structure of phonological systems, where each phoneme is described in terms of phonetic features demarcating all phonemes from one another. In the linguistic literature, various semantic domains have been subjected to componential analysis, but the classical example is the kinship domain to which I turn below.

2.1.1 *Kinship semantics*

Every known language has a kinship terminology, however not every language uses the same system: different systems group together under one linguistic label, or kin term, different relatives, or kin types. The result is that different meaning structures underlie different kinship terminologies, hence the interest of structural linguistics (and other disciplines like anthropology, ethnology, etc.) in the formal description of these meaning structures in the diverse languages throughout the world.

Two basic approaches to the structural description of kinship semantics are usually employed. In componential analysis, having its roots in post-Saussurian phonological and morphological work, and initiated by Lounsbury (1956) and Goodenough (1956), common feature values are extracted for the whole range of kin types (=denotata) of one kin term, and a conjunctive definition (=a bundle of feature values) is produced of every kin term such that every term is distinguished from every other by the presence in its definition of at least one contrasting feature.

In the other approach, usually referred to as "extensionist" (Lounsbury 1964, 1965), a componential analysis is made only of a small part of the kin types, called the "core", "kernel" or "foci", and the remaining denotata are described by rewrite rules, stating their similarity or proximity to the core denotata. Both these approaches assume as primary data a universal genealogical grid, or space of relatives (kin types), and inspect how this space is partitioned into subregions by kin terms.

The ultimate goal of both componential and extensionist analysis is to discover the structure of kinship systems, which amounts to concisely and intelligibly summarizing the kin domain, correctly predicting the usage of kin terms in a linguistic community. That is, given any pair of kinsmen in a society, alongside some (minimum) items of information about these kinsmen, such as their sex, generation, etc., from such a componential or extensionist model the analyst can infer whether they are kinfolk and what terms they would use to refer to one another. This has been occasionally termed "(social) structural reality" (Wallace and Atkins 1960, Wallace 1965), i.e. descriptions in which there are no *explicit* claims, or indeed relevant evidence, as to the cognitive reality of the outcome (i.e. how the individuals in a society actually construe the world of experience (kins) from their linguistic (kin term) system). This will be our basic concern in this chapter as well. It is worth mentioning nevertheless that the more ambitious goal of searching for cognitive validity (by psychological tests[1] of cognitive validity of alternative models, see e.g. Romney and D'Andrade 1964, Wallace 1965, Rose and Romney 1979) is a subsequent goal, and hence presupposes the availability of componential models, which I address here. Besides, if cognitive validity is correlated with the simplicity of analyses, as suggested e.g. by Sheffler and Lounsbury (1971), Noricks (1987), and elsewhere, then our simplest models are good candidates for psychological plausibility, but in any case this requires further study which is beyond the scope of this chapter.

The discovery of the structure of kinship systems has been recognized as a difficult problem for human analysts. Leech (1974) e.g. writes:

> kinship analyses have a mind-teasing quality of mathematical puzzles.
> The only cure for bafflement is to think hard and hope that the light will
> dawn!" (p. 239)

Some work has been done on automating part of the kinship analysis within the framework of the extensionist approach (cf. e.g. Kronenfeld 1976). I am not aware of similar attempts for the componential approach, which will be addressed here. It may be noted that by choosing to implement the componential method, I am not intending to imply its superiority over the extensionist method. In fact I believe that any one of them can reveal some important aspect of structure that escapes the others. The extensionist paradigm e.g., which assumes kernel kin types, while describing the remaining, more distant, kin types in terms of extensions of kernels, raises the interesting questions of the rules governing these extensions (incl. figurative extensions), the semantic relationships between narrow meanings and broader extensions, and lots of others that do not at all occur in pure componential analysis, where all kin types are viewed on a par with one another. It goes without saying that such concerns are beyond the scope of the present chapter.

---

[1] Such psychological tests include the listing of kin terms in free recall, semantic differentials, the triad method, etc.

2.1.2 The method of componential analysis

Componential analysis as applied to kinship is familiar to linguists (e.g. Greenberg 1949, Goodenough 1956, Lounsbury 1956, Lounsbury 1964, Wallace and Atkins 1960, Hammel 1965, Leech 1974, etc.). Below I briefly review some basic notions and aspects of the method.

The *kin terms* of a language, such as the English *father*, *uncle*, *mother-in-law*, etc., are linguistic labels for a range of *kin types* (=denotata), which specify the genealogical position of one's kin with respect to oneself. We shall use the following standard abbreviations (Murdock 1949) of atomic genealogical relationships in terms of which the kin types are expressed: Fa = "father", Mo = "mother", Br = "brother", Si = "sister", So = "son", Da = "daughter", Hu = "husband", Wi = "wife". These atomic relationships are juxtaposed to express more distant kin types (relatives), as e.g.: Fa "father", FaBr "father's brother", MoBr "mother's brother", FaSiHu "father's sister's husband", MoSiHu "mother's sister's husband", etc. The set of all kin terms in a language is the *kinship vocabulary* of this language.

The job of the linguist is to determine the relevant conditions for distinguishing the meaning of any of the kin terms within the semantic domain from any other. Componential analysis, as commonly conceived, consists of the following stages:

(1) The linguist isolates the kin terms of a language, and identifies the range of reference of each by a list of kin types (denotata), expressed in terms of the above primary relationships symbols.[2] Thus the range of the English kin term *uncle* (somewhat narrowly conceived) can be specified as: FaBr "father's brother", MoBr "mother's brother", FaSiHu "father's sister's husband", and MoSiHu "mother's sister's husband".

(2) The feature-value pairs, or *components*, of each kin term are found, which are the common components in each of the kin types covered by a kin term (as sex=male, lineality=collateral, and generation=1 are components common to all the four denotata of *uncle* listed above).

(3) The significant dimensions of contrast, or the overall *contrasting features* (or *dimensions*), are found, which are sufficient to describe the kinship vocabulary.

(4) Finally, a *conjunctive definition* of each kin term in the kinship vocabulary is produced, in which the meaning of any one term is

---

[2] Sometimes, additional atomic symbols (such as 'younger', 'older', etc.) are needed to describe kin types.

distinguished from the meaning of every other term by at least one contrasting feature. (Notice that, in contrast, the definition of kin terms in terms of their denotata is a *disjunctive* one, e.g. *uncle* is FaBr *or* MoBr *or* FaSiHu, etc.)

A basic criterion for adequacy (besides the obvious requirement for the consistency of the terms' definitions) is the *simplicity* of the componential analysis. The requirement for parsimony actually embodies two distinct criteria, applied at stages 3 and 4, respectively:

(i) choose the smallest number of contrasting features (dimensions) sufficient to describe the kinship vocabulary; and

(ii) choose the smallest number of components in the definitions of every kin term in the vocabulary.

Put differently, the problem of performing componential analysis reduces to parsimonious discrimination.

2.2 The KINSHIP Program

Below we describe the basics of the KINSHIP program. We begin with the input of the system, and proceed with its activities in modelling the various stages of componential analysis as sketched above. Finally, three distinct types of conducting componential analysis are isolated, all of which are encountered in actual kinship practice, and are supported by our program.

2.2.1 The program's input

KINSHIP accepts as input a set of kin terms, with their attendant kin types. For simplicity of exposition, we shall use as an illustrative example a small subset of the English consanguineal kin terms: *uncle, aunt, father, mother, brother, sister, son, daughter.*

Table 2.1. A subset of English consanguineal kinship terms

uncle	FaBr, MoBr
aunt	FaSi, MoSi
father	Fa
mother	Mo
brother	Br
sister	Si
son	So
daughter	Da

2.2.2 The program's algorithm

KINSHIP uses a domain-dependent process, which computes the feature values of kin types, and a domain-independent one, which performs parsimonious discrimination. The latter process comprises sub-processes for multiple concept discrimination and for ensuring the simplicity of the demarcation. The program thus follows the following basic steps:

I. Extraction of feature values of kin types

The program is endowed with a set of features (or dimensions) and with subroutines that determine, for each kin type, the value the kin type has for the inspected feature. For simplicity, in what follows I assume just four features: "generation", "sex", "distance" and "lineality". Given the input in Table 2.1, the program determines the values for some of the above features as follows. For instance, the values of a kin type for the feature "sex" can be determined by the system by its last symbol (=link), knowing further the sex of all atomic relationships. Thus, the program can find that the kin type FaBr is sex=male, since its last link, viz. Br, is male, while FaSi is sex=female, since Si is female. The feature generation of a kin type is determined as a sum of the generations of the links constituting this kin type, where the latter are +1 for the parental relationships Fa and Mo, −1 for the filial relationships So and Da, and 0 for all remaining relationships Br, Si, Hu, and Wi; thus the program can compute that the kin type FaBr is generation=1, since +1 +0 = 1. Similarly, all feature values (components) are computed, and this is done for all kin types in the data set. The result of this computation for our illustrative kinship domain, in which bundles of feature values are substituted for kin types, is given as Table 2.2:

Table 2.2. Determining feature values of kin types

uncle	[generation=1,sex=male,distance=2,lineality=collateral]
	[generation=1,sex=male,distance=2,lineality=collateral]
aunt	[generation=1,sex=female,distance=2,lineality=collateral]
	[generation=1,sex=female,distance=2,lineality=collateral]
father	[generation=1,sex=male,distance=1,lineality=lineal]
mother	[generation=1,sex=female,distance=1,lineality=lineal]
brother	[generation=0,sex=male,distance=1,lineality=collateral]
sister	[generation=0,sex=female,distance=1,lineality=collateral]
son	[generation=−1,sex=male,distance=1,lineality=lineal]
daughter	[generation=0,sex=female,distance=1,lineality=lineal]

II. Multiple concept (kin term) discrimination

The discrimination of kin terms comprises several steps, as follows.

II.1. Determining kin term components

The program then transfers the components of the kin types into components of kin terms by finding those components that are possessed by *all* the kin types covered by a kin term. For example, the kin term *uncle* will have the components [generation=1, sex=male, distance=2, lineality=collateral] since all its attendant kin types, FaBr and MoBr, have the same feature values. The program will produce the result shown in Table 2.3. For convenience, we shall say in such situations that a kin term possesses some feature, as all the terms in the figure possess the features generation, sex, distance, and lineality; conversely, a kin term will be said not to possess some feature if not all of its attendant kin types have the same value for that feature (e.g. the English word *cousin* does not have the feature sex), or, alternatively, some feature is irrelevant for certain kin types (as e.g. the feature matrilateral is irrelevant for *son* 'So').

Table 2.3. Determining the kin term components

uncle	[generation=1,sex=male,distance=2,lineality=collateral]
aunt	[generation=1,sex=female,distance=2,lineality=collateral]
father	[generation=1,sex=male,distance=1,lineality=lineal]
mother	[generation=1,sex=female,distance=1,lineality=lineal]
brother	[generation=0,sex=male,distance=1,lineality=collateral]
sister	[generation=0,sex=female,distance=1,lineality=collateral]
son	[generation=−1,sex=male,distance=1,lineality=lineal]
daughter	[generation=0,sex=female,distance=1,lineality=lineal]

II.2. Determining contrasting features between pairs of kin terms

The program then proceeds with computing the dimensions of contrast, or contrasting features, that demarcate one kin term from another. This entails forming all unordered pairs from the analysed terms (i.e. combining the first kin term with the second, third, fourth, and so on, the second with the third, fourth, and so on until all possibilities are exhausted), and then computing all the possible contrasts for each pair.

Table 2.4. Contrasting features between pairs of kin terms

	uncle	aunt	father	mother	brother	sister	son	*daughter*
uncle		sex	dist/lin	sex/dist/lin	gener/dist	gener/sex/dist	gener/dist/lin	gener/sex/dist/lin
aunt	sex		sex/dist/lin	dist/lin	gener/sex/dist	gener/dist	gener/sex/dist/lin	gener/dist
father	dist/lin	sex/dist/lin		sex	gener/lin	gener/sex/lin	gener	gener/sex
mother	sex/dist/lin	dist/lin	sex		gener/sex/lin	gener/lin	gener/sex	gener
brother	gener/dist	gener/sex/dist	gener/dist	gener/sex/lin		sex	gener/lin	gener/sex/lin
sister	gener/sex/dist	gener/dist	gener/sex/lin	gener/lin	sex		gener/sex/lin	gener/lin
son	gener/dist/lin	gener/sex/dist/lin	gener	gener/sex	gener/lin	gener/sex/lin		sex
daughter	gener/sex/dist/lin	gener/dist/lin	gener/sex	gener	gener/sex/lin	gener/lin	sex	

NOTE: A slash "/" stands for a logical disjunction *or*.

The result of the computation of the contrasting features in our illustrative example is given in Table 2.4, where the slant line "/" stands for a logical disjunction, "*or*".

Two terms are said to contrast with respect to some feature (dimension) just in case they have *different values* for this feature. Thus, *uncle* and *aunt* contrast along the dimension of sex since the former has feature value 'male' and the latter the feature value 'female'; *uncle* and *father* contrast along two dimensions, distance and lineality, insofar as *uncle* is distance=2 and lineality=collateral, whereas *father* is distance=1 and lineality=lineal, and so on.[3] If no contrast is found between two kin terms, this fact is signaled by KINSHIP, and the program proceeds smoothly.

As can be seen from Table 2.4, the contrasting features for the pair *son−uncle* are (generation *or* distance *or* lineality), those for *mother−aunt* are (distance *or* lineality), and so on.

The task of concept (kin term) discrimination can be completed by choosing arbitrarily, for each concept (kin term), one contrasting feature from the alternatives given in Table 2.4, such that distinguishes this concept from another concept, then choosing another feature distinguishing the concept from still another one, and so on, until the concept is demarcated from all others. Thus, e.g. to discriminate *uncle*, one needs to choose arbitrarily a feature (with its corresponding value) from each cell of the first row in Table 2.4; one such definition of *uncle* is [generation=1, sex=male, distance=2, lineality=collateral]. However, our program cares for simplicity of the kinship model and proceeds differently.

III. Ensuring the simplicity of kinship models

To find the simplest model(s), the program needs first to find the shortest overall feature (dimension) set that is necessary and sufficient to demarcate all the words in the kinship vocabulary, and then to find the shortest definitions (bundles of features) that are necessary and sufficient to demarcate each of the kin terms.

III.1. Determining simplest overall feature sets

To fulfil the first simplicity constraint, pertaining to choosing the minimum number of overall features, KINSHIP needs to find a minimum set of features that covers *all* pair-wise contrasts between the kin terms. (Note that Table 2.4, for obvious reasons, is symmetrical with respect to the empty-cells diagonal, implying that we may consider only half of it in order to find those contrasts.)

---

[3] In the case when the values of a feature are integers, we also admit values such "greater or equal to" (e.g. the feature value generation= ≥3 will contrast with another that is generation=2, but not with one that is generation=3 or generation=5.

What does this task mean, and how shall we perform its computation? This task can actually be reduced to the familiar one from algorithmic theory of finding a *minimum set-cover*,[4] or equivalently, the conversion of a *conjunctive normal form* (i.e. a conjunction of disjunctions — CNF) into a *disjunctive normal form* (a disjunction of conjunctions — DNF). In our particular case, we obtain two alternative minimal set-covers, each having three features: {generation, sex, distance} or {generation, sex, lineality}. (For convenience, here and in the following we use a comma in these expressions to represent conjunctive "and", i.e. we have e.g. {generation *and* sex *and* lineality}.) It will be easy to verify that either of these sets of features covers all cells of pair-wise contrasts, e.g. taking the feature set {generation, sex, distance}, it is seen from Table 2.4 that at least one of these features occurs in every cell of pair-wise contrasts.

Finally, it remains to construct a conjunctive definition (feature bundle) of each kin term, using one of the minimal sets of features (or both sets, in case we want to get alternatives with equally succinct feature sets).

III.2. Determining simplest definitions of kin terms

The procedure uses as input information the simplest overall feature set(s), obtained at step III.1, as well as the set of contrasting features, obtained at step II.2, and given in Table 2.4. The simplest definition of a kin term, then, must use *only* features from the simplest feature set, and, additionally, must use the *smallest* number of features, such that are members of this simplest feature set. In order to achieve the second goal, the very same procedure of conversion of CNF into DNF is used as in step II.1, converting the conjunction of alternative pair-wise contrasting features of a kin term with all other kin terms from Table 2.4 into a DNF formula, in which every resultant disjunct represents a potential kin term definition.

---

[4] Given a set, whose members are other sets, a "set cover" is a set whose members include at least one member of each constituent set. A "minimum set cover" is the set cover with the smallest cardinality (or the shortest set). We return to these notions, with examples, in Chapter 6 of the book.

Table 2.5. Contrasts with *uncle*

(sex)	/contrast with *aunt*/
(distance *or* lineality)	/contrast with *father*/
(sex *or* distance *or* lineality)	/contrast with *mother*/
(generation *or* distance)	/contrast with *brother*/
(generation *or* sex *or* distance)	/contrast with *sister*/
(generation *or* distance *or* lineality)	/contrast with *son*/
(generation *or* sex *or* distance *or* lineality)	/contrast with *daughter*/

For example, let us find the definition of the kin term *uncle*. Let us first assume that we are given the simplest overall feature set {generation, sex, distance} found above. Table 2.5, which is actually the first row of Table 2.4, gives the contrasts of *uncle* with all other kin terms in our illustrative kin domain. To find a definition of *uncle*, we need to convert the above CNF into a DNF, which yields the two expressions: {sex, distance} or {generation, sex, lineality}. Both these definitions of *uncle* are subsumed by the simplest feature set assumed, but the program will choose the first, as it is shorter.

Proceeding in an analogous manner with all kin terms from the examined kinship vocabulary, and again assuming the minimal feature set {generation, sex, distance}, gives the following simplest componential analysis:

Table 2.6. Simplest componential model

	Generation	*Sex*	***Distance***
uncle		male	2
aunt		female	2
father	1	male	1
mother	1	female	1
brother	0	male	
sister	0	female	
son	−1	male	
daughter	−1	female	

An alternative simplest model (cf. Table 2.7) is obtained using the minimal feature set {generation, sex, lineality}.

Table 2.7. Another simplest componential model

	Generation	Sex	Lineality
uncle		male	collateral
aunt		female	collateral
father	1	male	lineal
mother	1	female	lineal
brother	0	male	
sister	0	female	
son	−1	male	
daughter	−1	female	

2.2.3 *Three styles of componential analysis*

Behind the general statement that the bundle of feature values (=definition) of each kin term should distinguish it from all the remaining kin terms, *three styles* of kin term componential definitions are discernible. This distinction of styles depends on the presence or absence of redundant values (components) in the definition of some kin term. A *redundant* value is one that is not *necessary* for accomplishing the demarcation of kin terms (and can therefore be deleted from the resultant description without destroying this demarcation). All three styles are actually observed in kinship practice. To describe these styles in what follows, we will assume that a minimum set S of features has already been identified.

The first style, which we call a *nonredundant* kin term definition, is one in which each kin term is defined only with components which are both necessary and jointly sufficient to discriminate it from all other kin terms. The componential analyses, given in Tables 2.6 and 2.7, e.g. are nonredundant. In Table 2.6, for instance, in the definition of *uncle* the components sex=male and distance=2, jointly, suffice to discriminate the term from all others: distance=2 makes it distinct from *father, mother, brother, sister,* and *son* which all have distance=1; sex=male distinguishes the concept from *aunt* which has sex=female. Any of these components is also necessary for the distinction: removing distance=2 will lead to confusion of the term with all others possessing male sex (viz. *father, brother,* and *son*); removing sex=male will cause ambiguity with the other kin terms in the corpus that have distance=2, viz. *aunt*. It is worth noting that a simplest componential model is necessarily nonredundant, but of course there are non-simplest models which are also nonredundant.

The second style, which may be called a *fully redundant* kin term definition, simply lists, for every kin term, its value for every feature in *S*, without caring whether all these values are actually necessary for the demarcation. The resultant fully redundant componential analysis of our illustrative example — assuming the minimal feature set *S* = {generation, sex, distance} — will be seen shortly. In this analysis, the feature values will be sufficient to distinguish every kin term from all the rest. However, it will also be clear that some definitions will contain redundant values.

Table 2.8. A fully redundant componential model

	Generation	Sex	Distance
uncle	1	male	2
aunt	1	female	2
father	1	male	1
mother	1	female	1
brother	0	male	1
sister	0	female	1
son	−1	male	1
daughter	−1	female	1

Thus (cf. Table 2.8), on the basis of the values for generation, the kin terms are apportioned into three subsets: *uncle, aunt, father, mother* (generation=1), *brother* and *sister* (generation=0), and *son* and *daughter* (generation= −1); within the first subset, the values of distance, further break it down into *uncle* and *aunt* on the one hand (having distance=2), and *father* and *mother* on the other (having distance=1), each individual term being distinguished from the rest by being either of male or female sex. The feature sex suffices to completely demarcate each term within the remaining two subsets, those of generation=0 and those of generation= −1. It thus turns out that the values for distance of all the terms *sister, brother, son,* and *daughter* are not strictly necessary.

The third style of kin term definition, which is only *partially redundant*, does not list indiscriminately for every kin term the values of all features in *S*. Rather, it embodies a consecutive partitioning of the space of kin terms along the given dimensions, which is very much like that described in the previous paragraph (why this definition is redundant, we shall see shortly). In the procedure, leading to this definition, a feature is selected and the values for this feature are listed in the definitions of all kin terms, unless a term is already completely discriminated from all remaining in the corpus; if a term is already completely discriminated, the term's value for this feature is discarded, and does not enter as a component in its definition.

Two partially redundant componential analyses are shown in Table 2.9: in the first, only the bare values and the values in square brackets count (i.e. the components in angular brackets are ignored), whereas in the second only the bare values and those in angular brackets are valid components (i.e. the components in square brackets are ignored):

Table 2.9. Styles of kin term definitions

	Generation	Sex	Distance
uncle	<1>	male	2
aunt	<1>	female	2
father	1	male	[1]
mother	1	female	[1]
brother	0	male	[1]
sister	0	female	[1]
son	−1	male	[1]
daughter	−1	female	[1]

NOTE: Styles of kinship definitions: all three styles include the values not in brackets. Additionally, (1) "fully redundant" definitions include all items in brackets; (2) "partially redundant" include all items in angle brackets (< >) *or* in square brackets ([ ]), but not both; and (3) "nonredundant" does not include any values in brackets.

Let us now see how the first alternative partially redundant kin term definition is obtained. We start with the same feature set S = {generation, sex, distance} and select the first feature, viz. generation. Since no kin term is yet completely discriminated, the values for generation are included in the definitions of all kin terms. (This gives column 1 of Table 2.9.) The kin terms are partitioned into three subsets, and no term is completely discriminated by the generation feature. Then we take the second feature (sex), and, as no term is decisively demarcated, we list its corresponding values in the definitions of all kin terms. (This gives column 2 of Table 2.9.) The terms *brother, sister, son,* and *daughter* are now completely distinguished from the remaining terms because generation and sex cover all their cells of contrast, cf. Table 2.4. Finally, the last feature (distance) is chosen and its corresponding values are included in the definition of *uncle, aunt, father,* and *mother,* but *not* in the definitions of *brother, sister, son,* and *daughter,* which completes the analysis. It is now clear why the values for distance do not occur in the definitions of the latter terms.

The consecutive partitioning, described above, suggests that the *order* of applying the features may matter, and in fact it does. Thus, if we start the partitioning with distance, instead of with generation, we shall obtain the second alternative partially redundant definition (see Table 2.9, and note again that here only bare values, and those in square brackets, actually count). Starting with distance, the definitions of all kin terms will contain the corresponding values for this feature (column 3 of Table 2.9). No term is decisively demarcated, so we use the second feature sex, and include its corresponding values in the definitions of all kin terms. Now, distance and sex jointly suffice to discriminate completely *uncle* and *aunt*, which may be verified from Table 2.9, so when, finally, the feature generation is used, its corresponding values will not be included in the definitions of these two kin terms, but only in those of the remaining ones. (The relative order of using sex is irrelevant as regards the introduction of a new alternative analysis.)

It will be now clear why these two analyses are redundant. The first contains the component generation=1 in both the definition of *uncle* and in the definition of *aunt*, but in both cases this is not necessary since the components distance=2 and sex=male suffice to completely discriminate *uncle* (FaBr or MoBr), and the components distance=2 and sex=female do likewise for *aunt* (FaSi or MoSi). Similar considerations hold for the second analysis where the occurrence of distance=1 in the definitions of *brother*, *sister*, *son*, and *daughter* are redundant. Thus, *brother* is distinguished by having generation=0 and sex=male, *sister* by having generation=0 and sex=female, and so on. The analyses are only partially redundant since anyone of them avoids some redundancy, unlike the fully redundant componential analysis.

All three styles of componential definitions may be encountered in the work of kinship analysts, though indeed these researchers do not explicitly make our distinctions (this claim, of course, should not be interpreted in the sense that previous researchers have not noted the existence of redundant analyses). Giving but one example of each, Wallace and Atkins (1960) provide a fully redundant componential analysis of English consanguineals, Goodenough (1967) (and elsewhere) shows a partially redundant one of Lapp consanguineals, and Lounsbury insists on a nonredundant analysis saying that "[the] bundle of features states the necessary and sufficient conditions which an object must satisfy if it is to be a *denotatum* of the term so defined" (1964: 1074) (cf. also "A significatum is a statement of various necessary and sufficient conditions for a kin-type to belong to the class of kin-types denoted by a term" Wallace and Atkins 1960: 67).

In the remaining part of the chapter, we shall stick to *simplest* componential analyses, i.e. such that fulfil both requirements as to parsimony, viz. minimum of overall features and minimum components in kin term definitions, noting at the same time that, optionally, the user of KINSHIP can obtain all other non-simplest (and all simplest) alternatives.

2.3 Some discoveries of KINSHIP

Currently, KINSHIP uses more than twenty features. It employs those of Kroeber (1909), viz. generation, lineal vs. collateral, age difference in one generation, sex of the relative, sex of the first connecting relative, sex of the speaker, consanguineal vs. affinal, and condition of the connecting relative. Greenberg writes about these features: "Leaving aside some difficulties and complications, in principle any kin term in any language can be specified by means of them" (1980: 13). To alleviate some potential difficulties envisaged by Greenberg, we have also included the features distance, same vs. different sex of ego and alter, sex of the second connecting relative, Iroquois parallel, matrilateral, and some others.

So far we have applied KINSHIP on data from more than twenty languages belonging to different language families.

In this section, we apply the program to three data sets, those of Bulgarian, American English (Yankee), and Seneca. A componential analysis of Turkish can be found in Pericliev and Valdés-Pérez (1998a: 297–299) and an analysis of Swedish consanguineals in Pericliev and Valdés-Pérez (1998b).

2.3.1. Bulgarian: a novel analysis

A major application of KINSHIP is to perform componential analysis of kinship terminologies of unanalysed languages. Many terminologies of non-Indo-European languages have been the object of componential analyses; a lot of other languages, much better studied in other respects, however, have remained unstudied as regards their kinship systems. We turn to one such example from the Slavic language family, viz. Bulgarian.

Data on Bulgarian kinship can be found in various places, notably in Mladenov (1929[1979: 188–190]). Consanguineals are listed in Comrie and Corbett (1993). (Other aspects of kin terms are studied elsewhere, e.g. meaning shifts in Stoeva 1972 or the origin and dialectal distribution of some terms in Gălăbov 1986.) Bulgarian has the following basic lexemes for designating relatives, which we give with glosses: *pradjado* "great grandfather", *prababa* "great grandmother", *djado* "grandfather", *baba* "grandmother", *bašta* "father", *majka* "mother", *vujčo* "maternal uncle", *čičo* "paternal uncle", *lelja* "aunt", *brat* "brother", *sestra* "sister", *batko* "elder brother", *kaka* "elder sister", *bratovčedka* "female cousin", *bratovčed* "male cousin", *sin* "son", *dăšterja* "daughter", *plemennik* "nephew", *plemennica* "niece", *vnuc* "grandson", *vnučka* "granddaughter", *pravnuc* "great grandson", *pravnučka* "great granddaughter", *măž* "husband", *žena* "wife", *šurej* "brother-in-law", *šurenajka* "brother-in-law's wife", *dever* and *zet* and *badžanak* "brother-in-law", *zălva* and *baldăza* and *snaha* and *etărva* "sister-in-law", *svekăr* and *tăst* "father-in-law", *svekărva* and *tăšta* "mother-in-law", *vujna* and *strina* "aunt".

These lexemes with their range of denotata are given below. We note that this list is not exhaustive both as regards kin terms and their attendant kin types. Some other points should also be made in connection with this corpus. First, only the lexemes for reference, and not those for address, are listed (Bulgarian normally uses a vocative form, however some referential lexemes never form a vocative for address, so a different lexeme is used for this purpose, e.g. *bašta* "father" (ref.) vs. *tate* (voc.); other lexemes not used for address have no address counterparts, e.g. *dever*, *etărva*, etc.). Secondly, we omit numerous synonymous forms of the lexemes listed, which are basically dialectal variations (e.g. for *dăšterja* we have also *šterka*, *k'erka* (south-eastern dialects), *čerka* (north-west dialects)). Thirdly, also omitted are certain definitely dialectal lexemes for designating relatives, such as *sestrinik* (SiSo) or *bratanec* (BrSo).[5] Fourthly, insofar as the range of denotata of kin terms is concerned, we also follow literary, rather than dialectal, usages (thus e.g. for the lexeme *baba* "grandmother" we list only the kin types FaMo and MoMo, given in standard Bulgarian dictionaries, but not also FaMoSi and MoMoSi, as the kin term is somewhere used). Finally, we note that for our purposes it is sufficient to limit the terminology to

---

[5] Notable among these are a group of words for designating husband's sisters according to their relative age: *kalina* (oldest HuSi), *malina* (HuSi younger than *kalina*), *hubavka* (HuSi younger than *malina*), *jabălka* (HuSi younger than *hubavka*), and *dunka* (youngest HuSi). No such detailed distinction is attested in any other Slavic language, and we have not been able to find a comparably detailed system among those we are acquainted with. These Bulgarian kin terms were firstly noted by Marinov (1892: 172–173), and were (independently) included in the first significant dictionary of the Bulgarian language by Gerov (1897: 159); cf. also Gălăbov (1986).

three generations above and below ego, though the Bulgarian prefix *pra*–
just as the English word *great*, may be used any number of times to
denote one-generation removal.

1. *pradjado*, FaFaFa, FaMoFa, MoFaFa, MoMo.
2. *prababa*, FaFaMo, FaMoMo, MoFaMo, MoMoMo.
3. *djado*, FaFa, MoFa.
4. *baba*, FaMo, MoMo.
5. *bašta* , Fa.
6. *majka*, Mo.
7. *vujčo*, MoBr.
8. *čičo* , FaBr.
9. *lelja*, MoSi,FaSi.
10. *brat*, Br.
11. *sestra*, Si.
12. *batko*, elderBr.
13. *kaka*, elderSi.
14. *bratovčedka*, MoSiDa, MoBrDa, FaSiDa, FaBrDa, MoMoSiDa-
Da, MoMoSiSoDa, MoMoBrDaDa, MoMoBrSoDa, MoFaSiDaDa,
MoFaSiSoDa, MoFaBrDaDa, MoFaBrSoDa, FaMoSiDaDa, FaMo-
SiSoDa, FaMoBrDaDa, FaMoBrSoDa, FaFaSiDaDa, FaFaSiSoDa,
FaFaBrDaDa, FaFaBrSoDa.
15. *bratovčed*, MoSiSo, MoBrSo, FaSiSo, FaBrSo, MoMoSiDaSo,
MoMoSiSoSo, MoMoBrDaSo, MoMoBrSoSo, MoFaSiDaSo,
MoFaSiSoSo, MoFaBrDaSo, MoFaBrSoSo, FaMoSiDaSo, FaMoSi-
SoSo, FaMoBrDaSo, FaMoBrSoSo, FaFaSiDaSo, FaFaSiSoSo,
FaFaBrDaSo, FaFaBrSoSo.
16. *sin*, So.
17. *dăšterja*, Da.
18. *plemennik*, BrSo, SiSo.
19. *plemennitsa*, BrDa, SiDa.
20. *vnuc*, SoSo, DaSo.
21. *vnučka*, DaDa, SoDa.
22. *pravnuc*, SoSoSo, SoDaSo, DaSoSo, DaDaSo.
23. *pravnučka*, DaDaDa, SoSoDa, SoDaDa, DaSoDa.
24. *măž*, Hu.
25. *žena*, Wi.
26. *šurej*, WiBr.
27. *šurerenajka*, WiBrWi.
28. *dever*, HuBr.
29. *zet*, SiHu, DaHu.
30. *badžanak*, WiSiHu.

31. *zălva*, HuSi.
32. *baldăza*, WiSi.
33. *snaha*, BrWi, SoWi.
34. *etărva*, HuBrWi.
35. *svekăr*, HuFa.
36. *svekărva*, HuMo.
37. *tăst*, WiFa.
38. *tăšta*, WiMo.
39. *vujna*, MoBrWi.
40. *strina*, FaBrWi.

Running KINSHIP on the Bulgarian data, we obtained two simplest feature sets, each consisting of 7 features (we also got two feature sets of 8 features and one of 9). Componential analyses with these simplest feature sets are presented in Table 2.10 and Table 2.11. Each of the analyses uses seven out of the eight features listed below:

1. Generation of relative, with integer values from –3 to 3.
2. Sex of alter, with values 'male' or 'female'.
3. Distance, with integer values ranging from 1 to 3.
4. Affinity of relative, with 3 values: 'consanguineal' (absence of a marital tie), 'affinal-ego' (marital tie to ego), 'affinal' (marital tie not to ego).
5. Affinity of the first connecting relative (link), with values 'consanguineal' (first link is a blood relative) or 'affinal' (first link is a relative by marriage).
6. Sex of the first connecting relative (link), with values 'male' or 'female'.
7. Generation of the last link, with 3 values –1, 0, 1 (the generations of the last links will be: Fa and Mo = 1; Si, Br, Hu and Wi = 0; So and Da =–1, hence FaMo e.g. will have the value 1 for this feature, while So or SoSo will have the value –1).
8. Seniority within one generation, with values 'elder' or 'younger'.

Both analyses show that two words, viz. *batko* "elder brother" and *kaka* "elder sister", have no complementary lexemes, i.e. lexemes having an explicit value 'younger' for the feature seniority; thus, *brat* 'Br' and *sestra* 'Si' are unmarked with respect to seniority. In effect, two places are filled by "no lexeme" (cf. Wallace and Atkins 1960: 69).[6]

---

[6] We actually manually filled the "no-lexeme" places on the basis of the report from KINSHIP that brat and *batko* on the one hand, and *sestra* and *kaka* on the other, cannot be properly distinguished.

Table 2.10. Simplest componential analysis of Bulgarian kinterms

	Gene-ration of relative	Sex of alter	Distance	Affinity of relative	Affinity of 1st link	Sex of 1st link	Seniority
pradjado	3	male					
prababa	3	female					
djado	2	male					
baba	2	female					
bašta	1	male	1				
majka	1	female	1				
vujčo	1	male		consang		female	
čičo	1	male	2	consang		male	
lelja	1	female	2	consang			
brat	0	male	1	consang			
sestra	0	female	1	consang			
batko	0	male	1	consang			elder
/no lexeme/	–	–	–	–	–	–	younger
kaka	0	female	1	consang			elder
/no lexeme/	–	–	–	–	–	–	younger
bratovčedka	0	female	≥3	consang			
bratovčed	0	male	≥3	consang			
sin	–1	male	1				
dăšterja	–1	female	1				
plemennik	–1	male	2	consang			
plemennitsa	–1	female	2	consang			
vnuc	–2	male		consang			
vnučka	–2	female		consang			
pravnuc	–3	male	3				
pravnučka	–3	female	3				
măž		male		affin.-ego			
žena		female		affin.-ego			
šurej	0	male	2		affinal	female	
šurenajka		female	3		affinal	female	
dever	0	male	2			male	
zet		male	2	affinal	consang		
badžanak		male	3	affinal			
zălva	0	female	2		affinal	male	
baldăza	0	female	2			female	
snaha	≤0	female		affinal	consang		
etărva	0	female	3	affinal		male	
svekăr	1	male	2		affinal	male	
svekărva	1	female			affinal	male	
tăst	1	male		affinal		female	
tăšta	1	female	2			female	
vujna	1		3			female	
strina	1		3			male	

Table 2.11. Another simplest componential analysis of Bulgarian

	Gene-ration of relative	Sex of alter	Distance	Gener-ation of last link or str.equiv.	Affinity of 1st link	Sex of 1st link	Seniority
pradjado	3	male					
prababa	3	female					
djado	2	male					
baba	2	female					
bašta	1	male	1				
majka	1	female	1				
vujčo	1	male		0		female	
čičo	1	male		0		male	
lelja	1	female	2	0			
brat	0	male	1		consang		
sestra	0	female	1		consang		
batko	0	male	1				elder
/no lexeme/	–	–	–	–	–	–	younger
kaka	0	female	1				elder
/no lexeme/	–	–	–	–	–	–	younger
bratovčedka	0	female		–1			
bratovčed	0	male		–1			
sin	–1	male	1				
dăšterja	–1	female	1				
plemennik	–1	male	2	–1			
plemennitsa	–1	female	2	–1			
vnuc	–2	male		–1			
vnučka	–2	female		–1			
pravnuc	–3	male	3				
pravnučka	–3	female	3				
măž		male	1		affinal		
žena		female	1		affinal		
šurej	0	male	2		affinal	female	
šurenajka		female	3		affinal	female	
dever	0	male	2			male	
zet	≤0	male	2	0	consang		
badžanak		male	3	0			
zălva	0	female	2		affinal	male	
baldăza	0	female	2			female	
snaha	≤0	female	2		consang		
etărva			3		affinal	male	
svekăr	1	male			affinal	male	
svekărva	1	female			affinal	male	
tăst	1	male	2		affinal	female	
tăšta	1	female	2		affinal	female	
vujna	1		3			female	
strina	1		3			male	

Looking just at the first analysis (Table 2.10), we see that the feature affinity of 1st connecting relative serves basically to demarcate *zet*

'SiHu' or 'DaHu' from *šurej* 'WiBr', and *snaha* 'BrWi' or 'SoWi' from *zălva* 'HuSi'. The cross-generational terms are *snaha* and *zet* (e.g. for *snaha*, BrWi has generation=0 and SoWi has generation= −1), though in the case of *zet* this is not seen in Table 2.10 since the component is not needed for demarcation, in contrast to Table 2.11. The cross-distance terms are *bratovčed* "male cousin" and *bratovčedka* "female cousin", the former e.g. has distance=3 (MoSiSo), in which case it is often referred to in Bulgarian as "first cousin", or distance=5 (MoMoSiSoSo), when the relative is usually known as "second cousin". The basic difference of the second componential analysis (Table 2.11) from the first (Table 2.10) is that in place of the feature affinity of relative, the second uses the feature generation of last link. The lack of the feature affinity of relative in the second componential analysis should not be hurriedly proclaimed as calling into question the universality of the affinity/consanguinity distinction (assumed e.g. by Greenberg 1966b: 87), for the distinction is here present in the feature affinity of the 1st connecting relative.

We have also run KINSHIP with the terminologies of the other Slavic languages (with data taken from Comrie and Corbett 1993, and other sources). A detailed comparison of the Slavic kinship systems is beyond the scope of the present chapter, so we confine to just a few remarks. Bulgarian, in contrast to all the other Slavic terminologies, makes use of the feature seniority in one generation, though only partially, because it does not have any lexemes with seniority=younger; this feature is actually rather common in many systems throughout the world (from the languages spoken in Europe, Hungarian, distinguishing elder brother (*bátya*) from younger brother (*öccs*), and elder sister (*néne*) from younger sister (*húg*) is a popular example, known from illustrations of the componential method by L. Hjelmslev, e.g. Hjelmslev 1958).[7] The remaining features are employed by the other Slavic languages as well. KINSHIP found that a feature that Bulgarian does *not* use, while another Slavic language does, is the feature sex of the second connecting relative. This dimension of contrast (along with the feature sex of the first connecting relative) is necessary in Polish to discriminate the lexemes for male cousin, viz. *brat stryjeczny* 'FaBrSo', *brat cioteczny* 'FaSiSo' or 'MoSiSo', and *brat wujeczny* 'MoBrSo', as well as those for female cousin, *sestra stryjeczna* 'FaBrDa', *sestra cioteczna* 'FaSiDa' or

---

[7] It is interesting to recall that the different partitioning of the universe of relatives by kin terms in different languages, as in the Hungarian example vs. English with its two terms (*brother/sister*) vs. Malayan with just one word (*sudarā*), was known as far back as August Friedrich Pott in the 60s of 19th c.

'MoSiDa', and *sestra wujeczna* 'MoBrDa'. (KINSHIP also discovered that this feature would be necessary in languages like Turkish and Hindi as well.)

2.3.2 English: a reanalysis

A further application of KINSHIP is the reanalysis of languages that have been previously subjected to componential treatment. The program would be likely to notice semantic structuring of kinship paradigms that have remained unnoticed by human analysts. As an illustration we present a reanalysis of the American English (Yankee) kinship system, as presented by Goodenough (1965). The full listing of denotata is given below. It reflects Goodenough's symbolically expressed denotata (but not the "[natural language] descriptions of how the kinship terms are used when usual expectations about biological procreation, marriage, etc., are not met" (p. 264). This corpus, to our knowledge, is the most complete list of kin types for the kin terms in the American Yankee kinship terminology.

1. *great-grandfather*, FaFaFa, FaMoFa, MoFaFa, MoMoFa.
2. *great-grandmother*, FaFaMo, FaMoMo, MoFaMo, MoMoMo.
3. *great-uncle*, MoMoBr, MoFaBr, FaMoBr, FaFaBr.
4. *great-aunt*, MoMoSi, MoFaSi, FaMoSi, FaFaSi.
5. *grandfather*, FaFa, MoFa.
6. *grandmother*, FaMo, MoMo.
7. *uncle*, MoBr, FaBr, FaFaSo, FaMoSo, MoFaSo, MoMoSo, FaSiHu, MoSiHu, FaFaDaHu, FaMoDaHu, MoMoDaHu, MoFaDaHu.
8. *aunt*, MoSi, FaSi, FaFaDa, FaMoDa, MoFaDa, MoMoDa, FaBrWi, MoBrWi, FaFaSoWi, FaMoSoWi, MoMoSoWi, MoFaSoWi.
9. *father*, Fa.
10. *mother*, Mo.
11. *son*, So.
12. *daughter*, Da.
13. *brother*, Br, FaSo, MoSo.
14. *sister*, Si, FaDa, MoDa.
15. *cousin*, MoSiDa, MoBrDa, FaSiDa, FaBrDa, MoSiSo, MoBrSo, FaSiSo, FaBrSo, FaFaSoSo, FaFaSoDa, FaFaDaSo, FaFaDaDa, FaMoSoSo, FaMoSoDa, FaMoDaSo, FaMoDaDa, MoFaSoSo, MoFaSoDa, MoFaDaSo, MoFaDaDa, MoMoSoSo, MoMoSoDa, MoMoDaSo, MoMoDaDa, etc.
16. *nephew*, BrSo, SiSo, FaSoSo, MoSoSo, FaDaSo, MoDaSo, WiSiSo, WiBrSo, HuSiSo, HuBrSo, WiMoDaSo, WiFaSoSo, WiFaDaSo, WiMoSoSo, HuMoDaSo, HuFaSoSo, HuFaDaSo, HuMoSoSo.

17. *niece*, BrDa, SiDa, FaSoDa, MoSoDa, FaDaDa, MoDaDa, WiSi-Da, WiBrDa, HuSiDa, HuBrDa, WiMoDaDa, WiFaSoDa, WiFaDaDa, WiMoSoDa, HuMoDaDa, HuFaSoDa, HuFaDaDa, HuMoSoDa.

18. *grandson*, SoSo, DaSo.

19. *granddaughter*, DaDa, SoDa.

20. *great-grandson*, SoSoSo, SoDaSo, DaSoSo, DaDaSo.

21. *great-granddaughter*, DaDaDa, SoSoDa, SoDaDa, DaSoDa.

22. *husband*, Hu.

23. *wife*, Wi.

24. *father-in-law*, WiFa, HuFa, WiMoHu, HuMoHu.

25. *mother-in-law*, WiMo, HuMo, WiFaWi, HuFaWi.

26. *son-in-law*, DaHu, WiDaHu, HuDaHu.

27. *daughter-in-law*, SoWi, WiSoWi, HuSoWi.

28. *brother-in-law*, HuBr, WiBr, WiMoSo, WiFaSo, HuMoSo, HuFaSo, WiMoHuSo, WiFaWiSo, HuMoHuSo, HuFaWiSo, SiHu, FaDaHu, MoDaHu, MoHuDaHu, FaWiDaHu.

29. *sister-in-law*, HuSi, WiSi, WiFaDa, WiMoDa, HuFaDa, HuMoDa, WiMoHuDa, WiFaWiDa, HuMoHuDa, HuFaWiDa, BrWi, FaSoWi, MoSoWi, MoHuSoWi, FaWiSoWi.

30. *step-father*, MoHu.

31. *step-mother*, FaWi.

32. *step-son*, HuSo, WiSo.

33. *step-daughter*, HuDa, WiDa.

34. *step-brother*, MoHuSo, FaWiSo.

35. *step-sister*, MoHuDa, FaWiDa.

Running KINSHIP on the above data, we obtained just one simplest dimension set, comprising the following 5 features (cf. Table 2.12):

1. Generation of relative, with integer values from −3 to 3.

2. Sex of alter, with 2 values 'male'/'female'.

3. Generation of last link or its structural equivalent, with 3 values − 1, 0, 1.

4. Structural equivalence, with 3 values 'equivalent-c', 'equivalent-a', 'non-equivalent' (see below).

5. Affinity of relative, with 3 values: 'consanguineal' (absence of marital tie), 'affinal-ego' (marital tie to ego), 'affinal' (marital tie not to ego).

Table 2.12. Simplest componential analysis of American kinterms

	Generation of relative	Sex of alter	Generation of last link or str. equiv.	Structural equivalence	Affinity of relative
great-grandfather	3	male			
great-grandmother	3	female			
great-uncle	2	male	0		
great-aunt	2	female	0		
grandfather	2	male	1		
grandmother	2	female	1		
uncle	1	male	0		
aunt	1	female	0		
father	1	male		equiv-c	
mother	1	female		equiv-c	
son	−1	male		equiv-c	
daughter	−1	female		equiv-c	
brother	0	male	0		consang
sister	0	female	0		consang
cousin	0		−1		
nephew	−1	male	−1	non-equiv	
niece	−1	female	−1	non-equiv	
grandson	−2	male			
granddaughter	−2	female			
great-grandson	−3	male			
great-granddaughter	−3	female			
husband	0	male			affinal-ego
wife	0	female			affinal-ego
father-in-law	1	male	1	non-equiv	
mother-in-law	1	female	1	non-equiv	
son-in-law	−1	male	0	non-equiv	
daughter-in-law	−1	female	0	non-equiv	
brother-in-law	0	male		non-equiv	affinal
sister-in-law	0	female		non-equiv	affinal
step-father	1	male		equiv-a	
step-mother	1	female		equiv-a	
step-son	−1	male		equiv-a	
step-daughter	−1	female		equiv-a	
step-brother	0	male		equiv-a	affinal
step-sister	0	female		equiv-a	affinal

Two of the features merit an explanation. We start with structural equivalence. Goodenough (1964: 231–232) and Goodenough (1965: 277) use the fact that certain affinal kin types, viz. the step-relatives, are *structurally equivalent* to primary consanguineal kin types; for example, under normal expectations, one's father's wife will be one's mother, etc. Thus, the following equivalences are valid:

    (1) FaWi=Mo
    (2) MoHu=Fa
    (3) SpSo=So
    (4) SpDa=Da

(5) PaSpSo=Br

(6) PaSpDa=Si (Sp=spouse, Pa=parent; below we shall also use the common abbreviations Ch=child and Sb=sibling).

In our definition of this feature, one of the elements of the equivalence relation, viz. the primary *consanguineal* kin types, will get the value 'equivalent-c', the other elements, viz. the structurally equivalent *affinal* types, will get the value 'equivalent-a', and all the remaining kin types — which do not participate in the equivalence relation — will be 'non-equivalent' (Goodenough's feature is binary). For example, *step-father* (MoHu) will have the value 'equivalent-a' (by equivalence rule (2)), *father* (Fa) the value 'equivalent-c' (by the same equivalence rule), while *grandson* (SoSo, DaSo) the value 'non-=equivalent', since neither of its kin types form a part of any equivalence relation.

We may now look at the feature generation of last link or its structural equivalent. We first observe that an equivalence relation may exist not only between whole kin types and primary consanguines, a fact we used in the definition of the feature equivalence above, but also between parts, or sequences of links within a kin type, and primary consanguines. For example, under normal expectations, my mother's husband's daughter's husband is actually my sister's husband, i.e. *MoHuDa*Hu should be considered as SiHu, since the initial, italicized, sequence of the former kin type is of course equivalent to Si (cf. rule (6)) and can be substituted for it. Analogously, Wi*MoHuSo* can naturally be considered as WiBr since the italicized last sequence of the kin type is structurally equivalent to Br (by rule (5)) and hence can be substituted for it. We use the foregoing natural transformations in the definition of our feature generation of the last link, and determine the generation of the last link *only after* the equivalence substitution has been made (if possible); thus, the generation of the last link of the above kin type WiMoHuSo will be 0 since it is equivalent to WiBr, and the generation of Br is 0. (In a similar manner, we shall later use the feature generation of first link or its structural equivalent.)

Next, we observe that besides the structural equivalence between affinal and primary consanguineal kin types (i.e. rules (1)–(6)), there exists structural equivalence between some consanguineal and primary consanguineal kin types. These are:

(7) PaSo=Br

(8) PaDa=Si.

One can verify whether the kin types of a kin term possess the feature in the following way. If the last two/three symbols of a kin type are structurally equivalents to some primary consanguine — according to the above list of 8 equivalences — the generation of this consanguine is taken as the feature value. If not, then the generation of the last symbol (=link) is the feature value. Table 2.13 shows how one determines that *brother-in-law* is generation-of-last-link-or-structural-equivalent=0 (the last link/structural equivalent is underlined):

Table 2.13. "Generation of last link" of *brother-in-law*

brother-in-law	Ultimate value	Reasoning
Hu<u>Br</u>	= 0	since Br=0
Wi<u>Br</u>	= 0	since Br=0
Wi<u>Mo</u>So	= 0	since PaSo=Br=0 (by (7))
Wi<u>Fa</u>So	= 0	since PaSo=Br=0 (by (7))
Hu<u>Mo</u>So	= 0	since PaSo=Br=0 (by (7))
Hu<u>Fa</u>So	= 0	since PaSo=Br=0 (by (7))
Wi<u>Mo</u>HuSo	= 0	since PaSpSo=Br=0 (by (5))
Wi<u>Fa</u>WiSo	= 0	since PaSpSo=Br=0 (by (5))
Hu<u>Mo</u>HuSo	= 0	since PaSpSo=Br=0 (by (5))
Hu<u>Fa</u>WiSo	= 0	since PaSpSo=Br=0 (by (5))
Si<u>Hu</u>	= 0	since Hu=0
FaDa<u>Hu</u>	= 0	since Hu=0
MoDa<u>Hu</u>	= 0	since Hu=0
MoHuDa<u>Hu</u>	= 0	since Hu=0
FaWiDa<u>Hu</u>	= 0	since Hu=0

The second column shows the ultimate value and the third column the reason for assigning this value (the relevant substitutions made). In the first two, and in the last five, rows there are no valid structural equivalents, and hence the last links Br and Hu are considered, which are both of generation=0, while in the remaining cases there is a valid structural equivalence whose primary consanguineal counterpart is in all cases Br=0. (It should be clear from the above discussion, that despite its verbal formulation, containing an 'or', the feature generation of last link or its structural equivalent in no way smuggles disjunctivity; thus, a conjunctive, but somewhat less clear, wording of the same feature might have been just "generation of last link" where "last link" is conceived as the final symbol remaining after all relevant equivalence substitutions have already been made.)

It is worthwhile to briefly compare our analysis with componential analyses known in the literature, specifically with regards to parsimony and conjunctiveness of definitions. In comparison with Goodenough

(1965), who uses 9 features, the model discovered by KINSHIP is more economical. This is basically due to our use of multiple-valued features whereas Goodenough shows preference for binary, or sometimes ternary, features. Also, Goodenough seems unable to give a *conjunctive* definition of a number of kin terms, and lists as separate lexemes e.g. *uncle* (consanguineal meaning) and *uncle* (affinal meaning) and some others, like *nephew*, *niece*, etc. (cf. Table VI on p. 279, and Table X on p. 285, where this is less evident, but is nevertheless seen in the use of features, and the "same-as-above" entry in the table). Put differently, for these kin terms Goodenough has not found components shared by all their attendant kin types such that they also serve to contrast these from other kin terms. Our analysis does not encounter this problem, say with a kin term like *uncle*, owing to the introduction of the new feature generation of last link or its structural equivalent. Referring to Table 2.12, *uncle* is described with three features, generation of relative, sex of alter (both used by Goodenough), but also with generation of last link or its structural equivalent, the latter feature possessed by all its attendant kin types, both consanguineal and affinal, and hence eliminating the need to artificially introduce homonymity in the term. Besides, since the first two features, generation and sex of alter, are insufficient to demarcate the term from all remaining terms, the third feature — in conjunction with the other two — does the job. We note that disjunctive definitions would generally be conceived as a major shortcoming by kinship analysts, Lounsbury e.g. writing on this occasion:

> We feel that we have failed if we cannot achieve conjunctive definitions for every terminological class in the system. Were we to compromise on this point and admit disjunctive definitions (class sums, alternative criteria for membership) as on a par with conjunctive definitions (class products, uniform criteria for membership), there would be no motivation for analysis in the first place, for definitions of kin classes by summing of discrete members ... are disjunctive definitions par excellence. (Lounsbury 1965: 1074)

There is also empirical evidence that kin terms are actually conjunctive notions, coming from typological studies. Thus, in a study of grandparent terminology (Greenberg 1966b), involving the four kin types FaFa, MoFa, FaMo, and MoMo, 15 grandparental kin terms are possible, resulting from the different groupings of the kin types. Of these 15 possible kin terms, it was found, inspecting about one hundred languages, that four did not actually occur in the sample, and these were exactly the kin terms that involved logically disjunctive definitions. Very impressive results in this vein were found for sibling terminology as well

(Nerlove and Romney 1967, Kronenfeld 1974, Epling, Kirk, and Boyd 1973).

As a final contrast, our analysis does *not* have "no-lexeme" entries, whereas Goodenough's has three, thus showing a somewhat better regularity in the English kinship paradigm. Schneider (1965: 295) also notes an excessive use of empty lexemes in Goodenough's treatment.

Wallace and Atkins (1960), Wallace (1962), and Romney and D'Andrade (1964) are more economic treatments than ours (they use only three features each), but encompass a more limited data set, and the problem with disjunctive definitions in these analyses still remains (c.f. e.g. Wallace and Atkins 1960: 61 or Wallace 1962). It must be pointed out however that these analyses pursued different goals than parsimony, which was our predominant concern here, and much subsequent work was based on them.

Nogle (1974: 62–64) however claims to have based his analysis on the extensive Goodenough's data, so we should examine his proposal more closely. He uses the following dimensions of contrast: (1) nuclear family vs. nonnuclear family;[8] (2) affinal vs. consanguineal; (3) ascending vs. contemporary vs. descending generation; (4) consanguineal 1st link vs. affinal 1st link; (5) lineal vs. collateral; and (6) male vs. female. We easily tested Nogle's analysis by simply adding the first feature to the program, and slightly redefining the second (our previous feature was ternary-valued) and the third (our generation feature could take any number as value). With these modifications, we again ran KINSHIP on Goodenough's data. The program signaled that it is unable to distinguish between all pairs of the type *great–X* vs. *X*, as *great grandfather* vs. *grandfather*, *great grandmother* vs. *grandmother*, *great uncle* vs. *uncle*, etc. Clearly, the problem here comes from Nogle's only ternary value of generation, and to be fair, he does not list in his data the *great–X* terms (although Goodenough does). More importantly, we noted the following.

First, Nogle believes *not* to be able to give a conjunctive definition of *uncle* and *aunt* — and just as previous analysts — lists them as separate entries, with affinal or consanguineal meaning. However in actual fact his features are perfectly sufficient to make the demarcation. Thus, for *uncle* our program yielded the definition [nonnuclear, generation=ascending, consanguineal 1st link, collateral, male], and for *aunt*

---

[8] The nuclear family in Nogle's view includes Fa, Mo, Br, Si, So, Da, Hu, Wi, as well as all step-relatives.

the definition [nonnuclear, generation=ascending, consanguineal 1st link, collateral, female].

Table 2.14. Contrasts demarcating *uncle*

uncle (collateral)	vs.	*grandfather* (lineal)
uncle (collateral *or* nonnuclear)	vs.	*father* (lineal *or* nuclear)
uncle (consanguineal 1st link)	vs.	*father-in-law* (affinal 1st link)
uncle (nonnuclear)	vs.	*step-father* (nuclear)

Let us now show (cf. Table 2.14) how e.g. *uncle* contrasts with the other terms from the domain (the situation with *aunt* will be analogous). It will be clear that *uncle* stays distinct from all female terms, and all terms that are not of ascending generation. So let us just focus on contrasts with the remaining terms, viz. *grandfather*, *father*, *father-in-law*, and *step-father*. Table 2.14 lists the actual contrasts that might be used to accomplish the demarcation.

Our second observation is that Nogle believes, again mistakenly, to be able to demarcate *nephew* from *son-in-law*, and *niece* from *daughter-in-law* by stating in his analysis that the first terms in both pairs are consanguineal whereas the second terms are affinal. However, *nephew* and *niece* both do not possess the component consanguineal since they have each some kin types which are consanguineal, and others which are affinal (e.g. *nephew* ('BrSo', etc., but also 'WiSiSo', etc.); *niece* ('BrDa', etc. but also 'WiSiDa', etc.)).

Summarizing all the previous analyses from the point of view of interest to us, the analysis KINSHIP discovered, as far as we know, is the only one that manages to provide conjunctive definitions of all kin terms. Also, as far as we are aware, it is also the most parsimonious analysis, using 5 features, of the detailed data on English kinship. Claims as that by Wordick (1973: 1249), though indeed made in passing, that English can be handled by just 3 dimenisons, viz. (1) type, with values lineal vs. collateral vs. affinal, (2) generation removal, with values 1, 0, -1, and (3) sex of referent, with values male vs. female, cannot be taken very seriously. Thus, from a first glance it is seen that we cannot distinguish between *father*, *grandfather*, *great grandfather*, etc. insofar as they are all lineal males of ascending generation; the same applies to the female counterparts of these words, *mother*, *grandmother*, and *great grandmother*, which are all lineal females of ascending generation. Things however cannot be remedied by simply letting generation take further numbers as values. There is a problem with the first feature, type, for its values lineal, collateral and affinal — under their usual interpretations — are not mutually exclusive, as feature values should be. Thus, relatives can be *both* collateral *and* affinal (e.g. those designating *uncle, aunt*, etc. according to Wallace and Atkins (1960: 61); Goodenough (1965: 285); Nogle (1974: 64) and elsewhere); under Goodenough's conception (p. 285), though we do not follow it in our program, relatives may be both lineal and affinal (e.g. *father-in-law*, etc.). A reinterpretation that does make these values mutually exclusive is also not a way out. For example, defining lineal and collateral to apply just to consanguineals, but not to affinals, we run into an impossibility to demarcate, say, *uncle* and *father*, for *uncle* would be neither lineal (obviously), nor collateral (having affinal kin types like FaSiHu), nor affinal (having consanguineal kin types like FaBr). So failing to achieve a contrast on the dimension of type, the terms will not contrast on the other two dimensions generation and sex as well, for which they have the same values.

2.3.3 Seneca: a rediscovery of Lounsbury's analysis

Although my primary concern in this book is the discovery of new linguistic knowledge, the computational machinery described can be used to replicate discoveries of other analysts, the goal of most previous research on machine scientific discovery.

In this section, KINSHIP rediscovers the classical analysis of Lounsbury (1965) of the kinship system of the Amerindian language Seneca belonging to the Iroquoian family.

The data on consanguineal relations, as presented in Leech (1974), are given below. In a kin type formula:

(i) the prefixes *m* and *f* denote the sex, respectively 'male' or 'female', of the speaker;

(ii) the suffixes *e* and *y* denote seniority, respectively 'elder' or 'younger', within one generation.

1. *haʔnih*, Fa, FaBr, FaMoSiSo, FaFaBrSo, FaMoBrSo, FaFaSiSo, FaFaFaBrSoSo.
2. *noʔyēh*, Mo, MoSi, MoMoSiDa, MoFaBrDa, MoMoBrDa, MoFaSiDa, MoMoMoSiDaDa.[9]

---

[9] Our kin formula MoMoMoSiDaDa is incorrectly given as MoMoSiDaDa by Leech, which was signaled by KINSHIP.

3. *hakhno?sẽh*, MoBr, MoMoSiSo, MoFaBrSo, MoMoBrSo, MoFaSiSo, MoMoMoSiDaSo.

4. *ake:hak*, FaSi, FaMoSiDa, FaFaBrDa, FaMoBrDa, FaFaSiDa, FaFaFaBrSoDa.

5. *hahtsi?*, Bre, MoSiSoe, FaBrSoe, MoMoSiDaSoe, FaFaBrSoSoe, MoFaBrDaSoe, FaMoSiSoSoe, MoMoBrDaSoe.

6. *he?kẽ:?*, Bry, MoSiSoy, FaBrSoy, MoMoSiDaSoy, FaFaBrSoSoy, MoFaBrDaSoy, FaMoSiSoSoy, MoMoBrDaSoy.

7. *ahtsi?*, Sie, MoSiDae, FaBrDae, MoMoSiDaDae, FaFaBrSoDae, MoFaBrDaDae, FaMoSiSoDae, MoMoBrDaDae.

8. *khe?kẽ:?*, Siy, MoSiDay, FaBrDay, MoMoSiDaDay, FaFaBrSoDay, MoFaBrDaDay, FaMoSiSoDay, MoMoBrDaDay.

9. *akyã:?se:?*, MoBrSo, FaSiSo, MoMoSiSoSo, FaFaBrDaSo, MoFaBrSoSo, FaMoSiDaSo, MoMoBrSoSo, MoBrDa, FaSiDa.

10a. *he:awak* (for male Speaker) mSo, mBrSo, mMoSiSoSo, mFaBrSoSo, mMoBrSoSo, mFaSiSoSo, mMoMoSiDaSoSo.

10b. *he:awak* (for female Speaker) fSo, fSiSo, fMoSiDaSo, fFaBrDaSo, fMoBrDaSo, fFaSiDaSo, fMoMoSiDaDaSo.

11a. *khe:awak* (for male Speaker), mDa, mBrDa, mMoSiSoDa, mFaBrSoDa, mMoBrSoDa, mFaSiSoDa, mMoMoSiDaSoDa.

11b. *khe:awak* (for female Speaker), fDa, fSiDa, fMoSiDaDa, fFaBrDaDa, fMoBrDaDA, fFaSiDaDa, fMoMoSiDaDaDa.

12. *heyẽ:wõ:tẽ?*, mSiSo, mMoSiDaSo, mFaBrDaSo, mMoBrDaSo, mFaSiDaSo, mMoMoSiDaDaSo.

13. *hehsõ?neh*, fBrSo, fMoSiSoSo, fFaBrSoSo, fMoBrSoSo, fFaSiSoSo, fMoMoSiDaSoSo.

14. *kheyẽ:wõ:t~e?*, mSiDa, mMoSiDaDa, mFaBrDaDa, mMoBrDaDa, mFaSiDaDa, mMoMoSiDaDaDa.

15. *khehsõ?neh*, fBrDa, fMoSiSoDa, fFaBrSoDa, fMoBrSoDa, fFaSiSoDa, fMoMoSiDaSoDa.

Running KINSHIP on the above data, we obtained a simplest dimension set, comprising the following 5 features:

1. Generation of relative, with the integer values $-1, 0, 1$.
2. Parallelity, with values 'parallel'/'non-parallel' (cf. below)
3. Sex of alter, with 2 values 'male'/'female'.
4. Seniority within one generation, with values 'elder'/'younger'.
5. Sex of ego (speaker), with values 'male'/'female'.

The feature "parallelity" reflects the anthropological distinction between parallel and cross cousins, and for a kin type to have the value 'parallel' there should be an equivalence of sex between the two kin of the generation above ego (whichever of those is junior); otherwise, the

kin type is 'non-parallel' (or cross). This means that, for senior
generation kin, a kin type is parallel only if there is a sex equivalence
between ego's linking parent (=first link in formula) and alter (=last link
in formula); for junior generation, sex equivalence between ego and
alter's linking parent (penultimate link in formula); and for kin of the
same generation as ego, sex equivalence between ego's linking parent
and alter's linking parent.

Table 2.15. Simplest componential analysis of Seneca

	Generation	Parallelity	Sex of alter	Seniority	*Sex of speaker*
haʔnih	1	parallel	male		
noʔyẽh	1	parallel	female		
hakhnoʔsẽh	1	non- parallel	male		
ake:hak	1	non-parallel	female		
hahtsiʔ	0	parallel	male	elder	
heʔkẽ:ʔ	0	parallel	male	younger	
ahtsiʔ	0	parallel	female	elder	
kheʔkẽ:ʔ	0	parallel	female	younger	
akyã:ʔse:ʔ	0	non-parallel			
he:awak	−1	parallel	male		
khe:awak	−1	parallel	female		
heyẽ:wõ:tẽʔ	−1	non-parallel	male		male
hehsõʔnẽh	−1	non- parallel	male		female
kheyẽ:wõ:t~eʔ	−1	non- parallel	female		male
khehsõʔneh	−1	non- parallel	male		female

Table 2.15 gives the componential analysis of Seneca as produced by
KINSHIP. This componential model is the most simple one with the
available features and coincides with that of Lounsbury. Both discoveries
are performed under the same initial conditions, or have started with the
same data, so KINSHIP may be said to replicate an outstanding
linguistic achievement. At the same time, we note that one of the
contributions of Lounsbury was the invention of a new feature
"parallelity", which KINSHIP only used as previously defined by us, so
its discovery does not fully measure up to Lounsbury's achievement (but
see the "invented features" of our multiple concept discrimination
program introduced further in the book in Chapter 3).

2.4 An old problem from a new perspective: alternative componential models and how to choose among them

2.4.1. The problem

It is well known that kin domains admit alternative componential analyses. This is seen as a major difficulty in works where cognitive validity is conceived as the express goal of componential models, for it will not be clear which (if any) individual, or groups of, model(s) reflect the cognitive world of the native speakers of the language. Goodenough, an advocate and indeed one of the initiators of this cognitive view, showed three distinct paradigms for Trukese kinship terms, but was not really bothered by this variation of analyses, believing all three to be a part of the psychological world of Truks (1956: 213). In a famous paper however Burling (1964) drew the attention of analysts to the problem of alternatives by showing the logically admissible ones to be an immense number. Burling also argued that this is not only a theoretical concern, but also a practical matter, and that though this may seem a harsh conclusion for structural semantics, a large degree of indeterminacy will always remain (p. 27). In response to Burling, Dell Hymes (1964) argued that not all logical possibilities have equal chance of being arrived at in practice (by appealing basically to some external constraints like questioning the participants in the culture), but anyway the problem of whether the multiplicity of solutions is a real practical or a merely hypothetical formal issue remained unsolved. Thus, on the one hand kinship practitioners continued to provide componential analyses of further languages paying little, or no attention at all, to alternative solutions; on the other hand some theorists, appealing to Burling's results, presented alternatives to the "standard" componential analysis, which were assumed to evade the multiple solutions problem (cf. e.g. Wierzbicka 1991, Wierzbicka 1992, chapter V).

The multiplicity of solutions issue, if real, will be a problem not only to the approach emphasizing cognitive reality, but also to the more modest one, adopted here, whose prevalent concern is the discovery of structural reality, or rules, which, though not necessarily a part of a native's thinking, correctly and economically predict kin terms usage. Indeed, if a cognitively-oriented analyst would not like to face an intolerably great number of models to test psychologically, an analyst seeking simplicity would not be appeased presenting thousands or hundreds of thousands of models as (equally) parsimonious and intelligible summarization(s) of the data. In what follows we look at the problem from the latter perspective.

KINSHIP can shed some light on the problem. What we need is empirical data in addition to the previous basically theoretical considerations, and the system can provide these data by being capable to display, for any analysed language, all relevant feature (dimension) sets alongside with all alternative kin term definitions conforming to every particular feature (dimension) set.

We need to distinguish two aspects of the multiple solutions problem. First, we may just be interested in the number of feature sets that that might describe a kin domain. Secondly, we may be interested in the number of actual componential analyses, i.e. collections, comprising one definition of each kin term, of a kin domain.

Now, if we are interested in the multiplicity of feature sets only, our data from the analysis of more than twenty languages suggests that the multiple solutions problem is not particularly troublesome. Possible feature sets — assuming the features available to the system — vary from one (e.g. English, Seneca) to twenty (Hindi's consanguineals). Most systems however use only a couple of dimension sets. The simplicity constraint on the number of dimension sets further limits the empirical possibilities even in languages allowing a significant number of solutions. For example, in Hindi just four solutions are simplest, having five features (from the remaining ones, five solutions have six features, another five seven features, and six eight features); the Polish and Swedish consanguineal terminologies have only two simplest dimension sets out of a total of 12, etc.

We have also observed that with the increase of the completeness of the kin domain the number of adequate feature sets tends to decrease. Thus, our miniature illustrative data set of English (cf. Table 2.1), is describable with 12 dimensions, six of which are simplest (having three features), whereas the fullest available data set of Goodenough (1965), as we saw, is describable with just one feature set.

We may now look at the multiplicity of actual componential analyses. It will be observed that, adopting the style of writing componential analyses with fully redundant kin term definitions (cf. Section 2.2.3), the number of actual componential analyses and the number of possible feature sets will in fact be the same (recall that each term definition there contains a value corresponding to every applicable feature), so there does not exist a possibility for alternative kin term definitions within a pre-specified feature set. Alternative kin term definitions however occur using both partially redundant and nonredundant term descriptions. We concentrate below on the case of simplest nonredundant term definitions.

As already mentioned, KINSHIP is capable of displaying all different admissible feature sets, together with all admissible simplest term definitions, complying with each feature set.

Let us examine the results we got for English. The system showed that eight terms of the whole semantic field treated have two definitions each, while the remaining ones got just one. However, let us first see how we can express the total number of logically possible componential analyses, Q, in terms of the number of alternative definitions, N_i, each individual kin term has obtained. Since each individual definition may theoretically be combined with all remaining ones, the logical number of componential analyses will be determined by the formula $Q = N_1 \times N_2 \times N_3 \dots \times N_m$, that is the number of all admissible componential analyses will be equal to the product of the number of definitions of each individual kin term. For example, assuming our domain to comprise only three terms, the first having two definitions, the second one, and the third four, we have $Q = 2 \times 1 \times 4 = 8$ componential analyses in all. For English, where we have eight terms having two definitions each, $Q = 2^8 = 256$ solutions in all.

We may also adduce data for another analysed language, e.g. Bulgarian. In the case when Bulgarian is described with the feature set {generation of relative, sex of alter, distance, affinity of relative, affinity of 1st link, sex of 1st link, seniority}, 13 terms obtain two definitions, and one term gets four, which, calculated by the above formula, gives 32 768 analyses. When Bulgarian is described with the feature set {generation of relative, sex of alter, distance, generation of last link, affinity of 1st link, sex of 1st link, seniority}, 18 terms obtain two definitions, which amounts to 262 144 componential analyses!

Summarizing our results so far, the multiplicity of solutions problem stands out as a real rather than purely hypothetical one, for these are not only *logically* possible, but also *empirically* relevant solutions. The simplicity constraints on both feature sets and kin term definitions are indeed insufficient by themselves to limit the solutions to just a few analyses that would be an acceptable number for a linguist or anthropologist. (On the other hand these simplicity constraints really fare well, since without them, i.e. in a completely unconstrained analysis, the solutions for our two languages would become astronomical.)

However, is the situation really so hopeless? The answer to this question will entirely depend on whether we would be satisfied by *freely* combining kin term definitions with each other. To decide this we should examine more closely the alternative outputs provided by KINSHIP.

2.4.2 A simplicity constraint on alternative kin term definitions

Consider just the alternatives that KINSHIP reported for the American kinship terms *father* and *mother* (Table 2.16):

Table 2.16. Kin terms definitions for *father* and *mother*

father1	generation=1	sex=male	str.-equiv.=equiv-c
father2	sex=male	str.-equiv.=equiv-c	generation-of-last-link=1
mother1	generation=1	sex=female	str.-equiv.=equiv-c
mother2	sex=female	str.-equiv.=equiv-c	generation-of-last-link=1

These alternative kin term definitions yield $2 \times 2 = 4$ componential analyses, resulting from the combinations (cf. Table 2.17):

Table 2.17. Combinations of kin term definitions

COMBINATION 1 (*father1, mother1*)			
father	generation=1	sex=male	str.-equiv.=equiv-c
mother	generation=1	sex=female	str.-equiv.=equiv-c
COMBINATION 2 (*father1, mother2*)			
father	sex=male	str.-equiv.=equiv-c	generation=1
mother	sex=female	str.-equiv.=equiv-c	generation-of-last-link=1
COMBINATION 3 (*father2, mother1*)			
father	sex=male	str.-equiv.=equiv-c	generation-of-last-link=1
mother	sex=female	str.-equiv.=equiv-c	generation=1
COMBINATION 4 (*father2, mother2*)			
father	sex=male	str.-equiv.=equiv-c	generation-of-last-link=1
mother	sex=female	str.-equiv.=equiv-c	generation-of-last-link=1

Are all combinations equally satisfactory componential analyses? Hardly, so. Combination 2 and Combination 3 for instance give definitions of *mother* and *father*, using a different set of features for both words, when these terms have actually definitions with pair-wise identical features (Fa1−Mo1 and Fa2−Mo2), the latter fact adequately reflecting our intuition that their meanings differ only as regards the *value*, male or female, of one feature they both share, viz. sex. We would expect componential paradigms to respect our intuitions in this regard; hence we need a filtering device for "cross-definitions", as those occurring in Combination 2 and Combination 3. (Requiring lexemes like *father* and *mother* to get maximally close definitions, using the same features, seems to be in accord with the results of Romney and D'Andrade who found that such pairs, differing only as regards sex, are placed by subjects adjacently 98 per cent of the time in a free recall experiment (1964: 156).)

To handle this, we introduce a third simplicity criterion of *coherence*, that allows reducing the choice of alternative kin term definitions in a principled manner. To capture the above intuition, our third criterion minimizes the choices we can make in any such definition. Thus, note that our definition of *father* has components which *must* be used, since they occur in both alternatives Fa1 and Fa2 (which we call the *core*), and alternative components from which we should make choice (which we call the *remainder*). That is, the definition of *father*, and analogously that for *mother*, may be stated as Table 2.18:

Table 2.18. Application of the coherence criterion to *father* and *mother*

	Core	Remainder
father	[sex=male,str.-equiv=equiv-c] *and*	[gener=1 *or* gener-of-last-link=1]
mother	[sex=female,str.-equiv=equiv-c] *and*	[gener=1 *or* gener-of-last-link=1]

NOTE: Abbreviation: gener = generation.

The criterion simply minimizes the number of features that are used in the remainders. This means that, in the particular case, we should choose either the single feature generation, and hence the component generation=1 in the definitions of both words (which yields Combination 1) or the single feature generation-of-last-link, and hence the component generation-of-last-link=1 in both terms (which yields Combination 4). The criterion forbids using *both* features, which would have resulted in the cross-definitions Combination 3 and Combination 4, in addition to the first two combinations. Thus instead of four, we get just two componential models.

We may now see how our third simplicity criterion applies to English. As already mentioned, KINSHIP reported two alternatives for any of the 8 kin terms, which we list below as Table 2.19:

Table 2.19. American kin terms under the coherence criterion

	Core	Remainder
father	[sex=male,str.-equiv=equiv-c] *and*	[gener=1 *or* gener-of-last-link=1]
mother	[sex=female,str.-equiv=equiv-c] *and*	[gener=1 *or* gener-of-last-link=1]
son	[sex=male,str.-equiv=equiv-c] *and*	[gener=-1 *or* gener-of-last-link=1]
daughter	[sex=female,str.-equiv=equiv-c] *and*	[gener=-1 *or* gener-of-last-link=1]
father-in-law	[sex=male,str.-equiv=nonequiv] *and*	[gener=1 *or* affinity=affinal]
mother-in-law	[sex=female,str.-equiv=nonequiv] *and*	[gener=1 *or* affinity=affinal]
step-father	[sex=male,str.-equiv=equiv-a] *and*	[gener=1 *or* gener-of-last-link=1]
step-mother	[sex=female,str.-equiv=equiv-a] *and*	[gener=1 *or* gener-of-last-link=1]

NOTE: Abbreviation: gener = generation.

Looking at the remainders, it is obvious that only the single feature generation is a valid choice according to our criterion, since otherwise we should use not one, but two features, viz. generation-of-last-link and affinity. Selecting just the components having the feature generation for each kin term definition, we get a *unique* analysis for English out of the 256 models admissible without the criterion; this is actually the analysis shown in Table 2.12.

It is not guaranteed that each kin term will now have a unique model, and occasionally such redundancy has been observed in our applications. However, the gain is the application of a third simplicity criterion that (1) captures our intuitions on simple examples, (2) is based on a principle of maximizing the coherence among the remaining choices (blocking cross-definitions), and (3) is computed in an almost identical way to the first two simplicity criteria.[10]

-----

[10] The third criterion is implemented in KINSHIP by formulating a Boolean expression which is then converted to DNF, exactly as with the first two simplicity criteria. First, the intersection of the alternatives for a kin term is defined as the core for that kin term. Remove the core from each alternative model for a kin term. The remaining components yield a Boolean expression of this form:

(component *and* component …) *or* (component *and* component …) *or* …

2.4.3 Summing up

Multiple componential models may arise from two sources: (1) the existence of various dimension sets describing the kin domain, and (2) the existence of alternative definitions of kin terms within a pre-specified dimension set (this occurs with partially redundant and nonredundant kin term definitions).

From a practical point of view, the first source does not seem particularly troublesome, and multiple feature sets tend markedly to decrease with the increase of the completeness of the data set studied (this is a familiar idea that recurs e.g. in Nogle 1974). The requirement for using the shortest feature sets further limits possible choices. The second source, however, is more vexatious from this perspective and normally gives a flood of alternative models; here we focused just on simplest nonredundant kin term definitions, but allowing non-simplest nonredundant or partially redundant ones would even increase the indeterminacy.

Thus, indeterminacy stands out as a real, rather than a purely hypothetical, problem, for even if we somehow isolate the dimensions (by appealing to psychological, cultural or whatever reasons), there normally would still be an enormous amount of models.

Addressing this issue, here we introduced a structural constraint for choosing among alternative kin term definitions, based on the idea of economical use of features and very much in the vein of the other two and familiar parsimony criteria.[11] It seems intuitive, applied on simple examples, and attempts to reduce choices in some principled way (i.e. one independent of any particular language or culture). Componential analysis using all four criteria we use will as a rule result in one or just a couple of models, which is a favourable outcome if the conciseness and intelligibility of models is the primary goal of analysis.

---

for each kin term. (The exception is that when there is only a single choice for a kin term, that kin term is skipped.) All such expressions are then conjoined, and then converted to DNF. Finally, each minimal disjunct of the DNF yields a different parsimonious choice set S_i. To arrive at a specific componential model, for each kin term, we select one of its models only if the model's components lie either in the core or in S_i. (Of course, each S_i can lead to a different result.)

[11] An alternative simplicity criterion, based on the idea of focality of features (assuming frequency of occurrence as some measure of focality) is discussed in detail in Pericliev and Valdés-Pérez (1998a: 304–307).

2.5 KINSHIP as a tool

The examples we considered above are illustrations of one standard approach to componential analysis, fitting with what has been occasionally termed "(social) structural reality" (Wallace and Atkins 1960, Wallace 1965), from the point of view of which the parsimony and logical consistency with which kin terms usage is predicted are generally conceded as the basic criteria by which the relative merit of (alternative) solutions are assessed. It is important to emphasize, however, that KINSHIP is designed as a *computational tool* for performing componential analysis, and is thus not necessarily committed to this particular approach. In other words, though we consider structural reality an essential aspect of kinship structure, and have implemented the system to be capable of quite faithful mimicking of this approach, the user of the system is not forced to employ the system with the particular goal of parsimony in mind: one can obtain all, and not only the most concise, feature sets, alongside all, and not only the shortest, nonredundant kin term definitions; the system, as already mentioned, may also produce fully redundant or partially redundant componential models. In general, the kinship analyst may utilize the potential outputs of the system in ways that fit the particular goals pursued, if these outputs are in any sense relevant to these goals. (By the way, insofar as the extensionist paradigm also implies performing componential analysis, it will be clear that our system can be used to this end as well, though indeed it would be practically more helpful in "pure" componential analysis, which is as a rule much more difficult, owing to the need to find contrasting features covering all, not only the kernel, kin types of a kin term.)

KINSHIP has a number of facilities, making it a convenient investigatory tool, some of which are worth mentioning here. Importantly, the system disposes of a mechanism for *inventing derived features*, formed combining old features by means of the logical operations conjunction, disjunction, implication, and implication. This mechanism, reflecting interactions between features, can be used in the cases when the available features are insufficient to discriminate all kin terms, and is illustrated on kinship data in Pericliev and Valdés-Pérez (1998b). More recently, a means for statistical discrimination between kin terms was added, computing what percentage of the kin types should be retracted to obtain clean contrasts between terms. However, we cannot go into details here.

Also, the user can query the system in a variety of ways, as e.g.:

- what the attendant kin types of a given kin term are or what kin term corresponds to a given (set of) kin type(s);
- whether there exists cross-classification of kin types, i.e. one kin type is classed under two or more different kin terms (such kind of data preclude complete discrimination of kin terms, so the system displays the faulty kin types);
- what the current features of the system are;
- what kin type/kin term possesses what features;
- what semantic contrasts exist between a selected pair of kin terms; and
- what pairs of kin terms are indiscriminable.

Besides making these queries, the user is also free to employ a pre-specified subset of the set of available features which is for some reason, structural, cultural or psychological, considered important by the analyst in a specific culture. (This allows an analyst to estimate say how the features suggested by Kroeber fare, applied on a group of languages.)

It is not our purpose here to enter into a discussion of how these facilities might be used (in general, being a tool, the success of the system's use will depend on the analyst's skill and ingenuity), but will confine to giving an example of how the system's report of its failure to discriminate between a pair of kin terms may suggest the postulation of a novel feature to accomplish the discrimination.

The careful reader may have noticed that in our English data — following closely the symbolically expressed kin types in Goodenough (1965) — the kin term *cousin* encompasses only relatives of zero generation, whereas the extended meaning of the term may include relatives of any generation, a fact questioning the possibility to give a conjunctive definition of this kin term. We added to the English data the additional kin types and reran the system with the features that were available then. The program reported that it cannot cleanly discriminate the pairs *cousin* and *grandson*; *cousin* and *grandaughter*; *cousin* and *nephew*; *cousin* and *niece*. This suggested that we look at the kin types of these pairs, given as Table 2.20.

Now, what feature is possessed by all kin types of *cousin* that could serve as a potential contrast with the remaining kin terms? It is quite conspicuous in the data that all attendant kin types of *cousin* have as their first connecting link Pa, which is a relative of ascending generation, so a potential candidate is the feature "generation of the first connecting link". This feature indeed can discriminate *cousin* from *grandson/granddaughter* whose first connecting relative is Ch, that is of generation= −1.

Table 2.20. Kin types of certain American kin terms

cousin	grandson/granddaughter	nephew/niece
PaSbCh	ChCh	SbCh
PaPaChCh		PaChCh
PaPaSbCh		SpPaChCh
PaPaPaSbCh		
PaSbChCh		
PaSbChChCh		
PaPaSbChCh		
PaPaPaChChCh		
PaPaPaSbChChCh		
PaPaSbChChCh		
etc.		

NOTE: Abbreviations: Pa = parent, Sb = sibling, Ch = child, Sp = spouse.

How about the demarcation with *nephew/niece*? Two of their kin types, viz. SbCh and SpPaChCh, have as their first link Sb, which is of generation=0, and Sp, which is also of generation=0. As far as the third kin type PaChCh is concerned, its initial PaCh part is of course structurally equivalent to Sb (cf. equivalence rules 7 and 8 from Section 2.3.2), and hence also of generation=0. Thus we easily come up with a new feature "generation of the first connecting link or its structural equivalent", which, together with the previous five features, suffices to discriminate conjunctively all English kin terms. For brevity, we shall not list the componential analysis of all kin terms, but only of those that are actually discriminated by this feature (cf. Table 2.21):

Table 2.21. American kin terms discriminated by the feature "generation of the first connecting relative"

cousin			
		gener-of-last-link or str.eq=−1	gener-of-1-link or str.-eq=1
nephew			
sex=male		gener-of-last-link or str.eq=−1	gener-of-1-link or str.-eq=0
niece			
sex=female		gener-of-last-link or str.eq=−1	gener-of-1-link or str.-eq=0
grandson			
sex=male	gener=−2		gener-of-1-link or str.-eq=−1
granddaughter			
sex=female	gener=−2		gener-of-1-link or str.-eq=−1

NOTE: Abbreviation: gener = generation.

We thus see that the seemingly problematic kin term *cousin* can in fact be elegantly described conjunctively with just two components, viz. "generation of last link or structural equivalence = –1" and "generation of first connecting relative = 1". This is an important contribution of KINSHIP to the understanding of English kinship terminology, insofar as no previous analysis, as far as we know, has managed to give a conjunctive definition of *cousin*.

Also, although we have not implemented this so far, we can trivially extend the program to handle different (say, Romney style) input. Or we can incorporate additional features, as required by kinship analysts, which, of course, need not be limited to genealogies, but may involve other factors recognized as significant in the field; thus, the very way symbols like 'elder/younger' are sometimes added to the atomic genealogical ones Fa, Mo, ... , we may introduce further symbols, reflecting any aspect of social life, and then define features taking these symbols into account in the discrimination of kin terms.

2.6 Conclusion

In the chapter, we presented the first automation of componential analysis of kinship semantics. We described KINSHIP, a program which, with its capabilities to produce the guaranteed-simplest models, as well as all other non-simplest alternatives, its support of fully redundant, partially redundant and nonredundant styles of kin term definitions, and other accompanying facilities, may serve as a practical tool in the study of kinship vocabularies by the componential method. We suggested an intuitive structural constraint on the choice of alternative kin term definitions, which, coupled with the usual requirements for parsimony of overall features and components used, yields (nearly) unique models, characterizing the kin domain comprehensibly in terms of Kroeber's and some further features, added to the program. We presented the first analysis of Bulgarian. We believe the system to have discovered a noteworthy solution for English where a lot of human effort has previously been invested in the task. The componential model found is both the most parsimonious known today and has "correct", conjunctive, definitions for all terms, including *cousin*. The re-discovery of the classic analysis by Lounsbury (1964) is another achievement of the program. As we saw in the case with Nogle (1974), human analysts are not immune to providing logically inconsistent models, and our feeling is that this case is by no means an exception.

Chapter 3. Parsimonious Discrimination II: MPD and Other Applications

The multiple concept discrimination component of KINSHIP, described in the previous chapter, is in no way tied to kinship terms, but is domain-independent, and hence applicable for demarcation to any linguistic or non-linguistic objects. This allows the isolation of this computational mechanism into a separate program for parsimonious discrimination, called the Maximally Parsimonious Discrimination (MPD) program. In this chapter, MPD is enriched with the capabilities of performing partial, or statistical, contrasts, as well as with a facility for inventing derived features by combining primitive features via logical operations. Diverse linguistic problems may be reduced to performing parsimonious discrimination. In this chapter, I sketch a number of such problems, illustrating the different capabilities of MPD. One of the notable discoveries of MPD briefly dealt with is a more economical distinctive feature analysis of Russian phonemes than that of Cherry, Halle, and Jakobson (1953), who state parsimony as their express goal. We then describe in more detail an application of MPD to the profiling the world's languages in terms of their segments inventories. The profiles of the 451 languages in the USPID database are computed, some observations on their size and structure are made, and a criterion is suggested for choosing among alternatives. The chapter concludes by evaluating the MPD and the KINSHIP systems.

3.1 The Maximally Parsimonious Discrimination program (MPD)

A common task of knowledge discovery is multiple concept learning, in which from multiple given concepts, or classes,[1] the *profiles* of these classes are inferred, such that every class is contrasted from every other class by feature values. Ideally, good profiles should be concise, intelligible, and comprehensive (i.e. yielding all alternatives).

---

[1] The terms "concept" and "class" are used here synonymously and interchangeably.

To achieve these goals, the MPD (Maximally Parsimonious Discrimination) program we describe here (1) carries out a global optimization guaranteeing the minimum use of features; (2) produces conjunctive or nearly conjunctive, profiles for the sake of intelligibility; and (3) gives all alternative solutions. The first goal stems from the familiar requirement (as far back as Aristotle) that classes be distinguished by necessary and jointly sufficient descriptions. The second accords with the also familiar thesis that conjunctive descriptions are more comprehensible (they are the norm for typological classification (Hempel 1965), and they are more readily acquired by experimental subjects than disjunctive ones (Bruner, Goodnow, and Austin 1956)); we have already stressed in the previous chapter their importance for kinship terms analysis specifically. The third goal expresses the usefulness, for a diversity of reasons, of having all alternatives. Linguists would generally subscribe to all three requirements, hence the need for a computational tool with such focus.

The Maximally Parsimonious Discrimination (MPD) program is a general computational tool for inferring, given multiple classes (or, a classification), with attendant instances of these classes, the profiles (=descriptions) of these classes such that every class is contrasted from all remaining classes on the basis of feature values.

Expressing contrasts

The MPD program uses *Boolean*, *nominal* and *numeric* features to express contrasts, as follows:

- Two classes C1 and C2 contrast by a Boolean or nominal feature if neither of the instances of C1 and the instances of C2 have a common value.
- Two classes C1 and C2 contrast by a numeric feature if the *ranges* of the instances of C1 and of C2 do not overlap. (Besides these atomic feature values we may also support (hierarchically) structured values, but this will be of no concern here.)

MPD distinguishes two types of contrasts: (1) *absolute contrasts* when all the classes can be cleanly distinguished, and (2) *partial* (or *statistical*) *contrasts* when no absolute contrasts are possible between some pair-wise classes, but absolute contrasts can nevertheless be achieved by deleting up to N per cent of the instances, where N is specified by the user.

Derived features

The program can also invent *derived features* — in the case when no successful (absolute) contrasts are so far achieved — the key idea of which is to express interactions between the given primitive features. Currently, we have implemented inventing novel derived features via combining two primitive features (combining three or more primitive features is also possible, but has not so far been done owing to the likelihood of a combinatorial explosion):

- Two Boolean features P and Q are combined into a set of two-place functions, none of which is reducible to a one-place function or to the negation of another two-place function in the set. The resulting set consists of P–and–Q, P–or–Q, P–iff–Q,[2] P–implies–Q, and Q–implies–P.
- Two nominal features M and N are combined into a single two-place nominal function M×N.
- Two numeric features X and Y are combined by forming their product and their quotient.

Both primitive and derived features are treated analogously in deciding whether two classes contrast by a feature, since derived features are legitimate Boolean, nominal or numeric features.

It will be observed that contrasts by a nominal or numeric feature may (but will not necessarily) introduce a slight degree of disjunctiveness, which is to a somewhat greater extent the case in contrasts accomplished by derived features.

In the case of *missing values* for some features, MPD has two alternatives. By default, two classes do not contrast by a feature if some instance of either class is missing a value for that feature, but, at the option of the user, 'missing' can be viewed as a legitimate (nominal) value, making its contribution to the class contrasting.

The simplicity criteria

MPD uses three intuitive criteria to guarantee the uncovering of the most parsimonious discrimination among classes:

1. Minimize overall features. A set of classes may be demarcatable, using a number of overall feature sets of different cardinality; this criterion chooses those overall feature sets which have the smallest cardinality (i.e. are the shortest).

---

[2] "iff" is an abbreviation for "if and only if", i.e. logical equivalence.

2. Minimize profiles. Given some overall feature set, one class may be demarcatable — using only features from this set — by a number of profiles of different cardinality; this criterion chooses those profiles, which have the smallest cardinality.

3. Maximize coherence. This criterion maximizes the cohesion or coordination between class profiles in one discrimination model,[3] in the case when alternative profiles remain even after the application of the previous two simplicity criteria. The basic idea is the alternative features which are used in the equally simple alternative profiles to be minimized in a discrimination model.

We note that the processes MPD employs are computationally very costly, and this especially applies to criterion 1, which is the most expensive mechanism of the program. All the simplicity criteria are, technically speaking, NP-complete.[4] They are implemented in a uniform way (in all three cases computing minimum set covers, or equivalently, converting CNFs to DNFs), and use sound heuristics significantly increasing the efficiency, making MPD applicable to practical problems.

MPD is not the only program addressing discrimination, but the previous approaches like ID3 (Quinlan 1986) or C4.5 (Quinlan 1993), which use variations on greedy search, i.e. localized best-next-step search (typically based on information-gain heuristics), have as their major goal prediction on unseen instances, and therefore do not have as an explicit concern the conciseness, intelligibility, and comprehensiveness of the output, our concern here. A detailed computational description of the program and comparison with related work is given in Valdés-Pérez, Pereira, and Pericliev (2000: 417–422; 428–430; 432–436).

MPD can be used as tool in various ways, but a typical scenario would be the following:

> Using all 3 simplicity criteria, and finding all alternative models, follow the feature/contrast hierarchy: primitive & absolute > derived & absolute > primitive & partial > derived & partial.

This scenario reflects the desiderata of conciseness, comprehensiveness, and intelligibility (as far as the latter is concerned, the primitive

---

[3] In a "discrimination model", each class is described with a *unique* profile.

[4] Informally, NP-complete problems are such problems for which there is no known quick algorithm, and the time required to solve the problem using any known algorithm increases drastically with the increase of the size of the problem, thus making even moderately large problems unsolvable with the computing power available today.

features (normally user-supplied) are preferable to the computer-invented, and partially disjunctive, derived features). Note however that in some specific tasks, another hierarchy seems preferable, which the user is free to follow.

We can now come back shortly to the KINSHIP program. Its concept discrimination component accepts as input classes (the kin terms of a language), and instances of these classes (their attendant kin types), where each instance is described in terms of feature values. Then, the most parsimonious profile of the classes is computed, employing the three simplicity criteria. The contrasts KINSHIP uses to single out classes are normally absolute contrasts. The features the program is endowed with are of all types: binary (e.g. male=$\{+/-\}$), nominal (e.g. lineal=$\{$lineal, co-lineal, ablineal$\}$), and numeric (e.g. generation=$\{1, 2, ..., n\}$).

In the long history of this area of study, practitioners of the art have come up with explicit requirements as regards the adequacy of a componential analysis:

(1) *Parsimony*, including both overall features and kin term descriptions (=profiles).

(2) *Conjunctiveness* of kin term descriptions.

(3) *Comprehensiveness* in displaying all alternative componential models.

As seen, these requirements very nicely fit with most of the capabilities of MPD. This is not accidental, since, historically, we started our investigations with modelling the important discovery task of componential analysis, and then, realizing the generic nature of the discrimination subtask, isolated this part of the program, which was later extended with the mechanisms for derived features and partial contrasts.

The facility for inventing derived features may be useful when kinship terms fail discrimination with the available inventory of features. As an illustration, let us look at an indiscriminable pair of terms from the Australian aboriginal language Gooniyandi (McGregor 1996):

jaja   MoMo, MoMoSi, MoMoBr, MoFaSiHu, WiFaMo, MoBrSoWi, fDaSo, fDaDa
ngoomara   WiMoFa

KINSHIP/MPD would form derived features, and would find that e.g. the derived (binary) feature +/–[affinal-1st-link–<u>and</u>–male-alter] discriminates the terms:

> *jaja*   –[affinal-1st-link–<u>and</u>–male-alter]
> *ngoomara* +[affinal-1st-link–<u>and</u>–male-alter]

Indeed, the sole kin type of *ngoomara*, viz. WiMoFa, is +affinal-1st-link (Wi) *and* +male-alter, whereas neither of the kin types of *jaja* have *both* these feature values at the same time.

If one wishes, he/she may employ partial contrasts for making the discrimination. Thus, deleting one kin type, viz. WiFaMo, from the eight kin types of the kin term *jaja*, i.e. 1/8 = 87.5%, KINSHIP/MPD would find the following statistical demarcation:

> *jaja*   87.5% –[affinal-1st-link]
> *ngoomara*   +[affinal-1st-link]

In principle, using the facility of partial contrasts in KINSHIP may provide hints as to possibly incorrect inclusion of a kin type under a kin term, especially in insufficiently well understood kinship systems.

3.2 Some brief illustrations of applications from diverse fields

The goal of this section is to briefly sketch diverse problems that can be reduced to profiling multiple concepts, and therefore handled by the MPD machinery. A detailed study of the discrimination of the world languages in terms of their segment inventories is given in Section 3.3.

3.2.1 Inferring translational equivalents from verbal frames

In computational linguistics, the application areas commonly associated with concept discrimination algorithms are e.g. the learning of morphological rules (Daelemans, Berck, and Gillis 1996) or the learning of translational correspondences from verbal case frames (e.g. Tanaka 1996, Li and Abe 1996). By way of illustration of some of the capabilities of MPD on the latter problem, let us consider the learning of the Bulgarian translational equivalents of the English verb *feed* on the basis of the case frames of the latter.

Assume the following features/values, corresponding to the verbal slots. (Abbreviations: hum = human, phys-obj = physical object.):

(1) NP1 = {hum,beast,phys-obj};

(2) VTR = binary feature denoting whether the verb is transitive or not;

(3) NP2 = {hum,beast,phys-obj};

(4) PP = binary feature expressing the obligatory presense or absence of a prepositional phrase.

An illustrative input to MPD is given in Table 3.1 (the sentences in the third column of the table are not a part of the input, and are only given for the sake of clarity).

Table 3.1. Classes and instances

Classes	Instances	Illustrations
1.otglezdam	1.NP1=hum VTR NP2=beast not-PP	1.He feeds pigs
	2.NP1=hum VTR NP2=beast not-PP	2.Jane feeds cattle
2.xranja	1.NP1=hum VTR NP2=hum not-PP	1.Nurses feed invalids
	2.NP1=beast VTR NP2=beast not-PP	2.Wild animals feed their cubs regularly
3.xranja-se	1.NP1=beast not-VTR PP	1.Horses feed on grass
	2.NP1=beast not-VTR PP	2.Cows feed on hay
4.zaxranvam	1.NP1=hum VTR NP2=phys-obj PP	1.Farmers feed corn to fowls
	2.NP1=hum VTR NP2=phys-obj PP	2.This family feeds meat to their dog
5.podavam	1.NP1=phys-obj VTR NP2=phys-obj PP	1.The production line feeds cloth in the machine
	2.NP1=phys-obj VTR NP2=phys-obj PP	2.The trace feeds paper to the printer
	3.NP1=hum VTR NP2=phys-obj PP	3.Jim feeds coal to a furnace

MPD needs to find 10 pair-wise contrasts between the 5 classes (i.e. *N–choose–2*, calculable by the formula $N(N-1)/2$), and it has sucessfully discriminated all classes, as seen from the resultant demarcation in Table 3.2. This is done by the overall feature set {NP1, PP, NP1×NP2}, whose first two features are primitive, and the third is a derived nominal feature. Not all classes are absolutely discriminated: Class 4 (*zaxranvam*) and Class 5 (*podavam*) are only partially contrasted by the feature NP1. Thus, Class 5 is 66.6% NP1=phys-obj since we need to retract 1/3 of its instances (particularly, sentence (3) from Table 3.1 whose NP1=hum) in order to get a clean contrast by that feature. Class 1 (*otglezdam*) and Class 2 (*xranja*) use in their profiles the derived nominal feature

NP1xNP2; they actually contrast because all instances of Class 1 have the value 'hum' for NP1 and the value 'beast' for NP2, and hence the "derived value" [hum beast], whereas *neither* of the instances of Class 2 has an identical derived value (indeed, referring to Table 3.1, the first instance of Class 2 has NP1×NP2=[hum hum] and the second instance NP1×NP2=[beast beast]). The resultant profiling on Table 3.2 is the *simplest* in the sense that there are no more concise overall feature sets that discriminate the classes, and the profiles — using only features from the overall feature set — are the shortest.

Table 3.2. Classes and their profiles

Classes	Profiles
1.otglezdam	not-PP NP1×NP2=([hum beast])
2.xranja	not-PP NP1×NP2=([hum hum] or [beast beast])
3.xranja-se	NP1=beast PP
4.zaxranvam	NP1=hum PP
5.podavam	66.6% NP1=phys-obj PP

3.2.2 Distinctive feature analysis

A standard method in phonology is distinctive feature analysis. Distinctive feature analysis amounts to finding the distinctive features of a phonemic system, differentiating each phoneme from the phonemic system of a language from all other phonemes. The adequacy requirements of the method are the same as those in lexicology/semantics, and indeed they have been borrowed in lexicology (and morphology for that matter) from phonological work which chronologically preceded the former.

MPD was applied to the Russian phonemic system, the data coming from a paper by Cherry, Halle, and Jakobson (1953), who also explicitly state as one of their goals the finding of minimum phoneme descriptions.

The data consisted of 42 Russian phonemes, i.e. the transfer of feature values from instances (=allophones) to their respective classes (=phonemes) had been previously performed. The phonemes were described in terms of the following 11 binary features: (1) vocalic, (2) consonantal, (3) compact, (4) diffuse, (5) grave, (6) nasal, (7) continuant, (8) voiced, (9) sharp, (10) strident, and (11) stressed.

Running MPD on this dataset confirmed that the 11 primitive overall features are indeed needed, but it found 12 simpler phoneme profiles than those proposed in this classic article. Table 3.3 is a comparison of our results with those of Cherry, Halle, and Jakobson (1953); the redundant feature values are enclosed in brackets.

Table 3.3. MPD's analysis in comparison to that of Cherry *et al.* (1953)

Class	1	2	3	4	5	6	7	8	9	10	11
k	−	+	+		+		−	−	−		
k'	−	+	+		+		−	−	+		
g	−	+	+		+		−	+	−		
g'	(−)	+	+		+		−	+	+		
x	−	+	+		+		+				
c	−	+	+		−		−				
ʃ	−	+	+		−		+	−			
3	−	+	+		−		+	+			
t	−	+	−		−	−	−	−	−	−	
t'	−	+	−		−	−	−	−	+	−	
d	−	+	−		−	(−)	−	+	−	(−)	
d'	(−)	+	−		−	(−)	−	+	+	(−)	
s	−	+	−		−	−	+	−	−		
s'	−	+	−		−	−	+	−	+		
z	−	+	−		−	(−)	+	+	−		
z'	−	+	−		−	(−)	+	+	+		
ŝ	−	+	−		−	−	−	(−)	(−)	+	
n	−	+	−		−	+		−			
n'	−	+	−		−	+		+			
p	−	+	−		+	−	−	−	−		
p'	−	+	−		+	−	−	−	+		
b	−	+	−		+	(−)	−	+	−		
b'	(−)	+	−		+	(−)	−	+	+		
f	−	+	−		+	(−)	+	−	−		
f'	−	+	−		+	(−)	+	−	+		
v	−	+	−		+	(−)	+	+	−		
v'	−	+	−		+	(−)	+	+	+		
m	−	+	−		+	+		−			
m'	−	+	−		+	+		+			
'u	+	−	−	+	+					+	
u	+	−	−	+	+						−
'o	+	−	−	−	+						
'e	+	−	−	−	−						
'i	+	−	−	+	−						+

i	+	−	−	+	−		−
'a	+	−	+				+
a	+	−	+				−
r	+	+			−	−	
r'	+	+			−	+	
l	+	+			+	−	
l'	+	+			+	+	
j	−	−					

NOTE: The brackets enclose those feature values given in Cherry *et al.* (1953) which are redundant.

The first observation one can make from the comparison is that there is a lot of redundancy in these authors analysis: the 17 feature values enclosed in brackets are those components which are superfluous for the demarcation. Eleven out of a total of 42 phonemes have an incorrect description. As a result of this, the average phoneme profile turned out to comprise 6.14, rather than 6.5, components as suggested by Cherry, Halle, and Jakobson (1953). Also, some feature bundles are incorrect in more than one way; thus, the phoneme *d'* is assigned three superfluous feature values, and *d*, *ŝ*, and *b'* two such values.

The distinctive feature analysis of the Russian phonemic system discovered by MPD should be of interest to phonologists, as it is, to my knowledge, the most concise and also nonredundant model proposed in the literature. MPD is thus an advanced tool for conducting economic and nonredundant distinctive feature analysis of languages, awaiting further applications. The capability of MPD to treat not just binary, but also non-binary (nominal) features, it should be noted, makes it applicable to datasets of a newer trend in phonology which are not limited to using binary features, and instead exploit multivalued symbolic features as legitimate phonological building blocks.

3.2.3 *Profiling languages in terms of their word order*

A class may consist of a single member; hence MPD can be used for discovery of discriminations between individuals. One such example is the problem of profiling individual languages.

One application, which will only be mentioned here, is the processing of MPD of the dataset from the paper by Greenberg (1966a) on word order universals, a corpus that has previously been used to uncover linguistic universals, or similarities between languages; apparently, such data are feasible for uncovering the differences between languages. The data consist of a 30–language sample with a wide genetic and areal coverage. The individual languages are described in terms of 15 features, both nominal and binary, such as the position of Verb, Subject, and Object, the use of prepositions or postpositions, the positions of Noun and Relative Clause, Numeral and Noun, etc.

Running MPD on this dataset with these primitive absolute features showed that at least eight features were required to achieve contrasts, and from 435 (*30–Choose–2*) pair-wise discriminations to be made, just 12 turned out to be impossible, viz. the pairs:

[berber,zapotec], [berber,welsh], [berber,hebrew], [fulani,swahili],
[greek,serbian], [greek,maya], [hebrew,zapotec], [japanese,turkish],
[japanese,kannada], [kannada,turkish], [malay,yoruba], [maya,serbian].

In the processed dataset, for a number of languages, there missed values. The linguistic reasons for this were two-fold: (i) lack of reliable information; or (ii) non-applicability of the feature for a specific language. The above result reflects our default treatment of missing values as making no contribution to the contrast of language pairs. Following the other alternative path, and allowing 'missing' as a distinct value, will result in the successful discrimination of most language pairs. Indiscriminable would remain Greek and Serbian, which is no surprise given their genetic and areal affinity.

3.2.4 Profiling language disorders

This application concerns the discrimination of different forms of aphasia on the basis of their language behaviour.

There exist different methods for lesion location in aphasics, but determining the precise location and the exact extent of the damage is difficult, expensive and uncertain, therefore the need arises that patients be classified into aphasic disorders on the basis of their language behaviour rather than on neurological-location criteria. A battery of such tests have previously been used to this end, and MPD could be employed to suggest new (and hopefully useful) ones.

We addressed the profiling of aphasic patients, using the CAP dataset from the CHILDES database (MacWhinney 1995), containing (among others) 22 English subjects: 5 controls, and the others suffering from: anomia (3 patients), Broca's disorder (6 patients), Wernicke's disorder (5 patients), nonfluents (3 patients), the patients being grouped into classes according to their fit to a prototype used by neurologists and speech pathologists. The patients' records — verbal responses to pictorial stimuli — are transcribed in the database, and are coded with linguistic errors from a priorly identified set, containing such pertaining to phonology, morphology, syntax and semantics.

As a first step in our study, we attempted a profiling, using just the errors as they were coded in the transcripts. This provided a feature set of 26 binary features, based on the occurrence or non-occurrence of an error (feature) in the transcript of each patient. We ran MPD with primitive absolute features and found that from a total of 10 pair-wise contrasts to be made between 5 classes, 7 turned out to be impossible, and only 3 possible. We then used derived absolute features, but still one pair (Broca's and Wernicke's patients) remained uncontrasted. We obtained 80 simplest models with 5 features (two primitive and three derived) discriminating the four remaining classes.

We found this profiling unsatisfactory from a domain point of view, for a number of reasons. First, one pair remained uncontrasted. Secondly, only 3 pair-wise contrasts were made with absolute primitive features, which are as a rule most intuitively acceptable as regards the comprehensibility of the demarcations (in this specific case they correspond to "standard" errors, antecedently and independently identified from the task under consideration). And, thirdly, some of the derived features necessary for the profiling lacked the necessary plausibility for domain scientists, which led us to re-examining the transcripts (amounting roughly to 80 pages of written text) and adding manually some new features that could eventually result in more intelligible profiling. Some of the new features attempt to model pragmatic aspects of speech (especially some of Grices's conversational maxims), which, to our knowledge, have not been used in aphasics tests so far.

To give just an idea of this subsequent study, below is a brief description of only some of the new relevant features and how they apply to the different classes of language impairs.

(1) Prolixity

This feature is intended to simulate an aspect of the Grice's Maxim of Manner, viz. "Avoid unnecessary prolixity". We try to model it by computing the average number of words pronounced per individual pictorial stimulus, so each patient is assigned a number (at present, each word-like speech segment is taken into account). Wernicke's patients seem most prolix, in general.

(2) Truthfulness

This feature attempts to simulate Grices' Maxim of Quality: "Be truthful. Do not say that for which you lack adequate evidence". Wernicke's patients are most persistent in violating this maxim by fabricating things not seen in the pictorial stimuli. All other patients seem to conform to the maxim, except the nonfluents whose speech is difficult to characterize either way (so this feature is considered irrelevant for contrasting).

(3) Fluency

By this we mean general fluency, normal intonation contour, absence of many and long pauses, etc. The Broca's and non-fluent patients have negative value for this feature, in contrast to all others.

(4) Average number of errors

This is the second numerical feature, beside prolixity. It counts the average number of errors per individual stimulus (picture). Included are all coder's markings in the patients text, some explicitly marked as errors, others being pauses, retracings, etc.

Re-running MPD with absolute primitive features on the new data, now having more than 30 features, resulted in 9 successful demarcations out of 10. Two sets of primitive features were used to this end: {average errors, fluency, prolixity} and {average errors, fluency, truthfulness}. The Broca's patients and the nonfluent ones, which still persisted discrimination, could be successfully handled with nine alternative derived Boolean features, formed from different combinations of the coded errors (a handful of which are also plausible).

We also ran MPD with absolute primitive features and partial contrasts (cf. Table 3.4). The analysis uses four features {average errors, fluency, prolixity, semi-intelligible speech}, the latter feature coming from the inventory of CHILDES and described as a "Best guess at a word". Retracting one of the six Broca's subjects allows all classes to be completely discriminated.

Table 3.4. Profiles of Aphasic Patients with Absolute Features and Partial Contrasts

Classes	Profiles
Control Subjects	average errors=[0–1.3]
Anomic Subjects	average errors=[1.7,4.6]
	prolixity=[7,7.5]
	fluency
Broca's Subjects	not–fluency
	87% not–semi-intelligible
Wernicke's Subjects	prolixity=[12,30.1]
	fluency
Nonfluent Subjects	not–fluency
	semi-intelligible

These results may be considered reasonable from the point of view of aphasiology. First of all, now all disorders are successfully discriminated, and this is done with predominantly absolute primitive features, which, furthermore, make good sense to domain specialists: control subjects are singled out by the least number of mistakes they make, Wernicke's patients are contrasted from anomic ones by their greater prolixity, anomics contrast Broca's and nonfluent patients by their fluent speech, etc.

3.2.5 Applications outside of linguistics

The MPD machinery is general, and hence applicable to problems outside of linguistics. Below are briefly mentioned two applications of the program to psychology and chemistry, based on their exposition in Valdés-Pérez, Pereira, and Pericliev (2000). The idea is to illustrate the commonality of scientific inferences across sciences.

Unlike the original linguistics problems, these applications involve strictly numeric features. Also, these applications are instances of a general class of scientific application to which MPD is very suited: relating classes based on structure (brain lesions, chemical elements) to behavioural features, or classes based on behaviour to structural features. In all cases, the goal is to understand better, in the absence of an accurate theory that links the two, how structure relates to behaviour.

Psychology. A substantial application to psychology involved profiling children with different types of brain lesion with respect to their behavioural characteristics (MacWhinney *et al.* 2000). There were six structural classes (five types of brain lesion and one control group), 170 examples (children, of whom 150 were in the control group), and 18 numeric behavioural features that measured how well the children did in verbal laboratory tests. MPD found that three features were enough to profile all the classes at an overlap ceiling of 40%. The following qualitative, English-rendered excerpt consists of two profiles: one for the control group and another for the group of left-side focal lesions resulting from cerebral infarct:

> The control group (150 children) is better at visual naming than the minimal damage, hydrocephalus, left periventricular hemorrhage, and left cerebral infarct groups, and better at storing, elaborating, and following oral directions than the minimal damage, left periventricular hemorrhage, and right lesion groups.
>
> The left cerebral infarct group (7 children) is worse at storing, elaborating, and following oral directions than the right lesion and

control groups, is better at word repetition than the hydrocephalus group, but worse at word repetition than the minimal damage and left periventricular hemorrhage groups.

The full MPD profiles for brain lesions are reported elsewhere (McWhinney *et al.* 2000).

Chemistry. The goal of this application was to profile a set of eight metal catalysts in terms of their comparative ability to carry out types of chemical reactions, using data on 168 reactions and their energies (activation energy barriers) published earlier (for details, cf. Zeigarnik *et al.* 2000). Thus, the eight classes correspond to metal catalysts (iron, copper, nickel, palladium, platinum, rhodium, iridium, and ruthenium), an example corresponds to a specific chemical reaction, and the several dozen numeric features (which were defined by the authors) are mainly of the form energy of a reaction of a type X, where the definition of a type refers to the bonds broken and formed as a reaction converts the reactants to the products. If a given reaction (out of the 168 in the dataset) is not of a type X, then the feature energy of a reaction of a type X has the value not applicable. An example of a discovered profile at an overlap ceiling of 43% (Zeigarnik *et al.* 2000), expressed qualitatively and in English for convenience, is the following for iron (Fe):

> Fe is worse than Cu, Ni, Pd, Pt, Rh, and Ir in its ability to carry out reactions of the type M-x-C-H-x-M, and worse than Cu, Pd, Pt, Rh, Ru, and Ir in its ability to carry out reactions of the type M-x-C-O-x-M.

M-x-C-H-x-M is the notation for a reaction type that involves breaking a Metal-Carbon (M-x-C) and a Metal-Hydrogen (H-x-M) bond, and forming a Carbon-Hydrogen (C-H) bond. Unlike the applications to linguistics and psychology, in this case the global minimization of features was judged as less important, partly because one pair of metals was not sharply distinguished, hence the overlap ceiling would be set too high and the other metals would get profiles that were too crude, i.e., gave too much weight to conciseness over sharpness of contrast. Hence, the feature set for each of the metal classes was minimized separately. That is, the stage of minimization of the overall features was skipped, and the individual minimizations of profiles made use of the entire original feature set, rather than the globally minimized feature set.

3.3 Profiling the world's languages in terms of their segments

3.3.1 The problem

Two basic and interrelated goals of linguistic typology are to describe the similarities and the differences between the languages of the world (often referred to as the "generalizing" and the "individualizing" approach respectively, e.g. Greenberg 1973: 163, Croft 1990: 43).

In this section, I address in some detail the task of language individualization, computing the differences between the world languages in terms of the segment inventories these languages employ. In a historical perspective, the individualizing typological approach has typically emphasized the global, grammatico-semantic, characteristics of a language as forming an organic unity. Sapir (1921: 127), for instance, talks about a "basic plan, a certain cut", or a "structural genius" of each language which is much more fundamental than each individual feature. This overall genius of a language, in the Humboldtian and Whorfian linguistic traditions, was believed to have reflexes in the culture and national character of the speakers of that language. The same approach, however, perhaps with less far-reaching consequences — but still insightfully — has been applied for contrasting different linguistic sub-systems in an attempt to reveal the uniqueness of each studied language with respect to the sub-systems investigated. Indeed, languages differ from one another both when viewed from a more global perspective and when viewed from a more local one, involving linguistically significant individual traits of their phonology, grammar or semantics. And describing the differences between diverse language sub-systems is an important task of contemporary linguistics. Here, we confine to computing contrasts between languages at the level of phonology.

A "segment profile" for a language is a subset of its segment inventory that can distinguish this language from all other languages. In this chapter, the computer-generated segment profiles for the 451 languages in the UCLA Phonological Segment Inventory Database (UPSID-451) will be presented. It will be shown that languages usually possess a multitude of segment profiles, but not all of these alternatives are equally representative of a language's idiosyncrasy. A criterion will be suggested for choosing among these alternatives: Preferring the profile for a language which contains segments with the smallest frequencies of occurrence in other languages (this profile, in effect, can be considered as more "typical" for the language). Some patterns will emerge regarding the size and structure of the computed "typical" profiles.

The basic questions we ask are the following: What exactly is (are) the identifying profile(s) of a language discriminating it from all other languages in the database? Do any patterns in profiles emerge or are the profiles simply arbitrary sets of segments? In the case of alternative profiles for one language, is there a profile that better characterizes the typical phonological traits of this language than the other profiles, and how can we identify this profile?

We base our investigation on the most detailed collection of segment inventories of the world languages, compiled by Maddieson and colleagues at UCLA (Maddieson 1984). Originally, the *UCLA Phonological Segment Inventory Database* (UPSID) consisted of 371 languages. A later corrected and expanded version (Maddieson and Precoda 1991) contains already a 451 language sample, and we use this later version, known as UPSID-451, for our computations.

UPSID-451 contains phonologically contrastive segments of the world languages. For each language in the database, a segment inventory is included containing segments that have lexically contrastive function. The features assigned to a segment exhibit its most characteristic phonetic form. They all are (with rare exceptions) positively specified. The languages included are chosen on a quota principle, to the effect that all major language families are covered, but only one language from any small grouping is included. The language chosen to cover a small grouping would as a rule be described in trustworthy linguistic sources.

Our goal was to compute how the world languages contrast in terms of their segment inventories. In particular, we wanted to find the segment profiles for the languages in the database, whereby by a *segment profile* for a language (or *profile* for short), we understand the collection of one or more segments from its segment inventory that distinguishes this language from all other languages.

In general, a language L1 may be said to differ from the remaining languages L2...Ln in terms of their segment inventories in two distinct ways. First, L1 may differ from L2...Ln by a set consisting of only positively specified segments actually possessed by L1 (a *positive profile*). Secondly, L1 may differ from L2...Ln by a set comprising some negatively specified, or segment(s) absent from L1 (a *negative profile*). Thus, for instance, one (of many) positive profiles for Hungarian is [ø:, ø], signifying that Hungarian possesses a long mid front rounded vowel and a mid front rounded vowel, which taken together are unique to this language; the negative profile [ø:, not–ʏ], states that Hungarian possesses the first segment, a long mid front rounded vowel, but lacks the second, a lowered high front rounded vowel, and these circumstances distinguish it from the remaining languages.

Clearly, the use of negative profiles allows the discrimination of some languages that may not possess positive profiles. A case in point is the situation when a language has a segment inventory that is a proper subset of the segment inventory of another language. The language with the subsumed inventory cannot have a positive profile because it cannot possess a segment absent in the other language. The absence of a segment, which is present in the language with subsuming inventory, will allow formulating a negative profile.

We have developed techniques for discovery of both types of differences, but in the present study stick to positive profiles, using negative only when the positive ones fail to provide discrimination. We believe that for the task at hand it is more intuitive to describe differences between languages in terms of segments the languages do have rather than in terms of segments they do not have.

By way of a simple illustration of positive and negative profiles, consider three languages having the following segment inventories:

L1 [A, B]
L2 [A, B, C]
L3 [A, C, D]

The profiles for these languages are as follows:

L1 [B, not–C]
L2 [B, C]
L3 [D]

The profile for L1, [B, not–C], is a negative two-segment profile, in which the segment B serves to discriminate L1 from L3, which lacks B, whereas the absence of C (i.e. not–C) serves to discriminate L1 from L2, which does have C. L1 is indistinguishable from L2 unless a negatively specified, or lacking, segment is used in its profile. The profiles for L2 and L3 are both positive. In the profile for L2, the segments B and C demarcate L2 from L3 and L1, respectively. The one-segment profile [D] discriminates L3 from both L1 and L2, in which the segment D is absent.

Two specifics in the design of UPSID-451, viz. the presence of ambiguous and anomalous segments in inventories, are of direct relevance as to whether two languages contrast or not, so we turn to how we handle these problems.

In the cases when there is insufficient information about some specific segment in some language UPSID-451 will use this segment ambiguously. For instance, the segment ["tʲ"] in UPSID-451 denotes *either* a palatalized dental plosive *or* a palatalized alveolar plosive and the presence of this segment in the inventory of some language implies that it is unknown to the database whether the segment is actually a palatalized dental plosive (notated [t̪ʲ] in UPSID-451) or a palatalized alveolar plosive (notated [tʲ]). The consequence of this is that the superficially different pairs of segments ["tʲ"]–[t̪ʲ] and ["tʲ"]–[tʲ] cannot reliably contrast. Accordingly, our programs forbid differentiation between two languages based on such *uncontrastable* (pairs of) segments. It may be noted that the ambiguous segment ["tʲ"] is but one example of the large class of consonants for which it is not specified in the descriptive sources whether they are dental or alveolar (and there are further ambiguous codings in UPSID-451 which our programs take into consideration).

Besides ambiguous segments, the segment inventories of languages in UPSID-451 may include a set (possibly empty) of segments which can be considered anomalous in a language. These are segments "with a somewhat doubtful or marginal status in an inventory, but with sufficient claim to be included that they were not simply eliminated from consideration" (Maddieson 1984: 170). A segment is classed as "anomalous" if any of the following conditions holds: The segment is (1) rare (extremely low lexical frequency), (2) loan (occurs in unassimilated loans), (3) abstract (posited underlying segment), (4) derived (segment possibly derivable from others), or (5) obscure (occurring in a particularly vague or contradictory description). To make the generated positive profiles plausible and reliable, we stipulate that profiles must not contain an anomalous segment (to avoid claiming that a language L1 discriminates from another language L2 by a segment which is doubtful or marginal for L1). So for constructing a profile for L1 we choose segments from the *reduced segment inventory* of L1, i.e. the inventory resulting from removing all anomalous segments from it. And, secondly, to ensure that L2 indeed does not possess the segment included in the profile of L1, and used to contrast L1 from L2, we check that this segment is reliably absent from L2, which requires this check to be made in the *non-reduced segment inventory* of L2 (i.e. the inventory containing all segments, the anomalous ones including).

It should be noted that our conservative policy in discrimination — both as regards the treatment of ambiguous and of anomalous segments — ensures maximal reliability of the resultant positive profiles.

Returning to our simplistic illustration of profiles above, let us see what our conservative policy in discrimination implies for instance for the profile for L3, viz. the one-segment profile [D]. What our discrimination strategy implies is that, first, the segment D is non-anomalous in the language L3, and secondly, this segment is non-ambiguous in the sense that it does *not* stand in UPSID-451 for either of the segments A, B or C.

The original MPD program, with all the computationally complex processes it uses, is not particularly suited for the tasks at hand of discriminating such a sizable number of individual languages. In addition to the processing cost, there is no conceptual reason in this particular case to employ a mechanism for global minimization of the features used in discrimination. For these reasons, versions of the MPD program were implemented. In broad outline, the algorithm of the version for discovery of positive profiles is the following. The program selects a language from the database and inspects whether any one of its (non-anomalous) segments is absent from the (non-reduced) segment inventories of all other languages. If this is the case, the program finds all other idiosyncratic segments and the result is reported as (alternative) 1-segment profiles for that language. If not, the program hypothesizes 2-segment profiles (by forming all unordered pairs of segments from the language's (reduced) segment inventory) and checks which of these hypotheses hold in the database. This failing, the program consecutively hypothesizes and tests more complex profiles of size 3, then of size 4, then of size 5 etc. until a solution is found (or a failure is reported on exhausting all hypotheses).

It will be clear from this outline of the basic algorithm, that our tools find the *minimum* (=shortest) profiles, individuating the languages, as well as all their *alternatives* of the same length.

The search for negative profiles is carried out by a more complicated algorithm that compares the target language against each other language, then minimizes the segments that are needed to differentiate the target from every other language. These comparisons are not limited to segments that the target language possesses, which is why the profiles can turn out negative. Anomalous segments are treated as "missing values", which means that two languages are never contrasted by a segment if either language has an anomalous value for that segment. This conservative procedure guarantees stable profiles: resolving an anomalous value either way (as truly belonging to the language or as extraneous) will not change the accuracy of the profiles we have found.

Finally, it may be noted that the UPSID-451 database is designed to support machine investigations, and Maddieson and Precoda (1991) do provide some useful programming facilities (UPSID and PHONEME) that can be used as a quick reference to find occurrences of some particular segment or to look up the segment inventory of a particular language. These facilities however cannot be used for more complex computations, as required by our task of segment inventories contrasts.

3.3.2 The discovered profiles

Below are listed the machine discovered profiles of the languages in UPSID-451. First, the languages using positive profiles are given, followed by those needing negative profiles to individuate them from the rest of the languages. Languages are given in alphabetical order, starting with the languages employing profiles of minimum size. This section includes the "typical" segment profiles for the languages in UPSID-451, i.e. those profiles that pass the selection criterion elaborated later in Section 3.3.5.

The notation of segments below (and throughout the chapter) is that of Maddieson and Precoda (1991), which basically follows the IPA conventions. To alleviate reading, here we give a listing of some diacritic marks or other symbols used, some of which may *not* be standard IPA conventions (e.g. double quotes "b" denote an unspecified dental or alveolar consonant or is undifferentiated 'mid' for vowels). The complete notational details can be found in Maddieson and Precoda (1991).

b velarized
b^w labialized
b^j palatalized
$b̰$ laryngealized
$b?$ glottalized
$b^ˤ$ pharyngealized
$ɓ$ nasalized (of flaps approximants, vowels)
ŋb nasalized (of clicks)
gb voiced (of clicks)
bx velar-fricated (of clicks)
b^h aspirated or breathy
$b̤$ with breathy release
^hb preaspirated (of stops) or voiceless (of nasals, approximants, vowels, clicks)
$b̪$ dental
"b" unspecified dental or alveolar for consonants; undifferentiated 'mid' for vowels
b. retroflex
b< implosive

b' ejective
ⁿb prenasalized (also ᵑb)
b̆ overshort (of vowels)
rr voiced r-sound
D voiced tap

I. Languages discriminated by positive profiles

1-segment profiles

ACOMA — [ɕ'] or ["D̥"] or [s.']
AKAN — [çʷ] or [cçʷ] or [ɟjʷ] or [ɲʷ]
ALAWA — [ⁿ·d.]
AO — [ʐ̩.]
ARAUCANIAN — [t.θ.]
ARCHI — ["ɬʷ:"] or [χˤ:] or [χʷˤ:] or [qχ'] or [qχˤ] or [qχˤ'] or [qχˤ':] or [qχʷ'] or [qχʷˤ] or [qχʷˤ']
ARRERNTE — [bᵐ] or [d.ⁿ·] or [d̪ⁿ] or [d̪ⁿ] or [dⁿ] or [gⁿ]
ASHUSLAY — ["ts"]
AVAR — ["tɬ':"] or ["tɬ:"] or [kx':] or [kx:] or [qχ:]
BEEMBE — [pfʰ]
BRETON — ["ø"] or [ɛ̃õ] or [ɛo] or [ae] or [ãõ]
BRUU — [ʌ] or [ɒ]
BULGARIAN — [ts̺ʲ]
BURMESE — [õ̯ũ]
CHANGZHOU — ["tʰ··"] or ["tsʰ··"]
CHIPEWYAN — ["tʰ··"] or [kxʷʰ] or [tθ̬ʰ]
CHUVASH — [ŏ̆]
DAHALO — [d̪]
DAN — [d.]
EKARI — [gᴸ]

EPENA — [ĩ-]
EVEN — [ia̠]
EWE — [ɾ]
EWONDO — [i̠] or [u̠]
FIJIAN — [ⁿr]
FRENCH — [œ̃]
GA — [tʃʷ]
GELAO — ["ⁿts"] or [əɯ] or [ᶮcç]
HAMER — [eˤ]
HMONG — [ɛɯ] or [ᵑkʰ] or [ᵑq] or [ᵑqʰ] or [ⁿ·t.s.] or [ⁿ·t.s.ʰ] or [ⁿts̺ʰ] or [ⁿtʃʰ]
HOPI — [θ.]
HUASTECO — [ʒ]
IAI — [ŋ͡m̥] or [l̥.] or [n̥.]
IGBO — ["ⁿrʲ"] or [b̥ʲʰ] or [gʷ]
IK — ["e̥"] or ["o̥"] or [a̠]
INUIT — [f:]
IRANXE — [ãĩ] or [bʷ] or [f̃i]
IRISH — [βʲ] or [ɸʷ] or [bʷ] or [mʷ] or [m̩] or [pʷʰ] or [ꞙ]
ITELMEN — [ʐʲ]
JACALTEC — [qˁ]
JAPANESE — [ɴ]
JAVANESE — [tsʰ]
KABARDIAN — [θ] or [ð̬] or [ʔʷ] or [f'] or [ɣʲ] or [ɬʲ'] or [ʐʲ] or [xʲ]
KAROK — [ʊ:]
KASHMIRI — [ə̃:] or [dʒʲ] or [ɨ:] or [tʃʲ]
KHALKHA — [ʊi]
KHANTY — ["ĕ"] or ["o"] or [ŏ̆]

KHMER — [eə] or [ɯː]
KHMU? — [ɨa]
KIOWA — [ai̯] or [ãi̯] or [ᵈl̩]
KOHUMONO — [k͡pʰ]
KOLOKUMA — [g͡bʷ] or [k͡pʷ]
KONYAGI — [ᵑkʷ] or [ᶮc]
KOREAN — [s̰]
KOTOKO — [pf']
KWOMA — [ɸʷ]
LAI — [ˮɬʲˮ] or [ˮⁿdʲˮ] or [ˮtʲʰˮ] or [ᵐbʲ]
LAK — [ˮøˤˮ] or [ˮtsʷːˮ] or [qː] or [qʷː] or [tʃʷː] or [xʷː]
LAKKIA — [ŋʲ] or [ĩẽ]
LUNGCHOW — [ĭ] or [ŭ] or [ŭ̯]
LUO — [d̪ɵ̃]
MALAGASY — [d.r̩ʔ] or [t.r̩ʔ]
MALAKMALAK — [ø]
MANDARIN — [cçʰ]
MBUM — [ⱱ]
NAHUATL — [ɸ]
NAMA — [!xʰ] or [ǁxʰ] or [ǀx̥ʰ] or [ŋ!ʰ] or [ŋǁʰ] or [ǀxʰ]
NAMBAKAENGO—[ˮⁿdʷˮ]
NAXI — [ᶮɟʐ]
NENETS — [ɵ̃ʲ]
NEO-ARAMAIC — [iˤː] or [uˤː]
NEWARI — [ˮd̠zˮ]
NGANASAN — [kx]
NGIZIM — [ɟ]
NIVKH — [ɪe] or [t̪ʰ]
NORWEGIAN — [ɒ̥] or [æʉ] or [øy] or [ʉː]
NYAH — [iə] or [uə] or [ɯə]
OCAINA — [ɲː]
PACOH — [d̡] or [ɨə]
PAEZ — [ʎʲ]

PARAUK — [ŋ] or [ɔi̯] or [ʒ] or [ai] or [au] or [aɯ] or [iɛ] or [iɛ] or [i̯a] or [io] or [i̯u] or [l̩] or [n̩] or [ɣi] or [ɤi] or [oi] or [ua] or [ui] or [ɯi]
PHLONG — [vʷ]
ROMANIAN — [ea]
RUSSIAN — [f] or [ʒ]
RUTUL — [ɢˤ] or [ɢʷˤ] or [qˤ'] or [qˤʰ] or [qʷˤ'] or [qʷˤʰ]
SAAMI — [ˮdzʲˮ] or [ßʲ] or [hʲ]
SAMA — [ˮⁿsˮ]
SANDAWE — [!ʔ] or [ǁʔ] or [g!] or [gǁ] or [ǀʔ]
SEBEI — [ŭ]
SELEPET — [ɑ]
SELKUP — [ˮɣːˮ]
SENADI — [ˮzʲˮ]
SHILHA — [ˮdˤˮ] or [ˮlˤˮ] or [ˮrˤˮ] or [ˮsˤˮ] or [ˮtˤˮ] or [ˮzˤˮ] or [kˤ]
SHUSWAP — [ˮtɬˮ] or [ʁʷ] or [ʁ̥ʷ] or [q] or [qʷ]
SIONA — [t̠.]
SOMALI — [ʉ] or [d̠.]
SOUTH_NAMBIQUARA — [ˮẽˮ] or [ˮoˮ] or [ˮõˮ] or [ã] or [j̃] or [ʎ̠.]
SUI — [ɣ]
TACANA — [ɾ̩]
TAMANG — [tθʰ]
TARASCAN — [ɨʲ]
TEHUELCHE — [cɕ']
TEKE — [ɱ]
TELUGU — [ßː]
TERA — [ɓʲ] or [ᶮɟj]
TLINGIT — [χ'] or [χʷ'] or [xʷ']
UZBEK — [ʂ̰]

VANIMO — [ẽ]
VIETNAMESE — [iʌ] or [uʌ] or [ɯʌ]
WAHGI — [ʟ̩]
WANTOAT — ["ⁿz"]
WAPISHANA — [z̺.]
WARAY — [c:]
WICHITA — ["n:"] or [ɒ:]
WOISIKA — ["e̞"] or ["o̞"]
WOLOF — [b:] or [ɟ:] or [l̩:]
XO'Ū — ["oˤ:"] or ["õˤ"] or [‖] or [‖ⁿ] or [‖x] or [ǂ] or [ǂʰ] or [ǂx] or [lʰ] or [lx] or [ŋˤ] or [õˤ:] or [ãˤ] or [ãˤ:] or [aeˤ] or [ãẽˤ] or [aoˤ] or [ãõˤ] or [b'] or [d'] or [ɗ] or [dʒ'] or [dʒ] or [dz'] or [dz] or [ẽũˤ] or [g‖] or [g‖x] or [g‖x ʔ] or [g'] or [gl] or [gǂ] or [gǂ] or [gǂx] or [gǂxʔ] or [gl] or [glx] or [glxʔ] or [g|] or [g|x] or [g|xʔ] or [ŋ‖ʔ] or [ŋ‖ⁿ] or [ŋ‖xʔ] or [ŋǂʔ] or [ŋǂʰ] or [ŋǂxʔ] or [ŋ|xʔ] or [ŋ|xʔ] or [ŋ‖] or [ŋ‖] or [ŋǂ] or [ŋǂ] or [ŋl] or [ŋ|] or [oaˤ] or [õãˤ] or [õã] or [oe] or [oiˤ] or [õiˤ] or [t] or [tʃ] or [ts] or [|x]
YAGARIA — [ʟ]
YAKUT — [yø]
YANYUWA — [ⁿkʲ] or [ⁿt̪]
YUCHI — [ɸ']
YUKAGHIR — ["ғ"]
ZOQUE — ["ɣ̃"]
ZULU — [lˢ] or [kʟ̥']

2-segment profiles
ACHE — ["ʝ", "ⁿd"]
ADZERA — ["dz", "o:"] or ["dz",ɥ]

AGHEM — [ɒ, bv]
AHTNA — [dʒ, ɟ]
AIZI — [ɯ, k͡p]
AKAWAIO — ["z", ɔi]
ALAMBLAK — [D, tʰ]
ALBANIAN — [ɟʝ, ɬ]
ALEUT — [ð̞, j]
ALLADIAN — [ɟ, ɥ]
AMAHUACA — [ĩ, ũ]
AMELE — [ɡ͡b, ɟ]
AMHARIC — ["sʷ", hʷ]
AMUESHA — [lʲ, t.s.ʰ]
AMUZGO — [b̪, kʲ]
ANDOKE — [ã̝, ã]
ANGAATIHA — ["ə̆", ɺ]
ANGAS — [bʲ, ɨ:]
APINAYE — [Λ̃, ⁿɟ]
ARABIC — [æ:, sˤ]
ARMENIAN — [ð., ʀ]
ATAYAL — ["ts", ħ]
AWIYA — [ɢʷ, ŋʷ]
AZANDE — ["ʒ̃", ɺ]
AZERBAIJANI — [ɣ, ɣ̟]
BAI — [ɞ, ɯ]
BAINING — [ɛi, ai]
BARDI — [a:, l̩]
BASHKIR — ["ɣ", θ]
BASQUE — [ɟ, t.s.]
BATS — [ʔ, ã]
BEJA — [ɡʷ, t.]
BENGALI — [æ̃, d̪]
BERTA — ["ⁿd", "s'"]
BETE — [ɨ, ɯ]
BOBO-FING — [k͡p, tʰ]
BRAHUI — ["ɬ", e:]
BRAO — [cç, ⁿtʃ]
BRIBRI — ["ẽ", "z"]
BURUSHASKI — [ð., d.s.]
CADDO — ["ts'", ʊ]
CAMSA — [ɨ, t.s.]

CAYAPA — [d̪, l̠]

CAYUVAVA — [æ̃, ɨ]

CHAM — [cʰ, d̪]

CHAMORRO — [dz, ɹ.]

CHUKCHI — ["ə̆", ð̪.]

COFAN — [ɰ, ʑ]

CUBEO — ["ɟ", d̪]

DAFLA — [ʌ, i̥] or [ʌ, u̥]

DAGBANI — ["ə", ŋ͡m]

DAJU — [ʄ, ɾ.]

DAKOTA — [ʃ', x']

DANGALEAT — [ʄ, l̠]

DANI — [kʷ, oi]

DIEGUEÑO — [ʐ, ɹ]

DINKA — [ɛ, e̙] or [ɛ, o̙] or [ɔ, e̙] or [ɔ, o̙]

DIYARI — [n., D]

DOGON — ["d", D]

EJAGHAM — [ʌ, d̪]

EYAK — ["tɬʰ", ã:]

FARSI — [ɢ, a̙]

FE'FE' — ["ɣ̟ ", "z"]

FUZHOU — ["tsʰ", œ]

GADSUP — [ß, a̙:]

GARAWA — [c, t̪]

GBEYA — [ŋ͡mg͡b, n̠]

GEORGIAN — ["ə̆", "ɬ "]

GERMAN — [ø:, pf]

GREEK — [ð̠, ɑ]

GUAHIBO — ["ə̆", r]

GUAJIRO — ["ɟ", "r"]

GUAMBIANO — [ß, t.s.]

GUARANI — [ŋʷ, ɨ]

GUGU-YALANDYI — ["rr", ɹ.]

HADZA — [ǃʰ, ŋǃʔ] or [ǃʰ, ŋǁʔ] or [ǃʰ, ᵐpʰ] or [ǃʰ, ⁿt̪ʰ] or [ǁʰ, ŋǃʔ] or [ǁʰ, ŋǁʔ] or [ǁʰ, ᵐpʰ] or [ǁʰ, ⁿt̪ʰ] or [ŋǃʔ, ᵐpʰ] or [ŋǃʔ, ⁿt̪ʰ] or [ŋǁʔ, ᵐpʰ] or [ŋǁʔ, ⁿt̪ʰ]

HAIDA — [ɴ, qʷʰ]

HAKKA — ["ⁿd", "tsʰ"]

HAUSA — [kʲ', s̙]

HIGHLAND — ["ð", n̠]

HINDI-URDU — [ẽ:, n̠]

HIXKARYANA — [d̪, ɹ.]

HUARI — [ɪ̃, ɹ.]

HUAVE — ["ð", ᵑgʷ]

HUNGARIAN — [ɟj, ø:]

HUPA — [hʷ, tʃʷʰ]

IATE — [cʰ, ẽ]

IRAQW — [ɑ:, s:]

IRARUTU — [j̊, ⁿd]

ISLAND — ["ɣ̆", aɯ]

ISOKO — [p˂, v̙]

ITONAMA — ["t'", "tʲ"]

JAQARU — [t.s., t.s.']

JEBERO — [k̠, ɹ]

JIVARO — ["r", n̠]

K'EKCHI — [b̙, q']

KAINGANG — [ə̃, ⁿd̪]

KALIAI — [ʍ, ɾ.]

KAM — [e̙, lʲ]

KANAKURU — [d̪, ⁿʄ]

KANURI — [l., z]

KAREN — [ð, e̙]

KAWAIISU — ["r", ɣʷ]

KERA — [d̪, dʒ]

KET — ["ɵ", "dʲ"] or ["dʲ", "ɬ "]

KEWA — [ɸ, ɭ]

KHARIA — [ɦ, ɾ.]

KHASI — [ia, uo]

KIRGHIZ — [ɨ, ø]

KLAMATH — [c', l̥]

KLAO — [ɔ̃, ɟj]

KOMI — [ç, ɟj]

KONKANI — [ã̟, ɟʑ]

KORYAK — [ʙ̥, j̊]
KOTA — [r̪., s.]
KOYA — [ɐ, ɑ]
KPELLE — [gʷ, k͡p]
KUNIMAIPA — [ɢ, r̪.]
KURDISH — [əi, lˤ] or [əi,sˤ]
KURUKH — [″õ″, ɟ]
KWAKW'ALA — [n̠, tɬʰ] or [qʷʰ,tɬʰ]
LAME — [ao, eo]
LELEMI — [d., k͡p]
LENAKEL — [ɥ, pʷ]
LITHUANIAN — [æi, rʲ] or [æi,sʲ]
LUE — [kʷʰ, ɣ]
LUGBARA — [d̪̥, ʎ]
LUISENO — [qʷ, s.]
MAASAI — [ɠ, r̥]
MAMBILA — [bv, n̠]
MANCHU — [″ɵ″, ø]
MARI — [ʌ, ʎ]
MAUNG — [r̪., ɹ]
MAXAKALI — [ⁿdʒ, ũ]
MAZAHUA — [″sʰ″, ɲ]
MAZATEC — [ⁿ.d.z., ⁿdz]
MBA-NE — [ŋ͡m g͡b, ⁿdʒ]
MBABARAM — [d̪, ⁿd̪]
MIEN — [cʰ, ŋ̟]
MIXE — [æ, tθ]
MOGHOL — [ʀ, j̊]
MONGUOR — [ɢ, j̊]
MORO — [ʎ., ɣ]
MOVIMA — [ɬ, s.]
MUINANE — [rrʲ, ʐ]
MUMUYE — [ŋʷ, ʒ]
MUNDARI — [d̠ʒ, n.]
NANAI — [ɪ, j̊]
NAVAJO — [″dʐ″, ɛ̃:] or [″dʐ″,õ:]
NDUT — [″d″, ⁿɟ]

NEPALI — [d̪., dz]
NEZ — [n̠, qχ]
NGARINJIN — [ɨ, ɹ.]
NIMBORAN — [″ɣ″, ɨ]
NONI — [″d″, ″e:″]
NUNGGUBUYU — [ɰ, ɹ.]
NYANGI — [ɠ, s̠]
NYIMANG — [ɟ, ʎ]
OGBIA — [″d″, ″nʷ″] or [″nʷ″,ɐ]
OJIBWA — [ɛ̃:, ʊ]
PAIWAN — [″dʲ″, ʎ.]
PANARE — [″ə̃″, ″ɣ ″]
PAPAGO — [d., n̠]
PASHTO — [ɑ:, ʎ.]
PAYA — [″r″, w̃]
PICURIS — [″ə̃″, ″ɬ″]
PO-AI — [ɛ̆, aɨ] or [ɛ̆,ĩ] or [ɛ̆,ɨ̆] or [ɛ̆,ŭ] or [aɨ,ŏ] or [ĩ,ŏ] or [ɨ̆,ŏ] or [ŏ,ŭ]
POHNPEIAN — [pʷ, t.s.]
QUECHUA — [″t″, ʎ]
RESIGARO — [dʲ, n̥]
RUKAI — [t., v]
SALIBA — [″ẽ″, gʷ]
SANGO — [ʎ., ⁿʒ]
SAVOSAVO — [ⁿɟ, z]
SEDANG — [″r̥″, ″r̥″]
SHIRIANA — [″ə̃″, ũ]
SINHALESE — [ɟj̊, ʊ]
SIRIONO — [kʲ, ⁿdʒ]
SOCOTRI — [″ʓ″, ″rr″]
SOUTH_KIWAI — [″rr″, ou]
SPANISH — [θ, D]
SRE — [ɒ, cʰ]
TAISHAN — [æ, kʷʰ]
TAMA — [ħ, ɟ]
TAMASHEQ — [″e:″, d̥ˤ] or [″e:″,t̥ˤ] or [″e:″,z̥ˤ]
TAMPULMA — [ŋ͡m, ɟ]

THAI — [ɾ, t͜s̪ʰ]
TIGAK — [ɐ, ʤ]
TIGRE — [a̰ː, ts']
TIWI — [ⁿt̪., ɻ.]
TOL — [t͜s̪, tsʰ]
TRUMAI — [m̥, xː]
TSESHAHT — [''tɬ'', ʔˤ]
TSIMSHIAN — [ɰ, kʲ']
TSOU — ['']'', ɥ]
TULU — [s̪., ʊ]
TURKISH — [ɰ, ɣ]
TUVA — [ß, ɣ]
TZELTAL — [t͜s', y]
UPPER — [''ə'', ''tɬ''']
WARAO — [ß, ɟ]
WARIS — [''ⁿd'', ɒ]
WINTU — [q', ɹ]
WIYOT — [ɻ., ɹ]
YAGUA — [ŭ, ɨ̃]
YAWA — [nʲ, ɾ]
YAY — [ua, ɰa]
YESSAN-MAYO — [ⁿgʷ, ɒ]
YOLNGU — [ɐ, ɾ.] or [ɹ.,ɾ.]
YUCATEC — [''t''', ɛ] or [''t''',ɔ̞] or [''t''',u̞]
YUCUNA — [ʎ, tʰ]
YULU — [ɖ, ⁿẕ]
YUPIK — [''ʲ̥'', ɣʷ]

3-segment profiles
ABIPON — [ʁ, ɨ, q]
ALABAMA — [''ɬ'', ɸ, m]
AMO — [ɐ, k͡p, ts]
ANDAMANESE — [''d'', ''ʲ̥'', æ]
ARABELA — [''s'', ʃ, au]
ASMAT — [''ə'', ɔ, ɟ]
AUCA — [''ẽ'', æ̃, ĩ]
BAKAIRI — [''d'', ʒ, ẽ]
BAMBARA — [õ, ẽ, D]

BARASANO — [''ẽ'', ɨ̃, ɾ]
BELLA — [''tɬ''', c', ts']
CACUA — [ə̃, ɛ̃, ʍ]
CARIB — [ɐ, ß, ɯ]
CHEROKEE — [''ə̃'', d, dz]
DADIBI — [''ẽ'', tʰ, ũ]
DAGUR — [''l'', dʒ, y]
DIOLA — [ə, ɟ, ɾ]
DIZI — [''ts''', ɐ, ß]
DOAYO — [''d'', õ, k͡p]
FINNISH — [æ, lð, ø]
JAPRERIA — [''t'', ɨ̃, ɭ]
KADUGLI — [''e'', ɖ, ʄ]
KALA — [''ə'', n̠, z]
KOMA — [ɓ, p', s']
KPAN — [õ, dz, ⁿd]
KULLO — [''d'', ''d<'', ''ts''']
KWAIO — [ŋʷ, ⁿgʷ, xʷ]
LAHU — [ə, ɨ, qʰ]
LUA — [''ə̃'', ''ẽ'', ɗ]
LUSHOOTSEED — [ʊ, dz, tɬ']
MABA — [d., ɟ, z]
MAIDU — [c', cʰ, ɗ]
MARGI — [ɗ, dz, ʤ]
MIXTEC — [''õ'', ɖ̥, kʷ]
MURINHPATHA — [d, ɾ., t.]
MURSI — [''d'', θ̱, ɟ]
NGIYAMBAA — [ɹ., D, t̠]
NICOBARESE — [ə, ɒ, ɯ]
ORMURI — [''dz'', ß, a̰]
POMO — [ʊ, p', x]
SENECA — [''dz'', ''o'', ɛ̃]
TABI — [θ, ɖ̥, ɟ]
TAROK — [''d<'', ʒ, k͡p]
TEMNE — [ɑ, g͡b, t̠]
TICUNA — [''õ'', ''ɾ'', ɨ̃]
TIDDIM — [l, w̱, z]
TIRURAY — [ŋ, ɸ, ɨ]
TLAPANEC — [dʒ, ĩ, ts]
TONKAWA — [''ts'', eː, xʷ]

TOTONAC — [aː, ɬ, uː]
USAN — [ʌ, d, ⁿd]
WAPPO — ["l̰", "ts'", m̩]
WEST — ["r̰", ɸ, n̲]
WIK-MUNKAN — [ɔ, ʊ, t̲]
YANA — ["rr", tð', ui]
YAREBA — ["e", ɸ, dz]
YORUBA — [dʒ, k͡p, r]

4-segment profiles
ACHUMAWI — ["ə", "rr", χ, dʒ]
BURARRA — [ɛ, n., ɹ., u]
CHATINO — ["d", "ẽ", ʃ, ĩ]
CUNA — ["d", "r", gʷ, tʃ]
FASU — ["ẽ", ɸ, ɾ, w]
FUR — ["ə", aː, d, r]
JINGPHO — ["dz", "rr", "tʰ", "ts"]
JOMANG — [ʊ, d, d̲, ɟ]
KALKATUNGU — [lð, ʌ, ɹ., r]
KEFA — ["rr", "t", f, p']
KUNAMA — ["o", ʊ, ɲ, r]
QAWASQAR — ["ə", t', tʃ', x]
QUILEUTE — [l, qʷ', tɬ, ts']
SENTANI — ["ə", "d", a̰, f]
XIAMEN — ["dz", "t", "tsʰ", ɔ]
ZUNI — ["ɬ", "t", "tsʰ", kʷ']

5-segment profiles
BODO — ["ə", ŋ, d, ɾ, z]
BORORO — ["ə", "d", "rr", dʒ, ɨ]
GWARI — ["e", "o", ĩ, k͡p, z]
MARANAO — ["o", ŋ, h, ɨ, r]
MOR — ["e", "rr", ʔ, ß, w]
SA'BAN — ["ə", ŋ, d, ɨ, r]
SHASTA — ["rr", "t", p', tʃ', x]

TUNICA — [e, r, tʃʰ, tʰ, w]

6-segment profiles
BARIBA — [e, k͡p, r, t, ũ, z]
IVATAN — ["ə", d, h, r, t̲, v]
SIERRA — [ʔ, ɛ, ŋ, ʃ, ɨ, s̲]
TAGALOG — [ɪ, ŋ, n̲, r, s, t̲]
TEMEIN — [ɟ, n̲, ɲ, r, s, w]

7-segment profiles
TETUN — ["d", "e", "r", "s", ʔ, f, p]

II. Languages discriminated by negative profiles

3-segment profiles
BIROM — [c, k͡p, not–ɲ]
EFIK — [k͡p, not–g, not–"d"]
NASIOI — ["r", not–w, not–"l"]
RORO — [ɾ̥, "o", not–"n"]

4-segment profiles
BANDJALANG — [n̲, r, not–k, not–"d"]
CAMPA — [t̲, e, ß, not–"e"]
KOIARI — [ð̰, h, r, not–"l"]
PIRAHA — [not–ᵐb, not–j, not–m, not–u]
ROTOKAS — [D, t, ß, not–ʔ]
SUENA — ["dz", "r", not–"r",not–"e"]
WESTERN DESERT — [r, ḻ, not–bᵐ, not–ʔ]

5-segment profiles
CHUAVE — [f, ɾ, not–p, not–

h, not–ŋ]
DERA — ["ə", ŋ, "d", not–"l",
not–"dʲ"]
IWAM — ["ə", ŋ, not–b, not–l,
not–"n"]
MOXO — [ɛ, n̪, ɾ, ß, not–"o"]
NUBIAN — ["l", "e", d̪, ɲ,
not–"d"]

6-segment profiles
BATAK — ["l", "s", "o", ɛ,
dʒ, not–"e"]
BISA — [v, z, not–x, not–h,
not–tʃ, not–ɛ]
IBAN — ["ə", "e", dʒ, r, not–
"s", not–ʃ]
NERA — ["d", not–p, not–ʔ,
not–x, not–n̪, not–"t̺"]
SONGHAI — ["e", o, not–ɛ,
not–h, not–ʃ, not–"o"]

7-segment profiles
AINU — [ɾ, not–l, not–b, not–
"e", not–ʔ, not–ʃ, not-e]
HAWAIIAN — ["l", "n", "o",
ɛ, ʔ, h, not–"e"]
TAORIPI — ["e", "l", "s", not–
b, not–w, not–x, not–ß]

8-segment profiles
YAQUI — ["e", ɾ, ʔ, u, not–ã,
not–ʃ, not–ɬ, not–"d"]

**Two indistinguishable
languages**

Dyirbal and Yidiny cannot be
distinguished from one another,
but the shared profile [ɟ,ɻ]
distinguishes them from all
remaining languages.

3.3.3 *Overview of the results*

One can read off from the list of profiles in Section 3.3.2 that, for
example, Fijian has the 1-segment profile [ⁿr] (a prenasalized voiced
alveolar trill), which differentiates it from all other languages in UPSID-
451, that for Papago this is the 2-segment profile, [d̺, n̪] (a voiced
retroflex plosive and a voiced palato-alveolar nasal), that Tarok needs a
3-segment profile ["d<", ʒ, k͡p] (a voiced dental/alveolar implosive and a
voiced palato-alveolar sibilant fricative and a voiceless labial-velar
plosive), and so on.

Two languages, Dyirbal and Yidiny (both belonging to the
Australian family, Pama-Nyungan subfamily) are in principle indistinguishable from one another since they have identical (reduced)
segment inventories. They have a shared profile, making them distinct
from the rest of the languages, given at the end of Section 3.3.2. Twenty-
five further languages cannot be distinguished — employing only
positive profiles — from some other language(s). Below, we show the 25
languages that fail discrimination in the left-hand column, and the
language(s) with which they fail to discriminate in the right-hand
column.

Languages failing discrimination	Languages causing the failure of discrimination
Ainu	Sa'ban, Cayuvava
Chuave	Kanuri, Luo, Sandawe, Camsa, Gwari, Yaqui
Dera	Dagbani, Tarok, Sama
Birom	Tampulma
Bisa	Amo, Tampulma
Efik	Aghem, Amo, Bete, Lelemi, Tampulma
Western Desert	Arrernte
Piraha	Jingpho, Kurukh, Sama, Cofan, Huari, Chatino
Yaqui	Kanuri, Luo, Lua
Bandjalang	Ivatan
Songhai	Burushaski, Bambara, Kolokuma, Tampulma, Tarok, Tera
Iwam	Tarok, Iban
Koiari	Dahalo
Nasioi	Jingpho, South Kiwai, Bruu, Nyah, Itonama, Paya, Ticuna, Chatino, Kawaiisu, Kefa
Rotokas	Dahalo
Suena	Jingpho
Taoripi	Saami, Burushaski, Tarok, Gelao, Lai, Tetun, Amharic
Nera	Burushaski, Tarok
Nubian	Saami
Batak	Jingpho,Burushaski, Tarok, Sama
Hawaiian	Jingpho, Dani, Kurukh, Sama, Sui, Tetun, Itonama, Paya, Chatino, Kawaiisu, Tol, Kefa
Iban	Sama
Roro	Itonama, Paya
Campa	Amuzgo
Moxo	Amuzgo, Dahalo

The first ten languages above fail discrimination since their (reduced) segment inventories are subsumed by the inventories of the languages in the right-hand column, whereas the remaining 15 languages happen not to have a non-anomalous segment contrastable with the segments of some other languages. Section 3.3.2 lists the negative profiles that these languages need.

Table 3.5 presents some statistics on positive profiles, concerning their size (column 1), the number of languages using a profile of this size (column 2), the average sizes of the reduced segment inventories of these languages (column 3), and the corresponding average number of alternative profiles (column 4). Thus, row 2 e.g. indicates that 213 languages, whose mean reduced segment inventory size is 29.5, need at least the simultaneous presence of 2 segments to put them apart from the rest of the languages, and that, on the average, there are 19 alternative 2-segment profiles per language.

Table 3.5. Some statistics on positive profiles

Size of profiles	Number of languages distinguished by a profile of some size	Average sizes of reduced segment inventories of languages distinguished by a profile of some size	Average number of alternatives within profiles of some size
1	124	37.1	2.8
2	213	29.5	19
3	57	25.4	29.9
4	16	24	30.1
5	8	20.6	13.1
6	5	23	18
7	1	18	4

NOTE: Two languages are indistinguishable from one another, and 25 other languages can only be differentiated with negative profiles.

3.3.4 A new problem: inspecting the size and structure of profiles

Table 3.5 (column 1) shows that positive profiles vary in size from 1 to 7 segments. From columns 1 and 2 it is seen that about 3/4 of the languages from the database have profiles of one or two segments. Most numerous (viz. 213) are the languages needing 2-segment profiles.

Comparing the sizes of the positive profiles (hereafter just "profiles") and the average sizes of the corresponding segment inventories (columns 1 and 3), we see a (negative) correlation between these two parameters, viz. the smaller the profiles able to distinguish some languages, the larger their average segment inventories, and the larger the profiles, the smaller the inventories. This correlation is very slightly violated only in the case of languages needing 6-segment profiles (row 6 of Table 3.5). The correlation could be attributed to the interaction of the following two circumstances. The first one (noted by Maddieson 1984: 10) is that a smaller inventory has a greater probability of including a given common (frequent) segment than a larger one, and a larger segment inventory has a greater probability of including an unusual (infrequent) segment type than a smaller one. The second circumstance is that a segment set of a fixed cardinality (=size) is more likely to distinguish a given language if it consisted of unusual segments rather than if it consisted of more common segments. Therefore the languages with larger segment inventories, which will presumably contain unusual segments, will use for discrimination a smaller number of these than the languages with the smaller segment inventories, containing exclusively more common segments. On the other hand, a negative correlation between profile size and the number of segments can be expected even if all segments occurred with equal frequency.

Do any patterns emerge regarding the structure of profiles? In the first place, we examined the distribution of vowels and consonants in profiles, grouping under the class of vowels all segments marked as (simple) vowels and diphthongs in UPSID-451, and under the class of consonants all remaining segments. The results are summarized in Table 3.6.

Table 3.6 reveals patterns like the following: If a language uses a 1-segment profile, then it is more likely that it consists of a single consonant rather than a single vowel (240 out of 342 total 1-segment profiles or 70.1%); or within profiles of equal size, the most frequently occurring profiles are those in which consonants outnumber vowels, etc. The general conclusion to be drawn from the table is that consonants are more frequently used in profiles than vowels, a fact that can simply be attributed to their higher overall frequency of occurrence within the segment inventories in UPSID (Maddieson 1984: 9).

In the second place, we looked for other patterns in the profiles. As mentioned above, profiles will tend to comprise rarer segments, since these will generally have a higher discriminative power and we explored this line of research. At present, we dispose of no definitive answer to the question of what *types* of segments are rare in the world's languages (for a general discussion, and a discussion of cross-linguistic frequency of some specific types of sounds, cf. e.g. Maddieson 1984; Lindblom and Maddieson 1988; Laver 1991).

Table 3.6. Distribution of vowels and consonants computed from positive profiles

Size of profiles	Structure of profiles	Number of exemplifying profiles
1-segment profiles	C	240
	V	102
2-segment profiles	C + C	132
	V + C	82
	V + V	33
3-segment profiles	V + C + C	25
	C + C + C	17
	V + V + C	13
	V + V + V	2
4-segment profiles	V + C + C + C	5
	V + V + C + C	5
	C + C + C + C	6
5-segment profiles	C + C + C + C + C	1
	V + C + C + C + C	3
	V + V + C + C + C	3
	V + V + V + C + C	1
6-segment profiles	C + C + C + C + C + C	1
	V + C + C + C + C + C	2
	V + V + C + C + C + C	2
7-segment profiles	V + C + C + C + C + C + C	1
	Total	676

For the purposes of our study, we investigated the occurrence in segments of features singled out under the rubrics "secondary articulations or accompanying features" and "phonation and other types" by Maddieson and Precoda (1991). In particular, these included the features labialized, palatalized, velarized, pharyngealized, nasalized, nasal release, prestopped and lateral release (under the first rubric), and the features voiceless, voiced, aspirated, laryngealized, long, breathy, overshort and preaspirated (under the second rubric). Most of these features signify a certain articulatory complexity of segments in comparison with the segments' "basic" (non-labialized, non-palatalized, etc.) counterparts, and can hence be expected to be less frequent cross-linguistically.

There are 676 (positive) profiles listed in Section 3.3.2, comprising a total of 1148 segment tokens (occurrences). Of these, 985 segments or 85.8% contain at least one feature of the above list. The number of features from this list these segments use is 1577, or about 1.6 features per segment. The segments occurring in profiles therefore may be said to typically comprise features indicating secondary articulation, accompanying features or different phonation types.

In the third place, we investigated the least frequent segment in each profile, or what is the same, the segment with the highest discriminative power. 1-segment profiles, of course, will contain only (non-anomalous and contrastable) segments occurring in a single language, so we addressed larger profiles. It was found that the most infrequent segments in 2-segment profiles fall in the range 1–35 segment occurrences in UPSID-451, 3-segment profiles fall in the range 1–60 segment occurrences, 4-segment profiles in the range 5–66, 5-segment profiles in the range 33–61, 6-segment profiles in the range 33–74, and 7-segment profiles in the range 50–50 (Section 3.3.2 contains only one 7-segment profile, for Tetun). These figures are yet another indication of the correlation between a profile's size and the frequency of its constituent segments. At the same time, the overlap of the ranges of pairs of consecutively larger profiles (disregarding only profiles of size=1) shows the more complex interaction between segments, as they jointly act as discriminants.

Finally, we investigated whether the profiles' constituent segments share some features that bind these segments together (making sense only in profiles larger than 1-segment). Of course, those profiles from Table 3.6 that consist of vowel segments only, or of consonantal segments only, are exemplary, since they share the feature vowel or consonant, respectively. However, there exist further possibilities for feature sharing in segments belonging to the same profile, and we explore these next.

We found that out of 334 profiles that possess more than one segment, 193 (i.e. 57.7%) have all their component segments share *at least* one feature with all other component segments. The shared features may significantly exceed one, as in most of the following examples:

Hadza

2-segment profile:	[‖ʰ, ŋ‖ʔ]
Segment feature description:	[‖ʰ]–[voiceless aspirated alveolar lateral affricated click]
Segment feature description:	[ŋ‖ʔ]–[glottalized nasalized voiceless alveolar lateral affricated click]
Shared features (5):	[voiceless alveolar lateral affricated click]

Andoke

2-segment profile:	[ã̟, ɑ̃]
Segment feature description:	[ã̟]–[nasalized low front unrounded vowel]
Segment feature description:	[ɑ̃]–[nasalized low back unrounded vowel]
Shared features (4):	[nasalized low unrounded vowel]

Mazatec

2-segment profile:	[ⁿ·d.z., ⁿdz]
Segment feature description:	[ⁿ·d.z.]–[prenasalized voiced retroflex sibilant affricate]
Segment feature description:	[ⁿdz]–[prenasalized voiced alveolar sibilant affricate]
Shared features (4):	[prenasalized voiced sibilant affricate]

Auca

3-segment profile:	[”ẽ”, æ̃, ĩ]
Segment feature description:	[”ẽ”]–[nasalized mid front unrounded vowel]
Segment feature description:	[æ̃]–[nasalized raised low front unrounded vowel]
Segment feature description:	[ĩ]–[nasalized high front unrounded vowel]
Shared features (4):	[nasalized front unrounded vowel]

Kwaio

3-segment profile:	[ŋ^w, ⁿg^w, x^w]

3-segment profile: [ŋ^w, ^{n}g^w, x^w]
Segment feature description: [ŋ^w]–[labialized voiced velar nasal]
Segment feature description: [^{n}g^w]–[prenasalized labialized voiced velar plosive]
Segment feature description: [x^w]–[labialized voiceless velar fricative]
Shared features (3):   [labialized velar consonant]

The common features in all the segments of a profile allow characterizing the profile. For example, we may say that Kwaio differs from all other languages (in UPSID-451) by a combination of 3 of its labialized velar consonants, Auca by a combination of 3 of its nasalized front unrounded vowels, etc. Thus, our counts show integrity of profiles that apparently exceeds randomness. Thus, profiles can be described in more general, feature-centred ways.

3.3.5 A new problem: alternative profiles and how to choose among them

Languages discriminate from one another in a great number of ways, as shown by column 4 of Table 3.5, which gives the average number of alternative profiles of different sizes. These averages, however, conceal much variation.

Let us look at the alternatives within 1-segment profiles, i.e. cases where each of many single segments of a language can discriminate it from the other languages. Here, 71 languages do not actually have alternatives (i.e. possess only one idiosyncratic segment), while most of the other 53 languages have only a couple of such alternatives. Several languages however have a significant number of alternatives relative to their total (reduced) segment inventories. The leader is Xóũ with 65 alternatives, which amounts to 46% of its total (reduced) segment inventory of 140 segments. There follow several languages with considerably fewer alternatives (from 7 to 19), but whose idiosyncrasy is still impressive in that the unique segments they possess form a large part of their total sound inventories: Parauk (19/77 24%), Shilha (7/31 22%), Kabardian (8/55 14%) and Hmong (8/55 14%), Archi (10/75 13%), and Irish (7/63 11%). Though the Caucasian languages Kabardian and Archi might belong to the same language family, as believed by some linguists, it is seen that the large proportion of idiosyncratic segments in a language is not correlated with its genetic origin, as the other languages above belong to widely diverse language families. It seems to be correlated (as could be expected from our discussion in the previous section) with the largeness of inventories, but is not entirely limited to such languages, as Shilha shows, which has the average of 31 segments for this corpus.

Of the 213 languages with two-segment profiles only 37 do not have some alternative. Here the mean number of alternatives drastically increases (more than six times in comparison with 1-segment profiles), and one language, Hadza, has 320 alternative idiosyncratic segment pairs. Those exceeding 100 alternatives, in diminishing order, are Sedang (306), Lithuanian (208), Mazahua (165), Hindi-Urdu (137), and Kurdish (136).

From the 57 languages with distinctive triplets, 10 do not have alternatives, their mean number now being 29.9 triplets per language. Bella has 220 alternatives. Ormuri with 120 and Lushootseed with 115 are the only other languages in which this number exceeds 100.

From the 16 languages with distinctive 4-tuples, 2 have a single profile. The mean number of alternatives increases to 30.1, and the language with a maximum of alternatives, viz. 228, is Quileute. No other language exceeds 100 alternatives.

Only 14 languages need 5-segment, 6-segment or 7-segment profiles to be distinguished from the other languages and they generally have a smaller number of alternatives (Sa'ban is an exception with its 43 alternative quintuples, and so is Tagalog with 40 alternative sextuples).

The existence of this multitude of ways to differentiate a language from the others creates some problems. In the first place, we would like to limit these possibilities, especially if we want to view profiles as phonetic-phonological definitions of languages (it would be simplest to have just one definition of one and the same object). In the second place, and more importantly, our treatment of alternative profiles so far implies that all of them are *equally* representative of a language's idiosyncrasy, which turns out not to be the case. An example will make this point clearer.

Tigre, for instance, has the following 8 alternative profiles:

[aː"ə"]   [aːdʒ]   [aːg]   [aːkʼ]
[aːtʃ]   [aːtʃʼ]   [aːtsʼ]   [aːz]

any one of which is perfectly legitimate in the sense that it suffices to discriminate this language from all other languages. On a closer look, however, it may be seen that not all of these profiles represent equally well the specificity of Tigre, or its sound traits that put it apart from all the other languages of the world. Thus, the segment [aː] recurs in all 8 profiles, so it must be a component of any profile we might choose to use, but, as far as the second component of the profile is concerned, we have a choice between 8 alternative segments, viz. ["ə", dʒ, g, k', tʃ, tʃ', ts', z]. Some of these Tigre segments occur infrequently in other languages, hence they can be considered more "typical" of Tigre than the more widespread segments. Looking at their frequencies of occurrence in UPSID-451 (abstracting from their occurrence in Tigre itself), we get the following picture: ["ə"] (72 occurrences), [dʒ] (107), [g] (235), [k'] (62), [tʃ] (181), [tʃ'] (43), [ts'] (25), and [z] (58). Clearly, then, if we are after typicality, we should choose the most infrequent segment in the list, [a:], occurring in only 5 other languages, which together with [ts'] (occurring in only 26 other languages), would yield the most "typical" profile for Tigre. More generally, a *typical* profile for a language will comprise the more unusual segments occurring in that language in comparison with the other, less typical, alternatives. We thus come up with the following simple intuitive criterion for choosing a *typical profile* from all alternative profiles:

Typical profile

From a set of alternative profiles for a given language, choose the profile(s) containing the segments with the lowest frequency in the database.

This criterion was implemented in our system by counting the occurrences in the segment database, summing these counts for each profile, and then choosing the profile with the smallest count. The results in Section 3.3.2 reflect this criterion and list only typical profiles for the languages. After applying this filter some alternative typical profiles may still remain. Of course, this will be the case in all 1-segment profiles, since all the alternatives for one language will consist of a segment with zero frequency of occurrence in the remaining languages. So would alternatives with equal total frequencies in profiles larger than 1-segment. But these are not unwelcome consequences insofar as we would as a rule be interested in showing all segments occurring in just one language and, more generally, have all equally intuitive larger profiles, from which we could choose randomly, if need be (e.g. for providing a phonetic-phonological definition of some language).

3.3.6. A new problem: does feature relatedness exist between alternative 1-segment profiles?

1-segment profiles are of considerable interest since they pertain to segments unique to a particular language. We posed the question: If one language possesses several idiosyncratic segments, are these segments related in terms of their feature specifications? In other words, do these segments share some features that bind them together?

There are several cases of languages possessing idiosyncratic segments, which we present below, accompanying each with an example:

Case 1: All unique segments share some feature(s)
Akan
[çʷ]–[labialized voiceless palatal fricative]
[cçʷ]–[labialized voiceless palatal affricate]
[ɟjʷ]–[labialized voiced palatal affricate]
[ɲʷ]–[labialized voiced palatal nasal]
Shared features (3):   [labialized palatal consonant]

Case 2: A group of unique segments shares some feature(s), another group shares other feature(s)
Kashmiri
[dʒʲ]–[palatalized voiced palato-alveolar sibilant affricate]
[tʃʲ]–[palatalized voiceless palato-alveolar sibilant affricate]
Shared features (4):   [palatalized palato-alveolar sibilant affricate]

[ə̃ː]–[long nasalized higher mid central unrounded vowel]
[ɨ̃ː]–[long nasalized high central unrounded vowel]
Shared features (5):   [long nasalized central unrounded vowel]

Case 3: A group of unique segments share some feature(s), but an unrelated segment remains
Hmong
[ŋkʰ]–[prenasalized voiceless aspirated velar plosive]
[ɴq]–[prenasalized voiceless uvular plosive]
[ɴqʰ]–[prenasalized voiceless aspirated uvular plosive]
[nˌt.s.]–[prenasalized voiceless retroflex sibilant affricate]
[nˌt.s.ʰ]–[prenasalized voiceless aspirated retroflex sibilant affricate]
[n̪tsʰ]–[prenasalized voiceless aspirated dental sibilant affricate]

[ⁿtʃʰ]–[prenasalized voiceless aspirated palato-alveolar sibilant affricate]
Shared features (3)   [prenasalized voiceless consonant]

[ɛɯ]–[lower mid front unrounded to high back unrounded diphthong]
(Isolated segment)

Case 4: No group of unique segments shares any feature(s)
Somali
[d̠.]–[laryngealized voiced retroflex plosive]
(Isolated segment)
[ʉ]–[lowered high central rounded vowel]
(Isolated segment)

In case 1, all alternative unique segments for a language have one or more features in common. In Akan, all alternatives are grouped together by the feature set [labialized palatal consonant]. In case 2, the alternative unique segments for a language can be partitioned in two or more groups, the segments in each group being bound together by a feature set. The four alternatives of Kashmiri form two groups of segments, the palatalized palato-alveolar sibilant affricate group, consisting of two segments, and the long nasalized central unrounded vowel group, consisting also of two segments. In case 3, some of the segments are tied into groups by a set of features, but an isolated segment remains, sharing no features with the group. In Hmong, seven segments are classed together by the feature set [prenasalized voiceless consonant], while the segment [ɛɯ] remains unrelated to the rest of alternatives. Finally, in case 4, the segments exhibit no feature similarity, as in Somali which differentiates from the other languages in UPSID-451 by the consonantal segment [d̠.] and the vowel segment [ʉ] which are completely unrelated insofar as their feature specifications are concerned.

In each of the cases 1, 2, and 3 there exists a noticeable relatedness between the alternative idiosyncratic segments for one language, in the sense that all alternatives can be clustered into one or a couple of groups of segments sharing some feature(s), and only in case 4 is such a relatedness absent. The degree of this relatedness can further be judged by the number of shared features defining a cluster. We conducted estimates of the number of languages falling under each of these cases, as well as of the degree of segment relatedness in each cluster-defining feature set.

Our counts showed the following. First, from a total of 53 languages having alternative idiosyncratic segments, 49 (i.e. 92%) fall under one of the Cases 1, 2 or 3. More exactly, the distribution among the 4 cases is: Case 1 = 41 languages, Case 2 = 3 languages, Case 3 = 5, Case 4 = 4 languages. These figures indicate that, in their vast majority (92%), the corresponding languages individuate by segments which are themselves related; besides, most often all the segments group into just one cluster, defined by a set of the features these segments share. Secondly, we computed the degree of relatedness, or the strength of similarity, holding together the segments in one grouping. We found that their similarity is quite significant, amounting to an average of 2.7 shared features per grouping.

Thus, it turns out to be an interesting characteristic of languages that, if they possess several unique segments, they would tend to significantly relate to one another. Indeed, it is a remarkable fact that, for example, all the idiosyncratic segments of Shilha, which are 7 in number, are pharyngealized consonants; all 6 segments of Arrernte are voiced plosives, those of Rutul are pharyngealized uvular consonants, while all 6 segments of Nama are aspirated voiceless clicks; all 6 segments of South Nambiquara are laryngealized sounds (vowels or consonants). Or, that all 7 unique segments that Irish has should turn out to be consonants, or that all 10 such segments of Archi should also be consonants, but all of them voiceless. Or, further, that in languages having 2 or 3 unique segments these segments should share as much as three or four features, as in Wolof, Russian, Changzhou, Lungchow, Bruu, Neo-Aramaic, Vietnamese. The alternative unique segments a language possesses are not random segments from its inventory, but are rather ones that are strongly bound together by the features they share.

3.3.7. Conclusion

We have described how the languages of the world differ in terms of the segment inventories they employ, listing the profiles for the languages contained in the UPSID-451 database. In general, there is a significant variety of profiles discriminating a language from all the others, but some profile(s) can be considered more typical for a given language in that they contain segments that are less usual in the other languages, and we listed these typical profiles in Section 3.3.2. Additional computational machinery to that used for the discrimination was built to alleviate further comparisons. It was found that the size of (positive) profiles varies from 1 to 7 segments, but by far the most common are the 1-segment and 2-segment profiles, utilized by nearly 3/4 of all languages. We made also some quantitative and qualitative observations on the content of the generated profiles. A (positive) profile will generally tend to include more consonants than vowels, and more unusual, rather than more usual, segments, which further, share some features in common. The segments in profiles tend to have features pertaining to secondary articulations or diverse phonation types. Alternative 1-segment profiles for one language show significant inter-relatedness in terms of their feature specifications.

A word of caution as regards the plausibility of the generated profiles is in order, as our study is based on less than 10% of the world's languages. It will be clear that the validity of profiles will depend on the coverage and reliability of segment inventories descriptions in UPSID. UPSID is a carefully organized sample, with a wide genetic and areal coverage, but still the addition of a new language to the database may lead to the need for re-computation of the "antecedently valid" profiles. Thus, a language possessing, say, an idiosyncratic segment with reference to UPSID may not be distinguishable from a newly added language that also happens to have that segment, hence the need to reconsider the profile of the former. One obvious way to handle insufficiency of data is, of course, adding much new data. A less strenuous effort is however possible in the case when we want to increase the plausibility of the profile for some specific language(s) beyond the present coverage of UPSID. UPSID is built on the quota principle, including only one representative language of a small language grouping, so if we want to increase the plausibility of a profile for some language, one good way would be to include only some further languages in the data set, especially such that are closely gene- tically/areally related to this language. The rationale behind this move is that these related languages would be most likely to contain identical segments to those included in the profile of the language we are considering, and thus invoke a need for re-computation. If no such situation occurs, then the profile considered quite plausibly is valid beyond UPSID since the less vexing more distant languages are well represented in the database (using the quota principle). As far as the reliability of inventories descriptions in UPSID is concerned, there exist problems arising from an indeterminacy in some of the linguistic analyses on which UPSID is based (e.g. Maddieson 1992 mentions that Xóũ which has 121 consonants in UPSID can have only 55 according to an alternative analysis). We can get better discriminations among languages in terms of their segment inventories when we have better inventories descriptions of these languages. For the moment, with this data at hand, what could be done to at least partially diminish these problems of reliability of inventories/profiles was to handle the anomalous segments in a language, which are explicitly marked in UPSID, in a cautious way. We cannot go into details here, but it is worth mentioning that the conservative discrimination policy adopted by us had some effect on the resultant profiles. One striking example is the language Ojibwa which, if we disregard anomalies, has 6 idiosyncratic segments, amounting to 22% of its total inventory, but not a single idiosyncratic segment in our present analysis and hence requiring a 2-segment profile.

Finally, we note that, since a profile is a sequence of segments, unique to just one language, it can be viewed as a universal prohibiting the co-occurrence of this sequence of segments. This interpretation allows us to look at a profile for some language as a nearly absolute universal, valid in all but this particular language, or in 450/451 (=99,8%) of the cases. Thus, 1-segment profiles of the form [A] state that segment A does not occur in any language, 2-segment profiles [A, B] state that segments A and B do not co-occur, and so on for larger profiles. For instance, Seneca's profile ["dz","o",ɛ̃] is a universal, stating that these three segments do not occur together in any language, and will be valid in all languages except Seneca. The dual interpretation of our results, as discriminant sets or nearly absolute universals, is yet another indication of the close relation between both approaches to language, the individualizing vs. the generalizing, we referred to at the beginning of this article. Our empirical study thus would be of potential interest also to investigators of phonological universals.

3.4 Summary of Chapters 2 and 3

In Chapters 2 and 3, I described an intelligent program MPD/KINSHIP that carries out the general-scientific task of concept (class) discrimination. Given a set of concepts (classes), represented by at least one instance each, and where each instance is stated in terms of feature values, MPD/KINSHIP profiles, or discriminates every concept from all other concepts. MPD/KINSHIP also handles the meta-scientific task of ensuring simplicity of the description in that the resultant discrimination uses a minimum number of overall features that are necessary and jointly sufficient to single out each concept, and produces the shortest profile of each individual concept.

MPD/KINSHIP builds conjunctive profiles (or nearly conjunctive ones, in case derived features are used), which strengthens the legibility of the output, as conjunctive notions are more readily understandable, as noted by philosophers and psychologists, and hence with wider applicability in science (and everyday life more generally).

The application of MPD/KINSHIP to diverse problems has made conspicuous the problem of the multiplicity of solutions that are possible summarizing the same data set. MPD/KINSHIP thus addresses the meta-scientific task of ensuring the completeness of the solution (being capable to produce all solutions), and the soundness of the solution (the solution being generated mechanically following approved method).

The combined task of parsimonious discrimination, addressed by MPD/KINSHIP, is computationally complex: the number of pair-wise contrasts between the concepts a linguist needs to make to achieve the discrimination (*N–choose–2*, calculable by the formula $N(N-1)/2$) is large even for medium-sized problems, where the number of concepts, N, is say 40–50, and exceeds a thousand demarcations; still worse, the problem of discovering simplest solutions by finding minimum set covers, or equivalently, converting CNFs into DNFs, is NP-complete, and therefore a major obstacle even to contemporary computers. Besides the computational complexity of parsimonious discrimination, the wide variety of problems reducible to parsimonious discrimination both within and outside of linguistics is another argument justifying the need for its automation.

Some of the results of KINSHIP and MPD are worth summarizing. The KINSHIP program has so far been applied to more than 20 languages of different language families. In some cases, the datasets were partial (only consanguineal, or blood) kin systems, but in others they were complete systems comprising 40–50 classes with several hundreds of instances. The program has re-discovered some classical analyses (of the Amerindian language Seneca by Lounsbury), has successfully analyzed previously unanalyzed languages (e.g., Bulgarian), and has improved on previous analyses of English. For English, the most parsimonious model has been found, and the only one giving conjunctive class profiles for all kinterms, which sounds impressive considering the massive efforts concentrated on analyzing the English kinship system.

Most importantly, KINSHIP has shown that the huge number of potential componential (=discrimination) models — a menace to the very foundations of the approach, which has made some linguists propose alternative analytic tools — are in fact reduced to (nearly) unique analyses by our three simplicity criteria. Our 3rd criterion, ensuring the coordination between equally simple alternative profiles, and with no precedence in the linguistic literature, proved essential in the pruning of solutions.

Other results, from applications of MPD, are also worth noting. Thus, in the investigation of the Russian phonemic system in a classic article by Cherry, Halle, and Jakobson (1953), MPD confirmed that the 11 primitive overall features are indeed needed, but it found 12 simpler phoneme profiles out of 42 in all than those proposed. Additionally, the average phoneme profile turned out to comprise 6.14, rather than 6.5, components as suggested by these authors. The program also found the "typical profiles" of the 451 languages in the UPSID database, which raised new problems that were subsequently handled. The choice among alternative solutions was a recurrent problem in this application as well.

Chapter 4. Inferring Plausible Laws/Patterns I: UNIVAUTO and the Problem of Language Universals

One of the most common tasks of the discovery of scientific knowledge is that of inferring patterns (i.e. non-random associations), generalizations, or laws from data. When the data are numerical, the derived laws/patterns are quantitative, and when the data are nominal, the derived laws/patterns are qualitative. "Hard" sciences usually operate with quantitative laws, while "soft" sciences, like linguistics, with qualitative laws. As mentioned in Chapter 1, Langley *et al.* (1987) have computationally replicated a number of first class discoveries of quantitative laws from early physics and chemistry. In what follows in this chapter, we shall be concerned with the acquisition of new qualitative generalizations.

Qualitative generalizations are inferences from propositions concerning individual observations to universal propositions, i.e. from a^1 is P, a^2 is P, ... a^n is P to *All A's are P*. When class A is "closed", the qualitative generalizations that can be made about it can be proved to be true or false by simple enumeration of all a's. The more challenging, and more common, case, however, is when class A is "open", i.e. it is infinite or at least much too large for enumeration. In an open class, the qualitative generalizations that can be made about this class can *only* be proved to be false (e.g. by showing counter-examples), but not true, inasmuch as we can never be sure whether such counter-evidence will not be produced at some future moment, inspecting some further a. All we can do to remedy this situation to some extent is to provide certain argumentation about the *plausibility* of our beliefs about the truthfulness of the generalization.

Three types of plausibility arguments are commonly used in science in support of generalizations involving open classes, involving: (i) the number of supporting examples (the greater their number the better), (ii) the structural diversity of the supporting examples (the more diverse they are from one another the better), and (iii) statistical significance (the more improbable the generalization the better).

The task of discovery of patterns, or generalizations from data in linguistics is very general, and recurs practically at all levels of language and in all sub-disciplines within linguistics (and outside of linguistics), so the computational machinery to be described in this chapter is equally applicable to other problems than those explicitly dealt with here. Here, we confine to the problem of language universals, which is an important one within linguistic typology, and linguistics more generally.

In this chapter, I describe a discovery program, called UNIVAUTO (UNIVersals AUthoring TOol), which discovers and verbalizes in English its discoveries. Accepting as input information about languages, presented in terms of feature-values, the discoveries of another human agent arising from the same data, as well as some additional data, the program discovers the universals in the data, compares them with the discoveries of the human agent and, if appropriate, generates a report in English on its discoveries. Running UNIVAUTO on the data from the paper by Greenberg (1966a) on word order universals, the system has produced several linguistically valuable texts, two of which were published in a refereed linguistic journal. Other discoveries of the system that do not involve verbalization will also be sketched in the chapter. These include the discovery of kinship semantic pattern universals, as well as the testing of a hypothesis, proposed by Trudgill (2004a), assuming a certain type of correlation between population size and the size of sound inventories.

4.1 The problem of language universals as inferring plausible patterns from data

The languages of the world are both different from one another in some respects and alike in others. The study of their common features is the object of investigation of the "universalist" trend in linguistics. Though historically this trend exists for centuries, a new turn has emerged from the work of Joseph Greenberg, initiated by his paper (Greenberg 1966a) on the order of meaningful elements in language. We briefly discussed some of Greenberg's contributions in Chapter 1, Section 1.1.1.3.

Language universals, broadly speaking, are propositions holding for all languages without exceptions (*absolute universals*) or with a small number of exceptions (*statistical universals*). They belong to different types, according to whether they hold for one variable (*unrestricted universals*), or for two (or more) variables, e.g. *implicational universals* (*if A, then B*), *conjunctive universals* (*A and B*), etc. The idea of universals, their types, and examples from different linguistic levels, are familiar to linguists (cf. e.g. Comrie 1981, Croft 1990), and hence here I will confine to matters of interest in the context of this book. Our central matter of concern is: "What counts as an adequate universal, and how does one go about searching for universals?". The newer developments in universals research have direct relevance for this problem, so we may look at their characteristic features.

First of all, the work of Greenberg and followers marks the beginning of the quest for *empirical* universals, in the sense that their inferences are based on an explicit sample of the world languages. Publishing language samples is important both in that we can test proposed universals and can further search for other, yet uncovered, ones. This is in sharp contrast to earlier research, which did not bother to list the language material for the generalizations made and was thus untestable. (Those concerned with "definitional" universals (cf. Chapter 1, Section 1.1.3), which are logically derived from higher-order principles, rather "bottom-up" from the data, cannot be otherwise, and hence do not require much further data for their support.)

Secondly, and related to the first point, the new approach emphasized the need for compiling *representative samples* from which both statistically and inductively justified conclusions can be drawn. Considerable attention has since then been focused on the question of linguistic sampling for cross-linguistic research (cf. e.g. Bell 1978, Dryer 1989 and elsewhere). The wide historical and areal coverage of the languages included in samples is considered essential for providing the structural diversity of the linguistic support for proposed universals. Thus, the more language families and geographical areas the languages supporting a generalization belong to, the more varied they are expected to be, and hence the stronger the support for the generalization.

And, finally, to enhance the plausibility of proposed universals, beside structural diversity, the language support to universals is required to be statistically significant. It may be observed that though the new approach explicitly recognized the need for estimating significance, this requirement was fulfilled more in words than in deeds, and most proposed universals in the literature have not been actually tested for significance.

We thus see that the Greenbergian method of search for universals reduces to the general-scientific task of inference of patterns from data and the meta-scientific task of ensuring the plausibility of the found patterns.

4.2 UNIVAUTO — a system for discovery and verbalization of universals

UNIVAUTO (UNIVersals AUthoring TOol) is a system whose domain of application is the study of language universals. Given as input information about languages presented in terms of feature-values, (eventually) the discoveries of another human agent arising from the same data, as well as some additional data, the program discovers the universals in the data, compares them with the discoveries of the human agent and, if appropriate, generates a report (in English) on its discoveries. Running UNIVAUTO on the data from the paper by Greenberg (1966a) on word order universals, the system has produced several linguistically valuable texts, one of which was submitted for publication to a refereed linguistic journal without any further human editing (except for the formatting needed to conform to the style-sheet of the journal), and without disclosing the "machine origin" of the article. The article was accepted for publication with practically no revisions. To the best of our knowledge, this is the first discovery program to generate a scientific article (Pericliev 2003).

4.2.1 Brief overview

Below is a brief description of UNIVAUTO (UNIVersals AUthoring TOol) in terms of the problem it handles as well as its input and output. The data for the illustration comes from the paper by Greenberg (1966a).

The input

UNIVAUTO accepts as input the following, manually prepared, information (in internal representation):

(1) a *database* (= a table), usually comprising a sizable number of languages, described in terms of some properties (feature-value pairs), as well as a list of the abbreviations used in the database. By way of illustration, below is a (simplified) description of the language Berber in terms of just 4 features: V–order (=the position of verb, subject and object), NA/AN (=the position of noun and adjective), CNPN/PNCN (=the position of common noun and proper noun), and Pref/Suff (=the presence of prefix or suffix):

data(berber,[V–order=VSO, NA/AN=NA, CNPN/PNCN=*, Pref/Suff=both])

The program also knows what the abbreviations used for feature values stand for, e.g. V=verb, A=adjective, N=noun, etc. The special value "*" for the feature CNPN/PNCN designates that either that feature is inapplicable for Berber or that the value for that feature is unknown.

(2) *human analyst's discoveries* (represented as simple propositions); e.g.:

discovery(agent=greenberg,no=3,implication(V–order=VSO,Pr/Po=Pr), non-statistical).
discovery(agent=greenberg,no=12,implication(V–order=VSO,Wh–word=first), non-statistical).

The first of these two records states that the human agent, Greenberg, has found the implicational universal, relating two variables, to the effect that for all languages, if a language has a Verb–Subject–Object order then this language has prepositions, that this universals is non-statistical (holds without exceptions in the studied database), and that it is stated as Universal 3 in the original publication of the human agent.

(3) *Other information.* Aside from these basic sources of information, the input includes information on: the origin of database, if any (the full citation of work where the database is given); reference name(s) of database, if any; the "is-a" relation of rows and columns in the database; citations regarding the original paper's importance, if any (including quotes, of pre-specified grammatical form, with associated full reference of the quotes). Also, the input to the program may contain a classification of the languages investigated into language families/areas.

The problem

The most common situation in the study of universals, as our study of the literature has revealed, is the one in which a linguist presents some data as well as the universals he has been able to derive from these data. UNIVAUTO was designed to handle this situation (the system can, of course, also handle the situation in which there is no other human discoverer involved).

The problem UNIVAUTO addresses can be formulated as follows: Given the input information, find the language universals valid in the data, compare them with those discovered by some human agent, and write an article, if appropriate. For example, a query to the system may look like:

–?–discover(implication(A,B), non_statistical,
        positive_examples=4,compare_with=greenberg).

It amounts to requesting that a non-statistical implicational universal holding between two variables and supported in at least 4 positive examples be found, the results be compared with the findings of Greenberg, and, if judged as interesting enough, a report of these discoveries be written. Other queries may also be formulated, requiring different logical types of universals, different statistical nature or supporting positive evidence.

The output

Depending on what the system has been able to discover, it will issue a message summarizing its findings, including: (1) the number of idiosyncratic machine-discovered universals, (2) the number of idiosyncratic man-discovered universals, and (3) the number and nature of the "problems" in the man-discovered universals (on the categorization of "problems" we are handling, see below). If the discoveries are judged unworthy (by a simple numeric evaluation metric the system disposes of), the session will terminate by writing (on the screen and/or in a file) the system's "insignificant" findings. Otherwise, on request, it will report in English its discoveries.

Below we list some excerpts from the article Pericliev (1999a), generated by UNIVAUTO as an illustration of its output. The program was run on the data from the paper by Greenberg (1966a), with the query in the preceding section. It discovered some problems in his analyses (which form the bulk of the text below) as well as 59 novel universals that have gone unnoticed by Greenberg. We give some comments in angular brackets. The paragraphs have bold face numeration to be used for later reference.

4.2.2 The UNIVAUTO System

UNIVAUTO is a large program, comprising two basic modules: one in charge of the discoveries of the program, called UNIV(ersals), and the other in charge of the verbalization of these discoveries, called AU(thoring)TO(ol).

Figure 4.1. Illustrative output of UNIVAUTO (excerpt from Pericliev 1999a)

---

[1]   *Further implicational universals in Greenberg's data*

[2]   *The goal of this article is to study the implicational universals in the 30 languages sample of Greenberg 1966 and compare the results of the two studies.*

<The generated text continues with description of what an implicational universal is, a table of Greenberg's 30 languages sample, accompanied by the abbreviations used, and a listing of the universals he found. His universals, verbalized by our program, are listed with their numeration in the original publication. An alpha-numeric numeration means that an originally complex universal has been split into elementary ones of the form "If A then B". >

[3]   *We confirmed the validity of universals [12,13,15-a,15-b,21-a,22-a,27-a].*

[4]   *Universal [27-b] is also true, however it violates our restriction pertaining to the occurrence of at least 4 positive examples in the dataset. [27-b] is supported in 1 language (Thai).*

[5]   *Universals [16-a,16-b,16-c] are uncertain, rather than indisputably valid in the database investigated, since they assume properties in languages, which are actually marked in the database as "unknown or inapplicable" (notated with "*" in Table 4.1). Universal [16-a] would hold only if the feature AuxV/VAux is applicable for Berber, Hebrew, and Maori and in these languages the inflected auxiliary precedes the verb. Universal [16-b] would hold only if the feature AuxV/VAux is applicable for Burmese and Japanese and in these languages the verb precedes the inflected auxiliary. Universal [16-c] would hold only if the feature AuxV/VAux is applicable for Loritja and in this language the verb precedes the inflected auxiliary.*

[6]   *Universal [23-a] is false. It is falsified in Basque, Burmese, Burushaski, Finnish, Japanese, Norwegian, Nubian, and Turkish, in which the proper noun precedes the common noun but in which the noun does not precede the genitive.*

[7]   *We found the following previously undiscovered universals in the data.*

[8]   *Universal 1. If in a language the adjective precedes the adverb then the main verb precedes the subordinate verb.*

[9]   *Examples of this universal are 8 languages: Fulani, Guarani, Hebrew, Malay, Swahili, Thai, Yoruba, and Zapotec.*

[10]   *Universal 59. If a language has an initial yes-no question particle then this language has the question word or phrase placed first in an interrogative word question.*

<There follows a conclusion which is a summary of the results.>

4.2.2.1 The discovery module UNIV

The discovery module UNIV is designed to handle two tasks, that of logical pattern, or universals, discovery, and that of estimating significance.

Pattern discovery

UNIV discovers logical patterns (or universals), holding between one or more variables, including:
- *A* (unrestricted, non-implicational universal)
- *If A^1 and A^2 and A^3 and A^n then B* (implication)[1]
- *A and B* (conjunction), *A or B* (disjunction) *A iff B* (equivalence)

UNIV can compute "absolute" universals (holding without exceptions) or "statistical" universals (holding with some user-specified percentage of exceptions).

Also, UNIV can compute universals valid in (at least) a user-specified number of positive examples (=languages) and a user-specified number of language families/areas. The former circumstance is essential in handling implications, since an implication A → B is always logically valid when the antecedent A is not present (irrespectively of the truth value of B), and therefore a universal like, say, "If a sound is nasal (=A), then it is voiced (=B)" will be valid even if in the database investigated no language has a nasal. To avoid this counterintuitive circumstance, UNIV, in the case of implications, counts as positive evidence only languages in which both A and B actually occur. The latter circumstance, viz. that of supporting universals with example languages from different language families/areas, is essential for ensuring the structural diversity of the supporting evidence. More generally, we can describe the discovery module UNIV as having a number of parameters, which can be tuned by the user, allowing him/her to vary the output of the program. Some parameters relate to the choice of a type of universal ("unrestricted universals" or "implicational"; "non-statistical" or "statistical"). In addition to the parameter for number of positive examples, other basic parameters which can be varied are:

(i) Number of language families ≥N1 (the number of language families the supporting languages belong to are greater than or equal to the number N1 set by user).

---

[1] To avoid combinatorial explosion, currently the program does not handle implications with more than 3 antecedents.

(ii) Number of geographical areas ≥N2 (the number of geographical areas the supporting languages belong to are greater than or equal to the number N2 set by user).

(iii) Percentage of validity of pattern ≥N3 (the percentage of validity of pattern in the investigated database is greater than or equal to the number N3 set by user).

(iv) Statistical significance of pattern ≥N4 (the statistical significance of a pattern relative to the examined data is greater than or equal to the threshold N4 set by user). The system disposes of two different methods to estimate significance: the chi-square test (χ^2), and the permutation test (see below, and further on in the book).

UNIV conducts an *exhaustive* search, hypothesizing and testing all possible combinations between variables.

Importantly, given the discoveries of another, human agent, UNIV employs a diagnostic program to find (eventual) errors in the humanly proposed universals. We identify as *problems* the following categories (as well as some others not mentioned here):

(1) Restriction Problem: Universals found by human analyst that are below a user-selected threshold of positive evidence and/or percentage of validity (the latter applying to statistical universals).

(2) Uncertainty Problem: Universals found by human analyst that tacitly assume a value for some linguistic property which is actually unknown or inapplicable.

(3) Falsity Problem: Universals found by human analyst that are false.

The discoveries of UNIV fall into two *types*: (1) a list of new universals (unrestricted/implicational, statistical/non-statistical), and (2) a list of problems (sub-categorized as above).

Significance estimation

Elementary statistical theory warns that whenever one carries out a search for many possible patterns, some patterns will seem significant *even if* the data are generated randomly. Therefore, some checks should be applied to the collection of universals, whether the universals are generated humanly or by machine.

UNIV supports two ways of estimating the significance of the patterns found. One of these is the permutation test (Good 1994). The logic is this: suppose one has some method for discovering patterns along with some measure of pattern strength. Given a tabular dataset in which the rows correspond to the language examples and the columns to the features, used to described these languages, randomly permute the values within every column. These permutations will not change the distributions of feature values, which remain as before; only the inter-column relationships will change into random associations. Then, applying UNIV to the permuted dataset gives one sample of what pattern strengths can be expected by chance. Applying UNIV to many permuted datasets will give a better sample of the chance patterns. We will apply this significance test in Section 4.3.2, by collecting the strongest "patterns" in many trials of permuted data, and identifying the maximum of these. Then we will reject any pattern from the real data whose strength does not exceed this maximum. Chapter 7 provides an example of a version of this significance test.

UNIV also supports estimation of significance based on the chi-square (χ^2) statistic. Chapter 5 provides further details and illustrates its use.

4.2.2.2 The authoring module AUTO

AUTO accepts as input the discoveries made by UNIV, but this module also has access to the input data to make further computations, as necessary.

AUTO can generally be characterized as a *practical* text generation system, of opportunistic type, intended to meet the needs of our particular task, rather than as a system intended to handle, in a general and principled way, scientific articles' composition or surface generation of a wide range of linguistic phenomena (reminiscent of earlier work on generation from formatted data of metereological bulletins (Kittredge *et al.*'s RAREAS) or stock market reports (Kukich's Ana)). For applied Natural Language Generation, cf. e.g. Reiter, Mellish, and Levine (1995); also *Computational Linguistics* 1998 4(23), Dale, Moisl, and H. Somers (2000), and elsewhere. Xuang and Fielder (1996) and later work verbalize machine-found mathematical proofs.

Assessment of interestingness

AUTO needs to know whether the discoveries of UNIV are interesting enough for generating a report. To this end, domain-dependent criteria may be used or domain-independent ones (e.g. such using statistical methods, computation of "unexpectedness", etc.). A generally accepted *post-factum* criterion (e.g. Langley 1998) is that a discovery is interesting if it is published in the respective specialized literature. This suggests a natural and simple numeric method, which we use here: UNIV's discoveries (novel universals plus problems) are judged worthy of generating a report if they are at least as many in number as the number of the published discoveries of the human agent studying the same database.

Determination of content

Having decided upon report generation, AUTO follows a fixed scenario for the discourse composition (scientific papers are known to follow such fixed structure in "genre analysis"). The details of this scenario, however, will vary in accordance with a number of parameters, related with the discoveries made and/or other considerations. The basic *components* of the scenario, where each component is structured as a separate text paragraph (possibly with sub-(sub)-paragraphs), are:

(1) Statement of title. A scientific article's title usually reflects the basic contributions of the article; hence a general constraint on the machine selection of a title will be the potential discoveries of a system (in our case, these are universals of different logical type and statistical nature plus problems). Which of these potentialities AUTO would choose in each particular session depends on the actual discoveries of the system made in response to a particular query. Depending on the relative weight of the types of the actual discoveries, AUTO will choose as the focus of the title one of the following alternatives: (i) *new_universals*, (ii) *problems*, or (iii) *new_universals+problems*. Currently, the focus selection is made in the following (somewhat arbitrary) manner: select whichever of alternatives (i) or (ii) is equal to or exceeds 70%, otherwise select alternative (iii). The content of the title will also include a reference to the database investigated/author criticized and, possibly, some quantitative expression. The surface generator, at a later stage of the processing, may produce outputs such as that on (Figure 4.1, par. [1]), where the selected focus is alternative (i) or phrases like "Some problematic statistical implicational universals in someone's analysis", where the selected focus is alternative (ii), etc.

(2) Introduction of goal. This paragraph includes two messages, in this order: one on goal, and the other (optional, cf. point (8) below) on the discussed paper's importance. To determine the report's goal, AUTO adopts one of the same alternatives as those of the title's foci above. The method of selection is, however, different, for some (perhaps minor) goals need not figure in the title. *New_universals* is selected when the number of *problems* is very insignificant[2] (analogously for *problems*);

---

[2] In the current version of the program ≤ 2.

otherwise, *new_universals+problems* is chosen. In Figure 4.1, **[2]** this third alternative is selected, but the surfacing template indirectly reflects this fact by appealing to "comparison of results".

(3) Elaboration of goal. This includes three messages, in this order: one sentence simply a canned cliché of what linguistic universals are, the second a logical definition of the specific type of universal to be investigated (whose construction is based on the elementary logic knowledge of AUTO), and the third (optional) message is an introduction of constraints (pertaining to positive evidence and/or per-centage of validity of universal).

(4) Description of the investigated data and the human discoveries. This paragraph includes several sub-paragraphs, in this order: a brief description of the investigated data, an (optional)[3] statement of these data (formulated in a Table), and a statement of the human discoveries[4] (each one of them shaped as a separate sub-sub-paragraph). To determine the content of these (sub)-paragraphs, AUTO draws on information from the input data. To construct a Table from the data studied, it will need to produce its caption ("Table 1. Someone's N–language sample"), its first line, consisting of the headings of columns (the first one being headed (by default) by "Languages" and the rest by the features used), proceeding with listing, on a separate line, of each language with its respective feature-values. The description of the Table involves mentioning what its rows and columns are, their number, and (if available in the input) what their attributes are. (This could result in verbalizations like "Author considers the following data comprising *N* languages of diverse genetic origin, described in terms of *N1* ordering features".) The human discoveries, also present in the input data, can either be cited (if the input contains their original verbal formulations; our illustrative input does *not*) or, alternatively, be synthesized by our surface generator.

(5) Explaining the problems in the human discoveries. This paragraph comprises 4 sub-paragraphs, in this order: one conveying information on the confirmed humanly found universals (Figure 4.1, **[3]**), and the remaining on problems of restrictions, uncertainty and falsity (Figure 4.1, **[4,5,6]**). Each sub-paragraph starts with an *intro_part*, making a statement about a collection of discoveries (e.g. "Universals [1,2,..] are under-confirmed/uncertain/false..."), possibly accompanied

---

[3] Listed data must not be disproportionately large (parameter currently set to ≤50 languages).

[4] Only problematic discoveries will be given if the number of confirmed ones is large (currently, ≥10).

by some clarification.[5] All but the first sub-paragraph (referring to confirmed discoveries) also have a *body_part*, justifying why these predications hold for each individual discovery in the collection.

Humans may use a variety of strategies to express justifications (well-studied in computational linguistics and Artificial Intelligence), but we stick, again, to a fixed scheme, viz. appealing to *examples* and explaining why they are indeed examples. Thus, the examples for justifying that a universal is under-confirmed are all the languages conforming to this universal, which, in their totality, are less in number than required number in the query. The examples justifying that a universal is false are actually its counter-examples. And the examples justifying that a universal is uncertain (in our sense) are the languages having inapplicable feature/unknown value for some feature mentioned in the criticized universal. AUTO does the necessary computations to find all kinds of examples.

(6) Statement of the machine discoveries. This paragraph starts with an introductory sentence (to the effect that there follow our novel discoveries), and continues with sub-paragraphs for each new universal. The list of novel universals has already been found by UNIV and passed on to AUTO, and the latter shapes these discoveries, in the order they have been inputted, into separate paragraphs, with supporting evidence, which AUTO computes at this stage, appearing as sub-sub-paragraphs. This organization is well seen on Figure 4.1, paragraphs **[7-10]**). We note that in the case of statistical universals, the generated text may contain, in addition, the percentage of validity of a universal as well as the languages that are exceptions to this universal.

(7) Conclusion. The content of this text component, analogously to component (2), depends on the actual discoveries made by the system. If only *new_universals* have been discovered, the content of the conclusion will reflect this, mentioning their number. If only *problems* have been found, an *intro_part* will mention the total number of problems found, and the *body_part* their distribution, in the order: under-supported, uncertain and false. Finally, if the discoveries made are *new_universals+problems*, the text will mention this, proceed with *problems* (treating them as above), and end up with how many new universals have been found.

(8) References. AUTO keeps track of the cited authors, and constructs a bibliography. An obligatory entry in the bibliography is the author of the investigated database. A second possible source of citation

---

[5] These clarifications (e.g. *Universals [16-a, 16b, 16-c] are uncertain ... since they assume properties ...*) rely on canned phrases for their surface generation.

is provided by the optional inclusion in the input data of quoted evaluations of the studied linguistic work (these "evaluations" should be in pre-specified form, currently only adjectives like "good", "pioneering", "seminal", etc.). Thus, if AUTO decides on citing (based on a simple procedure), the quoted authors will also be added to the bibliography.

Sentence planning and surfacing

"Sentence planning" problems (basically) involve the decisions as to how each paragraph's content is to be split up into sentences and clauses. We confine ourselves to giving two examples, a simple and a more complex one.

A simple sentence planning is involved e.g. when AUTO forms the definition of a universal. Giving the truth table of the logical expression, corresponding to the universal, the system groups into one sentence all cases whose outcome is *true,* and into another sentence those with the outcome *false* (rather than simply enumerate as separate sentences all cases in the order they appear in the truth-table). Besides some "connectives" may also be produced, e.g. "It is true when *both* the antecedent and the consequent are true ...".

Now, a more complex case. Assume that we need to verbalize an under-support body_part, like that on Figure 4.1, par. **[4]**, but, say, requiring at least 8 supporting languages. The input to the sentence planning facility of AUTO would look like this (the last constituents indicating the number of supporting languages):

```
[3]--is_supported--Berber,Hebrew,Maori,Masai,Welsh,Zapotec--6
[12]--is_supported--Berber,Hebrew,Maori,Masai,Welsh,Zapotec--6
[I5-a]--is_supported--Berber,Hebrew,Maori,Masai, Welsh,Zapotec--6
[27-b]--is_supported--Thai--1
[13]--is_supported--Burmese,Burushaski,Hindi,Japanese,Kannada, Turkish--6
```

AUTO will form separate sentences from the propositions having an equal number of supporting evidence. Within the framework of each such sentence, the system will group together the propositions supported by the same languages, taking care that the universals with smaller numeration appear first. After some further transformations, the system outputs this:

[27-b] is supported in 1 language (Thai). [13] is supported in 6 languages (Burmese, Burushaski, Hindi, Japanese, Kannada, and Turkish), and so are [3,12,15-a] (Berber, Hebrew, Maori, Masai, Welsh, and Zapotec).

For the "surface generation" we use a hybrid approach, employing both templates and grammar rules, as required by the needs at the specific portions of text we are producing.

The *.templates* consist of canned text, interspersed with variables whose values are to be computed. The canned text employed comprises phrases, commonly used in our type of linguistic discourse. The variables, as common, may stand for individual words whose correct grammatical form is computed and inserted. To produce correct grammatical forms of words AUTO employs agreement between subject and predicate, noun and determiner, demonstrative, relative-marker, apposition; between noun and pronoun (for pronominal reference); external sandhi, etc. The variables in templates, however, may stand for more abstract entities than words and their values be computed by grammar rules. A typical example in our domain is the case when a variable stands for a list of languages, which will be handled by a grammar rule for *and*–coordinated NP to get e.g. "Masai, Welsh, and Zapotec".

Another important point about our use of templates is that often they are randomly chosen among a set of "synonymous" alternatives (the same applies to the variables in them), the idea being to increase the variability of the produced texts.

We have *grammar rules* to handle a variety of syntactic constructions, but the most important of them are those responsible for the verbalization of universals (forming by far the largest bulk of the produced texts).

The input to the universals grammar is a structure like this:

[implication(an,cnpn),non_statistical]

The grammar disposes of a dictionary, stating the English correspondences to the abbreviations in the structure (here, a=adjective, n=noun, cn=common noun, pn=proper noun). (The abbreviations may stand also for larger English phrases, as e.g. wh_word=question word or phrase place first in an interrogative word question.) The grammar will decompose these abbreviations into smaller portions matching "meaningful" English phrases, and knowing that symbol juxtaposition expresses precedence, will transform the above structure into:

[implication(adjective–precedes=noun, 'common noun'– precedes–'proper noun',
    non_statistical}

From this input, the grammar rules will output e.g. "If in a language the adjective precedes the noun then the common noun precedes the proper noun". An appropriate phrase (e.g. "with greater than chance frequency") will be appended sentence-initially or after the connective *then* to obtain a statistical universal.

The universals grammar I use is, of course, far from being so straightforward. There are diverse ways of expressing implications in English (and we do not confine only to implications), and the grammar tries to attend to this fact. Also, a number of linguistic complications occur when surfacing more complex structures like "If A1 and A2 and ... An, then D", etc. An important characteristic of this grammar is that it is a *random generator*, ensuring the avoidance of intra-textual repetitions in the statement of the many universals UNIV usually finds.

Finally, we note that AUTO also supports formatting facilities, e.g. for capitalization, correct spacing around punctuation marks, etc.

4.3 Some discoveries of UNIVAUTO

4.3.1 Word order universals

UNIVAUTO was run on the data from the paper by Greenberg (1966a) on the ordering of meaningful elements with different queries. In these queries, no significance estimate was required to be made of the found patterns, owing to the quite small size of the sample (only 30 languages), although the generated formulations, in the case of statistical universals, and following Greenberg's phrasing, use the qualification "with greater than chance frequency". The system generated several interesting texts in response to these queries, two of which were submitted to a refereed linguistic journal and published with no further human editing. The first submission was made without disclosing the "machine origin" of the paper. Figure 4.1 above includes excerpts from one of these articles. Below is the full text of the other publication (Pericliev 2000), in the form produced by the system, followed by a fragment of a text describing the disjunctive universals found in the same dataset.

More statistical implicational universals in Greenberg's data

In this article we study the statistical implicational universals in the 30 languages sample of Greenberg 1966. We will show some problems in the analyses proposed by Greenberg and will list further universals that can be uncovered in these data. This paper by Greenberg is considered seminal in the field of language universals (cf. e.g. Comrie 1981, Hawkins 1983, and Dryer 1995).

Language universals express common features shared by all languages ("non-statistical universals") or by most languages ("statistical universals"). Universals may be absolute or implicational. Our concern in this paper will be statistical implicational universals. An implication is a proposition of the logical form "If P then Q", where P is called an antecedent and Q is called a consequent. It is true when both the antecedent P and the consequent Q are true, or the antecedent P is false and the consequent Q is true, or both the antecedent P and the consequent Q are false. It is false when the antecedent P is true and the consequent Q is false. In what follows, we introduce the following restriction on deriving a universal: we shall take into consideration only implicational universals valid in at least 85 percent of the data, that is in at least 85 percent of the languages where the antecedent (and therefore the consequent) of the implicational universal actually occur.

Greenberg 1966 considers data comprising 30 languages of diverse genetic origin described in terms of 15 word/morpheme ordering features, which we list here as Table 4.1.

The table employs the following abbreviations:
SOVr=rigid Subject–Object–Verb order
SOVnr=nonrigid Subject–Object–Verb order
VSO=Verb–Subject–Object order
SVO=Subject–Verb–Object order
Pr=preposition
Po=postposition
Rel=relative clause
N=noun
CN=common noun
PN=proper noun
A=adjective
Adj=adjective
G=genitive
D=demonstrative
Num=numeral
Aux=auxiliary
V=verb
MV=main verb
SV=subordinate verb
Adv=adverb
MS=standard marker
SM=standard marker
Wh=interrogative word or phrase

Pref=prefix
Suff=suffix
init=initial
fin=final
* *=inapplicable or unknown value of a feature*

Below we restate, in our wording, the statistical implicational universals of the type studied here which Greenberg 1966 found in these data, preserving for ease of reference their original numeration. If the original formulation expresses a complex implicational statement, it is split into elementary propositions of the type "If P then Q":

[2-a]. With greater than chance frequency, in languages with prepositions the noun precedes the genitive.

[2-b]. With greater than chance frequency, in languages with postpositions the genitive precedes the noun.

[4-a]. If a language has rigid SOV order then, with greater than chance frequency, this language is with postpositions.

[4-b]. With greater than chance frequency, if a language has nonrigid SOV order then this language has postpositions.

[9-a]. With greater than chance frequency, if a language has an initial yes–no question particle then this language has prepositions.

[9-b]. With greater than chance frequency, if a language has a final yes–no question particle then this language has postpositions.

[17]. With greater than chance frequency, if a language has dominant order VSO then the noun precedes the adjective.

[18-a]. With greater than chance frequency, if in a language the adjective precedes the noun then the demonstrative precedes the noun.

[18-b]. If in a language the adjective precedes the noun then, with greater than chance frequency, the numeral precedes the noun.

[22-b]. With greater than chance frequency, if a language has adjective-marker-standard order then this language is with prepositions.

[23-b]. If in a language the common noun precedes the proper noun then, with greater than chance frequency, the genitive precedes the noun.

We found that universals *[2-a,22-b]* are indeed supported in 85 or more percent of the languages in the database.

Universal *[9-b]* is also a valid statistical universal, however it is below our threshold requiring the presence of at least 85 percent positive examples in the dataset. *[9-b]* is supported in 5 languages (Burmese, Burushaski, Japanese, Kannada, and Nubian) and is invalidated in 2 languages (Thai and Yoruba), which is 71.43 percent validity.

.

Table 4.1. Greenberg's 30–language sample

V order	Pr/Po	NRel/RelN	NA/AN	NG/GN	ND/DN	NNum/NumN	AuxV/VAux	MVSV/SVMV	AdjAdv/AdvAdj	AdjMS/SMAdj	Yes–No Part.	Wh–word	C P
SOVnr	Po	RelN	NA	GN	ND	NumN	VAux	MVSV	AdvAdj	SMAdj	*	*	P
VSO	Pr	NRel	NA	NG	ND	NumN	*	MVSV	*	AdjMS	init	first	*
SOVr	Po	RelN	NA	GN	DN	NumN	*	SVMV	AdvAdj	SMAdj	fin	*	P
SOVr	Po	RelN	AN	GN	DN	NumN	VAux	SVMV	AdvAdj	SMAdj	fin	*	P
SOVnr	Po	RelN	NA	GN	DN	NNum	VAux	MVSV	AdvAdj	SMAdj	*	*	*
SVO	Po	both	AN	GN	DN	NumN	AuxV	MVSV	AdvAdj	both	*	first	P
SVO	Pr	NRel	NA	NG	ND	NNum	*	MVSV	AdjAdv	AdjMS	*	first	*
SVO	Pr	NRel	AN	NG	DN	NumN	AuxV	MVSV	AdvAdj	AdjMS	*	first	C
SVO	Po	NRel	NA	GN	DN	both	VAux	MVSV	AdjAdv	SMAdj	*	first	C
VSO	Pr	NRel	NA	NG	ND	NumN	*	MVSV	AdjAdv	AdjMS	init	first	*
SOVr	Po	NRel	AN	GN	DN	NumN	VAux	SVMV	AdvAdj	SMAdj	*	*	*
SVO	Pr	NRel	NA	NG	DN	NumN	AuxV	MVSV	AdvAdj	AdjMS	*	first	C
SOVr	Po	RelN	AN	GN	DN	NumN	*	SVMV	AdvAdj	SMAdj	fin	*	P
SOVr	Po	RelN	AN	GN	DN	NumN	VAux	SVMV	AdvAdj	SMAdj	fin	*	*
SOVnr	Po	*	NA	GN	ND	NNum	*	MVSV	AdvAdj	*	*	*	*
SVO	Pr	NRel	NA	NG	ND	NumN	*	MVSV	AdjAdv	AdjMS	*	first	C
VSO	Pr	NRel	NA	NG	DN	NumN	*	MVSV	both	AdjMS	init	first	*
VSO	Pr	NRel	NA	NG	DN	NNum	AuxV	MVSV	*	*	init	first	*
SVO	Pr	NRel	AN	NG	DN	NumN	AuxV	MVSV	AdvAdj	*	*	first	*
SVO	Pr	NRel	AN	GN	DN	NumN	AuxV	MVSV	AdvAdj	AdjMS	*	first	P
SOVnr	Po	both	NA	GN	DN	NNum	VAux	MVSV	*	SMAdj	fin	*	P
SOVnr	Po	NRel	AN	GN	DN	NumN	VAux	MVSV	*	*	*	*	*
SVO	Pr	NRel	AN	NG	DN	NumN	AuxV	MVSV	AdvAdj	AdjMS	*	first	C
SVO	Po	NRel	NA	GN	ND	NNum	*	MVSV	*	AdjMS	*	*	*
SVO	Pr	NRel	NA	NG	ND	NNum	AuxV	MVSV	AdjAdv	AdjMS	*	*	C
SVO	Pr	NRel	NA	NG	ND	NumN	*	MVSV	AdjAdv	AdjMS	fin	*	C
SOVr	Po	RelN	AN	GN	DN	NumN	VAux	SVMV	AdvAdj	SMAdj	*	*	P
VSO	Pr	NRel	NA	NG	ND	NumN	AuxV	MVSV	both	AdjMS	init	first	C
SVO	Pr	NRel	NA	NG	ND	NNum	*	MVSV	AdjAdv	*	fin	first	*
VSO	Pr	NRel	NA	NG	ND	NumN	AuxV	MVSV	AdjAdv	AdjMS	*	first	C

Universals [2-b,4-a,4-b,9-a,17,18-a,18-b] are in fact non-statistical, rather than statistical universals, since they hold without any exceptions in the investigated database.

Universal [23-b] is not a valid statistical universal. [23-b] is supported in 1 language (Guarani) and is falsified in 8 languages (Greek, Italian, Malay, Serbian, Swahili, Thai, Welsh, and Zapotec), which amounts to 11.11 percent validity.

We found the following previously undiscovered universals in the data.

Universal 1. With greater than chance frequency, if in a language the adjective precedes the adverb then the noun precedes the demonstrative.

This universal is supported in 7 languages: Fulani, Hebrew, Malay, Swahili, Thai, Yoruba, and Zapotec. The counterexample is Guarani. The universal is supported in 87.5 % of the data.

Universal 2. If in a language the adjective precedes the adverb then, with greater than chance frequency, the noun precedes the genitive.

Positive evidence for this pattern is provided by 7 languages: Fulani, Hebrew, Malay, Swahili, Thai, Yoruba, and Zapotec. The exception is Guarani. The universal is supported in 87.5 % of the data.

Universal 3. With greater than chance frequency, if in a language the adjective precedes the adverb then this language is with prepositions.

Positive evidence for this pattern is provided by 7 languages: Fulani, Hebrew, Malay, Swahili, Thai, Yoruba, and Zapotec. The exception is Guarani. The percentage of validity is 87.5 %.

Universal 4. With greater than chance frequency, if in a language the adjective precedes the adverb then this language has both prefixes and suffixes.

Positive evidence for this pattern is provided by 7 languages: Fulani, Guarani, Hebrew, Malay, Swahili, Yoruba, and Zapotec. The counterexample is Thai. The percentage of validity is 87.5 %.

Universal 5. If in a language the adverb precedes the adjective then, with greater than chance frequency, the demonstrative precedes the noun.

This universal is supported in 13 languages: Burmese, Burushaski, Chibcha, Finnish, Greek, Hindi, Italian, Japanese, Kannada, Maya, Norwegian, Serbian, and Turkish. The counterexamples are Basque and Loritja. The percentage of validity is 86.67 %.

Universal 6. With greater than chance frequency, if in a language the adverb precedes the adjective then the numeral precedes the noun.

The following 13 languages support this universal: Basque, Burmese, Burushaski, Finnish, Greek, Hindi, Italian, Japanese, Kannada, Maya, Norwegian, Serbian, and Turkish. The exceptions are Chibcha and Loritja. The validity of the universal is 86.67 %.

Universal 7. With greater than chance frequency, in languages with adjective-marker-standard order the noun precedes the genitive.

Examples of this universal are 12 languages: Berber, Fulani, Greek, Hebrew, Italian, Malay, Maori, Serbian, Swahili, Thai, Welsh, and Zapotec. The exceptions are Norwegian and Songhai. The validity of the universal is 85.71 %.

Universal 8. If a language has adjective-marker-standard order then, with greater than chance frequency, this language has both prefixes and suffixes.

This universal is supported in 12 languages: Berber, Fulani, Greek, Hebrew, Italian, Malay, Maori, Norwegian, Serbian, Swahili, Welsh, and Zapotec. The counterexamples are Songhai and Thai. The percentage of validity is 85.71 %.

Universal 9. If a language has standard-adjective-marker order then, with greater than chance frequency, the demonstrative precedes the noun.

This universal is supported in 9 languages: Burmese, Burushaski, Chibcha, Guarani, Hindi, Japanese, Kannada, Nubian, and Turkish. The exception is Basque. The validity of the universal is 90.0 %.

Universal 10. With greater than chance frequency, if in a language the inflected auxiliary precedes the verb then the noun precedes the relative expression.

This universal is supported in 9 languages: Greek, Italian, Masai, Maya, Norwegian, Serbian, Swahili, Welsh, and Zapotec. The exception is Finnish. The universal holds in 90.0 % of the languages.

Universal 11. With greater than chance frequency, if in a language the inflected auxiliary precedes the verb then this language has prepositions.

Examples of this universal are 9 languages: Greek, Italian, Masai, Maya, Norwegian, Serbian, Swahili, Welsh, and Zapotec. The counterexample is Finnish. The validity of the universal is 90.0 %.

Universal 12. If in a language the inflected auxiliary precedes the verb then, with greater than chance frequency, this language is with both prefixes and suffixes.

This universal is supported in 9 languages: Greek, Italian, Masai, Maya, Norwegian, Serbian, Swahili, Welsh, and Zapotec. The exception is Finnish. The universal is supported in 90.0 % of the data.

Universal 13. If in a language the inflected auxiliary precedes the verb then, with greater than chance frequency, this language has the question word or phrase placed first in an interrogative word question.

The following 9 languages support this universal: Finnish, Greek, Italian, Masai, Maya, Norwegian, Serbian, Welsh, and Zapotec. The exception is Swahili. The universal is supported in 90.0 % of the data.

Universal 14. With greater than chance frequency, if in a language the verb precedes the inflected auxiliary then this language has standard-adjective-marker order.

Positive evidence for this pattern is provided by 8 languages: Basque, Burushaski, Chibcha, Guarani, Hindi, Kannada, Nubian, and Turkish. The exception is Quechua. The universal is supported in 88.89 % of the data.

Universal 15. If in a language the verb precedes the inflected auxiliary then, with greater than chance frequency, the demonstrative precedes the noun.

This universal is supported in 8 languages: Burushaski, Chibcha, Guarani, Hindi, Kannada, Nubian, Quechua, and Turkish. The counterexample is Basque. The universal is supported in 88.89 % of the data.

Universal 16. If in a language the common noun precedes the proper noun then, with greater than chance frequency, this language has adjective-marker-standard order.

Examples of this universal are 8 languages: Greek, Italian, Malay, Serbian, Swahili, Thai, Welsh, and Zapotec. The counterexample is Guarani. The validity of the universal is 88.89 %.

Universal 17. With greater than chance frequency, if in a language the common noun precedes the proper noun then the noun precedes the genitive.

The following 8 languages support this universal: Greek, Italian, Malay, Serbian, Swahili, Thai, Welsh, and Zapotec. The counterexample is Guarani. The universal holds in 88.89 % of the languages.

Universal 18. If in a language the common noun precedes the proper noun then, with greater than chance frequency, this language has prepositions.

Examples of this universal are 8 languages: Greek, Italian, Malay, Serbian, Swahili, Thai, Welsh, and Zapotec. The counterexample is Guarani. The universal is supported in 88.89 % of the data.

Universal 19. With greater than chance frequency, if in a language the common noun precedes the proper noun then this language has both prefixes and suffixes.

Positive evidence for this pattern is provided by 8 languages: Greek, Guarani, Italian, Malay, Serbian, Swahili, Welsh, and Zapotec. The exception is Thai. The percentage of validity is 88.89 %.

Universal 20. With greater than chance frequency, if in a language the proper noun precedes the common noun then the adverb precedes the adjective.

Examples of this universal are 7 languages: Basque, Burmese, Burushaski, Finnish, Japanese, Norwegian, and Turkish. The counterexample is Nubian. The universal is supported in 87.5 % of the data.

Universal 21. If in a language the proper noun precedes the common noun then, with greater than chance frequency, the demonstrative precedes the noun.

This universal is supported in 7 languages: Burmese, Burushaski, Finnish, Japanese, Norwegian, Nubian, and Turkish. The exception is Basque. The validity of the universal is 87.5 %.

Universal 22. With greater than chance frequency, if in a language the proper noun precedes the common noun then the numeral precedes the noun.

Examples of this universal are 7 languages: Basque, Burmese, Burushaski, Finnish, Japanese, Norwegian, and Turkish. The counterexample is Nubian. The validity of the universal is 87.5 %.

Universal 23. With greater than chance frequency, if in a language the proper noun precedes the common noun then this language has postpositions.

This universal is supported in 7 languages: Basque, Burmese, Burushaski, Finnish, Japanese, Nubian, and Turkish. The counterexample is Norwegian. The universal holds in 87.5 % of the languages.

Universal 24. With greater than chance frequency, if in a language the adjective precedes the noun then the adverb precedes the adjective.

Examples of this universal are 10 languages: Burushaski, Finnish, Greek, Hindi, Japanese, Kannada, Maya, Norwegian, Serbian, and Turkish. The counterexample is Quechua. The percentage of validity is 90.91 %.

Universal 25. With greater than chance frequency, if in a language the noun precedes the adjective then the main verb precedes the subordinate verb.

The following 18 languages support this universal: Basque, Berber, Chibcha, Fulani, Guarani, Hebrew, Italian, Loritja, Malay, Maori, Masai, Nubian, Songhai, Swahili, Thai, Welsh, Yoruba, and Zapotec. The exception is Burmese. The universal is supported in 94.74 % of the data.

Universal 26. If in a language the genitive precedes the noun then, with greater than chance frequency, this language is with postpositions.

The following 14 languages support this universal: Basque, Burmese, Burushaski, Chibcha, Finnish, Guarani, Hindi, Japanese, Kannada, Loritja, Nubian, Quechua, Songhai, and Turkish. The counterexample is Norwegian. The universal holds in 93.33 % of the languages.

Universal 27. With greater than chance frequency, if in a language the noun precedes the genitive then this language has both prefixes and suffixes.

Examples of this universal are 14 languages: Berber, Fulani, Greek, Hebrew, Italian, Malay, Maori, Masai, Maya, Serbian, Swahili, Welsh, Yoruba, and Zapotec. The exception is Thai. The universal holds in 93.33 % of the languages.

Universal 28. If in a language the noun precedes the genitive then, with greater than chance frequency, this language is with the question word or phrase placed first in an interrogative word question.

Examples of this universal are 13 languages: Berber, Fulani, Greek, Hebrew, Italian, Malay, Maori, Masai, Maya, Serbian, Welsh, Yoruba, and Zapotec. The exceptions are Swahili and Thai. The percentage of validity is 86.67 %.

Universal 29. If in a language the noun precedes the relative expression then, with greater than chance frequency, the main verb precedes the subordinate verb.

Positive evidence for this pattern is provided by 19 languages: Berber, Fulani, Greek, Guarani, Hebrew, Italian, Malay, Maori, Masai, Maya, Norwegian, Quechua, Serbian, Songhai, Swahili, Thai, Welsh, Yoruba, and Zapotec. The counterexample is Hindi. The percentage of validity is 95.0 %.

Universal 30. If in a language the relative expression precedes the noun then, with greater than chance frequency, the demonstrative precedes the noun.

Positive evidence for this pattern is provided by 6 languages: Burmese, Burushaski, Chibcha, Japanese, Kannada, and Turkish. The counterexample is Basque. The universal is supported in 85.71 % of the data.

Universal 31. With greater than chance frequency, if in a language the relative expression precedes the noun then the numeral precedes the noun.

Positive evidence for this pattern is provided by 6 languages: Basque, Burmese, Burushaski, Japanese, Kannada, and Turkish. The counterexample is Chibcha. The universal is supported in 85.71 % of the data.

Universal 32. With greater than chance frequency, if in a language the relative expression precedes the noun then this language is with suffixes.

Positive evidence for this pattern is provided by 6 languages: Basque, Burmese, Chibcha, Japanese, Kannada, and Turkish. The counterexample is Burushaski. The universal is supported in 85.71 % of the data.

Universal 33. If a language has postpositions then, with greater than chance frequency, this language has suffixes.

This universal is supported in 12 languages: Basque, Burmese, Chibcha, Finnish, Hindi, Japanese, Kannada, Loritja, Nubian, Quechua, Songhai, and Turkish. The exceptions are Burushaski and Guarani. The universal holds in 85.71 % of the languages.

Universal 34. If a language has prepositions then, with greater than chance frequency, this language is with both prefixes and suffixes.

Examples of this universal are 15 languages: Berber, Fulani, Greek, Hebrew, Italian, Malay, Maori, Masai, Maya, Norwegian, Serbian, Swahili, Welsh, Yoruba, and Zapotec. The exception is Thai. The percentage of validity is 93.75 %.

Universal 35. If a language has prepositions then, with greater than chance frequency, this language is with the question word or phrase placed first in an interrogative word question.

Positive evidence for this pattern is provided by 14 languages: Berber, Fulani, Greek, Hebrew, Italian, Malay, Maori, Masai, Maya, Norwegian, Serbian, Welsh, Yoruba, and Zapotec. The exceptions are Swahili and Thai. The validity of the universal is 87.5 %.

Universal 36. With greater than chance frequency, in languages with both prefixes and suffixes the main verb precedes the subordinate verb.

This universal is supported in 16 languages: Berber, Fulani, Greek, Guarani, Hebrew, Italian, Malay, Maori, Masai, Maya, Norwegian, Serbian, Swahili, Welsh, Yoruba, and Zapotec. The exception is Burushaski. The validity of the universal is 94.12 %.

Universal 37. If a language has both prefixes and suffixes then, with greater than chance frequency, the noun precedes the relative expression.

Examples of this universal are 16 languages: Berber, Fulani, Greek, Guarani, Hebrew, Italian, Malay, Maori, Masai, Maya, Norwegian, Serbian, Swahili, Welsh, Yoruba, and Zapotec. The counterexample is Burushaski. The percentage of validity is 94.12 %.

Universal 38. If a language has both prefixes and suffixes then, with greater than chance frequency, this language is with prepositions.

The following 15 languages support this universal: Berber, Fulani, Greek, Hebrew, Italian, Malay, Maori, Masai, Maya, Norwegian, Serbian, Swahili, Welsh, Yoruba, and Zapotec. The exceptions are Burushaski and Guarani. The validity of the universal is 88.24 %.

Universal 39. With greater than chance frequency, if a language has both prefixes and suffixes then this language has the question word or phrase placed first in an interrogative word question.

The following 15 languages support this universal: Berber, Fulani, Greek, Guarani, Hebrew, Italian, Malay, Maori, Masai, Maya, Norwegian, Serbian, Welsh, Yoruba, and Zapotec. The counterexamples are Burushaski and Swahili. The percentage of validity is 88.24 %.

Universal 40. With greater than chance frequency, in languages with dominant order SVO the noun precedes the relative expression.

Examples of this universal are 12 languages: Fulani, Greek, Guarani, Italian, Malay, Maya, Norwegian, Serbian, Songhai, Swahili, Thai, and Yoruba. The exception is Finnish. The universal is supported in 92.31 % of the data.

Universal 41. If a language has the question word or phrase placed first in an interrogative word question then, with greater than chance frequency, the noun precedes the relative expression.

Examples of this universal are 15 languages: Berber, Fulani, Greek, Guarani, Hebrew, Italian, Malay, Maori, Masai, Maya, Norwegian, Serbian, Welsh, Yoruba, and Zapotec. The counterexample is Finnish. The validity of the universal is 93.75 %.

Universal 42. If a language has the question word or phrase placed first in an interrogative word question then, with greater than chance frequency, this language is with prepositions.

Examples of this universal are 14 languages: Berber, Fulani, Greek, Hebrew, Italian, Malay, Maori, Masai, Maya, Norwegian, Serbian, Welsh, Yoruba, and Zapotec. The exceptions are Finnish and Guarani. The percentage of validity is 87.5 %.

Universal 43. With greater than chance frequency, if a language has the question word or phrase placed first in an interrogative word question then this language has both prefixes and suffixes.

This universal is supported in 15 languages: Berber, Fulani, Greek, Guarani, Hebrew, Italian, Malay, Maori, Masai, Maya, Norwegian, Serbian, Welsh, Yoruba, and Zapotec. The exception is Finnish. The validity of the universal is 93.75 %.

Concluding, we may summarize the results of our comparative study. We confirmed the validity of 3 of Greenberg's universals, but noted that 1 of these is supported in less than 85 percent of the languages, a plausibility requirement we set up at the beginning of this article. 7 universals were seen to be non-statistical, i.e. holding without exceptions, rather than statistical. 1 universal was shown to be invalid. Finally, 43 novel previously undiscovered universals were found to hold in the data.

References

Comrie, B. (1981). Typology and Universals. Chicago: Chicago University Press.
Dryer, M. (1995). Word order typology. In: J. Jacobs, A. von Stechow, W. Sternefeld and T. Vennemann (eds.), Syntax: An International Handbook of Contemporary Research, 1050–1065. Berlin and New York: Walter de Gruyter.
Greenberg, J. (1966). Some universals of grammar with particular reference to the order of meaningful elements. In: J. Greenberg (ed.), Universals of Language, 73–113. Cambrdige: MIT Press.
Hawkins, J. (1983). Word Order Universals. New York: Academic Press.

There follows an excerpt from a text generated by UNIVAUTO, which addresses disjunctive universals in the 30–language sample from Greenberg (1966a).

Disjunctive universals in Greenberg's data

The aim of this article is to propose some novel disjunctive universals that can be derived from the 30 languages sample in Greenberg 1966.
[...]
*   A disjunction is a a proposition of the logical form P ∨ Q where P is called a disjunct and Q is called a disjunct. It is true when both the disjunct P and the disjunct Q are true or the disjunct P is true and the disjunct Q is false or the disjunct P is false and the disjunct Q is true. It is false when both the disjunct P and the disjunct Q are false.*
*   Greenberg 1966 considers the following data comprising 30 languages of diverse genetic origin described in terms of 15 ordering features.*
[...]
*   Greenberg 1966 did not find any universals of the type we study here.*
*   We found the following previously undiscovered universals in the data.*
*   Universal 1. A language either has postpositions or the noun precedes the relative expression.*
*   Universal 2. A language either has postpositions or the main verb precedes the subordinate verb.*
*   Universal 3. A language either has prepositions or the genitive precedes the noun.*
*   Universal 4. In a language either the noun precedes the relative expression or the genitive precedes the noun.*

Universal 5. In a language either the noun precedes the adjective or the demonstrative precedes the noun.

Universal 6. In a language either the noun precedes the adjective or the numeral precedes the noun.

Universal 7. In a language either the genitive precedes the noun or the main verb precedes the subordinate verb.

Universal 8. In a language either the demonstrative precedes the noun or the main verb precedes the subordinate verb.

Universal 9. In a language either the numeral precedes the noun or the main verb precedes the subordinate verb.

Universal 10. In a language either the main verb precedes the subordinate verb or the adverb precedes the adjective.

Universal 11. In a language either the main verb precedes the subordinate verb or the standard marker precedes the adjective.

Thus, we found 11 disjunctive universals previously undiscovered in the data investigated.

[...]

The discoveries of UNIVAUTO presented in this section are of historical interest only. To-date there are much larger word order databases (e.g. Hawkins 1983, Dryer 1992) that would provide the empirical material for drawing more adequate conclusions about ordering in the world languages. The system's discoveries nevertheless are instructive in showing the deficiency of human, manual search for universals even in a rather small sample, comprising only 30 languages. Thus, we see that the solution reached by Greenberg is neither complete (i.e. giving all universals) nor sound (i.e. giving only the correct universals).

First, regarding completeness, we observe that in all texts produced by the system the number of machine-generated universals is much larger than the number of human-found universals. This should come as no surprise, realizing that to get all universals, an exhaustive search should be performed of the database. Such an exhaustive search in this case would mean that all logically possible universals would have to be hypothesized, which, given the 15 binary or non-binary features, amounts to forming many hundreds of hypotheses to be subsequently tested against the data. Generally people tend to overlook some alternatives.

Secondly, some incorrect generalizations can also smuggle in. Thus, Greenberg suggests the following universal (under Number 23) which, for the need of my program, I have split into two independent statements, (23-a) and (23-b), the first being non-statistical and the second statistical:

Greenberg's Universal 23:

(23-a). If in apposition the proper noun usually precedes the common noun, then the language is one in which the governing noun precedes its dependent genitive. (Non-statistical)

(23-b). With much better than chance frequency, if the common noun usually precedes the proper noun, the dependent genitive precedes its governing noun. (Statistical)

UNIVAUTO has detected the invalidity of both claims, and has reported:

Universal (23-a) is false. It is falsified in Basque, Burmese, Burushaski, Finish, Japanese, Norwegian, Nubian, Turkish, in which the proper noun precedes the common noun but in which the noun does not precede the genitive. (cf. Figure 4.1); and

Universal (23-b) is not a valid statistical universal. (23-b) is supported in 1 language (Guarani) and is falsified in 8 languages (Greek, Italian, Malay, Serbian, Swahili, Thai, Welsh, and Zapotec), which amounts to 11.11 percent validity. (cf. the generated text entitled *More statistical implicational universals in Greenberg's data*)

Why has this problem occurred? In order to test manually these statements, let us summarize the relevant data from Greenberg's Appendix II, containing information on the order of genitives and governing nouns, and footnote 19, containing information on the order of common nouns and proper nouns (see also Hawkins's Table 4.1, (1983: 24–25) summarizing all data contained in Greenberg's paper, including that of interest to us). There are four theoretically possible distributions, which we list below with the languages conforming to each one of them:

Common Noun + Proper Noun   &   *Genitive + Noun*
1 language: Guarani

Proper Noun + Common Noun   &   *Genitive + Noun*
8 languages: Basque, Burmese, Burushaski, Finnish, Japanese, Norwegian, Nubian, Turkish

Common Noun + Proper Noun   &   *Noun + Genitive*
8 languages: Greek, Italian, Malay, Serbian, Swahili, Thai, Welsh, Zapotec

Proper Noun + Common Noun   &   *Noun + Genitive*
0 languages

The reason for these problems in Greenberg's formulations seems to be a purely technical mistake, which becomes obvious as we look at his Table 9 (p. 89) which is his own summary of the data on which he bases his actual formulations. We list this table below, giving in parentheses the correct numbers of conforming languages:

	Genitive + Noun	Noun + Genitive
Common Noun + Proper Noun	**8 (1)**	**1 (8)**
Proper Noun + Common Noun	**0 (8)**	**8 (0)**

The problem apparently arises from listing numbers under the wrong column, so swapping the headings for the two columns would set things right. Accordingly, we should reformulate the universal as follows:

Greenberg's Universal 23 (Corrected version):

(23-a). If in apposition the proper noun usually precedes the common noun, then the language is one in which the governing noun *follows* its dependent genitive.

(23-b). With much better than chance frequency, if the common noun usually precedes the proper noun, the dependent genitive *follows* its governing noun.

UNIVAUTO has done this in its own wording. The need for correction does not seem to have been noticed in the literature, and this empirically misleading claim is repeated e.g. in *The Linguistics Encyclopedia*, edited by Kirsten Malmkjær (1991: 281).

4.3.2 Kinship pattern universals

Our next example comes from kinship semantics. The discussion in this section is essentially a part of a previous publication of ours (Valdés-Pérez and Pericliev 1999).

Murdock (1970) describes the terminological classification system of 566 societies from 194 of the 200 cultural provinces he has isolated. These terminological systems include eight sets of kin: grandparents (abbreviated *GrPa*), grandchildren (*GrCh*), uncles (*PaBr*), aunts (*PaSi*), nephews and nieces (male speaker) (*SbCh*), siblings (*Sibl*), cross-cousins (*CrCo*), and siblings-in-law (*Sb-il*).

The kinship systems of these societies are described in terms of "kinship patterns", a list of some of which is given below. The list of kinship patterns will serve the purposes of illustration and of further reference.

List of Relevant Kinship Patterns from Murdock

GRANDPARENTS

Bisexual Two terms, distinguished by sex, which can be glossed as "grandfather" and "grandmother".

Merging A single undifferentiated term, which can be glossed as "grandparent".

GRANDCHILDREN

Bisexual Two terms, distinguished by sex, which can be glossed as "grandson" and "granddaughter".

Merging A single undifferentiated term, which can be glossed as "grandchild".

UNCLES

Simple Bifurcate Collateral Two special terms, distinguished by the sex of the connecting relative, which can be glossed as "paternal uncle" and "maternal uncle".

Skewed Bifurcate Collateral Three special terms, distinguished by the sex of the connecting relative and in the case of paternal uncles also by relative age, which can be glossed as "father's elder brother", "father's younger brother", and "mother's brother".

Simple Bifurcate Merging A single special term which can be glossed as "mother's brother", paternal uncles being terminologically equated with father. Analogous to Pattern *Bifurcate Merging* for aunts

Lineal A single special term, which can be glossed as "uncle", applying to both the father's and the mother's brothers and distinguishing them from father.

Generation Special terms are lacking for both paternal and maternal uncles, who are terminologically equated with father.

AUNTS

Relative Age Two special terms, distinguished by age relative to the connecting relative, which can be glossed as "parent's elder sister" and "parent's younger sister".

Simple Bifurcate Collateral Two special terms, distinguished by the sex of the connecting relative, which can be glossed as "paternal aunt" and "maternal aunt".

Lineal A single special term, which can be glossed as "aunt", applying to both the father's and the mother's sisters and distinguishing them from mother.

Generation Special terms are lacking for both maternal and paternal aunts, who are terminologically equated with mother.

Skewed Bifurcate Collateral Three special terms, distinguished by the sex of the connecting relative and in the case of maternal aunts also by relative age, which can be glossed as "father's sister", "mother's elder sister", and "mother's younger sister".

Bifurcate Merging A single special term which can be glossed as "father's sister", maternal aunts being terminologically equated with mother. Analogous to Pattern *Simple Bifurcate Merging* for uncles.

NEPHEWS & NIECES (male speaking)

Sex-Differentiated Lineal Two special terms, differentiated by sex, which can be glossed as "nephew" and "niece".

SIBLINGS

Algonkian Three terms, distinguished by relative age and for elder siblings also by sex, which can be glossed as "elder brother", "elder sister", and "younger sibling".

Kordofanian A single undifferentiated term, which can be glossed as "sibling".

Yoruban Two terms, distinguished by relative age, which can be glossed as "elder sibling" and "younger sibling".

CROSS-COUSINS

Iroquois One or more special terms for first cross-cousins, which differ from those for siblings, parallel cousins, and avuncular and nepotic relatives.

SIBLINGS-IN-LAW

Simple Bisexual Two terms, differentiated by sex, which can be glossed as "brother-in-law" and "sister-in-law".

Opposite Sex Three terms, distinguished by relative sex and for siblings-in-law of the speaker's sex also by sex, which can be glossed as "sibling-in-law of opposite sex", "brother-in-law (ms)", and "sister-in-law (ws)".

Null Special affinal terms are absent or rare, siblings-inlaw being called by terms for consanguineal relatives, mainly those applying primarily to cousins rather than siblings.

Strongly Differentiated Any pattern having more than eight distinct terms for siblings-in-law and thus necessarily involving a proliferation of terms based on distinctions of relative age.

Valdés-Pérez and Pericliev (1999) have explored Murdock's dataset for exceptionless universals, the results of which are reported below, based on the exposition in the original article. Since Murdock's data have a number of entries that are uncertain (i.e., a value with a question mark), it was decided to use the entry and ignore the uncertainty. Of course, when a value was missing entirely (denoted with a dot in his original paper), it was left as missing. After verifying that the Murdock data contained no unrestricted universals, the authors searched for exceptionless implicational universals, i.e., of the form A → B.

The universals searched were required to be statistically significant in order to minimize the role of chance associations in the data. The method of permutations for determining the significance of the found universals was used. The basic idea of the test is as follows. The original dataset is randomized by permutations and universals are searched in a series of such random trials (usually 1000 or more). The probabilities of the universals thus found reflect our expectations for universals to occur by chance, so only those universals arising from the original data are accepted which have smaller probabilities than the threshold of presumably chance ones.

There are different ways to implement the above idea. For the investigation at hand, the authors define the probability of an exceptionless implication $A \rightarrow B$ as b^k, where b is the frequency ratio of B, and k is the number of positive examples observed in the data. Thus, if $A \rightarrow B$ occurs without exceptions 10 times in the data, and the value B is found 20% of the time, then the probability is 0.2^{10}. Then, it was needed to define a significance threshold. To achieve this, implications were searched on 1000 permuted variations of the data, requiring further that each of them is supported by at least 10 positive examples. Only 39 times were any implications found in the permuted data, i.e., 3.9% of the time. Roughly, it was required 99% assurance (p < 0.01) that an implication is not chance, so the tenth smallest of these 39 values is taken, which turns out to be 0.0011 (the absolute smallest was 1.9×10^{-4}). Thus, a significance threshold with 99% assurance is empirically determined on Murdock's dataset, which accepts any implications in the real data whose probability is smaller than 0.0011, and rejects any implications having probability bigger than 0.0011.

The program's findings are summarized below.[6] Only one simple implicational universal was retrieved, conforming to our requirements for significance and support by at least 10 languages (the notation follows Murdock, the *List of Some Kinship Patterns* above contains an expanded description of the terms in this and all other universals below, verbalization is not performed by UNIVAUTO, which presently does not know the English names of kinship patterns):

Universal (simple implication). *PaSi=K $\rightarrow$ GrCh=A*. (Examples=15, prob=5.4 × 10^{-5}).

If the aunts pattern is *Relative Age*, then the grandchildren pattern is *Merging*.

---

[6] The actual computations were performed by a straightforward program implemented by Valdés-Pérez. For the purposes of this section, I re-ran UNIVAUTO on the same data; insofar as this yielded essentially the same results, here I stick to those reported in our original paper.

This simple implication seems a plausible universal in our sense, as it is supported by 15 positive examples, it is statistically highly significant with probability of 5.4×10^{-5} (which is even smaller than the smallest value seen among the 1000 permutations), and besides the examples are expected to be structurally diverse, as witnessed by the areal and genetic origin of the supporting languages. Thus, the 15 languages are spoken in the following Provinces originally assigned by Murdock: Daka (Adamawa), Rega (South Equatorial Bantu), Burmese (South Burma), Lepcha (Tibet), Lao, Siamese (Thai), Cambodians (Cambodia), Mnong Gar, Jarai (Montagnards), Semang (Semang-Sakai), Iban (Borneo), Mangarevans (Eastern Polynesia), Selung (Sea Gypsies), Miyakan (Japan and Ryukyus), and Wichita (Caddoans); they belong to the following language familes (source: *Ethnologue Language Family Index* at www.sil.org/ethnologue): Daka, Rega (Niger-Congo), Burmese, Lepcha (Sino-Tibetan), Lao, Siamese (Daic), Cambodians, Mnong Gar, Semang (Austro-Asiatic), Iban, Jarai, Mangarevans, Selung (Austronesian), Miyakans (Japanese), Wichita (Caddoan).

As a next step in the investigation, it was proceeded with a search for universals of the next simplest form $A \& B \rightarrow C$, i.e. complex universals, comprising three variables. A significance threshold had again to be determined, now for complex implications with three variables, so again 1000 trials of permutation tests were performed to estimate a. In this case, the smallest probability seen for "universals" supported by at least ten cases was 6.7×10^{-6}; the 11th smallest of 2.3×10^{-4} provides our desired 99% threshold. Thus, only universals whose probability falls below this value were accepted.

There were 14 complex implicational universals that passed the permutation test of significance and which met or exceeded the arbitrary minimum of 10 examples:

Universal 1. *PaSi = E & CrCo = B → PaBr = C.* (Examples=25, prob=6.0×10^{-21}).

If the aunts pattern is *Skewed Bifurcate Collateral* and the cross-cousins pattern is *Iroquois*, then the uncles pattern is *Skewed Bifurcate Collateral*.

Universal 2. *PaBr = E & SbCh = F → PaSi = D.* (Examples=19, prob=3.2×10^{-18}).

If the uncles pattern is *Generation* and the nephews and nieces (male speaking) pattern is *Sex-Differentiated Lineal*, then the aunts pattern is *Generation*.

Universal 3. *PaBr = E* & *GrPa = A* → *PaSi = D*. (Examples=13, prob=8.7×10^{-13}).

If the uncles pattern is *Generation* and the grandparents pattern is *Bisexual*, then the aunts pattern is *Generation*.

Universal 4. *PaBr = D* & *Sb-il = B* → *PaSi = C*. (Examples=14, prob=7.3×10^{-12}).

If the uncles pattern is *Lineal* and the siblings-in-law pattern is *Simple Bisexual*, then the aunts pattern is *Lineal*.

Universal 5. *PaBr = E* & *GrCh = A* → *PaSi = D*. (Examples=12, prob=7.8×10^{-12}).

If the uncles pattern is *Generation* and the grandchildren pattern is *Merging*, then the aunts pattern is *Generation*.

Universal 6. *PaSi = A* & *Sb-il = D* → *PaBr = B*. (Examples=18, prob=4.3×10^{-11}).

If the aunts pattern is *Simple Bifurcate Collateral* and the siblings-in-law pattern is *Opposite Sex*, then the uncles pattern is *Simple Bifurcate Collateral*.

Universal 7. *PaSi = A* & *Sb-il = B* → *PaBr = B*. (Examples=16, prob=6.1×10^{-10}).

If the aunts pattern is *Simple Bifurcate Collateral* and the siblings-in-law pattern is *Simple Bisexual*, then the uncles pattern is *Simple Bifurcate Collateral*.

Universal 8. *PaSi = C* & *Sibl = C* → *PaBr = D*. (Examples=11, prob=6.2×10^{-10}).

If the aunts pattern is *Lineal* and the siblings pattern is *Yoruban*, then the uncles pattern is *Lineal*.

Universal 9. *PaSi = E* & *GrPa = B* → *PaBr = C*. (Examples=10, prob=8.3×10^{-9}).

If the aunts pattern is *Skewed Bifurcate Collateral* and the grandparents pattern is *Merging*, then the uncles pattern is *Skewed Bifurcate Collateral*.

Universal 10. *PaSi = E* & *Sb-il = K* → *PaBr = C*. (Examples=10, prob=1.7×10^{-8}).

If the aunts pattern is *Skewed Bifurcate Collateral* and the siblings-in-law pattern is *Strongly Differentiated*, then the uncles pattern is *Skewed Bifurcate Collateral*.

Universal 11. *PaSi = B & Sibl = E → PaBr = A.* (Examples=12, prob=4.2×10^{-7}).
If the aunts pattern is *Bifurcate Merging* and the siblings pattern is *Kordofanian*, then the uncles pattern is *Simple Bifurcate Merging*.

Universal 12. *PaSi = B & Sibl = D → PaBr = A.* (Examples=11, prob=1.4×10^{-6}).
If the aunts pattern is *Bifurcate Merging* and the siblings pattern is *Algonkian*, then the uncles pattern is *Simple Bifurcate Merging*.

Universal 13. *PaSi = B & Sb-il = E → PaBr = A.* (Examples=10, prob=6.3×10^{-6}).
If the aunts pattern is *Bifurcate Merging* and the siblings-in-law pattern is *Null*, then the uncles pattern is *Simple Bifurcate Merging*.

Universal 14. *GrCh = B & PaSi = C → GrPa = A.* (Examples=16, prob=1.3×10^{-4}).
If the grandchildren pattern is *Bisexual* and the aunts pattern is *Lineal*, then the grandparents pattern is *Bisexual*.

The authors make the following observations regarding the found universals. First, some sets of universals, viz. (Nos. 1, 9, 10), (Nos. 2, 3, 5), (Nos. 6, 7), and (Nos. 11, 12, 13) may be collapsed into more compact formulae, using disjunction. For example, (Nos. 6, 7) can be expressed as:

PaSi = A & Sb-il = [D ∨ B] → PaBr = B.
If the aunts pattern is *Simple Bifurcate Collateral* and the siblings-in-law pattern is *Opposite Sex* or *Simple Bisexual*, then the uncles pattern is *Simple Bifurcate Collateral*.

Secondly, 14 universals involve an implication between the relatives uncle–aunt (or vice versa), and one universal (the last one) between grandchild and grandparent; all of these pairs of relatives are "symmetrical" with respect to ego in a genealogical grid: uncle and aunt along the dimension of collaterality, grandchild and grandparent along the dimension of lineality.

And, thirdly, all universals express a uniformity between the patterns for the pairs uncle–aunt and grandchild–grandparent (Murdock states that the aunt and uncle patterns in universals No. 11, No. 12, and No. 13 are analogous, even though the names differ; cf. also the *List of Some Kinship Patterns*). However, these uniformities are not absolute, otherwise they would have shown up as simple, two term, universals; rather, each is mediated by another pattern. For example, in the first universal, the relation between aunt and uncle is contingent on a value of Iroquois for the cross-cousins pattern. Looking more closely at why the simpler implication did not show up as an exceptionless universal, the data reveal that the aunt pattern occurs 63 times, but in only 56 of these does the uncle pattern hold (the seven exceptions are the Luguru, Akha, Eastern Pomo, Miwok, Southern Ute, Hano, and Tepehuan societies). Depending on taste, or better, the explanatoriness of the decision, one might prefer a simpler universal having an 11% exception rate to our more complex universals. Similarly, the data reveal that the simplified universals No. 6 and No. 7 (removing the contingencies on siblings-in-law) have an exception rate of 19%. On the other hand, the simplified universals Nos. 2, 3, and 5 would have an exception rate of only 0.04 (one — the Samoans — out of 28), so it is probably best to favor the singly-contingent, 1-exception universal in this case. The exception rates for all 14 simplified (i.e., keeping only the relation between aunt and uncle or grandparents and grandchildren) universals are No. 1 (7/63), No. 2 (1/28), No. 3 (1/28), No. 4 (8/81), No. 5 (1/28), No. 6 (29/152), No. 7 (29/152), No. 8 (15/88), No. 9 (7/63), No. 10 (7/63), No. 11 (22/144), No. 12 (22/144), No. 13 (22/144), and No. 14 (15/89).

4.3.3 Testing a hypothesis involving universals

In a paper whose basic concern is the search for significant correlations between societal types and linguistic structure, Peter Trudgill (2004a) makes (among others) the following two interrelated *factual* claims pertaining to an existence of a correlation between the size of a community speaking a language and the size of the phonological inventory of that language (cf. his Conclusions 4 and 5, respectively):

I. Large community size favours medium-sized phonological inventories; *and*

II. Small (=non-large) community size favours either small phonological inventories or large inventories (but not medium-sized ones).

In the paper, Trudgill is primarily concerned with Austrone-sian/Polynesian languages, and rightly notes that "In the absence of a large-scale database of evidence on this topic, taken from different language families in different parts of the world, any conclusions to be produced [...] can be only suggestive and tentative."

Using our machinery for discovery of universals, a cross-linguistic test of the above two claims will be made in this section, which was previously presented in Pericliev (2004a). A specification is in order. I should note at this stage that, judging from the context and the examples Trudgill gives, by "phonological inventory" he means the *consonantal* inventories of languages (rather than inventories including both consonants and vowels) and I will therefore focus on consonantal inventories, using the latter complex term for greater clarity of exposition.[7]

As a preliminary step of the testing, we need to collect data on the size of consonantal inventories of languages and the size of the populations speaking those languages. I therefore compiled such a database on the basis of the 451 languages and their phonological inventories as described in the UPSID-451 sample (Maddieson and Precoda 1991, Maddieson 1991; cf. also Maddieson 1984). The number of consonants for each of these 451 languages was computed, and then the corresponding sizes of the linguistic communities speaking the languages were added, based on the information to that effect contained in the electronic version of *Ethnologue*. For 23 languages (coming from different language families/areas of the UPSID sample) I could not supply information regarding the number of their speakers (the languages are extinct; there is no estimate about speakers, or they do not figure in *Ethnologue*). This left us with 428 odd languages containing the relevant information. The resultant sample clearly inherits UPSID's representativeness and, just as UPSID itself, can be used for making valid statistical inferences about the (consonantal) segment inventories of the languages of the world.

We can now look more closely at Claims I and II. The claims assume that the universe of all consonantal inventories is split exhaustively into three categories: "small inventory", "medium-sized inventory", and "large inventory", and the universe of all linguistic communities is split exhaustively into two categories: "small community", and "large (=non-small) community". The claims then can be represented as:

---

[7] In his response to Pericliev (2004a), Trudgill (2004b) states his concerns to have been whole inventories; adding vowels, however, would not lead to a need to change or modify the conclusions reached here.

	All communities	*All inventories*	
	large	medium-sized	*Claim I*
	small	small or large	
			Claim II
	(=non-large)	(non-medium-sized)	

meaning that languages spoken by large communities will favour medium-sized inventories and vice versa, languages having medium-sized inventories will favour large communities (Claim I), and languages spoken by small communities will favour either small or large inventories and vice versa, languages having either small or large inventories will favour small communities (Claim II). This is a one-to-one correspondence (=equivalence, two-way implication) between large communities and medium-sized inventories on the one hand, and small communities and small/large inventories on the other. Put still differently, the claims amount to saying that the space of all languages is partitioned in two: (i) languages that *both* have medium-sized inventories *and* are spoken by large communities; and (ii) languages that *both* have small/large inventories *and* are spoken by small communities.

In order to be able to inspect Claims I and II, we need to have a specific *numerical interpretation* of the meanings of the terms participating in the claims, especially as regards the meanings of "small inventory", "medium-sized inventory" and "large inventory", "large community", and "small community". Trudgill does not give an exact numerical interpretation of these terms. This makes the claims insufficiently specific and thus not amenable to direct testing. Indeed, is e.g. a "small community" one comprising 100, 1000, 10000, 25000 or more speakers? Or do 17 consonants constitute a "small" or a "medium-sized" inventory? Or do 26 consonants constitute a "medium-sized" or a "large" inventory? Depending on the specific numerical interpretations of these terms the outcomes of a test may vary.

There are two different approaches to handling this indeterminacy of terms in the inspected propositions:

A. We select some "reasonable" interpretations of the terms and test the claims with these interpretations.

B. We try to determine whether there exist such interpretations of the terms for which the claims are actually true.

We pursue both approaches below.

Let us first look for a "reasonable" numerical interpretation of "medium-sized inventory" (a "small inventory" will then be one which is smaller than the "medium-sized" one, and a "large inventory" one which is larger than the "medium-sized" one). The mean of consonantal inventories is about 22, and one standard deviation of the mean is 9, giving the interval 22 ±9 as a reasonable interpretation of a "typical" or "average" consonantal inventory. The interval 22 ±9 comprises 78% of all languages in our 428 language sample. Varying slightly this interval, I presume, will also yield intuitively credible average consonantal inventories.

Insofar as the demarcation between a "large community" and a "small community" is concerned, it seems to me that any number from, say, 1000 to 100000 can intuitively satisfactorily split the languages into such spoken by small vs. large populations.

We are now ready to test Claims I and II empirically for *different* reasonable interpretations of their component terms, by selecting some combinations of such interpretations. Let us call the interval 22±9 a (reasonable) *inventory size demarcator* and any integer within the interval 1000–100000 a (reasonable) *community size demarcator*. Selecting a specific value for each demarcator turns the indeterminate Claims I and II into completely definite statements amenable to testing. Thus, e.g. selecting

Community size demarcator	*Inventory size demarcator*
5000	13–31

turns Claims I and II respectively into:

I'. Community sizes > 5000 speakers (large ones) favour inventories between 13 and 31 consonants inclusive (i.e. medium-sized ones); *and*

II'. Community sizes ≤ 5000 speakers (small ones) favour either <13 consonants (small inventories) or > 31 consonants (large inventories).

Table 4.2 summarizes the results of a number of computationally performed tests of Claims I and II, using as a database our 428 language sample. The tests use different interpretations of Claims I and II component terms, which were chosen randomly from the intuitive values agreed upon above. The meanings of columns in Table 4.2 are self-explanatory. Columns 4 and 5 give the positive examples and all relevant examples (separated by slash) and the percentage of validity of the respective claim.[8]

---

[8] As usual, I count as positive examples the languages which both are spoken by large communities and have medium-sized inventories (Claim I) or both are spoken by small communities and have small or large inventories (Claim II). Counter-examples are the languages satisfying only one of the two conjoined

Table 4.2. Fourteen tests of Claims I and II under different "reasonable" interpretations of the terms "small" vs. "large" community size and "small" vs. "medium-sized" vs. "large" consonantal inventory

Test No.	Community size demarcator	Inventory size demarcator	Validity of Claim I	Validity of Claim II
1	1000	13–31	262/405 65%	23/166 14%
2	5000	13–31	226/387 58%	41/202 20%
3	25000	13–31	171/370 46%	58/257 23%
4	50000	13–31	149/364 41%	64/279 23%
5	100000	13–31	130/359 36%	69/298 23%
6	1000	18–26	162/365 44%	63/266 24%
7	5000	18–26	141/332 43%	96/287 33%
8	25000	18–26	114/287 40%	141/314 45%
9	50000	18–26	102/271 38%	157/326 48%
10	100000	18–26	89/260 34%	168/339 50%
11	10000	19–25	113/288 39%	140/315 44%
12	15000	19–25	110/279 39%	149/318 47%
13	35000	19–25	90/254 35%	174/338 51%
14	80000	19–25	76/240 32%	188/352 53%

conditions (e.g. a language spoken by a large community but having a small inventory will be a counter-example to either claim). The number of "relevant examples" is equal to the sum of positive examples and the counter-examples.

This suite of random tests strongly suggests that Trudgill's Claims I and II are not valid. Both claims are generally valid below or around the threshold of 50%, and therefore there are no linguistic *preferences* of the types suggested by Trudgill. Only in tests Nos. 1 and 2 does Claim I slightly exceed the 50% threshold, with values of 65% and 58% respectively. Unfortunately, these results also do not provide any (even minor) support for Trudgill's claims. There are two reasons for this. First, these language distributions are simply to be expected by chance, and therefore present no significant clustering indicative of a real linguistic preference.[9] And, secondly, in these two tests the corresponding two companion Claims II, which are also crucial to Trudgill's argumentation, are hopelessly unsupported (with validity of 14% and 20% respectively).

It could be (correctly) objected that a definite conclusion as to the validity of tested claims is a bit hurried since our suite of tests is by far not exhaustive and involves only a dozen combinations of terms interpretations, while there is a vast number of logically possible ones, leaving the theoretical possibility for finding term interpretations for which the claims are valid.

To remedy this, let us now pursue the second approach B, conducting a graphical test of Trudgill's claims. Let us plot the languages in the sample in a *xy* scatter diagram, where the *x*–axis displays the size of consonantal inventories and the *y*–axis the number of speakers. Each language in the sample will be represented by a point, whose position in this diagram will be determined by the number of consonants it has and by the number of people the language is spoken by.

---

[9] For example, let us look at test No. 1, Claim I (Table 4.2), which is supported in 262 languages (or $262/405 = 65\%$ validity) such that are spoken by > 1000 people and also have inventories from 13 to 31. As already mentioned, 78% of all languages in the sample (or 335 languages out of 428) have consonantal inventories in the interval 22 ± 9, i.e. from 13 to 31. I computed that 336 languages are spoken by > 1000 people, giving also 78% of all languages in the sample. Now, the probability of the occurrence of one language which both has > 1000 speakers and from 13 to 31 consonants will be equal to the product of these two percentages, i.e. $0.78 \times 0.78 = 0.61$ (or 61%). Now we ask: How many languages having both properties (=positive examples) are to be expected to occur by chance in the whole sample of 428 languages? To find this, we should multiply 428 by the probability 0.61, giving $428 \times 0.61 = 261$ languages. Thus, we expect 261 languages as chance support and we find almost the same number, 262, in the actual test.

What would Trudgill's claims amount to viewed from this graphical perspective?

Figure 4.2. Distribution of an artificial 428 language sample conforming 100% to Claims I and II

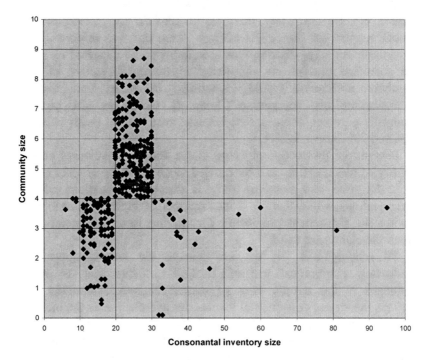

Figure 4.2 is a graphical representation of an artificial language data set I generated computationally,[10] consisting of 428 languages (as our original sample), which conforms 100% to Trudgill's Claims I and II. (Note that the y–axis is an exponential scale with a base of 10, i.e. $10^1 =$ 10 speakers, $10^2 = 100$ speakers, $10^3 = 1000$ speakers, etc.)

---

[10] The basics of the algorithm are as follows. First, the community size demarcator and the inventory size demarcator were chosen to be $10^4 = 10000$ speakers and 20–30 consonants, respectively. Then, for any language in our 428 language sample, the following was done: if it conforms to either claim, it is listed with unchanged descriptors in the artificial sample; if it does not conform to any of the two claims, the size of its consonantal inventory is randomly changed to conform to one of the claims (this category was chosen which was closer to the original consonantal number, e.g. for a language spoken by a small community but having a medium-sized inventory of 21 consonants, a random number would be chosen below (not above) this interval. In effect, the algorithm generates a "corrected version" of the original sample.

As Figure 4.2 clearly shows, and this would be the case for *any* conforming language sample, Claims I and II could be true[11] only if all (or at least, most) languages cluster in three regions:

- an upper middle region (corresponding to Claim I: large communities correlate with medium-sized inventories), and
- a lower left region *or* a lower right region (corresponding to Claim II: small communities correlate with either small or large inventories, respectively).

In the particular example, both claims are true under the following numerical interpretation of the claims' component terms:

Community size demarcator   *Inventory size demarcator*
$10^4 = 10000$ 20–30

(equivalent to saying that: a "small community" is smaller than or equal to $10^4 = 10000$, a "large community" is larger than $10^4 = 10000$; a "small inventory" is smaller than 20 consonants, a "medium-sized inventory" lies in the interval 20–30 consonants, and a "large inventory" is greater than 30 consonants).

Now we can look at the actual distribution of our original 428 language sample and compare the result to that of the artificial (and conforming) sample, given in Figure 4.2. The actual distribution is given in Figure 4.3.

The graph in Figure 4.3 is markedly different from that in Figure 4.2. There is not a trace of any of the three distinct clusters in Figure 4.2, meaning that Claims I and II are not really supported under *any interpretation* of their component terms. Our graphical testing thus enforces the preliminary impression of the falsehood of the claims, also arrived at by other means.

We can safely conclude then that there is no correlation of the type suggested by Trudgill between the size of a community speaking a language and the size of the consonantal inventory of that language. (Neither does such a correlation exist when whole inventories (consonants + vowels) are involved, as my preliminary looking at this problem suggests.)

---

[11] I say "could be true", and not "will be true" because clustering in the mentioned regions is a necessary, but not also a sufficient condition for Claims I and II to be true. Thus, some clusterings may arise due simply to chance, and therefore a candidate cluster should additionally be shown to be statistically significant.

Figure 4.3. Distribution of the actual 428 language sample

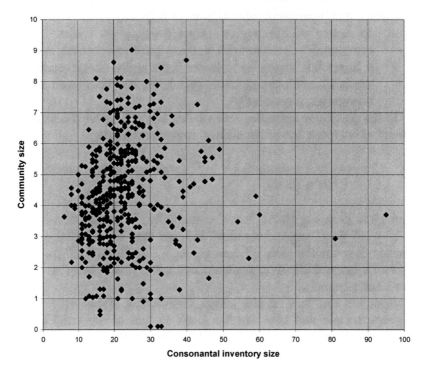

Finally, let me note that my considerations here in no way undermine Trudgill's more general concern for searching of significant correlations between societal types and linguistic structure. It seems however that such undoubtedly fruitful pursuits, of mostly theoretical nature, had better be complemented by extensive data collection and severe testing of the hypotheses arrived at theoretically.

4.3.4 Violation of universals as linguistic peculiarity

A language can be viewed as "peculiar" if it violates a universal pattern that admits only very few exceptions. Thus, if e.g. the implication A → B holds with only a very few exceptions, the counter-examples, i.e. the languages which have A but not B, are "peculiar" ("deviant", "rare") in that they behave unlike most other languages of the world. In this section, I sketch an experiment, in which UNIVAUTO was used to mine "near-universals" valid in at least 95% of the languages in the *UCLA Phonological Segment Inventory Database* (UPSID), comprising 451 languages (Maddieson 1984, Maddieson and Precoda 1991). For details, see Pericliev (2004b). We ran the program requiring that these "near-universals" are statistically highly significant universals ($p < 0.01$) (in order to minimize the smuggling of purely chance patterns) and are further supported in at least 2 distinct language families from 2 distinct large geographical areas (in order to minimize the smuggling of genetic/areal patterns). UNIVAUTO retrieved 33 near-universals (or phonological peculiarities) of implicational type. It turned out that 391 of these languages had no peculiarity of the type studied, 43 had one, and 17 more than one peculiarity, which may be called "strongly peculiar" languages. Table 4.3 lists the strongly peculiar languages with their deviancies.

Table 4.3. Strongly peculiar languages and their deviances

No. of Peculiarities	Language	Peculiarities
Two peculiarities	*Kewa* (Papuan/Trans-New-Guinea)	has [g] but lacks [b] has [t] but lacks [k]
"	*Usan* (Papuan/Trans-New-Guinea)	has [p] but lacks [k] has [t] but lacks [k]
"	*Vanimo* (Papuan/Sko)	has[p] but lacks [k] has [t] but lacks [k]
"	*Beembe* (Niger-Kordofanian/Bantoid)	has [p] but lacks [k] has [t] but lacks [k]
"	*Kohumono* (Niger-Kordofanian/Cross-River)	has [t] but lacks [k] has [tʃ] but lacks [k]
"	*Diyari* (Australian/Pama-Nyungan)	has [d.] but lacks [b] has [d.] but lacks [g]
"	*Wapishana* (South American/M.-Arawakan)	has [d] but lacks [b] has [g] but lacks [b]
"	*Bella Coola* (North American/Almosan)	has [p] but lacks [k] has [t̪] but lacks [k]
"	*Kwakw'ala* (North American/Almosan)	has [ɟ] but lacks [g] has [dz] but lacks [g]
"	*Mixe* (North American/Penutian)	has [d̪] but lacks [b] has [g] but lacks [b]
"	*Tzeltal* (North American/Penutian)	has [p] but lacks [k] has [t̪] but lacks [k]
"	*Zuni* (North American/Penutian)	has ["t"] but lacks [k] has [p] but lacks [k]

Three peculiarities	Eyak (Na-Dene/Eyak)	has ["d"] but lacks [b]
		has [g] but lacks [b]
		has [dʒ] but lacks [b]
"	Hupa (Na-Dene/Athabaskan)	has [t] but lacks [k]
		has [tʃ] but lacks [k]
		has [tʃ'] but lacks [k']
"	Cherokee (Northern American/Keresiouan)	has [d] but lacks [b]
		has [g] but lacks [b]
		has [dz] but lacks [b]
Four peculiarities	Klao (Niger-Kordofanian/Krue)	has ["t"] but lacks [k]
		has [p] but lacks [k]
		has [g͡b] but lacks [g]
		has ["d"] but lacks [˝n˝]
Six peculiarities	Irish (Indo-European/Celtic)	has [d] but lacks [b]
		has [d̪] but lacks [b]
		has [g] but lacks [b]
		has [dʒ] but lacks [b]
		has [tʃ] but lacks [k]
		has [ŋ] but lacks [m]

The following observations can be made from the results in Table 4.3:

First, no language was found that has more than six peculiarities, or violates more than six universals (Irish, the most strongly peculiar language in our data set, has six deviations). Generally, languages that have more than two peculiarities are rare (only five languages in our data set, viz. Eyak, Hupa, Cherokee, Klao, and Irish). This suggests some limit to language variation (relative to the examined peculiarity type): languages can indeed be idiosyncratic, but only to a certain limit, not exceeding six deviations.

Secondly, regarding the content of phonological peculiarities, it is seen that all strongly peculiar languages turn out to have a "gap" in their (oral or nasal) stop systems. Thus, they illegitimately lack only one of the following segments: [b], [k], [g], [k'], ["n"], and [m]. The missing segments belong to the bilabial, dental/alveolar and velar series.

It is interesting to note that many of the strongly peculiar languages lack only one segment, even though they have several peculiarities, or violate several diverse normative rules or universals. Examples are Usan, Vanimo, Beembe, Kohumono, Wapishana, Bella Coola, Kwakw'ala, Mixe, Tzeltal, Zuni, Eyak, and Cherokee. For example, say Eyak has just one gap in its segment inventory, viz. it lacks a [b], but violates three universals with the antecedents ["d"], [g], and [dʒ], any one of which implies the consequent [b].

The languages that lack most segments (=have most gaps) are: Klao (lacking three segments, [k], [g], and ["n"]), and Irish (also lacking three segments, [b], [k], and [m]). Thus, complementing the conclusion in point (1) above, we can say that the limit to language idiosyncrasy (relative to the examined peculiarity type) is violation of no more than six universals and no more than three gaps in segment inventory.

And, thirdly, regarding the language family/areal distribution of the strongly phonologically peculiar languages, it is interesting to note that they seem to be clustered into the Papuan family (3 languages), the Niger-Kordofanian family (3 languages), and the Amerindian languages (9 languages).

The observed circumstances do not seem random, and therefore call for an explanation. Indeed, why cannot languages violate more than six universals and cannot have more than three segment gaps? Or why are the missing segments only bilabial, dental/alveolar or velar stops to the exclusion of all other segments? Or why should the strongly peculiar languages be genetically and areally so unevenly distributed?

I will conclude this section noting that among other consequences, our results have an important consequence regarding historical reconstruction of languages. Universals have been traditionally invoked in language reconstruction (at least as far back as the work of Roman Jakobson). The rationale behind this is the assumption that extinct languages must not have been essentially different from extant languages, so that patterns or universals that have been established on the basis of extant languages must have held true also for the unknown proto-languages. Put differently, language reconstruction on a typological basis assumes that reconstructed languages "generally should not violate universals". Here, we make this assumption more specific, suggesting an upper bound on the number of universals violations and segment gaps.

4.4 Conclusion

In this chapter, I introduced UNIVAUTO, a system that can produce a coherent English text, describing its discoveries. Despite the seemingly bizarre nature of the task of article generation, this work was actually inspired by the practical need to verbalize the great number of universals UNIV has systematically found in the various databases we have explored, as well as by the need to compare these with the findings of previous researchers. Presumably, such problems have not confronted previous discovery programs because they searched nonconventional spaces (necessitating additional human interpretation of results), because their solution objects (e.g. numerical laws in physics or mathematics, reaction path-ways in chemistry, etc.) are not amenable to verbal expression or simply because the set of solution objects has been too small to require automated verbalization.

In sum, UNIVAUTO models scientific domains in which a machine is likely to find numerous and verbalizable solution objects (conceivably, low-level generalizations), and the scientific discourses in these domains are basically limited to description of these findings. I believe that such domains are not exceptional in empirical sciences generally, and hence systems like ours are not unlikely to emerge to aid scientists in these domains.

I have illustrated the full capacities of UNIVAUTO with one full text generated by the system and two fragments, all based on the data from Greenberg (1966a). These discoveries of the program are mostly historical because the database used is much too small for more definitive results. They however nicely show some difficulties usually encountered by human analysts in exploring data. A further example of the verbalization component of UNIVAUTO is provided in the next chapter, where I deal with phonological universals. The other illustrations, which do not use the verbalization component of the system, were concerned with universals from domains different from word order. The results obtained in these applications were found interesting and worthy of publication in specialized linguistic journals.

Chapter 5. Inferring Plausible Laws/Patterns II: UNIVAUTO and Implicational Phonological Universals

In this chapter, I describe the computational exploration of the UPSID database, comprising the segment inventories of 451 languages, for implicational universals of type $A \rightarrow B$ ("If Segment A, then Segment B"). UNIVAUTO found and verbalized 146 statistically significant (near) universals that are supported by languages from at least two language families from at least two geographical areas. Some implications of these findings are discussed. A universal principle (a meta-universal) holding for implicational phonological universals is proposed, stating that the antecedent and the consequent of an implicational universal must share at least one feature and, additionally, the consequent must have an equal or smaller number of features than the antecedent. The principle is both statistically significant and highly predictive (valid in 94.5% of all found universals).

5.1 The problem

In his paper on ordering universals, Greenberg (1966a) makes the following methodological remark:

> In a certain sense we would prefer to have as few universals as possible, not as many. That is, we would like to be able to deduce them from as small a number of general principles as possible. However, *the establishment of a relatively large number of empirical generalizations must, on the whole, come first*. For one thing, it would be embarrassing to deduce a particular universal from what seemed like a valid general principle, only to discover that the generalization was not empirically valid. (p.75; italics mine)

The discovery of a sizable number of (relatively low level) empirical generalizations is indeed an indispensable testbed for general deductive principles, once they have been found. To this remark one could add that such generalizations are also indispensable for hinting or arriving at general principles, for principles do not come from nowhere but are significantly, even if possibly indirectly, dependent on observation.

In this chapter, I will adopt an empirical approach to the study of phonological universals. In particular, I will address the study of implicational universals of type $A \rightarrow B$, where A and B are segments, which have been of common interest in linguistic research. The computer system UNIVAUTO, described in Chapter 4 and applied to the study of word order and universals from other domains in Chapter 4, will be used to uncover the universals of this type in the *UCLA Phonological Segment Inventory Database,* UPSID-451, one of the most representative phonological databases to-date. Then, based on the sizable number (viz. 146) of universals of type Segment $A \rightarrow$ Segment B found by the system, now represented in terms of feature structures rather than segments, an empirical principle, or a meta-universal, I call the "Principle of Antecedent–Consequent Compatibility", will be derived, stating that if $A \rightarrow B$ is a universal, then segment A and segment B share at least one feature and, besides, B never has more features than A. This principle will be shown to be highly statistically significant (and not due simply to chance) and highly predictive (valid in 94.5% of all 146 universals inspected).

The study of various phonological universals, including those of the type addressed here, is of course by no means a novel research problem. See e.g. Sedlak's (1969) and Crothers's (1978) work on vowels; Nartey's (1979) on fricatives and stops; or Ferguson's (1966, 1974) on nasals, to mention only some of the important work in the field. Another notable contribution, deserving special mention, is the book by Maddieson (1984). In this context, a chapter like this one requires some justification.

There are two basic justifications for the present chapter, one having to do with the data addressed, and the other with the approach to these data. Thus, in this chapter I explore the representative UPSID-451 database, which, to the best of my knowledge, has not been investigated for phonological universals so far. Maddieson's (1984) book is based on an earlier version of UPSID, comprising 317 languages, whereas this investigation uses the last corrected and expanded version, comprising 451 languages. Other previous researchers base their studies on smaller and/or possibly not fully compatible[1] databases.

---

[1] For example, the phonological decisions regarding the description of the segment inventory of a language in the UPSID database may differ from those taken in the Stanford Phonological Archive (Maddieson 1984: 6), another important database on which much of previous research on universals is based.

My second justification is that previous researchers have conducted manual searches, while the task of universals discovery is obviously computationally complex, requires a systematic, exhaustive search, and hence machine processing, the approach I adopt here. Thus, to find all valid patterns (relative to a database), say of the form "If Segment A, then Segment B" I address here, implies, first, finding all logically possible combinations from all segments used in the database, and secondly, testing all such hypotheses against the database. More technically, this reduces to finding all ordered pairs (=implications) of segments from the segments used and testing them. The number of ordered pairs of segments from a set of N segments is computed by the formula: $N^2 - N$. Thus, given that the number of segments used in UPSID-451 is N = 919 the number of potential hypotheses to construct and subsequently test equals $919^2 - 919 = 843\ 642$. Additionally, the found putative universals must be statistically significant to minimize mere chance as the reason for their occurrence, a task also difficult to achieve manually. Most previous research on phonological universals in contrast seems to have been appeased with those universals that just *happen* to be noticed by individual linguists, instead of trying an exhaustive (machine) search of the databases studied, and not infrequently posited universals without explicit concern for their statistical significance.

The chapter is organized as follows. Section 5.2 sketches the UPSID-451 database, which was also used previously in Chapters 3 and 4, and proceeds with showing how we tuned the relevant parameters of UNIVAUTO in our search for plausible universals. Section 5.3 is the computer enumeration of the universals found by the system, stated in English and in the form generated by the program. In Section 5.4, I summarize the results, compare them to those of Maddieson (1984) and make some further observations based on the found list of universals. Section 5.5 describes the Principle of Antecedent–Consequent Compatibility and in Section 6.6 I evaluate the UNIVAUTO system.

5.2 Searching for plausible universals with UNIVAUTO

The *UCLA Phonological Segment Inventory Database* (UPSID) is compiled by Maddieson and colleagues at UCLA and is one of the most detailed collections of segment inventories of the world languages. As already mentioned, originally, the database consisted of 371 languages (Maddieson 1984). A later corrected and expanded version (Maddieson and Precoda 1991, Maddieson 1991) contains already a 451 language sample, and I use this later version, usually referred to as UPSID-451, for the computations.

UPSID-451 contains phonologically contrastive segments of the world languages. For each language in the database, a segment inventory is included containing segments that have lexically contrastive function. The features assigned to a segment exhibit its most characteristic phonetic form. The phonetic features consist of an elaborated set of categories from standard phonetic theory, such as places and manners of articulation (for consonants), height, backness and roundness (for vowels), and so on.

UPSID-451 is compiled on a genetic principle, classifying the languages into 18 major genetic groupings (= language families). These language families fall into 4 large geographical areas:

I. EURASIA
1. Indo-European
2. Ural-Altaic
3. Austro-Asiatic
4. Austro-Tai
5. Sino-Tibetan
6. Caucasian
7. Other Eurasian minor families
8. Dravidian

III. AMERICAS
13. Na-Dene
14. North Amerind
15. South Amerind
16. Eskimo-Aleut

II. AFRICA
9. Niger-Kordofanian
10. Nilo-Saharan
11. Afro-Asiatic
12. Khoisan

IV. AUSTRALASIA
17. Australian
18. Papuan

The languages included are chosen on a quota principle, to the effect that all major language (sub-)families are covered, but only one language from any smaller grouping is included. The sample is designed to include one language from a grouping of about the level of affiliation of, say, the West Germanic branch of Indo-European, comprising German, English, Dutch, Frisian and their close relatives (in this particular case, the selected language is German). The language chosen to cover a small grouping would as a rule be described in trustworthy linguistic sources.

UPSID-451 can be assessed as a very representative sample. The primary goal of the database is to provide a sample from which statistically valid statements concerning frequency and co-occurrence can be drawn. The database is thus a reliable empirical source for a computational investigation of the sort undertaken in this chapter. For details concerning the design of UPSID, and some problems arising therefrom, the reader is referred to Maddieson (1984: Chapter 10; 1991), and Maddieson and Precoda (1991).

Our UNIVAUTO system uses as input the following information available in UPSID-451:

- segment inventories of languages;
- feature descriptions of segments used;
- language family membership of languages; and
- areal membership (=geographical affiliation) of languages.

We may now recollect that the *discovery module* UNIV of our system UNIVAUTO has a number of parameters, which can be tuned by the user, allowing him/her to vary the output of the program. In addition to the choice of a type of universal ("unrestricted universals" or "implicational"; "non-statistical" or "statistical"), etc., other parameters which can be varied are:

(a) Number of language families $\geq N1$ (the number of language families the supporting languages belong to are greater than or equal to the number N1 set by user).

(b) Number of geographical areas $\geq N2$ (the number of geographical areas the supporting languages belong to are greater than or equal to the number N2 set by user).

(c) Percentage of validity of pattern $\geq N3$ (the percentage of validity of pattern in the investigated database is greater than or equal to the number N3 set by user).

(d) Statistical significance of pattern $\geq N4$ (the statistical significance of a pattern relative to the examined data is greater than or equal to the threshold N4 set by user). For this application, I use the chi-square test, which is illustrated below.

We also recollect that the discovery module of the system conducts an "exhaustive search" of the database, meaning that all logically possible hypotheses, conforming to the user's query, are constructed and then tested against the data.

In our quest for plausible universals, I ran UNIVAUTO on the UPSID-451 data, requiring that the system discover implications of the logical form "If Segment A, then Segment B" such that these implications are:

(i) valid in at least 90% of the relevant languages;
(ii) statistically highly significant;
(iii) valid in two or more language families;

(iv) valid in two or more geographical areas.

Constraint (i) ensures that we find only absolute universals or near universals, rather than weaker claims, often referred to as "tendencies" or merely "preferences". (The exact threshold of 90% is, of course, somewhat randomly chosen for the notion "near universal".)

We know from elementary statistics that in searching a database some patterns may seem significant while in fact they occur simply by chance. This circumstance is widely recognized by typologists (e.g. Comrie 1981: 194, Dryer 2003). An investigator of phonological universals like Maddieson (1984, 1991, 1999) is also quite sensitive to this circumstance. Constraint (ii) ensures that we find only implications that have a reliable assurance that they have not occurred by chance in the studied database. I have chosen a confidence level which is equal or greater than 99% (or a significance of $p < 0.01$), a high significance level that is generally considered to be reliable and yield results that are beyond reasonable doubt in social science. For this study, I have basically used a standard statistical test to determine significance, viz. the chi-square (χ^2) test.[2]

Below is an illustration of how I employ the chi-square (χ^2) statistic to compute the significance of an implication $A \rightarrow B$. This statistic estimates the difference between the actual, or observed, number of examples/counter-examples to an implication and the number that may be expected to occur by chance. If the difference between observed and expected number is large, then the implication may be considered significant in that it is unlikely to have occurred by chance. If the difference between observed and expected number of examples/counter-examples to an implication is small, then the implication may be considered insignificant in the sense that the data suggests a chance origin of its actual occurrence. χ^2 is estimated by the following general formula:

(1)
$$\chi^2 = \frac{(\text{Observed Exs} - \text{Expected Exs})^2}{\text{Expected Exs}} + \frac{(\text{Observed Counterexs} - \text{Expected Counterexs})^2}{\text{Expected Counterexs}}$$

which is instantiated in our case to:

---

[2] Parenthetically, it might be interesting to note that the permutation test, as described in Chapter 4, Section 4.3.2, was also run to test the significance of the exceptionless implications found and the results of both tests are almost completely identical, suggesting that these tests can be used interchangeably.

(2)

$$\chi^2 = \frac{(N-np)^2}{np} + \frac{[n-N-n(1-p)]^2}{n(1-p)},$$

where:

- N is the number of observed examples of an implication A → B (or the languages that support the implication in the sense that do not falsify it)
- n is the size of the sample (or the examined database comprising 451 languages)
- p is the probability of an occurrence of an example of an implication
- $n - N$ is the number of observed counter-examples to an implication A → B
- $1 - p$ is the probability of an occurrence of a counter-example to an implication

Formula (2) for χ^2 is a sum of two addends, the first of which computes the difference between observed and expected examples, and the second the difference between observed and expected counter-examples to an implication. The probability, p, of an example of implication A → B is computed by the formula:

(3) $p = 1 - p(A)p(not-B),$

where the probabilities of the two multipliers, $p(A)$ and $p(not-B)$, are defined as the frequency ratios of A and $not-B$, respectively (e.g. if A occurs 100 times in the database of 451 languages its probability $p(A) =$ 100/451 or 0.22).

By way of illustration, consider the estimation of the significance of the universals [p] → [k] (Universal 38 below). Let us first find the values for n, N, and p and then substitute these values in formula (2) above. The size of the sample, n, is 451 (there are 451 languages in our database). The number of positive examples, N, of [p] → [k] is found by our program to be 446 (there are 5 counter-example languages that have [p] but lack [k], i.e. 451 – 5 = 446). Our program finds that the frequency of [p] is 375 and the frequency of not–[k] (the languages that lack [k]) is 46; therefore (by formula 3) the probability of a positive example of [p] → [k], p, will be: $p = 1 - 375/451 \times 46/451 = 0.92$. Substituting these values for the corresponding variables in formula (2), we get:

$$\chi^2 = \frac{(446 - 451 \times 0.92)^2}{451 \times 0.92} + \frac{[451 - 446 - 451(1 - 0.92)]^2}{451 \times (1 - 0.92)} = 31.14$$

Checking a table (to be found in most statistical textbooks) of critical values of χ^2 with 1 degree of freedom would provide the significance level. χ^2 of 6.63 or higher would be seen to yield our chosen level of $p <$ 0.01 (99% assurance of non-randomness). In doing such a check, we shall also see that the found χ^2 of 31.14 is very high and would not, as a rule, be listed in such tables, stopping at the level 0.001 (reached at $\chi^2 =$ 10.83 or higher). Thus, the assurance that the investigated universal [p] → [k] is not random approaches certainty.[3]

We can now return to our constraints. Constraint (iii) ensures that the system does not output as universals implications that might be specific to the languages in just one language family (*family generalizations*) and thus be likely to be simply inherited from their proto-language. The language families assumed by the system are the 18 major genetic groups, as defined in UPSID-451 and shown above (cf. Section 2).

Likewise, constraint (iv) ensures that the system does not output as universals implications that might be specific to the languages in only one linguistic area, *or Sprachbund* (*areal generalizations*) and thus potentially be due to contact and borrowing between these languages, rather than reflect genuine universal properties. The system assumes the four major geographical groupings, as defined in UPSID-451, viz. Eurasia, Africa, the Americas, and Australasia (cf. Section 2). Notice that it is possible to take into consideration *linguistic areas* by reference to UPSID's *geographical areas*, because the latter include as their proper subparts all less controversial linguistic areas[4] and therefore an implication supported by languages in at least two geographical areas is

---

[3] Tables with the critical values for the chi-square (χ^2) test can be found in practically any statistical textbook (cf. e.g. McClave and Dietrich 1988). In accordance with current practice, I call critical values higher than $\chi^2 = 6.64$ (=99% or greater assurance) "highly significant", those higher than $\chi^2 = 3.84$ (but smaller than $\chi^2 = 6.64$) are called simply "significant", and those below $\chi^2 = 3.84$ are called "non-significant".

[4] Thus, the Balkans (Sandfeld 1930), northwest Europe (Chambers and Trudgill 1980), South Asia (Masica 1976), South East Asia (Henderson 1965), and the Caucasus (Catford 1977) are all situated in Eurasia; sub-Saharan Africa (Greenberg 1959, 1984) is part of the African geographical area, and Meso-America (Campbell, Kaufman, and Smith-Stark 1986) is part of the Americas.

guaranteed to be supported by languages belonging to at least two distinct language areas.

It is important to note that constraint (iv) is intentionally chosen to be strong enough to remedy possibly controversial decisions that might have been made in UPSID-451 regarding the clustering of languages into genetic groups. Thus, the question of how the internal structure of a family tree has been determined –so long as the possible groupings are within the same geographical area– is of no practical importance for us. For instance, whether Hmong-Mien languages are assumed to be related to Sino-Tibetan (as done in UPSID-451) or to Austro-Tai (following Ruhlen 1987), an implication holding in, say, Hmong-Mien languages and Indo-European languages, but not in language(s) from another geographical area, cannot smuggle itself as a universal into our description since it will be considered by the program as an Eurasian areal generalization. Similarly, it does not matter whether, say, Nilo-Saharan is a valid language family (as UPSID-451 assumes following Greenberg 1963), whether it forms with Niger-Kordofanian a larger family (as assumed by e.g. Gregersen 1972) or whether either family is fictitious (as assumed e.g. by Dalby 1970). Whatever genetic affiliation we assume, with positive examples coming only from the geographical area of Africa, the system will not posit a universal. Finally, for analogous reasons the question whether a group of languages forms a genetic or an areal grouping (as in the case of the Caucasian languages for which both alternatives have their upholders) also cannot affect the universals to be discovered by the system. On the genetic affiliation assumption (taken in UPSID-451) an implication supported only in the Caucasus would be rejected as a genetic generalization, while on an areal affiliation assumption it would be rejected as an areal generalization. The particular reason for the rejection is of no interest insofar as our goal is concerned.

Summing up, the tuning of our system attempts to mimic the standard (manual) linguistic approach to the study of universals. It is well-known that observed similarities between languages, such as the implicational associations between two variables/segments I study here paper, can be due to one of the following reasons: (1) chance; (2) genetic affiliation between the languages; (3) areal contacts between the languages; (4) universal tendencies holding for all/most languages. The human analyst tries to eliminate (more accurately, minimize) the first three factors as a possible reason, so that ultimately we are left with just one option, viz. that a universal tendency is the most likely reason. Likewise, for each found implication in the database, our system inspects its probability of occurrence in the database comprising all languages, and if this probability is very low (meaning that chance can be safely excluded) it is required that the implication hold in several distinct language families/areas to discard the other two factors as a possible explanation.

Now, for the purposes of this computational experiment, we do not need the *authoring module* to generate a whole article, with all its discourse components (cf. Chapter 4 for checking what these components are). Rather, the discovery module here feeds the discovered patterns to the authoring module, together with their positive and negative examples, as well as the language families and geographical areas of both categories. And the system is restricted simply to the production of two paragraphs. The first paragraph states the universal itself, and the second one states the positive evidence in terms of number of supporting languages, language families and geographical areas, and (wherever applicable) the negative evidence in terms of counter-example languages. We need not go into the details of the generation process here (cf. Chapter 4), and will confine to saying that, for our particular task, we use a hybrid grammar consisting of templates (=canned text interspersed with variables, whose values are computed and inserted in the variable slots) and rules, which are randomly chosen from a set of alternative templates/rules in order to ensure variability of the text produced. For filling in the names of segments in the produced conditional sentences stating universals "If <Segment1>, then <Segment2>", the feature specifications of segments provided in UPSID-451 are used. The authoring module is also responsible for choosing the order of stating universals, the correct punctualization, capitalization, etc.

5.3 Computer verbalization of the implicational phonological universals in UPSID-451

The following description is structured as follows. First, universals are stated that hold between two segments of the same manner of articulation, and then follow those that hold between two segments with different manners of articulation. Within the first category, the universals are subcategorized according to the actual manner, in the order: plosives, implosives, ejective-stops, fricatives, affricates, approximants, nasals, and vowels (no patterns were found between diphthongs). Within the second category, universals are listed according to the antecedent of a universal, following a similar order. Every universal conforms to all of the four constraints given above. Its support in terms of number of relevant languages, their families and geographical areas are given, as well as eventual counter-evidence. The percentage of validity of each universal is also mentioned. The exact statistical significance is omitted from the text, since all patterns are highly significant (i.e. have equal or greater than 99% assurance of their being non-random). The entire text below is generated by UNIVAUTO, except for the headings, which were manually inserted (the ASCII–IPA symbol conversion is additionally done in MS Word by a further program of mine). Pericliev 2008, on which this chapter is based, states the system's discoveries only in terms of the participating segments and in a tabular form.

I. Universals involving segments of the same manner of articulation

I.1. Plosives

Universal 1. The presence of a voiced dental/alveolar plosive in a language implies the presence of a voiceless dental/alveolar plosive ([˝d ˝] → [˝t ˝]).
    Positive evidence for this pattern is provided by 82 languages belonging to 14 families from 4 geographical areas. The counter-examples in UPSID-451 are Khalkha, Berta, Eyak, Archi, Avar, Lak, Rutul, Adzera, and Mbabaram. The universal is supported in 82/91 or 90% of the languages in UPSID-451.
    Universal 2. The presence of a voiced dental/alveolar plosive in a language implies the presence of a voiced bilabial plosive ([˝d ˝] → [b]).
    This universal is supported in 89 languages from 16 families situated in 4 areas. The counter-examples in UPSID-451 are Sentani and Eyak. The percentage of validity of the pattern is 89/91 or 98%.
    Universal 3. The presence of a prenasalized voiced dental/alveolar plosive in a language implies the presence of a prenasalized voiced velar plosive ([ⁿd ˝] → [ᵑg]).
    Examples of this universal are 16 languages, members of 9 language families from 4 geographical areas. There is one counter-example, viz. Lai. The percentage of validity of the pattern is 16/17 or 94%.
    Universal 4. The presence of a prenasalized voiced dental/alveolar plosive in a language implies the presence of a prenasalized voiced bilabial plosive ([ⁿd ˝] → [ᵐb]).
    Positive evidence for this pattern is provided by 16 languages belonging to 9 families from 4 geographical areas. There is one counter-example, viz. Mazatec. The percentage of validity of the pattern is 16/17 or 94%.
    Universal 5. If a language has a voiceless dental/alveolar plosive then it also has a voiceless velar plosive ([˝t ˝] → [k]).

This universal is supported in 150 languages from 16 families situated in 4 areas. The exceptions to the pattern are Klao and Zuni. The percentage of validity of the pattern is 150/152 or 99%.

Universal 6. The presence of a palatalized voiceless dental/alveolar plosive in a language implies the presence of a voiceless dental/alveolar plosive ([″tʲ″] → [″t″]).

This pattern is corroborated in 11 languages from 7 families in 4 geographical areas. The pattern is exceptionless in UPSID-451 (11/11 or 100%).

Universal 7. A voiceless aspirated dental/alveolar plosive does not occur without a voiceless aspirated velar plosive ([″tʰ″] → [kʰ]).

Examples of this universal are 47 languages, members of 11 language families from 4 geographical areas. The counter-examples in UPSID-451 are Shiriana and Picuris. The universal is supported in 47/49 or 96% of the languages in UPSID-451.

Universal 8. If a language has a voiceless aspirated dental/alveolar plosive then it also has a voiceless aspirated bilabial plosive ([″tʰ″] → [pʰ]).

Examples of this universal are 45 languages, members of 11 language families from 4 geographical areas. The following languages are counter-examples: Eyak, Navajo, Shiriana, and Wichita. The percentage of validity of the pattern is 45/49 or 92%.

Universal 9. A prenasalized voiced velar plosive does not occur without a prenasalized voiced bilabial plosive ([ⁿg] → [ᵐb]).

This universal is supported in 44 languages from 11 families situated in 4 areas. There is one counter-example, viz. Mazatec. The percentage of validity of the pattern is 44/45 or 98%.

Universal 10. The presence of a prenasalized labialized voiced velar plosive in a language implies the presence of a prenasalized voiced velar plosive ([ⁿgʷ] → [ⁿg]).

Positive evidence for this pattern is provided by 10 languages belonging to 5 families from 4 geographical areas. There are no counter-examples to the pattern in UPSID-451 (10/10 or 100%).

Universal 11. The presence of a prenasalized labialized voiced velar plosive in a language implies the presence of a prenasalized voiced bilabial plosive ([ⁿgʷ] → [ᵐb]).

Positive evidence for this pattern is provided by 10 languages belonging to 5 families from 4 geographical areas. The pattern is exceptionless in UPSID-451 (10/10 or 100%).

Universal 12. If a language has a breathy voiced bilabial plosive then it also has a breathy voiced velar plosive ([b̤] → [g̤]).

This pattern is corroborated in 9 languages from 5 families in 2 geographical areas. This is an exceptionless universal (9/9 or 100%).

Universal 13. The presence of a breathy voiced bilabial plosive in a language implies the presence of a voiceless aspirated velar plosive ([b̤] → [kʰ]).

This universal is supported in 9 languages from 5 families situated in 2 areas. The pattern is exceptionless in UPSID-451 (9/9 or 100%).

Universal 14. The presence of a breathy voiced bilabial plosive in a language implies the presence of a voiceless aspirated bilabial plosive ([b̤] → [pʰ]).

Examples of this universal are 9 languages, members of 5 language families from 2 geographical areas. This is an exceptionless universal (9/9 or 100%).

Universal 15. If a language has a voiceless aspirated palatal plosive then it also has a voiceless aspirated bilabial plosive ([cʰ] → [pʰ]).

Examples of this universal are 16 languages, members of 6 language families from 2 geographical areas. An exception to the pattern is Hupa. The universal is supported in 16/17 or 94% of the languages in UPSID-451.

Universal 16. If a language has a voiced alveolar plosive then it also has a voiced bilabial plosive ([d] → [b]).

This pattern is corroborated in 116 languages from 15 families in 4 geographical areas. Gadsup, Irish, Wapishana, and Cherokee are negative instances to the universal. The percentage of validity of the pattern is 116/120 or 97%.

Universal 17. If a language has a laryngealized voiced alveolar plosive then it also has a laryngealized voiced bilabial plosive ([d̰] → [b̰]).

This pattern is corroborated in 7 languages from 4 families in 3 geographical areas. This is an exceptionless universal (7/7 or 100%).

Universal 18. If a language has a voiced retroflex plosive then it also has a voiced bilabial plosive ([d.] → [b]).

This universal is supported in 26 languages from 10 families situated in 4 areas. There is one counter-example, viz. Diyari. The universal is supported in 26/27 or 96% of the languages in UPSID-451.

Universal 19. A voiced retroflex plosive does not occur without a voiced velar plosive ([d.] → [g]).

This universal is supported in 26 languages from 10 families situated in 4 areas. Diyari is a negative instance to the universal. The universal is supported in 26/27 or 96% of the languages in UPSID-451.

Universal 20. If a language has a voiced dental plosive then it also has a voiced bilabial plosive ([d̪] → [b]).

This universal is supported in 78 languages from 15 families situated in 4 areas. Irish and Mixe are negative instances to the universal. The percentage of validity of the pattern is 78/80 or 98%.

Universal 21. If a language has a voiced dental plosive then it also has a voiced velar plosive ([d̪] → [g]).

Examples of this universal are 75 languages, members of 14 language families from 4 geographical areas. Kabardian, Thai, Andoke, Cayuvava, and Tehuelche are negative instances to the universal. The universal is supported in 75/80 or 94% of the languages in UPSID-451.

Universal 22. The presence of a voiced palatal plosive in a language implies the presence of a voiced bilabial plosive ([ɟ] → [b]).

This universal is supported in 43 languages from 12 families situated in 4 areas. There are no counter-examples to the pattern in UPSID-451 (43/43 or 100%).

Universal 23. A voiced palatal plosive does not occur without a voiced velar plosive ([ɟ] → [g]).

This universal is supported in 42 languages from 12 families situated in 4 areas. An exception to the pattern is Kwakw. The percentage of validity of the pattern is 42/43 or 98%.

Universal 24. A voiced velar plosive does not occur without a voiced bilabial plosive ([g] → [b]).

Positive evidence for this pattern is provided by 244 languages belonging to 17 families from 4 geographical areas. The exceptions to the pattern are Kewa, Rotokas, Eyak, Irish, Brao, Wapishana, Cherokee, Mazahua, and Mixe. The universal is supported in 244/253 or 96% of the languages in UPSID-451.

Universal 25. A labialized voiced velar plosive does not occur without a voiced velar plosive ([gʷ] → [g]).

Examples of this universal are 22 languages, members of 7 language families from 4 geographical areas. The counter-examples in UPSID-451 are Kabardian and Kwakw. The percentage of validity of the pattern is 22/24 or 92%.

Universal 26. If a language has a voiced labial-velar plosive then it also has a voiced bilabial plosive ([g͡b] → [b]).

This universal is supported in 39 languages from 5 families situated in 3 areas. The pattern is exceptionless in UPSID-451 (39/39 or 100%).

Universal 27. The presence of a voiced labial-velar plosive in a language implies the presence of a voiced velar plosive ([g͡b] → [g]).

Examples of this universal are 37 languages, members of 5 language families from 3 geographical areas. Klao and Temne are negative instances to the universal. The percentage of validity of the pattern is 37/39 or 95%.

Universal 28. A breathy voiced velar plosive does not occur without a breathy voiced bilabial plosive ([g] → [b̪]).

Examples of this universal are 9 languages, members of 5 language families from 2 geographical areas. !Xu is a negative instance to the universal. The percentage of validity of the pattern is 9/10 or 90%.

Universal 29. A breathy voiced velar plosive does not occur without a voiceless aspirated velar plosive ([g̤] → [kʰ]).

This universal is supported in 10 languages from 6 families situated in 2 areas. There are no counter-examples to the pattern in UPSID-451 (10/10 or 100%).

Universal 30. The presence of a breathy voiced velar plosive in a language implies the presence of a voiceless aspirated bilabial plosive ([g̤] → [pʰ]).

This pattern is corroborated in 10 languages from 6 families in 2 geographical areas. This is an exceptionless universal (10/10 or 100%).

Universal 31. A voiceless velar plosive does not occur without a voiceless bilabial plosive ([k] → [p]).

Examples of this universal are 368 languages, members of 18 language families from 4 geographical areas. The counter-examples in UPSID-451 are Amele, Chuave, Koiari, Kwoma, Yareba, Ket, Kunama, Maba, Nera, Nubian, Nyimang, Songhai, Tama, Aghem, Efik, Ewondo, Fe'fe', Noni, Yoruba, Aleut, Irarutu, Mor, Tiruray, Warao, Seneca, Wichita, Arabic, Beja, Dizi, Hausa, Kullo, Shilha, Socotri, Tamasheq, and Tigre. The percentage of validity of the pattern is 368/403 or 91%.

Universal 32. The presence of a labialized voiceless aspirated velar plosive in a language implies the presence of a voiceless aspirated velar plosive ([kʷʰ] → [kʰ]).

This universal is supported in 19 languages from 8 families situated in 3 areas. The exceptions to the pattern are Kabardian and Kwakw. The percentage of validity of the pattern is 19/21 or 90%.

Universal 33. A voiceless aspirated velar plosive does not occur without a voiceless aspirated bilabial plosive ([kʰ] → [pʰ]).

Positive evidence for this pattern is provided by 94 languages belonging to 14 families from 4 geographical areas. The exceptions to the pattern are Yessan-Mayo, Ahtna, Eyak, Navajo, Irish, Tzeltal, Wichita, Zuni, and Somali. The universal is supported in 94/103 or 91% of the languages in UPSID-451.

Universal 34. The presence of a prenasalized voiced bilabial plosive in a language implies the presence of a prenasalized voiced velar plosive ([ᵐb] → [ᵑg]).

This universal is supported in 44 languages from 11 families situated in 4 areas. The counter-examples in UPSID-451 are Kewa, Konyagi, Lai, and Sama. The universal is supported in 44/48 or 92% of the languages in UPSID-451.

Universal 35. The presence of a prenasalized voiced alveolar plosive in a language implies the presence of a prenasalized voiced velar plosive ($[^n d]$ → $[^\eta g]$).

Examples of this universal are 24 languages, members of 8 language families from 4 geographical areas. Kewa and Konyagi are negative instances to the universal. The percentage of validity of the pattern is 24/26 or 92%.

Universal 36. The presence of a prenasalized voiced alveolar plosive in a language implies the presence of a prenasalized voiced bilabial plosive ($[^n d]$ → $[^m b]$).

This pattern is corroborated in 26 languages from 8 families in 4 geographical areas. This is an exceptionless universal (26/26 or 100%).

Universal 37. A prenasalized voiced alveolar plosive does not occur without a voiceless alveolar plosive ($[^n d]$ → $[t]$).

This universal is supported in 25 languages from 8 families situated in 4 areas. An exception to the pattern is Yessan-Mayo. The percentage of validity of the pattern is 25/26 or 96%.

Universal 38. If a language has a voiceless bilabial plosive then it also has a voiceless velar plosive ($[p]$ → $[k]$).

Positive evidence for this pattern is provided by 368 languages belonging to 18 families from 4 geographical areas. The counter-examples in UPSID-451 are Usan, Vanimo, Beembe, Klao, Bella, Tzeltal, and Zuni. The universal is supported in 368/375 or 98% of the languages in UPSID-451.

Universal 39. A voiceless aspirated bilabial plosive does not occur without a voiceless aspirated velar plosive ($[p^h]$ → $[k^h]$).

This pattern is corroborated in 94 languages from 14 families in 4 geographical areas. Tiddim, Kabardian, Brao, Yucuna, Kwakw, Picuris, and Wintu are negative instances to the universal. The universal is supported in 94/101 or 93% of the languages in UPSID-451.

Universal 40. A labialized voiceless uvular plosive does not occur without a labialized voiceless velar plosive ($[q^w]$ → $[k^w]$).

Examples of this universal are 12 languages, members of 4 language families from 2 geographical areas. This is an exceptionless universal (12/12 or 100%).

Universal 41. The presence of a labialized voiceless uvular plosive in a language implies the presence of a voiceless uvular plosive ($[q^w]$ → $[q]$).

Positive evidence for this pattern is provided by 12 languages belonging to 4 families from 2 geographical areas. The pattern is exceptionless in UPSID-451 (12/12 or 100%).

Universal 42. If a language has a voiceless aspirated uvular plosive then it also has a voiceless aspirated velar plosive ([qʰ] → [kʰ]).

This pattern is corroborated in 16 languages from 7 families in 2 geographical areas. An exception to the pattern is Kwakw. The universal is supported in 16/17 or 94% of the languages in UPSID-451.

Universal 43. If a language has a voiceless alveolar plosive then it also has a voiceless velar plosive ([t] → [k]).

Examples of this universal are 174 languages, members of 15 language families from 4 geographical areas. The following languages are counter-examples: Kewa, Usan, Vanimo, Beembe, Kohumono, Hupa, and Kwaio. The universal is supported in 174/181 or 96% of the languages in UPSID-451.

Universal 44. If a language has a voiceless dental plosive then it also has a voiceless velar plosive ([t̪] → [k]).

Examples of this universal are 104 languages, members of 16 language families from 4 geographical areas. The exceptions to the pattern are Bella and Tzeltal. The percentage of validity of the pattern is 104/106 or 98%.

Universal 45. If a language has a voiceless aspirated dental plosive then it also has a voiceless aspirated velar plosive ([t̪ʰ] → [kʰ]).

Positive evidence for this pattern is provided by 27 languages belonging to 12 families from 4 geographical areas. The counter-examples in UPSID-451 are Kabardian, Vietnamese, and Guahibo. The universal is supported in 27/30 or 90% of the languages in UPSID-451.

Universal 46. A voiceless palato-alveolar plosive does not occur without a voiceless alveolar plosive ([t̠] → [t]).

This universal is supported in 18 languages from 6 families situated in 4 areas. The following languages are counter-examples: Panare and Highland. The percentage of validity of the pattern is 18/20 or 90%.

I.2. Implosives

Universal 47. If a language has a voiced alveolar implosive then it also has a voiced bilabial implosive ([ɗ] → [ɓ]).

Examples of this universal are 23 languages, members of 7 language families from 3 geographical areas. There are no counter-examples to the pattern in UPSID-451 (23/23 or 100%).

I.3. Ejective-stops

Universal 48. If a language has a voiceless dental/alveolar ejective-stop then it also has a voiceless velar ejective-stop ([''t' ''] → [k']).

This pattern is corroborated in 24 languages from 6 families in 3 geographical areas. The pattern is exceptionless in UPSID-451 (24/24 or 100%).

Universal 49. A voiceless bilabial ejective-stop does not occur without a voiceless velar ejective-stop ([p'] → [k']).

Positive evidence for this pattern is provided by 41 languages belonging to 10 families from 3 geographical areas. The exceptions to the pattern are Kabardian, Bella, and Kwakw. The universal is supported in 41/44 or 93% of the languages in UPSID-451.

Universal 50. The presence of a labialized voiceless uvular ejective-stop in a language implies the presence of a labialized voiceless velar ejective-stop ([qʷ'] → [kʷ']).

This universal is supported in 11 languages from 3 families situated in 2 areas. This is an exceptionless universal (11/11 or 100%).

Universal 51. If a language has a labialized voiceless uvular ejective-stop then it also has a voiceless bilabial ejective-stop ([qʷ'] → [p']).

Examples of this universal are 10 languages, members of 3 language families from 2 geographical areas. Haida is a negative instance to the universal. The percentage of validity of the pattern is 10/11 or 91%.

Universal 52. A labialized voiceless uvular ejective-stop does not occur without a voiceless uvular ejective-stop ([qʷ'] → [q']).

This pattern is corroborated in 11 languages from 3 families in 2 geographical areas. The pattern is exceptionless in UPSID-451 (11/11 or 100%).

Universal 53. If a language has a voiceless alveolar ejective-stop then it also has a voiceless velar ejective-stop ([t'] → [k']).

This pattern is corroborated in 22 languages from 7 families in 2 geographical areas. The following languages are counter-examples: Hupa and Kwakw. The universal is supported in 22/24 or 92% of the languages in UPSID-451.

Universal 54. If a language has a voiceless dental ejective-stop then it also has a voiceless bilabial ejective-stop ([tð'] → [p']).

This universal is supported in 15 languages from 5 families situated in 3 areas. There is one counter-example, viz. Tigre. The universal is supported in 15/16 or 94% of the languages in UPSID-451.

I.4. Fricatives

Universal 55. The presence of a voiced dental/alveolar sibilant fricative in a language implies the presence of a voiceless dental/alveolar sibilant fricative ([z̋] → [s̋]).
This universal is supported in 43 languages from 13 families situated in 4 areas. There are no counter-examples to the pattern in UPSID-451 (43/43 or 100%).

Universal 56. The presence of a voiced pharyngeal fricative in a language implies the presence of a voiceless pharyngeal fricative ([ʕ] → [ħ]).

Examples of this universal are 10 languages, members of 4 language families from 2 geographical areas. There are no counter-examples to the pattern in UPSID-451 (10/10 or 100%).

Universal 57. A labialized voiceless uvular fricative does not occur without a voiceless uvular fricative ([χʷ] → [χ]).

Examples of this universal are 14 languages, members of 4 language families from 2 geographical areas. The pattern is exceptionless in UPSID-451 (14/14 or 100%).

Universal 58. If a language has a labialized voiceless uvular fricative then it also has a labialized voiceless velar fricative ([χʷ] → [xʷ]).

This pattern is corroborated in 13 languages from 4 families in 2 geographical areas. Archi is a negative instance to the universal. The percentage of validity of the pattern is 13/14 or 93%.

Universal 59. If a language has a voiced palato-alveolar sibilant fricative then it also has a voiceless palato-alveolar sibilant fricative ([ʒ] → [ʃ]).

This pattern is corroborated in 58 languages from 13 families in 3 geographical areas. The counter-examples in UPSID-451 are Mbum, Atayal, and Apinaye. The percentage of validity of the pattern is 58/61 or 95%.

Universal 60. If a language has a voiced alveolar sibilant fricative then it also has a voiceless alveolar sibilant fricative ([z] → [s]).

This universal is supported in 62 languages from 15 families situated in 4 areas. The pattern is exceptionless in UPSID-451 (62/62 or 100%).

Universal 61. The presence of a voiced dental sibilant fricative in a language implies the presence of a voiceless dental sibilant fricative ([z̪] → [s̪]).

Positive evidence for this pattern is provided by 16 languages belonging to 6 families from 2 geographical areas. There is one counter-example, viz. Bai. The percentage of validity of the pattern is 16/17 or 94%.

I.5. Affricates

Universal 62. The presence of a voiced palatal affricate in a language implies the presence of a voiceless palatal affricate ([ɟʝ] → [cç]).
Examples of this universal are 8 languages, members of 5 language families from 3 geographical areas. The pattern is exceptionless in UPSID-451 (8/8 or 100%).

 Universal 63. The presence of a voiceless alveolar lateral ejective-affricate in a language implies the presence of a voiceless alveolar sibilant ejective-affricate ([tɬ'] → [ts']).
 Examples of this universal are 9 languages, members of 4 language families from 2 geographical areas. There are no counter-examples to the pattern in UPSID-451 (9/9 or 100%).

I.6. Approximants

Universal 64. A voiceless dental/alveolar lateral approximant does not occur without a voiced dental/alveolar lateral approximant ([̥l ̈] → [̈l ̈]).
Examples of this universal are 10 languages, members of 7 language families from 2 geographical areas. The pattern is exceptionless in UPSID-451 (10/10 or 100%).

 Universal 65. The presence of a voiceless palatal approximant in a language implies the presence of a voiceless labial-velar approximant ([j̊] → [ʍ]).
 Positive evidence for this pattern is provided by 9 languages belonging to 6 families from 2 geographical areas. The pattern is exceptionless in UPSID-451 (9/9 or 100%).

 Universal 66. A voiced labial-velar approximant does not occur without a voiced palatal approximant ([w] → [j]).
 Examples of this universal are 310 languages, members of 18 language families from 4 geographical areas. Moghol, Hakka, Hmong, Amele, Asmat, Baining, South-Kiwai, Fe'fe', Klao, Gelao, Hawaiian, Iai, Irarutu, Kwaio, Lenakel, Tetun, Auca, Cacua, Ticuna, Wapishana, Tzeltal, and Wichita are negative instances to the universal. The percentage of validity of the pattern is 310/332 or 93%.

I.7. Nasals

Universal 67. If a language has a voiceless dental/alveolar nasal then it also has a voiceless bilabial nasal ([̈n̥ ̈] → [m̥]).

Examples of this universal are 9 languages, members of 5 language families from 2 geographical areas. The pattern is exceptionless in UPSID-451 (9/9 or 100%).

Universal 68. The presence of a voiced velar nasal in a language implies the presence of a voiced bilabial nasal ([ŋ] → [m]).

This pattern is corroborated in 235 languages from 17 families in 4 geographical areas. The exceptions to the pattern are Irish and Mixtec. The universal is supported in 235/237 or 99% of the languages in UPSID-451.

Universal 69. A voiceless velar nasal does not occur without a voiceless bilabial nasal ([ŋ̊] → [m̥]).

Positive evidence for this pattern is provided by 9 languages belonging to 5 families from 2 geographical areas. There are no counter-examples to the pattern in UPSID-451 (9/9 or 100%).

Universal 70. If a language has a voiceless palatal nasal then it also has a voiceless bilabial nasal ([ɲ̊] → [m̥]).

Positive evidence for this pattern is provided by 8 languages belonging to 5 families from 2 geographical areas. There are no counter-examples to the pattern in UPSID-451 (8/8 or 100%).

Universal 71. If a language has a voiced alveolar nasal then it also has a voiced bilabial nasal ([n] → [m]).

This universal is supported in 200 languages from 17 families situated in 4 areas. The counter-examples in UPSID-451 are Konkani and South Nambiquara. The percentage of validity of the pattern is 200/202 or 99%.

Universal 72. The presence of a voiced palatal nasal in a language implies the presence of a voiced bilabial nasal ([ɲ] → [m]).

This universal is supported in 141 languages from 15 families situated in 4 areas. The pattern is exceptionless in UPSID-451 (141/141 or 100%).

I.8. Vowels

Universal 73. A nasalized mid central unrounded vowel does not occur without a nasalized high front unrounded vowel ([ə̃] → [ĩ]).
This pattern is corroborated in 11 languages from 5 families in 4 geographical areas. Cherokee is a negative instance to the universal. The universal is supported in 11/12 or 92% of the languages in UPSID-451.

Universal 74. If a language has a long mid front unrounded vowel then it also has a long mid back rounded vowel ([e:] → [o:]).

This universal is supported in 10 languages from 6 families situated in 3 areas. Noni is a negative instance to the universal. The percentage of validity of the pattern is 10/11 or 91%.

Universal 75. The presence of a nasalized mid front unrounded vowel in a language implies the presence of a mid front unrounded vowel ([̈ẽ ̈] → [̈e ̈]).

Positive evidence for this pattern is provided by 31 languages belonging to 7 families from 4 geographical areas. The exceptions to the pattern are Dan and Yuchi. The percentage of validity of the pattern is 31/33 or 94%.

Universal 76. If a language has a nasalized mid back rounded vowel then it also has a mid back rounded vowel ([̈õ ̈] → [̈o ̈]).

Positive evidence for this pattern is provided by 33 languages belonging to 8 families from 4 geographical areas. Dan and Yuchi are negative instances to the universal. The universal is supported in 33/35 or 94% of the languages in UPSID-451.

Universal 77. The presence of a nasalized lower-mid front unrounded vowel in a language implies the presence of a lower-mid front unrounded vowel ([ɛ̃] → [ɛ]).

This universal is supported in 34 languages from 7 families situated in 4 areas. Seneca is a negative instance to the universal. The universal is supported in 34/35 or 97% of the languages in UPSID-451.

Universal 78. A nasalized lower-mid back rounded vowel does not occur without a lower-mid back rounded vowel ([ɔ̃] → [ɔ]).

Positive evidence for this pattern is provided by 29 languages belonging to 6 families from 4 geographical areas. The counter-examples in UPSID-451 are Breton, Highland, and Seneca. The percentage of validity of the pattern is 29/32 or 91%.

Universal 79. A long raised low front unrounded vowel does not occur without a long high front unrounded vowel [æ:] → [i:].

Positive evidence for this pattern is provided by 8 languages belonging to 4 families from 2 geographical areas. This is an exceptionless universal (8/8 or 100%).

Universal 80. The presence of a long raised low front unrounded vowel in a language implies the presence of a long high back rounded vowel ([æ:] → [u:]).

Positive evidence for this pattern is provided by 8 languages belonging to 4 families from 2 geographical areas. There are no counter-examples to the pattern in UPSID-451 (8/8 or 100%).

Universal 81. If a language has a nasalized low central unrounded vowel then it also has a low central unrounded vowel ([ã] → [a]).

This pattern is corroborated in 82 languages from 10 families in 4 geographical areas. Kashmiri is a negative instance to the universal. The percentage of validity of the pattern is 82/83 or 99%.

Universal 82. If a language has a higher-mid front unrounded vowel then it also has a high back rounded vowel ([e] → [u]).

Positive evidence for this pattern is provided by 116 languages belonging to 15 families from 4 geographical areas. Uzbek, Ewondo, Ormuri, Vietnamese, Amuesha, Campa, Yagua, and Alabama are negative instances to the universal. The universal is supported in 116/124 or 94% of the languages in UPSID-451.

Universal 83. A long higher-mid front unrounded vowel does not occur without a long higher-mid back rounded vowel ([e:] → [o:]).

This pattern is corroborated in 20 languages from 9 families in 4 geographical areas. There is one counter-example, viz. Norwegian. The percentage of validity of the pattern is 20/21 or 95%.

Universal 84. The presence of a nasalized higher-mid front unrounded vowel in a language implies the presence of a higher-mid front unrounded vowel ([ẽ] → [e]).

Positive evidence for this pattern is provided by 17 languages belonging to 5 families from 4 geographical areas. There is one counter-example, viz. Bats. The universal is supported in 17/18 or 94% of the languages in UPSID-451.

Universal 85. If a language has a nasalized higher-mid front unrounded vowel then it also has a nasalized high front unrounded vowel ([ẽ] → [ĩ]).

Examples of this universal are 18 languages, members of 6 language families from 4 geographical areas. There are no counter-examples to the pattern in UPSID-451 (18/18 or 100%).

Universal 86. If a language has a nasalized higher-mid front unrounded vowel then it also has a nasalized high back rounded vowel ([ẽ] → [ũ]).

Positive evidence for this pattern is provided by 17 languages belonging to 6 families from 4 geographical areas. Yagua is a negative instance to the universal. The percentage of validity of the pattern is 17/18 or 94%.

Universal 87. If a language has a high front unrounded vowel then it also has a high back rounded vowel ([i] → [u]).

Positive evidence for this pattern is provided by 360 languages belonging to 18 families from 4 geographical areas. Bashkir, Japanese, Uzbek, Nimboran, Noni, Haida, Adzera, Malagasy, Maranao, Malakmalak, Murinhpatha, Wik-Munkan, Abipon, Auca, Cacua, Campa, Cayapa, Cofan, Jaqaru, Maxakali, Ocaina, Piraha, Resigaro, Shiriana, Tacana, Yagua, Hopi, Karok, Klamath, Mazatec, Nahuatl, Tseshaht, and Somali are negative instances to the universal. The percentage of validity of the pattern is 360/393 or 92%.

Universal 88. If a language has a long high front unrounded vowel then it also has a long high back rounded vowel ([i:] → [u:]).

This universal is supported in 36 languages from 13 families situated in 4 areas. The following languages are counter-examples: Navajo, Adzera, Karok, and Ojibwa. The percentage of validity of the pattern is 36/40 or 90%.

Universal 89. A nasalized high front unrounded vowel does not occur without a high front unrounded vowel ([ĩ] → [i]).

This universal is supported in 82 languages from 10 families situated in 4 areas. This is an exceptionless universal (82/82 or 100%).

Universal 90. A long nasalized high front unrounded vowel does not occur without a long high front unrounded vowel ([ĩ:] → [i:]).

Positive evidence for this pattern is provided by 8 languages belonging to 4 families from 2 geographical areas. The pattern is exceptionless in UPSID-451 (8/8 or 100%).

Universal 91. The presence of a nasalized higher-mid back rounded vowel in a language implies the presence of a higher-mid back rounded vowel ([õ] → [o]).

This pattern is corroborated in 25 languages from 7 families in 4 geographical areas. French and Lakkia are negative instances to the universal. The universal is supported in 25/27 or 93% of the languages in UPSID-451.

Universal 92. If a language has a high back rounded vowel then it also has a high front unrounded vowel ([u] → [i]).

This pattern is corroborated in 360 languages from 18 families in 4 geographical areas. The following languages are counter-examples: Even, Selkup, Yukaghir, Basque, Chukchi, Nivkh, Pohnpeian, Hixkaryana, and Angas. The universal is supported in 360/369 or 98% of the languages in UPSID-451.

Universal 93. If a language has a long high back rounded vowel then it also has a long high front unrounded vowel ([u:] → [i:]).

This universal is supported in 36 languages from 13 families situated in 4 areas. The pattern is exceptionless in UPSID-451 (36/36 or 100%).

Universal 94. A nasalized high back rounded vowel does not occur without a nasalized low central unrounded vowel ([ũ] → [ã]).

Positive evidence for this pattern is provided by 67 languages belonging to 10 families from 4 geographical areas. Newari, Yoruba, Eyak, Bats, Chatino, Kiowa, and Picuris are negative instances to the universal. The universal is supported in 67/74 or 91% of the languages in UPSID-451.

Universal 95. The presence of a nasalized high back rounded vowel in a language implies the presence of a high front unrounded vowel ([ũ] → [i]).

Positive evidence for this pattern is provided by 74 languages belonging to 12 families from 4 geographical areas. There are no counter-examples to the pattern in UPSID-451 (74/74 or 100%).

Universal 96. The presence of a nasalized high back rounded vowel in a language implies the presence of a nasalized high front unrounded vowel ([ũ] → [ĩ]).

Positive evidence for this pattern is provided by 69 languages belonging to 10 families from 4 geographical areas. Songhai, Sango, Lakkia, Bribri, and Huari are negative instances to the universal. The percentage of validity of the pattern is 69/74 or 93%.

Universal 97. A nasalized high back rounded vowel does not occur without a high back rounded vowel ([ũ] → [u]).

This universal is supported in 74 languages from 12 families situated in 4 areas. The pattern is exceptionless in UPSID-451 (74/74 or 100%).

II. Universals involving segments of different manner of articulation

II.1. Plosive antecedent

Universal 98. If a language has a voiced dental/alveolar plosive then it also has a voiced dental/alveolar nasal ([̈d ̈] → [̈n ̈]).
This universal is supported in 87 languages from 16 families situated in 4 areas. The exceptions to the pattern are Yakut, Maba, Klao, and Lithuanian. The universal is supported in 87/91 or 96% of the languages in UPSID-451.

Universal 99. If a language has a voiceless dental/alveolar plosive then it also has a voiced dental/alveolar nasal ([̈t ̈] → [̈n ̈]).

This universal is supported in 138 languages from 16 families situated in 4 areas. The counter-examples in UPSID-451 are Yakut, Hakka, Mandarin, Taoripi, Waris, Maba, Klao, Lithuanian, Ache, Piraha, Siriono, Mazatec, Mixtec, and Tonkawa. The percentage of validity of the pattern is 138/152 or 91%.

Universal 100. A voiceless aspirated dental/alveolar plosive does not occur without a voiced dental/alveolar nasal ([̈tʰ ̈] → [̈n ̈]).

This pattern is corroborated in 46 languages from 11 families in 4 geographical areas. The following languages are counter-examples: Hakka, Mandarin, and South Nambiquara. The universal is supported in 46/49 or 94% of the languages in UPSID-451.

Universal 101. The presence of a voiced labial-velar plosive in a language implies the presence of a lower-mid front unrounded vowel ([g͡b] → [ɛ]).

This pattern is corroborated in 35 languages from 5 families in 3 geographical areas. The counter-examples in UPSID-451 are Dagbani, Gwari, Mbum, and Tarok. The percentage of validity of the pattern is 35/39 or 90%.

Universal 102. If a language has a voiced labial-velar plosive then it also has a voiceless labiodental fricative ([g͡b] → [f]).

This universal is supported in 39 languages from 5 families situated in 3 areas. This is an exceptionless universal (39/39 or 100%).

Universal 103. If a language has a labialized voiceless uvular plosive then it also has a labialized voiceless velar fricative ([qʷ] → [xʷ]).

This pattern is corroborated in 11 languages from 4 families in 2 geographical areas. Awiya is a negative instance to the universal. The percentage of validity of the pattern is 11/12 or 92%.

Universal 104. The presence of a voiceless palato-alveolar plosive in a language implies the presence of a voiced alveolar nasal ([t̠] → [n]).

This universal is supported in 18 languages from 6 families situated in 4 areas. The exceptions to the pattern are Panare and Highland. The universal is supported in 18/20 or 90% of the languages in UPSID-451.

Universal 105. If a language has a voiceless palato-alveolar plosive then it also has a voiced palato-alveolar nasal ([t̠] → [n̠]).

Positive evidence for this pattern is provided by 18 languages belonging to 5 families from 3 geographical areas. The following languages are counter-examples: Ejagham and Panare. The percentage of validity of the pattern is 18/20 or 90%.

II.2. Implosive antecedent

Universal 106. A voiced dental/alveolar implosive does not occur without a voiced dental/alveolar nasal (["d "] → ["n "]).
Positive evidence for this pattern is provided by 13 languages belonging to 6 families from 3 geographical areas. An exception to the pattern is South Nambiquara. The universal is supported in 13/14 or 93% of the languages in UPSID-451.

Universal 107. The presence of a voiced alveolar implosive in a language implies the presence of a voiced alveolar nasal ([ɗ] → [n]).

Examples of this universal are 22 languages, members of 7 language families from 3 geographical areas. An exception to the pattern is Vietnamese. The percentage of validity of the pattern is 22/23 or 96%.

II.3. Ejective-stop antecedent

Universal 108. If a language has a voiceless dental/alveolar ejective-stop then it also has a voiced dental/alveolar nasal (["t' "] → ["n "]).

This universal is supported in 24 languages from 6 families situated in 3 areas. The pattern is exceptionless in UPSID-451 (24/24 or 100%).

Universal 109. A labialized voiceless velar ejective-stop does not occur without a glottal plosive ([kʷ'] → [ʔ]).

This pattern is corroborated in 22 languages from 6 families in 3 geographical areas. Amharic is a negative instance to the universal. The percentage of validity of the pattern is 22/23 or 96%.

Universal 110. The presence of a voiceless bilabial ejective-stop in a language implies the presence of a voiceless h-sound ([p'] → [h]).

Examples of this universal are 40 languages, members of 8 language families from 3 geographical areas. Itelmen, Tlingit, Kabardian, and Jaqaru are negative instances to the universal. The percentage of validity of the pattern is 40/44 or 91%.

Universal 111. If a language has a labialized voiceless uvular ejective-stop then it also has a voiceless uvular fricative ([qʷ'] → [χ]).

This universal is supported in 11 languages from 3 families situated in 2 areas. There are no counter-examples to the pattern in UPSID-451 (11/11 or 100%).

Universal 112. The presence of a labialized voiceless uvular ejective-stop in a language implies the presence of a labialized voiceless uvular fricative ([qʷ'] → [χʷ]).

This universal is supported in 11 languages from 3 families situated in 2 areas. This is an exceptionless universal (11/11 or 100%).

Universal 113. The presence of a labialized voiceless uvular ejective-stop in a language implies the presence of a labialized voiceless velar fricative ([qʷ'] → [xʷ]).

Positive evidence for this pattern is provided by 11 languages belonging to 3 families from 2 geographical areas. The pattern is exceptionless in UPSID-451 (11/11 or 100%).

II.4. Sibilant fricative antecedent

Universal 114. The presence of a voiced dental/alveolar sibilant fricative in a language implies the presence of a voiced dental/alveolar nasal ([z̈] → [n̈]).

This pattern is corroborated in 42 languages from 13 families in 4 geographical areas. An exception to the pattern is Hindi-Urdu. The percentage of validity of the pattern is 42/43 or 98%.

Universal 115. A voiceless palato-alveolar sibilant fricative does not occur without a voiced palatal approximant ([ʃ] → [j]).

This universal is supported in 171 languages from 17 families situated in 4 areas. The following languages are counter-examples: Moghol, Monguor, Hmong, Phlong, Basque, Nubian, Inuit, Georgian, Iai, Parauk, Muinane, Ocaina, Wapishana, Huasteco, Mixtec, and Ojibwa. The percentage of validity of the pattern is 171/187 or 91%.

Universal 116. A voiced alveolar sibilant fricative does not occur without a voiced bilabial plosive ([z] → [b]).

Positive evidence for this pattern is provided by 56 languages belonging to 11 families from 4 geographical areas. The counter-examples in UPSID-451 are Ao, Savosavo, Nivkh, Zulu, Georgian, and Vietnamese. The percentage of validity of the pattern is 56/62 or 90%.

Universal 117. The presence of a voiced alveolar sibilant fricative in a language implies the presence of a voiced velar plosive ([z] → [g]).

This universal is supported in 56 languages from 11 families situated in 4 areas. The following languages are counter-examples: Ao, Savosavo, Nivkh, Zulu, Georgian, and Vietnamese. The universal is supported in 56/62 or 90% of the languages in UPSID-451.

II.5. Affricate antecedent

Universal 118. A voiceless aspirated dental/alveolar sibilant affricate does not occur without a voiceless dental/alveolar sibilant fricative ([″tsʰ ″] → [″s ″]). Positive evidence for this pattern is provided by 23 languages belonging to 7 families from 2 geographical areas. The exceptions to the pattern are Lakkia and Iate. The percentage of validity of the pattern is 23/25 or 92%.

Universal 119. The presence of a voiceless aspirated dental/alveolar sibilant affricate in a language implies the presence of a voiceless aspirated velar plosive ([″tsʰ ″] → [kʰ]).

This pattern is corroborated in 24 languages from 8 families in 2 geographical areas. Chipewyan is a negative instance to the universal. The percentage of validity of the pattern is 24/25 or 96%.

Universal 120. If a language has a voiced palato-alveolar sibilant affricate then it also has a voiced bilabial plosive ([dʒ] → [b]).

This pattern is corroborated in 108 languages from 17 families in 4 geographical areas. The exceptions to the pattern are Zulu, Eyak, Irish, Ache, and Achumawi. The universal is supported in 108/113 or 96% of the languages in UPSID-451.

Universal 121. The presence of a voiced palato-alveolar sibilant affricate in a language implies the presence of a voiced velar plosive ([dʒ] → [g]).

Positive evidence for this pattern is provided by 105 languages belonging to 17 families from 4 geographical areas. The following languages are counter-examples: Yawa, Zulu, Khasi, Ache, Andoke, Cayuvava, Achumawi, and Wintu. The percentage of validity of the pattern is 105/113 or 93%.

Universal 122. A breathy voiced palato-alveolar sibilant affricate does not occur without a breathy voiced velar plosive ([d̤ʒ] → [g]).

Positive evidence for this pattern is provided by 7 languages belonging to 4 families from 2 geographical areas. This is an exceptionless universal (7/7 or 100%).

Universal 123. A voiced alveolar sibilant affricate does not occur without a voiced bilabial plosive ([dz] → [b]).

This universal is supported in 23 languages from 11 families situated in 4 areas. There is one counter-example, viz. Cherokee. The percentage of validity of the pattern is 23/24 or 96%.

Universal 124. If a language has a voiced alveolar sibilant affricate then it also has a voiced velar plosive ([dz] → [g]).

This universal is supported in 23 languages from 11 families situated in 4 areas. Kwakw is a negative instance to the universal. The percentage of validity of the pattern is 23/24 or 96%.

Universal 125. If a language has a voiced alveolar sibilant affricate then it also has a voiceless alveolar sibilant fricative ([dz] → [s]).

Examples of this universal are 22 languages, members of 10 language families from 4 geographical areas. The exceptions to the pattern are Chamorro and Cherokee. The percentage of validity of the pattern is 22/24 or 92%.

Universal 126. A prenasalized voiced palato-alveolar sibilant affricate does not occur without a prenasalized voiced velar plosive ([^{n}dʒ] → [^{n}g]).

Positive evidence for this pattern is provided by 9 languages belonging to 7 families from 4 geographical areas. Sama is a negative instance to the universal. The percentage of validity of the pattern is 9/10 or 90%.

Universal 127. A prenasalized voiced palato-alveolar sibilant affricate does not occur without a prenasalized voiced bilabial plosive ([^{n}dʒ] → [^{m}b]).

Positive evidence for this pattern is provided by 9 languages belonging to 7 families from 4 geographical areas. There is one counter-example, viz. Mazatec. The universal is supported in 9/10 or 90% of the languages in UPSID-451.

Universal 128. The presence of a voiceless palato-alveolar sibilant affricate in a language implies the presence of a voiceless velar plosive ([tʃ] → [k]).

Positive evidence for this pattern is provided by 182 languages belonging to 16 families from 4 geographical areas. Alamblak, Kohumono, Hupa, Farsi, Irish, and Somali are negative instances to the universal. The percentage of validity of the pattern is 182/188 or 97%.

Universal 129. A voiceless palato-alveolar sibilant affricate does not occur without a voiceless bilabial plosive ([tʃ] → [p]).

Positive evidence for this pattern is provided by 172 languages belonging to 16 families from 4 geographical areas. The counter-examples in UPSID-451 are Alamblak, Kwoma, Kunama, Nubian, Aghem, Fe'fe', Kohumono, Noni, Hupa, Farsi, Irish, Dizi, Hausa, Kullo, Somali, and Tigre. The percentage of validity of the pattern is 172/188 or 91%.

Universal 130. A voiceless aspirated palato-alveolar sibilant affricate does not occur without a voiceless aspirated velar plosive ([tʃʰ] → [kʰ]).

This pattern is corroborated in 48 languages from 13 families in 3 geographical areas. The counter-examples in UPSID-451 are Monguor, Chipewyan, and Amuesha. The percentage of validity of the pattern is 48/51 or 94%.

Universal 131. A voiceless dental/alveolar lateral ejective-affricate does not occur without a voiceless dental/alveolar lateral fricative ([˝tɬ' ˝] → [˝ɬ ˝]).

This pattern is corroborated in 10 languages from 5 families in 3 geographical areas. An exception to the pattern is Chipewyan. The percentage of validity of the pattern is 10/11 or 91%.

Universal 132. The presence of a voiceless dental/alveolar lateral ejective-affricate in a language implies the presence of a voiceless velar ejective-stop ([˝tɬ' ˝] → [k']).

This pattern is corroborated in 10 languages from 5 families in 3 geographical areas. Bella is a negative instance to the universal. The percentage of validity of the pattern is 10/11 or 91%.

Universal 133. The presence of a voiceless dental/alveolar sibilant ejective-affricate in a language implies the presence of a voiced dental/alveolar nasal ([˝ts' ˝] → [˝n ˝]).

Examples of this universal are 17 languages, members of 5 language families from 3 geographical areas. The pattern is exceptionless in UPSID-451 (17/17 or 100%).

Universal 134. If a language has a voiceless dental/alveolar sibilant ejective-affricate then it also has a voiceless dental/alveolar sibilant fricative ([˝ts' ˝] → [˝s ˝]).

This universal is supported in 17 languages from 5 families situated in 3 areas. There are no counter-examples to the pattern in UPSID-451 (17/17 or 100%).

Universal 135. A voiceless dental/alveolar sibilant ejective-affricate does not occur without a voiceless velar ejective-stop ([˝ts' ˝] → [k']).

Positive evidence for this pattern is provided by 17 languages belonging to 5 families from 3 geographical areas. There are no counter-examples to the pattern in UPSID-451 (17/17 or 100%).

Universal 136. A voiceless palato-alveolar sibilant ejective-affricate does not occur without a voiceless velar ejective-stop ([tʃ'] → [k']).

Positive evidence for this pattern is provided by 43 languages belonging to 8 families from 3 geographical areas. An exception to the pattern is Hupa. The universal is supported in 43/44 or 98% of the languages in UPSID-451.

Universal 137. The presence of a voiceless alveolar sibilant ejective-affricate in a language implies the presence of a voiceless alveolar sibilant fricative ([ts'] → [s]).

Positive evidence for this pattern is provided by 24 languages belonging to 7 families from 3 geographical areas. The following languages are counter-examples: Huasteco and Pomo. The percentage of validity of the pattern is 24/26 or 92%.

II.6. Miscellaneous antecedents

Universal 138. If a language has a voiced dental/alveolar r-sound then it also has a voiced dental/alveolar nasal ([″rr ″] → [″n ″]).

Positive evidence for this pattern is provided by 33 languages belonging to 12 families from 4 geographical areas. The following languages are counter-examples: Waris, Yana, and Beja. The percentage of validity of the pattern is 33/36 or 92%.

Universal 139. If a language has a voiced dental/alveolar r-sound then it also has a voiced labial-velar approximant ([″rr ″] → [w]).

Positive evidence for this pattern is provided by 35 languages belonging to 12 families from 4 geographical areas. An exception to the pattern is Wappo. The percentage of validity of the pattern is 35/36 or 97%.

Universal 140. A voiced dental trill does not occur without a voiceless dental plosive ([r̪] → [t̪]).

Positive evidence for this pattern is provided by 9 languages belonging to 6 families from 3 geographical areas. The pattern is exceptionless in UPSID-451 (9/9 or 100%).

Universal 141. A laryngealized voiced palatal approximant does not occur without a glottal plosive ([j̰] → [ʔ]).

Examples of this universal are 17 languages, members of 6 language families from 3 geographical areas. This is an exceptionless universal (17/17 or 100%).

Universal 142. The presence of a voiced dental lateral approximant in a language implies the presence of a voiced dental nasal ([lð̪] → [n̪]).

Positive evidence for this pattern is provided by 32 languages belonging to 12 families from 4 geographical areas. Dafla and Wolof are negative instances to the universal. The percentage of validity of the pattern is 32/34 or 94%.

Universal 143. The presence of a voiced dental lateral approximant in a language implies the presence of a voiceless dental plosive ([lð̪] → [t̪]).

This pattern is corroborated in 31 languages from 12 families in 4 geographical areas. Dafla, Wolof, and Tonkawa are negative instances to the universal. The percentage of validity of the pattern is 31/34 or 91%.

Universal 144. If a language has a laryngealized voiced labial-velar approximant then it also has a glottal plosive ([w̰] → [ʔ]).

This pattern is corroborated in 17 languages from 6 families in 3 geographical areas. This is an exceptionless universal (17/17 or 100%).

Universal 145. The presence of a palatalized voiced bilabial nasal in a language implies the presence of a palatalized voiceless bilabial plosive ([mʲ] → [pʲ]).

This universal is supported in 9 languages from 5 families situated in 3 areas. An exception to the pattern is Irish. The universal is supported in 9/10 or 90% of the languages in UPSID-451.

Universal 146. If a language has a voiced retroflex nasal then it also has a voiced retroflex lateral approximant ([n.] → [l.]).

Positive evidence for this pattern is provided by 22 languages belonging to 6 families from 2 geographical areas. The following languages are counter-examples: Pashto and Koya. The percentage of validity of the pattern is 22/24 or 92%.

5.4 Interpretation of results

5.4.1 Summary

The system found and verbalized 146 highly significant universals of type "If Segment A, then Segment B" that are valid in at least 90% of the languages in UPSID-451 and are supported by languages from at least two different language families from at least two different geographical areas. Of these 146 universals, 50 or 1/3 are exceptionless.

It may be noted that some of the exceptionless patterns can be combined by rules of logic into "hierarchies" or other more complex expressions; this, however, is beyond the scope of the present article. By way of an illustration, the universals

[b̪] → [g] (Universal No. 12)
[b̪] → [kʰ] (Universal No. 13)
[b̪] → [pʰ] (Universal No. 14)
[g] → [kʰ] (Universal No. 29)
[g] → [pʰ] (Universal No. 30)

can be collapsed into the more complex (and compact) universal, or hierarchy, viz.

[b̪] > [g] > ([kʰ] & [pʰ]).

This notation and the interpretation of the hierarchy are familiar to linguists: any segment implies all the segments lying on its right, e.g. a language having [b̪] will also necessarily have the segments [g], ([kʰ], and [pʰ]. It is worthwhile to repeat that such logical transformations can validly be made only with absolute universals, not statistical ones.[5]

5.4.2 Comparison with Maddieson (1984)

Maddieson (1984) proposes more than sixty generalizations in his book. They are of different nature. Two large categories are (1) universals referring to languages, and (2) universals referring to segments. Examples of the category (2) are "If a segment is nasal, it is voiced" (p. 69), "An ejective segment is likely to be a stop" (p. 120) or "An ejective affricate segment is usually sibilant" (p. 121). Within the framework of category (1), the proposed universals can be sub-categorized into (1.1) such referring to numerical properties of segment inventories (as e.g. "A language with two or more liquids is most likely to have at least one

---

[5] A very simple example may serve to illustrate the case. Consider the miniature data set consisting of only 2 languages, which have the following two-segment inventories: Language 1: a, b and Language 2: b, c. The following two implications are valid in this data set:
(i) a → b (absolute universal, one relevant case, Language 1, one positive example: 1/1 or 100% validity); *and*
(ii)   b → c (statistical universal, two relevant cases, since b occurs in both Language 1 and Language 2, one positive example, viz. Language 2, and one counterexample, viz. Language 1: ½ or 50% validity).
Now, given (i) and (ii), can we form a hierarchy, or what is the same, validly infer from a → b & b → c by the law of transitivity that a → c? Clearly not, since a → c is actually 100% false (falsified by Language 1, which has a but not c; Language 2 is irrelevant as it does not have an a). This remark is not to suggest that stating hierarchies containing also statistical universals is not possible, but only that the resulting hierarchies should be empirically tested in this situation insofar as traditional logic does not work in such cases.

lateral" (p. 88), "A language is most likely to have 2 series of stops" (p. 39)), and (1.2) such *not* referring to numerical properties, but only to inter-segmental relations. In turn, universals of the latter sub-category, (1.2), which can be appropriately called *inter-segmental universals*, cover statements, of different logical form, holding between *individual segments* (e.g. [p] → [k], p. 13) and/or *classes of segments* (e.g. "Nasal consonants do not occur unless stops (including affricates) occur at (broadly) the same place of articulation", p. 13; or [k] → [*t], p. 13, where [*t] stands for the class consisting of dental, alveolar and dental/alveolar plosives).

In this chapter, we are concerned with implicational patterns holding between individual segments, and there are about a dozen such patterns proposed by Maddieson. It is instructive to compare the discoveries of UNIVAUTO with those of Maddieson.

Some universals proposed by Maddieson, based on the smaller database of 371 languages, are amply corroborated in the larger data set of 451 languages and conform to all our "plausibility requirements", viz. high significance, validity in at least 90% of the languages, and supporting languages belonging to at least two language families situated in at least two geographical areas. Such universals will figure in both Maddieson's description and our list. Some examples are: [p] → [k] (Universal 38), [w] → [j] (Universal 66) or [ŋ] → [m] (Universal 68), etc.

There are some universals that are present in Maddieson (1984), but are absent from our list. Since our search is exhaustive, the only reason for this difference (apart from corrected segment inventory data in UPSID-451 as compared to UPSID-371) should be attributed to the fact that these proposals of Maddieson do not conform to one or more of our plausibility requirements. Examples include universals posited by Maddieson which nearly miss our plausibility criteria, such as [kʷ'] → [k'] (p. 120). In UPSID-317 this claim is supported in 17 out of 18 cases (94%). The assessment of this claim with regard to UPSID-451 however is as follows:

Validity: 20/23 (87%)
Significance: 14.84 (=highly significant)
Number of families: 6
Number of areas: 3

The claim thus passes all our plausibility conditions with the exception of percentage of validity, which is, in the larger database, below the required threshold of 90%.

Other universals posited by Maddieson (1984) violate our plausibility requirements to a greater extent. Consider e.g. "[ø] and [œ] do not occur (separately [...]) unless [y] also occurs" (p. 14). This claim encompasses two separate simpler claims, whose assessment with respect to UPSID-451 is as follows:

[ø] → [y].
Validity: 8/12 (67%)
Significance: 4.89 (=significant, but not highly significant)
Number of families: 2
Number of areas: 1

[œ] → [y].
Validity: 5/8 (62%)
Significance: 2.81 (=not significant)
Number of families: 5
Number of areas: 2

As seen, the first claim violates our requirements regarding validity, significance, and number of areas, whereas the second is below the thresholds for percentage of validity and significance.

Finally, there are universals — and this is the vast majority of listed patterns — appearing in our list but not in Maddieson (1984) (or any other source known to me). These patterns seem to have remained unnoticed by previous researchers.

It should be noted, however, that it is also theoretically possible that some of our "new" universals may happen to be subsumed by more general claims made in these sources, a circumstance precluding the need for our more specific claims to be listed separately in these sources. As an example of this situation, consider our "A voiceless dental/alveolar lateral approximant does not occur without a voiced dental/alveolar lateral approximant" ([l̥] → [l]) (Universal 64). This claim happens to be a particular instance of Maddieson's (1984: 14) more general claim "Voiceless nasals and approximants do not occur unless the language has the voiced counterpart" (exceptionless in UPSID-317, 4 exceptions in UPSID-451), and thus naturally does not appear in his book. A similar example is provided by our Universals Nos. 75–77, 81, 84, 89–91, and 97, all of which are particular cases of Greenberg's (1966b) more general claim (also well supported in UPSID-451) that nasal vowels are the marked and oral vowels are the unmarked members (meaning that nasal vowels imply their equivalent oral vowels).

It should be emphasized however that by far not all generalizations proposed in the literature, such that may turn out to be generalizations of some of the patterns listed here, are in fact true generalizations. Thus, our [z] → [b] (Universal 116) and [z] → [g] (Universal 117) cannot be properly regarded as subsumed, say, by Jakobson's claim that "In the linguistic systems of the world, fricatives cannot exist unless stops exist as well" (1941: 51), which amounts to saying that if a language has a fricative, then it also has a stop. This claim is actually a pseudo-universal since *all* languages have a stop, and therefore the presence (or absence) of a fricative is entirely unrelated to the presence or absence of a stop in a language.

5.4.3 How to use the results

The list of posited universals can serve as an empirical basis for conjecturing or testing of various issues concerning the structure of segment inventories of the world's languages. These could be of interest not only for phonology and phonetics, but also to fields like language acquisition, historical or areal linguistics. It is beyond the scope of the present chapter to pursue this line of research. In what follows in this section, I confine to making only several observations.

(1) Looking at our list of universals, we see that our Type I comprises 97 universals and Type II comprises 49 universals. This fact suggests that if two segments are in an implicational relationship the much more likely pattern is the one in which both the antecedent and the consequent of the implication have the same manner of articulation.

(2) No universals are found in our list that hold between a consonant and a vowel or vice versa, with the exception of [g͡b] → [ɛ] (Universal 101). I am not aware of similar correlation between a vowel and a consonant being seriously discussed in the literature. This pattern however is interesting in yet another respect. It is massively supported by 30 languages from all Niger-Kordofanian branches (aside from other languages). Importantly, all counter-examples also come from Niger-Kordofanian languages: Dagbani (Voltaic branch), Gwari (Kwa), Mbum (Adamawa), and Tarok (Plateau). How can we interpret this fact of a "common anomaly"? Does it suggest some closer historical relationship (genetic or areal) between these four languages that jointly violate a well-supported pattern or are there some other factors at play? In any case, this common anomaly calls for an explanation.

(3) It has been a common view in phonology that there exist only few generalizations that hold universally, i.e. are exceptionless. Maddieson (1984) e.g. writes in this context:

...there are many strong implicational hierarchies between particular types of segments (although *very few are exceptionless*) (p. 13; italics mine).

Most of these observations and hypotheses about phonological universals necessarily concern relative rather than absolute matters. Experience has shown that *few interesting things are to be said about phonological inventories that are truly universal, i.e. exceptionless* (p. 2; italics mine).

Our system found 50 exceptionless universals which have very strong support both from a statistical and a typological perspective. This circumstance seems to weaken to a certain extent claims similar to the one above. We explored only one logical type of universals, and there are other types among which additional exceptionless patterns can also be expected to be found.

(4) Our list of universals can be used as a point of reference for checking some proposals that have been made in the literature. For example, in a familiar paper Gamkrelidze (1978) has suggested that "the presence of the voiced velar fricative phoneme [ɣ] in a system presupposes the simultaneous presence of the voiceless velar fricative [x]" and that languages with [ɣ] but not [x] are "rare exceptions". We should therefore expect to find his proposal among the universals in our list. However this is not the case, which implies that Gamkrelidze's proposal violates some of our plausibility thresholds. For his hypothesis UNIVAUTO outputs:

Validity: 28/55 (51%)
Significance: 6.83 (almost highly significant)
Number of families: 14
Number of areas: 3

Thus, we can conclude that while Gamkrelidze is right in asserting a correlation between [ɣ] and [x], this correlation is not strong and indeed very far from being a rare exception as he claims and is valid in only 51% of the languages in UPSID-451.

If the presence of [ɣ] is only weakly correlated with the presence of [x], what about their *absences*? For example, we can inspect the contraposition of [ɣ] → [x], viz. not [x] → not [ɣ] (by the logic law of contraposition stating the equivalence of A → B and not B → not A). A contraposition of a statistical universal will as a rule have a different percentage of validity from the original universal (but will preserve the same (in our particular case, high) significance of the original universal). Interestingly, UNIVAUTO reveals a high validity of 330/357 or 92% for the contraposition not [x] → not [ɣ]. Gamkrelidze thus should have opted for this latter statement if he wished to posit a strong correlation between these two segments.

(5) Universals have been traditionally invoked in language reconstruction. The rationale behind this is the assumption that extinct languages must not have been essentially different from extant languages, so that patterns or universals that have been established on the basis of extant languages must have held true also for the unknown proto-languages. In particular, implicational universals of type A → B can be used in reconstruction in the following manner: If A → B is a known universal, and A is reconstructed in the proto-language, then B should also be reconstructed. Analogously, granted the validity of the same universal and assuming the reconstruction of the *absence* of the consequent B, the simultaneous absence of the antecedent A must be reconstructed (by contraposition; see above).

Our list of universals can be used as a point of reference for similar questions of language reconstruction. By way of illustration, consider the well-known absence (or extreme rarity) of the sound [b] in Proto-Indo-European (PIE). Can our universals throw some light on the distribution of sounds in PIE (given the general validity of current historical linguistics practices)? Put differently, what are the consequences of the absence of [b]? To see this we must explore our list for universals of type "If (some segment) A, then [b]", which are equivalent (by contraposition) to "If not [b], then not A". Such contrapositions will reveal the (potentially) absent segments in PIE owing to the absence of [b]. It turns out that the presumed PIE gap in the stop system implies quite a number of segments that probably must also have been absent. Below I list the relevant contrapositions alongside with their (recomputed) validity percentage. The third column gives the number of the original universal a contraposition is a transformation of. The contrapositions are highly significant because they are transformations of highly significant original universals.

Contrapositions	Percentage of Validity	Original Universal No.
not [b] → not [˝d˝]	162/164 (99%)	2
not [b] → not [d]	160/164 (98%)	16
not [b] → not [d.]	163/164 (99%)	18
not [b] → not [ḓ]	162/164 (99%)	20

not [b] → not [ɟ]	164/164 (100%)	22
not [b] → not [g]	155/164 (87%)	24
not [b] → not [g͡b]	164/164 (100%)	26
not [b] → not [z]	158/164 (96%)	116
not [b] → not [dʒ]	159/164 (97%)	120
not [b] → not [dz]	163/164 (99%)	123

It goes without saying that the brief discussion above is only an illustration of a potential use of our list of universals and is not intended as a real contribution to the reconstruction of PIE. If this typological methodology is to be taken seriously in historical linguistics, however, consequences like those mentioned above should be taken into consideration in any discussion of the problem.

5.5 A new problem: can the list of universals found be generalized?

Both members of the implications A → B we discussed are segments and therefore can be represented as feature bundles. I now address the question as to whether there exist some patterns between the antecedent A and the consequent B in terms of their feature structure representations.

It is instructive to look at the features which the antecedent A and the consequent B share, as well as at the features specific to A and those specific to B. In other words, let us look at the intersection of A and B (A ∩ B), the difference between A and B (A − B), and the difference between B and A (B − A). Below I show some universals from our list represented in this form.

Table 5.1. Feature differences between antecedent and consequent of a universal

Univ.No.	Universal A → B	A − B	A ∩ B	B − A
64.	[l̥˝]→[l˝]	voiceless	dental/alveolar lateral approximant	voiced
67.	[n̥˝]→[m̥]	dental/alveolar	voiceless nasal	bilabial
48.	[t'˝]→[k']	dental/alveolar	voiceless ejective-stop	velar
6.	[tʲ]→[t˝]	palatalized	voiceless dental/alveolar plosive	Ø

The first row e.g. states that in the universal [l̥˝] → [l˝], stated as Universal 64 in the previous section, the antecedent A is voiceless, the consequent B is voiced, and they both are dental/alveolar lateral approximants.

A closer look (here accomplished computationally) at the 146 universals, represented in the above form, reveals the following patterns:

(1) The antecedent A and the consequent B are *similar* in that they share at least one feature. (Cf. column 4 in Table 5.1.) This holds in the vast majority of cases (139 out of 146 or 95.2%); the exceptions are Universals Nos. 101, 102, 104, 115, 109, 141, 144 (the consequent in the latter three universals being the glottal plosive [ʔ]). The actual distribution is as follows: there are 7 universals with no overlapping features, 23 with 1 overlap, 60 with 2 overlaps, 42 with 3 overlaps, 13 with 4 overlaps, and 1 with 5 overlaps. The average feature overlap in the 146 universals is 2.23 features per universal.

(2) The consequent of an implication B is *equally or more simple* than the antecedent A, never more complex in terms of the number of features it has. Thus, the first three cases on Table 5.1 show that the consequent B has an equal number of features as the antecedent A, while in the fourth B has one feature less (viz. A has the additional feature "palatalized"). This state of affairs holds in 144 out of 146 universals (or in 99%); the exceptions are Universal No. 101 (an exception also to the previous condition) and No. 146 in which a (non-lateral) nasal implies a lateral approximant.

The above observations can be combined in the following empirically derived phonological principle, or meta-universal:

The principle of antecedent-consequent compatibility

The antecedent and the consequent of an implicational universal A → B (where A and B are feature bundles) are not arbitrary feature bundles, but are rather "compatible" ones in the sense that (i) they are similar (=share at least one feature), and (ii) the consequent is equally simple or simpler than the antecedent, never more complex (i.e. the former has an equal or smaller number of features than the antecedent, never greater).

138 out of 146 (or 94.5%) of the universals in our list conform to both conditions, and only 1 universal out of 146 (or 99.3%) violates both conditions.

To take such empirically derived claims seriously, however, we need to ascertain that they have not occurred simply by chance (or arise from noise from the data explored).

The estimation whether this principle is chance or not can be done, for instance, as follows. What we need is to find the number of universals conforming to the principle that could be expected to occur by chance in our data, and compare this number with the number of actually observed conforming universals. We first find the logically possible number of universals that can be formed from 919 segments (UPSID-451 uses 919 different segments). This number is 421,821 (computed by the formula $N2 - N$, where N is the number of segments). From this total of potential universals, some universals will comply with our principle, while the rest will not comply. I empirically computed the former number by checking in how many implications the antecedent and the consequent share at least one feature and, additionally, the consequent has at least as many features as the antecedent. I thus found 238,613 conforming universals. The non-conforming ones will therefore be the difference between all possible implications and the conforming ones, i.e. 421,821 − 238,613 = 183,208. The probability of occurrence of a conforming universal will be 238,613/421,821 (0.57) and the probability of occurrence of a non-conforming universal 183,208/421,821 (0.43) (it should be remembered that the probability of an event is computed by the ratio of the number of favourable cases against all possible cases). Now, we can ask: how many conforming and how many non-conforming universals should we expect in the sample of 146 universals? To calculate these numbers, we have to multiply individual probabilities by the size of the sample, viz. 146:

$0.57 \times 146 = 83$ conforming universals to be expected by chance in 146 universals

$0.43 \times 146 = 63$ non-conforming universals to be expected by chance in 146 universals

Thus, if the proposed principle depended on chance, we should expect to find in our list of 146 discovered universals 83 conforming universals and 63 exceptions to the principle. In sharp contrast to these chance expectations, we actually found 138 conforming universals and only 8 exceptions. Statistically, this is a highly significant result or practically a certainty that the principle is indeed valid. Our principle is thus both reliable (= statistically significant) and highly predictive (valid in 94.5% of the universals investigated).

The proposed principle (or "meta-universal") can be viewed as a strong constraint on what is a possible/impossible phonological universal of type A → B (A and B being feature bundles).

Thus, given two arbitrary segments, or feature bundles, we can predict that they are an *impossible* universal (or at least, a highly unlikely one) if they violate our principle. Thus e.g. the voiced bilabial plosive [b] and the voiceless velar fricative [x] are much too dissimilar in feature structure in order to form a universal ([b] → [x] or [x] → [b]). More generally, a vowel and a consonant or a consonant and a diphthong should also not be expected to form a universal for the same reason, as well as any two segments that are not "sufficiently similar" or "cognate". An implication like [b] → [bʷ], i.e. [voiced bilabial plosive] → [labialized voiced bilabial plosive], must also be ruled out since it violates the simplicity condition of our principle, requiring that the consequent does not have more features than the antecedent. It would be next to impossible for a universal like [x] → [bʷ], i.e. [voiceless velar fricative] → [labialized voiced bilabial plosive], to hold, since it violates both conditions of similarity and simplicity. All these predictions are amply substantiated by the facts.

On the other hand, given the principle of antecedent-consequent compatibility, one can predict (classes of) implications that are *possible* universals. All implications that conform to the principle are potential candidates (though, of course, none is guaranteed to be a valid universal). In any case, the principle can be viewed as a worthy heuristic. By way of illustration, consider the following two predictions:

(i) A segment, or feature bundle, A with secondary articulation or accompanying features implies its plain counterpart B. (This prediction is based on the fact that A and B will necessarily have greater than zero feature overlap; the greater complexity of A shows that it is this segment, and not B, that is the antecedent of the implication.);

(ii) Any segments, or feature bundles, A and B that differ only as regards their values for a single feature (=parameter) form a universal A → B (or B → A). (The prediction is based on the fact that A and B will necessarily have greater than zero feature overlap and besides A and B will have the same number of features.)

The reader would readily notice that such inferences conforming to our principle closely match current wisdom in the field, expressed impressionistically in "tendencies" such as "Secondary (articulation) consonants and vowels usually imply their primary equivalents" (cf. (i)) or "A voiced obstruent usually implies its voiceless cognate" (cf. (ii)). Other predictions from our principle that have no precedent in the literature will suggest presumably unexplored routes for manual search for implicational universals. Our principle thus can be viewed as a powerful explanatory/predictive tool in the study of implicational phonological universals.

The systematic study of universals is a computationally complex task and hence requires automation. In this chapter, the program UNIVAUTO was applied to the study of elementary implicational universals, A → B, based on the UPSID-451 database. One hundred and forty six highly significant phonological universals were found, which were then inspected to see whether some pattern occurs between the feature structures of the antecedent and the consequent of an implication. The principle of antecedent-consequent compatibility emerged as a result of this inspection. The principle is a necessary condition that any two segments, or feature bundles, that form an implicational universal must satisfy. It can serve as a heuristic or explanatory principle in the study of implicational phonological universals. I also showed how the list of computer-enumerated universals can serve as an empirical basis for conjecturing or testing of various problems concerning the structure of segment inventories of the world's languages, including important issues like language reconstruction.

5.6 Summary of Chapters 4 and 5

In Chapters 4 and 5, I described the UNIVAUTO system, which handles the general scientific task of detection of laws, or patterns, from data, as well as the meta-scientific task of inferring inductively plausible and significant laws/patterns. Both tasks are computationally complex and hence require automation. Thus, previous, human, search for universals yielded solutions which were as a rule non-complete relative to the databases explored, i.e. omitting a large number of valid universals (as e.g. was the case with Greenberg and Maddieson), and occasionally not sound, i.e. positing as universals patterns that actually were not "valid" in the sense that they undoubtedly lack empirical support or are not significant (as e.g. was the case with these two authors and Trudgill). All this could be expected, bearing in mind that these authors did not perform comprehensive search of their databases.

UNIVAUTO mimics the general task of discovery of inductive generalizations, and hence would be applicable not only to language universals discovery, where the objects described in the data are languages, but to any database describing any type of objects, be they linguistic or not. This however applies primarily to its discovery module. The text generation module, as it stands, is less flexible and most probably unportable to a domain outside of universals.

UNIVAUTO has so far produced around 60 pages of text, covering about 250 new universals from the fields of word order and phonology, of which we presented a small portion in Chapters 4 and 5. The system also found new (non-verbalized) universals from other subject domains, such as kinship semantics, "social typology", etc.

The plausibility of posited universals has been a major concern for UNIVAUTO. Universals are inductive generalizations from an observed sample to all human languages and as such they need substantial corroboration. The system disposes with two principled mechanisms to this end. The first is the mechanism ensuring statistical plausibility, allowing the user to specify a significance threshold for the system's inferences. It is embodied in two diverse methods, the chi-square test and the permutation method which can alternatively be used. The second plausibility mechanism attends to the need for qualitatively different languages to provide support for a hypothetical universal for it to be outputted by the program. The specific measure of "typological diversity" of the supporting languages is chosen by the user of the system, by selecting the minimum number of language families and geographical areas to which the supporting languages must belong.

UNIVAUTO achieves an unprecedented intelligibility of presenting its discoveries. With some discovery systems, the user/designer may encounter difficulties in interpreting the program's findings. With other systems, typically those that model previously defined domain-specific problems, and hence systems searching conventional problem spaces, the findings would as a rule be more intelligible. However, intelligibility is a matter of degree and UNIVAUTO seems unique in producing an understandable English text to describe its discoveries. UNIVAUTO both states in English its discoveries (universals+problems) and the supporting evidence that makes these discoveries plausible/valid. Additionally, it provides a general context into which it places these discoveries (in the introductory parts of the generated text), as well as a summary of the findings (in the conclusion part of the generated text). The self-contained nature of the texts the system produces is evident in the fact of the publication of two of the generated texts. A word regarding the unique capability of the program to verbalize its discoveries in English. Previous researchers in machine scientific discovery have not seriously considered extending their systems with text generation components basically because, presumably, their discovery objects are either non-verbally represented in their respective domains or are not sufficiently numerous to merit verbalization. Systems like UNIVAUTO are likely to emerge as an aid to scientists in the future as scientific discovery programs are built addressing tasks worthy of verbalization.

Chapter 6. Inferring Simplest Laws/Patterns: MINTYP and the Problem of Describing a Typology

Given a dataset, a common problem in scientific knowledge discovery is to summarize this set by a collection of rules (laws, patterns, etc.) such that the resultant description is the simplest, or most economic. In linguistics, the problem occurs e.g. in attempts to describe a linguistic typology in terms of the smallest set of implicational universals that allow all actually attested, and none of the unattested, language types.

In this chapter, I introduce the MINTYP (Minimum TYPological description) program, which handles this problem, illustrating it on the typologies in Greenberg's Appendix II (Greenberg 1966a) and Hawkins' Expanded Sample (Hawkins 1983). Hawkins has noticed that Greenberg's universals do not describe all and only the attested types in Appendix II, but our computational analysis shows that Hawkins himself has not been fully successful in describing the typology in his Expanded Sample either. I prove that for any typology with at least one unattested type there exists a minimum description, consisting of a conjunction of non-statistical (implicational) universals, defining all and only the attested types. Then I show the method by which MINTYP finds the minimum description(s) of a typology, as well as the discoveries of the system from Greenberg's and Hawkins' data.

Our discussion is organized as follows. Section 6.1 reviews the analyses of the word order typologies in Greenberg's Appendix II (Greenberg 1966a) and Hawkins' Expanded Sample (Hawkins 1983), as familiar illustrations of the kind of task we are discussing. Neither author has proposed a set of universals, defining all and only the attested types in his data. In Section 6.2, using some results from propositional logic, I postulate a principle stating the existence of a minimum account of typologies. This principle allows us to make the a priori judgment that both Greenberg's and Hawkins' analyses are, from a descriptive point of view, not fully adequate. Section 6.3 describes the method MINTYP employs for finding minimum account(s) of a typology in terms of implicational universals, which is illustrated on Hawkins' typology; the Expanded Sample turns out to have a number of alternative accounts, three of which are simplest in that they consist of the smallest number of universals. In this section, I also list the possible (simplest and non-simplest) accounts of Greenberg's Appendix II. Section 6.4 concludes with summary of the results and some remarks on the relation between non-statistical and statistical universals. The discussion in this chapter is based on Pericliev (2002).

6.1 The problem of describing a typology seen as the task of inferring the simplest laws/patterns

A linguistic typology states all logically possible types, and is typically accompanied by empirical facts as to which of these logically possible types are actually attested and which are not attested (relative to a sample). Given such a typology, linguists face the task of describing it by formulating statements that capture the distributional pattern shown by the typology. The typology's description would normally be required to be as simple as possible, in accordance with the meta-scientific principle of simplicity (*simplex sigillum veri*), which is widely endorsed in linguistics. The question arises of how we can find the simplest description(s) of a typology. The problem was distinctly stated by Hawkins (1983) in early work on word order universals, but as we shall see later, has not yet found its solution. We already saw the importance of simplicity in Chapter 2 in discussing componential analysis.

In his paper on the order of meaningful elements, Greenberg (1966a) proposes a typology of the world's languages in terms of their ordering properties, which he states as Appendix II in his article (for a review of the state of the art in word order typology, cf. e.g. Dryer 1995). This typology uses four dimensions (=properties of languages), viz. verb–subject–object order, adposition order (preposition or postposition), adjective–noun order, and genitive–noun order. Greenberg notes that only three out of the six logically admissible types verb–subject–object order are attested, viz. Subject–Verb–Object, Subject–Object–Verb, and Verb–Subject–Object, while the others are non-existent or extremely rare.[1] Then, assuming binary (Boolean, yes/no) attributes on the dimensions of adpositions, adjective–noun, and genitive–noun, he comes

---

[1] Later researchers indeed found that other orders, viz. Verb-Object-Subject (Keenan 1978, Tomlin 1986) or Object-Verb-Subject and Object-Subject-Verb (e.g. Derbyshire and Pullum 1981) are also attested, though rarely, in some of the world's languages. We note, however, that these further empirical findings have no bearing on our present discussion.

up with a typology classifying the languages of the world into 3x2x2x2=24 logically admissible types.

Table 6.1. The Typology in Greenberg's Appendix II

1.	VSO/ Pr/ NG/ NA	19
2.	VSO/ Pr/ NG/ AN	5
3.	VSO/ Pr/ GN/ AN	1
4.	VSO/ Pr/ GN/ NA	0
5.	VSO/ Po/ NG/ NA	0
6.	VSO/ Po/ NG/ AN	0
7.	VSO/ Po/ GN/ AN	0
8.	VSO/ Po/ GN/ NA	0
9.	SVO/ Pr/ NG/ NA	21
10.	SVO/ Pr/ NG/ AN	8
11.	SVO/ Pr/ GN/ AN	3
12.	SVO/ Pr/ GN/ NA	1
13.	SVO/ Po/ NG/ NA	0
14.	SVO/ Po/ NG/ AN	2
15.	SVO/ Po/ GN/ AN	6
16.	SVO/ Po/ GN/ NA	11
17.	SOV/ Pr/ NG/ NA	4
18.	SOV/ Pr/ NG/ AN	0
19.	SOV/ Pr/ GN/ AN	1
20.	SOV/ Pr/ GN/ NA	0
21.	SOV/ Po/ NG/ NA	7
22.	SOV/ Po/ NG/ AN	0
23.	SOV/ Po/ GN/ AN	28
24.	SOV/ Po/ GN/ NA	24

Basing his analysis on 142 (groups of) languages of wide genetic and areal coverage, he notes that 9 out of the 24 logically admissible types are actually unattested. This is seen from Table 6.1, which reproduces

Greenberg's Appendix II.[2] The disallowed Types are 4, 5, 6, 7, 8, 13, 18, 20, and 22.

In his paper, Greenberg proposes 28 non-statistical and statistical ordering universals, basing his analyses, in addition to Appendix II, on his 30–language sample (given in Appendix I), containing information also on other ordering properties such as noun–relative clause, auxiliary verb–main verb, etc. Here, we will be interested only in the non-statistical universals pertaining to the proposed four-dimensional typology, i.e. the ones referring to the ordering of verb–subject–object, adpositions, adjective–noun or genitive–noun, since only these could be relevant to our task of describing the typology.

Greenberg managed to find two exceptionless universals holding in Appendix II: his Universal (3) ("Languages with dominant VSO order are always prepositional")[3] and his Universal (5) ("If a language has dominant SOV and the genitive follows the governing noun, then the adjective likewise follows the noun").

The goal of positing universals, which Greenberg was in pursuit of, is to define all and only the attested types in a typology. Operating in conjunction with one another, a set of universals should predict which types would occur and which would not. Thus, a word order type would be attested if no one of its word orders violates any of the conjoined universals; otherwise, this type would be unattested. Or, putting it differently, any word order co-occurrence type would be attested if it satisfies the logical conjunction [Universal$_1$ & Universal$_2$,...& Universal$_n$], which means (recalling the definition of logical conjunction) that each of the conjuncts, Universal$_1$, Universal$_2$, etc., should be individually satisfied; if, in contrast, a type has some orderings that do not satisfy even one of the conjuncts, then this type ought to be unattested.

How successful has Greenberg been in describing his typology, and in doing it in the simplest possible way? Greenberg's concern for simplicity is manifest in words like "In a certain sense we would prefer

---

[2] The following common abbreviations are used: SVO = Subject-Verb-Object, SOV = Subject-Object-Verb, VSO = Verb-Subject-Object, V-1 = Verb-initial, AN = Adjective-Noun, NA = Noun-Adjective, GN = Genitive-Noun, NG = Noun-Genitive, Pr = Preposition, Po= Postposition.

[3] As a point of fact, this universal turned out to have a counterexample, viz. Papago. However, since this language was pointed out to Greenberg only after the completion of his article, its actual existence should be ignored as it will be irrelevant to our purely methodological discussion attempting to assess how successful Greenberg has been in describing the data at his disposal.

to have as few universals as possible, not as many. That is, we would like to be able to deduce them from as small a number of general principles as possible" (1966a: 75). Though the principles he had in mind would perhaps be of a more abstract and explanatory nature than those needed for a typology's description in terms of universals, we may safely assume that the simplest descriptive solutions would also be a worthy goal for him.

In order to evaluate Greenberg's proposal, below we list, in symbolic form,[4] his two universals, giving in parentheses the types excluded by each of them:

Universal (3):   VSO → Pr   (Types 5, 6, 7, 8)
Universal (5):   SOV & NG → NA   (Types 18, 22)

(It is easy to check in Table 6.1 that these universals block exactly these types, and no others.) If we compare all the types excluded by the universals with all the unattested ones, we see that Types 4, 13, and 20 are not ruled out by any of the generalizations even though they are unattested. Greenberg's generalizations did not constitute a descriptively adequate account of the data in Appendix II and therefore the question of whether his account is minimal or not simply does not arise.

In his book Hawkins (1983) extends and slightly corrects Greenberg's typology in Appendix II, using the data from his Expanded Sample of 336 (groups of) languages. Table 6.2 reproduces Hawkins' Expanded Sample (1983: 288).

Hawkins preserves the basic structure of Greenberg's typology in keeping the same dimensions and the same attributes on these dimensions, with one exception. Thus, instead of the attribute VSO, Hawkins introduces the attribute V-1, basically in order to admit both VSO languages and VOS languages, the latter discovered by Keenan (1978; for details, cf. p. 55).

---

[4] We use the following common logic notations: "~" (negation), "→" (implication), "&" (conjunction), "∨" (disjunction) "≡" (equivalence). In what follows, we shall state universals only in symbolic form, rather than also verbalize them, as their interpretation will be obvious to a linguistic audience conversant with typological and universals research.

Table 6.2. The Typology in Hawkins' Expanded Sample

1.	V-1/ Pr/ NG/ NA	38
2.	V-1/ Pr/ NG/ AN	13
3.	V-1/ Pr/ GN/ AN	1
4.	V-1/ Pr/ GN/ NA	0
5.	V-1/ Po/ NG/ NA	0
6.	V-1/ Po/ NG/ AN	0
7.	V-1/ Po/ GN/ AN	1
8.	V-1/ Po/ GN/ NA	0
9.	SVO/ Pr/ NG/ NA	56
10.	SVO/ Pr/ NG/ AN	17
11.	SVO/ Pr/ GN/ AN	7
12.	SVO/ Pr/ GN/ NA	4
13.	SVO/ Po/ NG/ NA	0
14.	SVO/ Po/ NG/ AN	0
15.	SVO/ Po/ GN/ AN	12
16.	SVO/ Po/ GN/ NA	13
17.	SOV/ Pr/ NG/ NA	10
18.	SOV/ Pr/ NG/ AN	0
19.	SOV/ Pr/ GN/ AN	2
20.	SOV/ Pr/ GN/ NA	0
21.	SOV/ Po/ NG/ NA	11
22.	SOV/ Po/ NG/ AN	0
23.	SOV/ Po/ GN/ AN	96
24.	SOV/ Po/ GN/ NA	55

As seen in Table 6.2, no explicit provision is made for the object-first languages found by Derbyshire and Pullum (1981). This typology, again, has 9 unattested word order types, which, however, are slightly different from those of Greenberg (cf. Table 6.1); non-occurring here are Types 4, 5, 6, 8, 13, 14, 18, 20, and 22.

Hawkins (1983) repeatedly states that the major goal of the linguist is to describe the data most simply in terms of implicational universals. Thus e.g. he writes that "the purpose of a set of implicational universals, operating collectively, is to define all and only the attested word order co-occurrences in the most revealing, and *simplest*, manner". (1983: 29; emphasis ours). He declares that Greenberg has only been partly successful in this task (Hawkins 1983: 27), and addresses the problem head-on in Section 3.2 of his book.

Below is the set of implicational universals he found, with the excluded co-occurrence types given in parentheses. In the sequel, we preserve, as in the original works, Arabic numerals for the enumeration of Greenberg's universals, related to Appendix II, and Roman numerals for Hawkins' universals, related to the Expanded Sample. The universals we posit will have a prime ('), added to an Arabic or Roman numeral, depending on whether they describe Appendix II or the Expanded Sample, respectively.

As regards the symbolic formulation of Hawkins' universals, we may note that his "complex" universals of type A → (B → C) are in fact logically equivalent (by an equivalence known in logic as "exportation") to A & B → C; the universals A → (B → (C → D)) are equivalent to A & B & C → D, etc. The latter symbolization seems more intuitive to us for the following reasons. First, it can be more naturally verbalized than the former statement (cf. "If A and B, then C" vs. "If A, then if B, then C"). Secondly, the truth tables for the latter formulae, containing & (and) are more immediately evident than in the former notation, viz. they are the same as for the two-termed implication A → B, in which the antecedent, A, is a conjunction of atomic terms. And, finally, since in the latter symbolization a conjunction of terms denotes the antecedent of an implication, and since a conjunction (like disjunction or equivalence) is commutative, it is obvious that the permutation of these terms is logically immaterial: A & B & C → D is equivalent to B & A & C → D, etc. In this context, it makes no sense from a logical (or linguistic) perspective to speak of an "ultimate antecedent", as it happens a number of times in Hawkins (1983). The greater legibility of a complex universal being stated with one conjunctive antecedent is also noted by Dryer (1997: 141). Despite these considerations, however, we shall keep Hawkins' original symbolization, as it has been widely used in the linguistic literature throughout the years.

Universal (I)	SOV → (AN → GN)	(Types 18, 22)
Universal (II)	V-1 → (NA → NG)	(Types 4, 8)

Universal (III)   Pr & ~SVO → (NA → NG)   (Types 4, 20)
Universal (IV)   Po → (AN → GN)   (Types 6, 14, 22)

Hawkins notes that two remaining unattested types, viz. Types 5 and 13, are not forbidden by his description in (I)–(IV). Apparently assuming that there exists no set of exceptionless universals that can fully describe the typology, including Types 5 and 13, he leaves them aside, suggesting that statistical generalizations should be invoked for explanation of their non-occurrence. Thus, Hawkins writes that these types "will be predicted by the distributional principle in Chapter 4 to be rare or nonoccurring in a sample this size" (Hawkins 1983: 69). Understandably, as with Greenberg, no attempt is made to justify the proposed universals as the simplest account.

Summarizing the discussion so far, we may conclude that while Greenberg's analysis of the data in his Appendix II has only been partially successful in that he failed to exclude three unattested types, Hawkins' account of his Expanded Sample is not fully satisfactory either because it still fails to exclude two unattested types. In both cases, the proclaimed goal of descriptive simplicity has been compromised owing to the failure of both authors either to find several complete solutions, a necessary prerequisite for selecting the simplest one, or alternatively, to demonstrate that some solution is unique, and hence the simplest.

These objections are valid only if there *do* exist sets (conjunctions) of non-statistical universals that define all and only the attested types in both Table 6.1 and Table 6.2 in a simplest way. In the next section, we postulate a descriptive principle stating that for typologies such as those in Table 6.1 and Table 6.2 such minimum accounts indeed do exist. This principle thus allows us to claim in an a priori way that both Greenberg's and Hawkins' analyses are not fully adequate, even if we do not know what the correct analyses actually are. From a purely heuristic perspective, it would be interesting to note that the actual hint for posing the novel question of whether or not a minimum account of a typology exists, as well as its positive answer, came from experiments with MINTYP on various typologies, which invariably ended with finding such accounts. All I had to do was to prove why this was the case.

6.2 A new problem: does a minimum account of a typology exist?

In a revealing article, Greenberg (1978a) brings to the attention of linguists some logical properties of the different types of typologies used in linguistics. He discusses typologies in terms of the number of their dimensions (one or multi-dimensional typologies), the attributes on these dimensions (categorical or numerical), and, for the case of one- and two-dimensional typologies, describes the logical form to which they correspond (e.g. one-dimensional typologies correspond to unrestricted universals, two-dimensional typologies to unilateral or bilateral implications, etc.). Greenberg does not enter into analysis of the logical expressions generated by typologies of more than two dimensions.

Before considering the question of describing arbitrary typologies in its full generality, let us limit our attention to typologies having only binary (i.e. Boolean, yes/no) attributes on all their dimensions.

From Greenberg's discussions, as well as from elementary knowledge of mathematical logic, it is clear that an n-dimensional typology ($n \geq 1$) with binary attributes for these dimensions is in fact an n-place (n-argument) truth function (truth table) in propositional logic.[5] Thus, the n dimensions of the typology correspond to the n places (=arguments) of the truth function, the binary yes/no attributes of the typology correspond to the values T(rue)/F(alse) the truth function's arguments take, and the attested vs. unattested types in a typology correspond to the two possible values, T(rue)/F(alse) of the truth function. An n-dimensional typology with binary attributes defines all logically possible types, whose number is 2^n, and 2^n is exactly the number of the rows in a truth function, resulting from all logically possible distributions of the values T/F of all the arguments of the truth function.

Now, let us state some relevant facts from propositional logic. For our discussion, we need only mention them rather than go into the details of how they may be formally proven in mathematical logic (the interested reader is referred e.g. to Mendelson (1963: Chapter 1); Quine (1965: Chapter 1)).

Fact 1. Every truth function can be generated by some propositional formula.

Fact 2. Every propositional formula can be represented as a *conjunctive normal form* (CNF). A Conjunctive Normal Form is a propositional formula of type $C_1 \& C_2 \& C_3 \ldots \& C_n$, in which every conjunct C_i is a disjunction of atomic propositions or their negations. Examples of CNFs are: $(A \vee B \vee {\sim}C) \& (A \vee D)$; $(A \vee B) \& (C \vee D)$; A, etc.

---

[5] A truth function of n arguments is any function of n arguments which takes the truth values True or False, its arguments also taking the same truth values.

Fact 3. Every compound (=non-atomic) propositional formula can be expressed by means of atomic propositions bound only by one minimum pair of logical connectives: the pair negation and implication ($\sim$ and $\rightarrow$), the pair negation and conjunction ($\sim$ and $\&$), or the pair negation and disjunction ($\sim$ and $\vee$); alternatively, several of these connectives may be used.

Now, given that an n-dimensional typology with binary attributes is equivalent to an n-place truth function, it will follow (by Fact 1) that it can be generated by some propositional formula (= a (compound) universal). This (compound) universal, in turn, can be expressed as a Conjunctive Normal Form (by Fact 2). And, finally, each individual conjunct in this (compound) universal in CNF, if compound, may be represented, among other alternatives, by an implicational expression, possibly containing negations, or optionally, other connectives as well (by Fact 3).

In purely linguistic terms, the argument above amounts to the following: Any n-dimensional typology with binary attributes can be described by a non-statistical (compound) universal, or what is the same, by a conjunction of universals, of the form:

[Universal$_1$ & Universal$_2$ & Universal$_3$...& Universal$_n$]

Besides, any of these conjoined universals, if compound, will consist of atomic propositions linked by disjunctions and negations, and can be represented either in implicational form (replacing the disjunctions and negations with implications and negations, and possibly some other connectives) or in some other logical form, which is less popular in linguistics. The details of a conversion of one logical formula into another equivalent formula will be of no great interest to a linguist. It suffices for the purposes of the present chapter that only the basic idea of our argument be grasped, or indeed only its ultimate result. Therefore, a single simple example of such a conversion will have to appease the more logically-minded linguist. Thus, let Universal$_1$ from the conjunction of universals [Universal$_1$& Universal$_2$ & Universal$_3$...& Universal$_n$] be the disjunction A $\vee$ B, and we want to get an implicational formula from this disjunction. First, we can substitute A by its equivalent formula $\sim(\sim A)$ (by the law of double negation, A $\equiv \sim(\sim A)$), and thus obtain $\sim(\sim A) \vee$ B. This result then is convertible into the implication $\sim A \rightarrow$ B by the "material conditional" A $\rightarrow$ B $\equiv \sim A \vee$ B.

These considerations allow us to postulate the following "existence" principle:

For any linguistic *n*-dimensional typology with binary attributes, there exists at least one set (conjunction) of non-statistical universals of implicational (or some other) form, which generates this typology (i.e. describes all and only its attested types).

Let us now turn to the typologies given in Table 6.1 and Table 6.2. The only difference between these typologies and one having binary attributes is the non-binary nature of their dimension for Verb Order. This dimension has three attributes, viz. SVO, SOV and VSO (or V-1), instead of only two; all other dimensions are binary. But obviously we can split up this 3-attribute dimension into three 2-attribute dimensions, SVO, SOV and VSO (or V-1), which are now binary, as each language type will either have or lack any one of the mentioned orders. More generally, any *n*-dimensional typology with non-binary attributes can be transformed into one with binary attributes by increasing the number of dimensions.[6]

Two specific types of *n*-dimensional typologies deserve special mention at this point. The first is the one in which *all* the types are actually attested, and the second is the one in which *none* of the types are attested. Typologies with no attested types can be regarded as non-occurring in linguistic practice, and hence ignored. The reason why such typologies are useless is simply that the properties they employ to classify languages must be irrelevant to natural languages, if indeed no language is either positively or negatively specified with respect to these properties. (An example would be a typology attempting to classify languages, say, on the basis of the properties "has feathers" and "can fly".) If typologies with no attested types are non-occurring, those with all types attested have been used in linguistics. They state that any combination of linguistic properties is realized, which means that no exceptionless generalization can formulated describing such typologies. The reason why this is so can easily be understood by appealing to the familiar fact that any universal *forbids* some co-occurrence of linguistic properties, or some type(s), while no type is forbidden by definition in the typologies at issue. In handling such typologies with no forbidden

---

[6] It is important to realize that this reduction move is only a mental operation in the construction of our argument, and therefore does not involve, in any literal sense, the transformation of non-binary to binary typologies. As a consequence, any questions naturally arising in linguistic feature theory, such as intuitiveness vs. unintuitiveness of binary typologies, the advantages and disadvantages of particular ways the reduction is achieved, etc. are completely beside the point in the present context. All that counts is the possibility of the reduction. Our illustrative examples in the next section are in fact both non-binary typologies.

types, which do not allow the formulation of non-statistical universals, the linguist has to look for statistical universals, if indeed some significant statistical correlations between the languages' attributes in the typology are discernible. (A statement to the same effect, but for the more specific case of two-dimensional typologies, is made by Greenberg, saying that for tetrachoric tables with 4 pluses "no exceptionless generalization is possible" (1978a: 54).)

The above considerations, pertaining to the reducibility of typologies to binary ones and to the generalizations corresponding to typologies with all/none forbidden types, allow us to reformulate our previous version of the existence principle as follows:

> For any linguistic *n*-dimensional typology such that it has some attested and some unattested type(s), there exists at least one set (conjunction) of non-statistical universals of implicational (or some other) form, which generates this typology (i.e. describes all and only its attested types).

This is a fundamental descriptive principle in typology since it tells us that any typology that has some attested and some unattested types does have some description in terms of a set of exceptionless universals covering all and only the attested language types, even if we do not know exactly what this set of universals actually is. The heuristic value of this "existence" principle is self-evident. Our knowledge that a solution of some pre-specified format exists is, in the first place, a good incentive for initiating the search for this solution. And, secondly, it will direct this search, precluding, as a side effect, the possibility of someone trying to pass as the correct solution an object that deviates from the pre-specified solution's format.

It may be worth noting at this point, following Greenberg (1978a: 41–49), that not all typological work necessarily employ typologies (=classifications) in the usual sense, in which there is a finite number of mutually exclusive types (=classes), and every language, relevant to the typology, falls under one and only one type (class). As a result, not all typological descriptions are summarizable in terms of universals. Thus, a characterization on the basis of continuous numerical attributes, as e.g. the use of morpheme-word ratio (M/W) as a measure of the degree of typological synthesis (Greenberg 1954), does not divide languages into mutually exclusive classes but orders them on a continuum. Indeed, if each language is assigned a number corresponding to its M/W ratio over a sample of texts from this language, the languages do not form classes, but are ordered on a numerical continuum, allowing us to claim, say, that Eskimo is more synthetic than Vietnamese, and German lies somewhere between them, but not the classes to which these languages belong. As Greenberg (1978a) notes, in this case the associated generalizations involved would be statistical measures of central tendency (e.g. averages and medians, dispersion, etc.), rather than (implicational) universals. Nonetheless, if desired, continuous numerical attributes can be reduced to categorical (nominal) attributes by defining number intervals, this reduction resulting in the usual typologies obeying the existence principle stated above. For example, introducing the three M/W ratio intervals < 2.00, 2.00–2.99, and ≥ 3.00, we introduce a dimension with three categorical attributes (corresponding to analytic, synthetic or polysynthetic language, respectively). This dimension, possibly with some further linguistic properties, then can be used to define an *n*-dimensional typology for which we can assess whether or not it is describable in terms of non-statistical universals appealing to our existence principle.

A remark on the *simplicity* of solutions to typologies. Our descriptive principle states that there would be at least one solution to a typology, comprising a set of (implicational) universals. If we can demonstrate that a solution is unique, then this solution is clearly the simplest. In the case when there are alternative solutions, it is natural to regard the set(s) of universals with the smallest cardinality (=size) as simplest (e.g. a set of three universals is simpler than a set of four universals). Thus, in effect, for any typology of the type we discuss, there exist(s) simplest solution(s).

Insofar as Table 6.1 and Table 6.2 do not belong to the class of typologies in which all or none of the logically possible types are attested, they will have minimum accounts in terms of non-statistical universals.

We are not aware of our descriptive principle having been previously stated in the linguistic literature. In any case, it seems unlikely that it was familiar to Greenberg or Hawkins (at the time of writing), for if it had been, they would probably have found a comprehensive account of their typologies. In particular, had this principle been known to Hawkins, it would have saved him the need to relegate Types 5 and 13 to his (statistical) distributional principle in a situation in which there exist non-statistical universals, so favoured by him, that are perfectly sufficient to do the job.

6.3 MINTYP and its discoveries

It is good to know that a (simplest) solution to a problem exists, but it is still better if you know how to find it. In this section, I deal with the method MINTYP employs to find the minimum description(s) of a typology in terms of a set of implicational universals.

MINTYP accepts as *input* information as that in Tables 1 and 2, i.e. the definitions (=co-occurrences) of all logically admissible types, alongside with information about the number of languages conforming to each type. That is, the typologies are inputted to the system in the form in which they are commonly stated in linguistics. (Insofar as only non-statistical universals are outputted by the system, the exact number of the languages conforming to a type is irrelevant, and the program runs smoothly with information only recording that some types are attested, while others are not.)

MINTYP *outputs* all descriptions of a typology, in ascending of order of complexity, i.e. starting with the simplest accounts.

In essence, MINTYP links two basic modules, one for discovery of universals and the other for finding minimum covers. Both have been previously built for the programs UNIVAUTO and KINSHIP, respectively, which we described previously in the book.

We illustrate our approach[7] on Hawkins' typology (cf. Table 6.2). MINTYP's method comprises the following steps:

Step 1. Find all logically nonequivalent implications holding over attested types; then associate each of the found implications with the type(s) it forbids.

In order to find a minimum set of universals describing a typology we first need to know all universals valid in the data. We may limit ourselves to finding only logically nonequivalent implications to avoid the proliferation of generalizations potentially discoverable in the data, as any generalization from a set of logically equivalent generalizations makes the same claim as any other.

Two propositions (= universals) P and Q are said to be *logically equivalent* if when P is true Q is also true, and when Q is true P is also true; otherwise they are *logically nonequivalent*. Such equivalence between two propositions (universals) can be ascertained by drawing their truth tables and checking that they have identical truth values in each row of their truth tables, or alternatively, by showing that P is convertible into Q by some known tautology (= law of logic).

As a familiar example, consider the universal SOV → (NG → NA), which is equivalent to Hawkins' universal (I), viz. SOV → (AN → GN).

---

[7] There are of course other approaches to the same problem, based on logic transformations, but we will not discuss them here.

Their equivalence can be shown, using the logic law of contraposition, viz. P → Q ≡ ~Q → ~P. Thus, under the assumption made in the typologies investigated of a basic word order for the adjective and the noun, and for the genitive and the noun, it is obvious that AN is the negation of NA (i.e. AN ≡ ~ NA), and GN is the negation of NG (i.e. GN ≡ ~ NG). From these facts it is easy to see how the former universal is derivable from that of Hawkins' by the appropriate substitutions. In an analogous manner, one can derive Hawkins' universal (I) from the former (for a linguistic discussion of contraposition, cf. e.g. Croft 1990: 49). For our descriptive purposes, obviously, we need only keep one of these redundant universals.

Below we list nine logically nonequivalent implications that we found in Table 6.2. To avoid the proliferation of redundant implications found, also excluded from this list are implications that logically follow from stronger implications, such as e.g. the four-termed universal Po → (SOV → (AN → GN)) which logically follows from Hawkins' three-termed universal (I), SOV → (AN → GN). In general, a proposition (universal) P is said to logically imply another proposition Q if when P is true, Q is also necessarily true. To see why Hawkins' universal logically implies the other universal, we first note that Hawkins' universal is equivalent (identical) to the antecedent of the latter implication. Denoting Hawkins' universal SOV → (AN → GN) by H, we therefore need to show that whenever H is true, Po → H is also true. That this is indeed the case follows from the fact that when the antecedent of an implication is true, the whole implication is also necessarily true.

The superfluousness of universals that are logically implied by stronger universals has long been noted in the typological literature. The standard example is the (unrestricted) universal "All languages have oral vowels" which logically implies the (implicational) universal "If a language has nasal vowels, then it also has oral vowels". Cf. e.g. Howard (1971), Greenberg (1978a: 50–51), Comrie (1981: 18).

In their formulation we use (explicitly) only the connective implication (→), although, as it should be clear from our previous considerations, they will be equivalent to the more legible statements, using also conjunction. Each of the implications is associated with the excluded co-occurrence types:

Universal (I')	SOV → (AN → GN)	(Types 18, 22)
Universal (II')	V-1 → (NA → NG)	(Types 4, 8)

Universal (III') Pr → (NA → (GN → SVO))[8]   (Types 4, 20)
Universal (IV') Po → (AN → GN)   (Types 6, 14, 22)
Universal (V') NA → (V-1 → Pr)   (Types 5, 8)
Universal (VI') NG → (V-1 → Pr)   (Types 5, 6)
Universal (VII')NG → (SVO → Pr)   (Types 13, 14)
Universal (VIII')   NG → (Po → SOV)   (Types 5, 6, 13, 14)
Universal (IX') GN → (NA → (SOV → Po))   (Type 20)

Our universals (I')–(IV') coincide with Hawkins' set (I)–(IV).

Step 2. Associate, with any unattested type, the universal(s) which exclude the type.

This step is unproblematic, once we have available all the implications found at Step 1. Thus, we have:

Excluded Types	Universals excluding the Types
4	(II', III')
5	(V', VI', VIII')
6	(IV', VI', VIII')
8	(II', V')
13	(VII', VIII')
14	(V', VII', VIII')
18	(I')
20	(III', IX')
22	(I', IV')

Step 3. Form a set S whose members are all sets consisting of the alternative universals excluding a type (i.e. the sets in right-hand column above), and then find the minimum set cover of S.

The set S will have as its members all nine sets of universals above, i.e.

S = { (II', III'), (V', VI', VIII'), (IV', VI', VIII'), (II', V'), (VII', VIII'), (V', VII', VIII'), (I'), (III', IX'), (I', IV') }.

A *cover* of a set S is called another set C which contains at least one member from each of the sets that are members of S. That is, the cover C

---

[8] This formulation is equivalent (by contraposition and exportation) to Hawkins' Universal (III), Pr & ~SVO → (NA → NG), which can also be seen from the same set of types they both rule out, viz. Types 4 and 20.

in the above case should contain at least one member from the first set (II', III'), at least one member from the second set (V', VI', VIII'), at least one member from the third set (IV', VI', VIII'), and so on for all the nine sets of universals which are members of S. We note that a cover must not contain redundant elements. It will be clear from this definition of a cover of a set that finding the cover of the set S will contain the universals needed to exclude *all* the nine unattested types. A *minimum cover* of a set S is the cover C_i having the smallest cardinality (=the smallest number of members, composing C_i). The minimum cover of S thus will yield the smallest number of universals that can block all the non-attested types.

Computing the minimum covers for the set S, we get the following three minimum sets of universals, each having four universals, which describe all and only the attested types in Table 6.2:

Account 1: Universals [I' & II' & III' & VIII']
Account 2: Universals [I' & II' & VIII' & IX']
Account 3: Universals [I' & III' & V' & VIII']

There also exist five other, non-minimum, accounts, consisting of 5 and 6 universals, as follows:

Account 4: Universals [I' & II' & VI' & VII' & IX']
Account 5: Universals [I' & III' & IV' & V' & VII']
Account 6: Universals [I' & II' & III' & VI' & VII']
Account 7: Universals [I' & III' & V' & VI' & VII']
Account 8: Universals [I' & II' & IV' & V' & VII' & IX']

For example, account 1 uses the first three of Hawkins' universals, plus Universal (VIII'), ruling out, among others, the non-attested Types 5 and 13, Hawkins had problems with. The correctness of the rest of the solutions is readily testable against the data from Table 6.2, and we leave this exercise to the reader. We may note that Hawkins' Universal (IV) does not actually figure in any one of the three simplest accounts. The reason is simply that it does not add any further information to the one already contained in any of these three accounts.

We should emphasize that, since a cover of a set does not contain redundant members (i.e. universals that are logically equivalent or logically implied by other universals), both the minimum and non-minimum accounts above contain all and only the universals needed to describe the typology studied. That is, adding a universal to any of the accounts would result in redundancy, whereas removing a universal would lead to a failure to describe the typology. This is the reason why a solution, say, having all nine universals found to hold in the Expanded

Sample, would not be a correct one; more precisely, its shortcoming will be the presence of superfluous universals.

We may now look at the accounts of Greenberg's typology in his Appendix II. At Step 1 of our method, we found the following implicational universals, which we list below, alongside with the co-occurrence types each of them excludes:

Universal (1')   VSO → Pr   (Types 5, 6, 7, 8)
Universal (2')   SOV → (NG → NA)[9]   (Types 18, 22)
Universal (3')   VSO → (NA → NG)   (Types 4, 8)
Universal (4')   AN → (NG → (Po → SVO))   (Types 6, 22)
Universal (5')   GN → (NA → (Pr → SVO))   (Types 4, 20)
Universal (6')   GN → (NA → (SOV → Po))   (Type 20)
Universal (7')   NA → (NG → (Po → SOV))   (Types 5, 13)
Universal (8')   NA → (NG → (SVO → Pr))   (Type 13)

The following two are the minimum sets of universals, defining Appendix II, and they comprise four universals:

Account 1: [1' & 2' & 5' & 7']
Account 2: [1' & 2' & 5' & 8']

There are also two non-simplest accounts, comprising five universals:

Account 3: [1' & 2' & 3' & 6' & 7']
Account 4: [1' & 2' & 3' & 6' & 8']

Universals (1') and (2') correspond to Greenberg's Universals (3) and (5), respectively. Hence both generalizations proposed by Greenberg should figure in both the simplest and non-simplest accounts of his typology (see above).

Concluding this section, a methodological remark is in order. As seen from our analyses above, both Appendix II and the Expanded Sample allow more than one simplest description (under our definition of "simplicity" as the minimum number of universals in an account of a typology). None of the simplest solutions can be considered "better" than any other from a purely descriptive point of view, as all of them are equally empirically adequate. If simplicity is the seal of truth, as the Latin saying quoted at the beginning of this chapter goes, then we have to concede that there exist in this case more than one solution marked with this seal.

---

[9] This universal is equivalent (by exportation) to Greenberg's SOV & NG → NA.

The reader would have noticed by now that the execution of our method is not straightforward as far as Step 1 and Step 3 are concerned. The tasks defined at these steps are indeed quite complex computationally, and hence very difficult to perform manually, even for the relatively small typologies we are considering.

6.4 Conclusion

The contributions of this chapter may be summarized as follows. I proposed a principle asserting, for any typology with some unattested types, the existence of a (simplest) set of non-statistical universals of some logical form (e.g. implications) that define all and only its attested types. This was made possible by building on the insightful logical analysis of linguistic typologies by Greenberg (1978a) and linking his analysis to certain relevant results from propositional logic. The postulated principle allowed us to judge both Greenberg's and Hawkins' descriptions as not fully descriptively adequate, even without knowing what exactly the descriptions of their typologies would be. I also suggested a method of discovery of (minimum) description(s) of a typology in terms of implicational universals, and briefly outlined a computer program, MINTYP, which executes this computationally costly task. Running the program on the data from Greenberg's Appendix II and Hawkins' Expanded Sample, we found the minimum (as well as the non-minimum) sets of universals defining all and only the attested types in these typologies, and showed that each set must consist of at least four implicational universals. We also noted the existence of alternative simplest sets of universals defining the typologies studied.

The set of universals defining a typology may be viewed either as a set of grammar rules generating attested co-occurrences or as mere co-occurrence facts that need to be explained by some theory. Under both interpretations, disposing of a most economic description might be a virtue. In the first case, it would generally be preferable to have as few rules as possible; in the second case, again, the availability of a smaller number of facts to explain would generally be preferable to having a greater number of facts to explain. Though we have focused on finding guaranteed-simplest solutions, however, it will be clear from our discussion that finding *any* consistent description of a typology, be it simplest or not, would involve a similar method to the one we described here.

Finally, a word of caution against an eventual (mis)interpretation of our results as implying the superfluousness of statistical universals for the description of typologies. Indeed, one may feel tempted to claim that since for many typologies we face in practice there exist set(s) of non-statistical universals defining these typologies, there is no place for statistical universals in this enterprise. The debate in favour, or against, statistical universals is a complex matter in which the arguments of advocates of either position should be carefully weighed up (cf. e.g. Hawkins' 1983 defence of non-statistical universals, and Dryer's 1997 of statistical ones). And this is a task beyond the scope of the present chapter. Here, we shall have to limit ourselves to a few remarks as to why our results should *not* be conceived as downplaying the role of statistical universals. In the first place, and this is an obvious point, non-statistical universals cannot register prevailing co-occurrence tendencies, or significant correlations that have a limited number of exceptions; such important facts about language are only accountable for in terms of statistical universals. Secondly, on inspecting increasingly larger databases it may eventually turn out that all of the logically possible types are actually attested; in this case, again, as mentioned earlier, we ought to take recourse to statistical, rather than non-statistical, universals for a description of this typology. Thus, for instance, it was found that Type 4 (V-1&Pr&NA&GN) and Type 8 (V-1&Po&NA&GN), previously believed to be non-existent, actually occur in languages such as Kivila and Garawa, and Yagua and Guajajara, respectively (for a discussion, cf. e.g. Dryer 1991). If it is convincingly demonstrated that all types actually occur, we will be forced by these empirical data to replace the non-statistical descriptions of the four-dimensional typologies studied here with statistical ones.[10] And, finally, since the ultimate aim of describing typologies in terms of universals is to provide data that can be subsequently deduced from, or explained by, higher-order principles or theories, there is definitely a place for statistical universals if they happen to fit better into these higher-order explanatory frameworks than non-statistical universals do. We may recall in this context our discussion of complex non-statistical universals of kinship semantic patterns in Chapter 4, Section 4.3.2, where we reported the findings of Valdés–Pérez and Pericliev (1999) to the effect that all the complex non-statistical universals these authors uncovered could, perhaps more insightfully, be viewed as simple statistical universals

---

[10] An obvious implication of this point is that the only conclusive demonstration that some typology must be described in terms of statistical universals is showing that all its types are attested, *not* the piecemeal engineering of refuting any non-statistical universal that happens to be posited on these data. The reason is simply that, following the latter strategy, one can never be sure that there are no further, non-statistical, universals defining the typology after all.

between two kin patterns since all such universals involved the symmetrical kin pattern pairs uncle–aunt and grandchild–grandparent.

Chapter 7. Detecting Significant Similarities: RECLASS and the Problem of Genetic Language Classification

Given a set of languages described in terms of feature values or wordlists, as well as the current genetic classification of these languages, the RECLASS program, which will be the object of discussion in this chapter, finds all pairs of languages, such that the languages in each pair both exhibit statistically significant similarities and belong to *different* language families. The existence of such similarities suggests a possible historical (i.e. genealogical or diffusional) link between these languages, and hence eventually may lead to the need for revision of the current classification. Running RECLASS on a database of the kinship terminological patterns of 566 languages (Murdock 1970), it was found that significant similarities exist between two geographically distant language families: the Kaingang family, comprising Xokleng and Kaingang, spoken in South Eastern Brazil, on the Atlantic, and Austronesian, spoken in the Pacific. Then RECLASS compared wordlists of Kaingang and Austronesian languages, a comparison which also revealed non-chance matches between these language families. The computationally generated hypothesis of a possible existence of a linguistic link between the Kaingang and Austronesian language families was subsequently tested manually by comparing structural features of these languages and positing sound correspondences in lexicons, with results leading broadly in the same direction. One plausible explanation of the results found is a distant relationship between these families, a conclusion corroborated also by some extralinguistic facts. If such a hypothesis turns out to be true, one important implication would be some prehistoric contact between these two distant parts of the world.

7.1 The problem of genetic language classification and the detection of significant similarities

The discovery of patterned, non-chance phenomena is important in science because such phenomena require an explanation for their occurrence. The great philologer of 18th century Sir William Jones in his work "On the Gods of Greece, Italy and India", appearing in the *Asiatick Researches 1*, laid the foundations of comparative mythological research, making the following methodological remark at the very beginning of his work:

> when features of resemblance, too strong to have been accidental, are observable in different systems of polytheism, without fancy or prejudice to colour them and improve the likeness, we can scarce help believing, that some connection has immemorially subsisted between the several nations, who have adopted them. (Works 3: 319)

The same mode of reasoning, based on the discovery of non-random phenomena and their subsequent explanation, culminates in Jones's positing of the hypothesis of the existence of an Indo-European language family, invoked to explain the non-chance parallels that can be observed among Sanskrit and European languages. Thus, in Jones's famous pronouncement regarding the relationships of Sanskrit and Greek and Latin, which I quoted in full in Chapter 1, he wrote that these languages bear:

> a stronger affinity, both in the roots of verbs and in the forms of grammar, than could possibly have been produced by accident; so strong indeed that no philologer could examine them all three, without believing them to have sprung from some common source, which, perhaps, no longer exists.

The mentioned type of scientific inference is common in historical and other branches of linguistics and in science more generally, and therefore the question arises of how we can at least partly automate it in order to facilitate the process of making similar discoveries, similar at least in spirit or subject matter if not in grandeur. Addressing this problem is not an anachronism viewed from the perspective of present-day historical linguistics because even though much was achieved after Jones and currently we dispose of reliable standard language classification sources like *Ethnologue* (Gordon 2005) and Ruhlen (1987), many problems still persist. These problems are the existence of as yet unclassified languages, language isolates, some smaller language groupings, or the controversial "macro-families" (Nostratic, etc.), all of which have attracted a lot of attention and have given rise to heated disputes. The possible existence of some misclassifications in our current standard language classification sources is also not completely out of the question.

We may want to have a closer look at the basic logic stages of the discussed type of linguistic inference and how they could be reflected in a discovery like Jones's. From a purely analytical perspective, this mode of linguistic reasoning may be said to pass through three distinct, though related, logic stages:

    I. Hitting upon languages that share non-random properties, or choosing which languages to compare.

    II. Demonstrating in an objective way, with "no fancy and prejudice to improve the likeness", that the properties these languages share indeed exceed randomness.

    III. Finding an explanation for the observed non-random similarities between the languages.

The first stage seems crucial for a discovery like Jones's. Indeed, how can a linguist find or recall relevant properties from relevant languages in the face of more than 5000–6000 languages spoken in the world and describable in terms of thousands of essential properties relating to phonology, grammar or lexicon? From a mathematical perspective, there are billions of alternative combinations or routes to pursue before encountering even a very tiny portion of plausible candidates. A similar selection process is of course partly constrained by current linguistic (and extra-linguistic) knowledge, and this explains why, say, one would chose Greek and Latin for comparison with Sanskrit, as they were *known* to be related, and why one would focus on flexion ("forms of grammar") and lexicon ("roots of verbs"), which were *known* to be symptomatic/diagnostic for a relationship, but why also choose exactly Sanskrit to compare with them and not, say, Zulu, some Australian native language or any other of the remaining thousands of languages around the world or in comparable proximity? A similar selection presents a formidable computational problem to an investigator and no heuristics based on current linguistic or extra-linguistic knowledge can reasonably strongly constrain the process, so the discovery of a solution is to a considerable extent a matter of chance. If Jones independently of others conceived the idea for this comparison, this must have been triggered by the chance circumstance of his appointment as a judge in India. As I already mentioned in Chapter 1 of the book in relation to the origin of the ideas of a possible relationship between Ket and Na-Dene, conceived by Ruhlen (1998), and Proto-Ongan and Proto-Austronesian by Blevins (2007), fortuity has been a major factor in similar discoveries.

The second stage of the discovery process, or the justification or proof of an idea which is already at hand, is as a rule the less hard task, and it is no surprise that Greek mathematicians emphasized this point by a saying to the effect that what mathematicians don't know are the theorems, given the theorems, they can prove them themselves (Lakatos 1971). From a contemporary linguistic perspective, what is required is that computations be made showing that the probability of the resemblances between the languages observed is close to nil and therefore chance could be safely excluded as an explanation for the observations. Modern linguistics has devoted a lot of attention to this problem, especially in the context of historical linguistics, and I will briefly return to this question later in the chapter. Suffice it to say here that making such computations is generally hard and requires machine aid.

In the 18th century, the criteria for rigorousness in linguistic research were apparently less strict and Jones — without ever publishing or even caring to preserve his supportive data[1] — limited himself to a mere declaration that the parallels he observed indicate "stronger affinity [...] than could possibly have been produced by accident" and presented, and of course could not be expected to present, concrete probability estimations having in mind that the mathematical idea of probability gained popularity only after the publication in 1812 of Laplace's *Théorie Analytique des Probabilités*. Other scholars had just to trust him, which they did as he was probably the most distinguished and influential linguist of the century, and in his going to India "intellectuals were literally *expecting* major discoveries in colonial India" (Cannon 1991: 29; italics in original). At the same time, it should be conceded that such trust was well grounded for he was in no way negligent to method as e.g. the following quote shows:

> I beg leave, as a philologer, to enter my protest against conjectural etymology in historical researches, and principally against the licentiousness of etymologists in transposing and inserting letters, in substituting, at pleasure, any consonant for another of the same order, and in totally disregarding the vowels ... I contend, that almost any word or nation, might be derived from any other, if such licenses as I am opposing, were permitted in etymological histories.

Regarding his particular assessment of the non-randomness of the similarities he noticed to exist among Greek and Latin on the one hand and Sanskrit on the other, it was based on the long tradition of empirical

---

[1] A characteristic trait of Jones's style of scientific exposition was that he only included in his writing the conclusions he had reached and did not describe in more detail either the data or the argumentation leading to these conclusions.

language investigation which had convincingly shown that parallels in inflexion ("forms of grammar") and in "basic vocabulary" ("roots of verbs") are highly unlikely to occur in languages non-related by kinship or diffusion. Besides, it was understood that his claims were based on systematic comparisons of multitude of cases.

Finally, at the third stage of the linguistic inference at issue, one needs to find an explanation for the observed non-random similarities between the languages. As we well know today, and was known at Jones's time, similarities between languages in principle can be due to several reasons: (i) chance, (ii) borrowing, (iii) the operation of some universals, or (iv) genetic affinity between the languages. Jones excluded chance (even if on impressionistic grounds by contemporary standards) and borrowing (owing to the nature of the similarities) and because "Common origin was a vastly better hypothesis than coincidence and borrowing, where each similar pair of items would require a separate hypothesis, rather than fitting all the similarities into one cosmopolitan explanation" (Cannon 1991: 31); he never considered explicitly the possibility for universals being a potential reason, and rightly, because no universals can explain similarities in lexicon, so the only viable hypothesis remained genetic relationship.[2]

These considerations are instructive and suggest some steps in the investigation process that are amenable, or indeed advisable, for automation. In this chapter, I will address the automation of stages I and II raised by this great linguistic discovery. They obviously require such automation if linguistics is not to rely to a considerable extent on chance circumstances or on impressionistic judgements rather than on accurate demonstration.

The complex task we need to carry out in order to handle our problem comprises the general scientific task of finding similarities and the meta-scientific task of estimating their statistical significance, which can be broadly described as follows:

Given:

(1) A set of languages described in terms of: (a) feature values, or (b) wordlists;

(2) The currently accepted genetic classification of each language.

---

[2] This analysis, leading to the claim that Greek, Latin and Sanskrit are affiliated of course is not the whole story, since Jones additionally postulated a parent language (Indo-European) of which these languages are direct descendants or "sisters", as he called them. The more involved question of how one can arrive at this particular conclusion, or how Jones might have, will be ignored here.

Find:

All pairs of languages such that both exhibit "similarities" in feature values/wordlist exceeding chance and belong to distinct genetic groupings.

It will be observed that with such a formulation of the task we directly attack the problem of possible misclassifications (or lack of classification) in current linguistic sources, and make provision for handling similarities in both language properties of arbitrary nature (phonological, grammatical, etc.) and lexicon. Also, such an approach presupposes the availability of databases of relevant linguistic information on the world's languages (linguistic features and/or comparative wordlists), a need well understood in contemporary linguistics. Ferguson (1978: 26), for instance, wrote in this context "The need is urgent for reliable, detailed, comparable cross-linguistic data, accessible to researchers by topic", and to-date notable success has been achieved in this direction, culminating in the *World Atlas of Language Structures*, (WALS, Haspelmath *et al.* 2005), now also available online; another ambitious undertaking for archiving information about 1500 languages, the Rosetta Project, is underway. Other noteworthy earlier databases, some of which we explored with different goals in mind in this book, include the Stanford Phonological Archive, the UCLA Phonological Segment Inventory Database in phonetics–phonology; Greenberg (1966a), Hawkins (1983), Dryer (1992) in word order; Murdock (1970) in kinship terminology, to mention but a few of the familiar databases in some areas. A complementary step is the automated discovery of new and interesting knowledge in the large bulks of data already available, because such searches would normally be computationally hard, and hence beyond human reach.

Before proceeding with our discussion, it is worth mentioning again that the discovery of non-random phenomena and their subsequent explanation is a familiar method in linguistics generally and is by no means limited only to applications in historical linguistics, which are the subject of this chapter. Hurford (1977) for instance cites a number of other examples from the literature related to the theoretical study of language. We saw the importance of the notion of statistical significance in our discussion of language universals in Chapters 4 and 5.

7.2 The RECLASS program and its discoveries

Given a set of languages, described either in terms of feature values or, alternatively, in terms of wordlists, alongside the current phylogenetic classification of the languages, the RECLASS program compares exhaustively the similarities in all pairs of languages belonging to different families, and outputs those pairs, which happen to bear greater similarities than could be expected by mere chance.

In what follows in this section, we explain both modes of operation of RECLASS, with features and wordlists, and illustrate some of its discoveries.

7.2.1 RECLASS and the exploration of kinship pattern similarities

7.2.1.1 RECLASS operating with features

In the mode working with features, RECLASS accepts as input languages, described in terms of feature-values, as well as their genetic affiliation. For each language pair, such that the constituent languages in it belong to different families, the program computes their common feature-values and then assesses the statistical significance of these similarities. The program discards as uninteresting/chance any language pair whose feature-value associations (=similarities) are not statistically significant. If, in contrast, the feature-value overlap of two languages belonging to two different language families turns out to be statistically significant, or greater-than-chance, the program outputs that pair of languages alongside their coinciding feature-values as facts requiring an explanation.

For estimation of statistical significance, I use the permutation method, as described in Chapter 4, Section 4.3.2 (for a general discussion of the permutation method, cf. e.g. Good 1994). The permutation method compares feature-value similarities in original and scrambled data. The probability of occurrence of shared feature-values in two languages is calculated as follows. Let F^1, F^2,...F^n are feature-values that two languages share. Then we define the probability of occurrence of F^1, F^2,...F^n in both languages as the product $R^1 \times R^2$, ... $\times R^n$, where the R's are the frequency ratios of F^1, F^2, ... F^n, respectively. For example, if, in our database of 566 languages, two languages, L^1 and L^2, share 3 feature-values, F^1, F^2, and F^3, and F^1 occurs 10 times, F^2 15 times, and F^3 2 times, then the probability of F^1, F^2, and F^3 occurring in both L^1 and L^2 will be $10/566 \times 15/566 \times 2/566 = 1.65.10^{-6}$.

A significance threshold is determined as follows. The original data, in which rows are languages and columns are feature-values, is permuted, meaning that each column is randomly permuted, thus creating random inter-row associations, while preserving the original distributions of feature-values. For each permuted data set, all pairs of languages belonging to different language families are compared as to feature-value sharing. This procedure is repeated 1000 times, recording the result from each trial. The results from all trials, indicating the number of chance feature-value coincidences that may arise between two languages in 1000 trials, are ordered in ascending order of their probability. Now, significance can be determined by *ranking*, or positioning in this ordered list of the probabilities of the similarities between language pairs found in the original data. Taking the 10th smallest probability from this ordered list provides a threshold below which all language pairs with smaller probabilities of their coincident feature-values will have smaller significance than $10/1000=0.01$ or $p < 0.01$ (=99% or greater assurance for non-randomness, often referred to as "high significance"). Taking the 50th smallest probability from the ordered list yields a threshold below which all language pairs with smaller probabilities of their coincident feature-values will have smaller significance than $50/1000=0.05$ or $p < 0.05$ (=95% or greater assurance for non-randomness, referred to merely as "significance"). Both significance thresholds are used in social science and I will follow common practice here. We shall look at particular examples below.

Before turning to examples, we mention that the assessment of similarities between languages has been a common task in linguistics for handling different problems, such as subgrouping (in historical linguistics), measuring the degree of mutual intelligibility (in dialectology), etc., and it has been addressed in lexicostatistics well before the advent of computers the 70s of last century. For example, in what seems to be the first proposal in this direction, Kroeber and Chrétien (1937) construct a table of the following form (where L1 and L2 are a pair of languages):

Table 7.1. Similarities of features

	No. of features exhibited by L1	No. of features not exhibited by L1	Total
No. of features exhibited by L2	a	b	a + b
No. of features not exhibited by L2	c	d	c + d
Total	a + c	b + d	N

Then, Nr^2, where

$$r = \frac{ad - bc}{\sqrt{(a+b)(c+d)(a+c)(b+d)}}$$

is chi-square (χ^2) with one degree of freedom, which allows the estimation of statistical significance of the relationship between languages L1 and L2. There are, of course, different ways of estimating significance and therefore different methods for achieving the same goal, and we need not go into details here. For example, Embleton (1986) provides further information on similar attempts in linguistics.

7.2.1.2 The data

For the purposes of the investigation reported in this chapter, the program is used on data comprising kinship semantic patterns contributed by G. P. Murdock (Murdock 1970), and discussed previously (cf. Chapter 4, Section 4.3.2). Here, we recollect the basic relevant points.

Murdock (1970) describes the terminological classification system of 566 languages from 194 of the 200 cultural provinces that he had previously isolated (Murdock 1968). This data set is the most representative compilation of kinship terminologies to date. The data includes virtually all systems published for Africa and aboriginal North and South America, and is only slightly less exhaustive for Eurasia and Oceania. Moreover, the data set is based on files of over one thousand complete systems; the published data set includes only those systems which differ from the remaining systems within the same sampled province in order to evade duplication.

The Murdock data set focuses on eight sets of kin ("features" in our sense): grandparents (*GrPa*), grandchildren (*GrCh*), uncles (*PaBr*), aunts (*PaSi*), nephews and nieces (male speaker, ms) (*SbCh*), siblings (*Sibl*), cross-cousins (*CrCo*), and siblings-in-law (*Sb-Inl*). Every type of kin is described in terms of "kin term patterns" ("features-values" in our sense), showing the number of kin terms used for that kin as well as their range of reference. Examples of kin term patterns are given in the *List of Relevant Kinship Patterns from Murdock* (cf. Chapter 4, Section 4.3.2).

For the eight sets of kin Murdock describes, he uses 192 patterns in all, distributed as follows: GrP (20), GrCh (20), PaBr (13), PaSi (14), SbCh (26), Sibl (43), CrCo (18) and Sb-Inl (38).

For our purposes we needed to associate each language in Murdock's sample with the language family to which this language belongs. To this end, *Ethnologue*, a standard and constantly updated reference on world languages and language families, was used.

7.2.1.3 The discoveries

The results from running the program may be summarized as follows. Three language pairs turned out to have similarities which are "highly significant" ($p < 0.01$), or what is the same we have assurance of at least 99% that these similarities are non-chance. Four language pairs turned out to have similarities that are "significant" ($p < 0.05$), or for which we have assurance of at least 95% that their similarities are non-chance. Below I list these language pairs, together with the language families they belong to according to *Ethnologue*. The number of overlapping kinship semantic patterns is also given as well as their probability.

The language pairs having "highly significant" similarities ($p < 0.01$) are:

1. Xokleng (Macro-Ge) – Ami (Austronesian), seven common patterns with probability of 6.3×10^{-8}
2. Xokleng (Macro-Ge) – Trukese (Austronesian), six common patterns with probability of 3×10^{-8}
3. Xokleng (Macro-Ge) – Ulithian (Austronesian), six common patterns with probability of 7.2×10^{-8}

From the computation of the probabilities of kinship pattern similarities in the 1000 random permutations, it turns out that the 10th smallest probability is 1.1×10^{-7}. All the three pairs of languages above have similarities whose probability of occurrence is smaller than this threshold; hence all three have significance which is smaller than 0.01, or $p < 0.01$.[3]

The language pairs having similarities at the significance level of $p < 0.05$ are the following (the 50th smallest probability in the random trials turning out to be 3.5×10^{-7}):

4. Rwala-Bedouin (Afro-Asiatic) – Anatolian-Turkish (Altaic), seven common patterns with probability of 1.1×10^{-7}

---

[3] A more accurate significance estimation, than just saying that it is smaller than 0.01, can of course also be accomplished. Thus, within the ascending-order list of random-trial probabilities of kinship pattern similarities, the similarities actually found to exist between Xokleng and Trukese, with a probability of 3×10^{-8}, come second, with only one random trial before it (with probability of 2.16×10^{-8}) and thus have significance of 2/1000, or $p = 0.002$. Xokleng and Ami, with probability of 6.3×10^{-8}, come fifth and have significance of $p = 0.005$, and Xokleng and Ulithian, with probability of 7.2×10^{-8}, come eighth and have significance of $p = 0.008$.

5. Icelandic (Indo-European) – Egyptian (Afro-Asiatic), 8 common patterns with probability of 1.5×10^{-7}
6. Iban (Austronesian) – Khmer (Cambodia) (Austro-Asiatic), 7 common patterns with probability of 1.9×10^{-7}
7. Maria-Gond (Dravidian) – Baiga (Indo-European), 7 common patterns with probability of 3.3×10^{-7}

Many borderline significant similarities between pairs of languages emerged, but I ignore them inasmuch as I am interested here only in commonalities that are very unlikely to have occurred simply by chance.

Our program has thus generated the problems of having to explain cases 1–7. For example, as regards the Indo-European language Baiga and the Dravidian language Maria-Gond (case 7), one may speculate that perhaps contact and borrowing are involved inasmuch as both languages are spoken in the Indian region Madhya Pradesh. The Indo-European language Icelandic and the Afro-Asiatic language Egyptian (case 5) share all 8 compared patterns, and are too distant in space to assume borrowing; and indeed, genetic relationship between these two families is sometimes posited in the literature. Austronesian and Austro-Asiatic (cf. case 6) are also believed by some linguists to be genetically related under the Austric macro-family. Both most reliable statistically and most interesting linguistically, however, are undoubtedly cases 1–3 and below I turn to their discussion.

Xokleng is spoken by about 750 people in the eastern, Atlantic, part of Brazil, viz. in the state of Santa Catarina, along the tributary of the Itají River, and its classification according to *Ethnologue* is Macro-Ge/Ge-Kaingang/Kaingang/Northern. Its alternate names are Aweikoma, Shokleng, Kaingang, Bugre, Botocudos. The three Austronesian languages, Ulithian, Trukese, and Ami, are spoken in the Pacific. Trukese (also known as Chuuk, Truk) is spoken by some 40,000 people on the Caroline Islands and Ponape, Micronesia, and is an Austronesian language of the Oceanic branch. Ulithian is also spoken on the Caroline Islands of Micronesia (3,000 people) and belongs to the same branch. Ami is a language of Taiwan (130,000 speakers), and is an Austronesian language of the Formosan/Paiwanic branch.

Below is an explanation of Xokleng's kinship semantic patterns. For ease of reference, further on I shall use their abbreviations (note that patterns denoted by initial letters in the alphabet, A, B, C are used for common and those denoted by final letters are used for rare patterns; e.g. Sb-Inl=A means that the pattern A for siblings-in-law is the most common one in the database, Sb-Inl=B that the pattern B for siblings-in-law is the next common, and so on).

1. GrPa=L. "Null Pattern", in which special terms are lacking for grandparents, who are called by the same terms for parents.

2. GrCh=K. "Null Pattern", in which special terms are lacking for grandchildren, who are called by the same term or terms that the speaker applies to his own children.

3. PaBr=E. "Generation Pattern", in which special terms are lacking for both paternal and maternal uncles, who are terminologically equated with father.

4. PaSi=D. "Generation Pattern", in which special terms are lacking for both paternal and maternal aunts, who are terminologically equated with mother. Analogous to Pattern E for uncles.

5. SbCh=F. "Sex-Differentiated Lineal Pattern", in which there are two special terms, differentiated by sex, which can be glossed by as "nephew" and "niece".

6. Sibl=C. "Yoruban Pattern", in which there are two terms, distinguished by relative age, which can be glossed as "elder sibling" and "younger sibling".

7. CrCo=A. "Hawaiian Pattern", in which special cousin terms are lacking, both cross and parallel cousins called by the terms for siblings.

8. Sb-Inl=A. "Merging Pattern", in which there is a single undifferentiated term, which can be glossed as "sibling-in-law".

Xokleng exhibits seven identical patterns with Ami, out of eight types of patterns compared. These are the patterns GrCh=K, PaBr=E, PaSi=D, SbCh=F, Sibl=C, CrCo=A, and Sb-Inl=A. The language shows six matches with Trukese (viz. GrPa=L, GrCh=K, PaBr=E, PaSi=D, SbCh=F, Sb-Inl=A) and six matches with Ulithian (viz. GrPa=L, GrCh=K, PaBr=E, PaSi=D, SbCh=F, CrCo=A). Besides these highly statistically significant overlaps, we may mention some other Austronesian languages that notably resemble Xokleng, e.g. Malayan and Rotuman with five overlaps, Samoan, Merina, Kapingamarangi, Maori with four overlaps, etc.

Xokleng thus seems to follow an Austronesian type of kinship semantic patterning (in his original files, G. P. Murdock marks the structural type of Xokleng's terminology as "Normal Hawaiian", which is characterized by a generational-terminology structure for the parental generation, and in which there is no distinction between siblings and cousins, all called by the term for sibling). Table 7.2 summarizes the distribution of Xokleng's patterns in Austronesian languages on the one hand, and in all remaining languages (without the Macro-Ge ones) on the other.

Table 7.2. Comparison of the distribution of the patterns of Xokleng in Austronesian and in the remaining languages

Patterns of Xokleng	Austronesian lgs with same pattern		All remaining lgs with same pattern		
	Number	Average	Number	Average	Families
GrPa=L Null	4	**5.0**	2	0.4	2
GrCh=K Null	9	**11.2**	10	2.0	7
PaBr=E Generation	18	**22.5**	9	1.8	7
PaSi=D Generation	30	**37.5**	33	6.7	11
SbCh=F Sex-Differ. Lineal	18	**22.5**	34	6.9	17
SibI=C Yoruban	15	**18.8**	32	6.6	15
CrCo=A Hawaiian	38	**47.5**	136	28.0	35
Sb-Inl=A Merging	19	**23.8**	52	10.7	17

NOTE: Total number of: Austronesian languages=84, All remaining languages without Macro-Ge=473

As seen in Table 7.2, some of the rarer patterns of Xokleng (viz. GrPa=L, PaBr=E) are more frequent in Austronesian than in all remaining languages, even though the Austronesian languages in the examined database are only 84, while all remaining languages (without the Macro-Ge ones) are 473. Other rare patterns of Xokleng (viz. GrCh=K, PaSi=D) are comparably frequent in Austronesian and in all remaining languages (also bearing in mind the smaller number of Austronesian as compared to all remaining languages). For all eight investigated types of patterns, Xokleng shares a pattern that is, on the average, more common for Austronesian than for the class of all remaining languages (compare column 3 with column 5; the larger value of the two columns is given in bold). The patterns that are more frequent in absolute terms in non-Austronesian languages than in Austronesian seem to be distributed more or less randomly among a large number of language families.

In sum: In pair-wise comparisons, the Brazilian language Xokleng exhibits striking similarities in its kinship semantic patterns to each of the languages Ami, Ulithian, and Trukese, all belonging to the Austronesian language family. In each case, these similarities are statistically very significant (i.e. highly unlikely to have occurred simply by chance); the probability that the *joint* occurrence of all three events is only chance is practically nil. Besides these commonalties with the mentioned languages, Xokleng resembles significantly other Austronesian languages, showing a very Austronesian type of kinship system, labelled "Normal Hawaiian" by the famous anthropologist G. P. Murdock.

7.2.2 RECLASS and the exploration of lexical similarities

7.2.2.1 RECLASS operating with wordlists

The specific task we need to address is the following: *Given* a bilingual wordlist, *find* whether the form-meaning similarities between the two languages exceed chance (and therefore are probably related). This is a long-standing problem in linguistics, and there are lots of works devoted to its solution. Some investigations e.g. seek to find a heuristic for deciding whether two languages are related by investigating 100 wordlists of basic vocabulary. Thus, Swadesh (1954) calculates on purely mathematical backgrounds that two languages need to share four or more CVC (C=Consonant, V=Vowel) sequences in a 100 wordlist in order to be related at 95% confidence level ($p < 0.05$), while Cowan's computations (Cowan 1962) for the same issue suggest three or more CVC matches. Bender (1969) addresses the same question from an empirical, rather than purely mathematical, perspective and inspects empirically the chance word matches that occur in pair-wise comparisons of 21 genetically non-related languages. He finds that only two CVC matches out of 100 items are necessary to have a confidence level of 94%, and only three to reach the 99% level. Bender also makes similar computations for cases in which the phonetic similarity criteria are slightly relaxed (cf. below). More recently, Rosenfelder (2002) proposes a method calculating the probabilities of the resemblances between a pair of languages, and a computer program executing the method; his approach is not limited to inspection of wordlists of fixed length, and furthermore explicitly takes into account the variability (degree of laxness) of both the phonetic and the semantic similarity criteria used for matching two words. Two computational methods also not limited to wordlists of fixed length and fixed phonetic similarity criteria, and using the permutation test to estimate statistical significance of bilingual wordlists, are Oswalt (1970, 1991), and Kessler (2001).

RECLASS assesses the statistical significance of similarities in wordlists by the permutation method, and analogously to its operation on features. The number of matches found in the original, or non-permuted, data is compared to the numbers found in many (usually 1000 or more) random permutations of the original data. The program supports two regimes of calculating actual significance. In the first, which is analogous to the one used on features, the number of random scores is ranked and a significance threshold is determined, taking the 10th largest number in 1000 permutations as one ensuring the level of $p < 0.01$ (or 99% assurance). The second regime re-implements the received Oswalt's approach (Oswalt 1970, 1991), assuming that using a standard approach might increase the credibility of the results to be obtained following it.

In Oswalt's method, the number of matches found in the original data (called *actual score*) is compared to the numbers found in random permutations of the original data (called *background score*). Our data is permuted 1000 times, and the *random mean* is calculated, which is the average of the number of matches obtained in the 1000 random permutations. The *actual deviation* is computed (=actual score minus random mean), which is a figure, indicating the number of greater-than-chance similarities.

The distribution of random scores is sufficiently close to a normal (bell-shaped) curve, which allows the computation of statistical significance, which is a better measure of the strength of the relationship than the actual deviation, as follows. The *standard deviation*, a measure of the dispersal of random scores, is computed as the square root of the mean of the squares of the deviations of each random score from the random mean. The *standard score* is computed by dividing the actual deviation by the standard deviation. The standard score is an important figure in these computations, as it allows us to determine the significance of the similarities of the examined languages. The higher the standard score, the lower the probability of getting the result by chance and hence the higher the significance. Tables of areas under the standard normal curve (to be found in most statistical textbooks) show the probability (=significance) of finding such a score or one higher. It may be noted that the significance level of $p < 0.01$ ("high significance") corresponds to a standard score of 2.3 or higher, and also that one unit of standard score means a lot in terms of changing significance (e.g., the change from 2.5 to 3.5 yields a significance change from 0.0062 to 0.0002) and normally statistical tables stop at a standard score of 4, giving a significance of 0.0000 to four decimal places (or practically, a certainty).

7.2.2.2 The data

To be able to compare the lexicons of languages and evaluate the statistical significance of the similarities found between pairs of languages, we first need to compile wordlists of these languages. The languages from the Kaingang language family Xokleng and Kaingang were chosen to be pair-wise compared to the following languages from the Austronesian family: Tagalog and Malayan (languages of Southeast Asia) and Fijian, Samoan and Hawaiian (languages of Oceania), languages representative of the widely spread Austronesian family.

A list of around 100-item basic lexical meanings ($\approx$a Swadesh list) was selected, as follows: and, arm/hand, ashes, bad, beat, belly/stomach, big, bird, black/dark-brown, bone, breast, burn, child, cloud, cold, come, cut, day, die/dead, dig, dream, ear, eat, egg, eye, fall, far, fat, father, fear, feather, fire, fish, five, four, fruit, grass, green/blue, hair, head, hear, hit, strike, hunt, husband, I, in, inside, kill, leaf, leg/foot, lie down (sleep), lips, long, lot (a lot), louse, man, manure/shit, mother, mouth, no/not, near, nose, old, person/human being, pierce/stab, plant, rain, red, road/path, rope/cord, sand, say, see, sharp(en), shoot, sick, skin, sky, small, spider, split, stick (wood), stone, sun, tail, three, throw, thunder, tongue, tooth, turn, understand, water, we (incl/excl), wet, white, wife, wind, wing, woman, woods/forest, work, yellow, you (sg/pl).

Then we filled the meaning slots above with the Austronesian words, as they are given in *The Austronesian Basic Vocabulary Database*.[4] As far as Xokleng is concerned, the list was compiled basically from Gensch (1908) and Henry (1935, 1948), while Kaigang's data came from the dictionary by Wiesemann (2002). In the cases when more than one word was available to fill a slot (either because the two sources supply distinct forms or one source gives synonymous forms), one form is randomly selected in order to maintain the impartiality of the method.

7.2.2.3 The discoveries

We have now to define the phonetic similarity criteria, or what counts as a match, in comparing two word forms. One can define these criteria more strictly or more loosely, the latter choice generally resulting in increasing the number of matches found, but at the cost of deteriorated formal resemblances and lower significance level. In the statistical approach, in contrast to non-statistical studies usually aiming at unearthing more matches (or putative cognates), how one chooses to

---

[4] In a couple of cases, other sources are used, as for instance when the database does not include a word from our 100-word list.

define these criteria is not really crucial insofar as the statistical test is in control of the process. What really matters in language comparisons is not the number of matches, but the strength of the relationships, which is reflected in the statistical significance. For the purposes of this chapter, I compare all consonant–vowel–consonant (CVC) sequences in a word pair, following so-called "extended criteria method" in a familiar paper by Bender (1969). The criteria, then, are:

(i) $C^1V^1C^2$ in one language is accepted as corresponding to (=matching) $C^3V^2C^4$ in another if the vowels are identical (disregarding differences in length or nasality) and if one or both pairs of consonants are identical while the other pair differs by only one feature (occasionally a difference of two features is accepted; see point (v)).

(ii) $C^1V^1C^2$ in one language is accepted as corresponding to $C^3V^2C^4$ in another if C^1 is identical to C^3 and C^2 is identical to C^4, disregarding of the intervening vowels. This criterion makes explicit use of the general assumption that consonants count for more in correspondences than vowels.

(iii) An item consisting of a CV alone is counted in comparison with an identical CV standing alone or occurring in a larger item.

(iv) An item comprising any sequence of three sounds is counted in comparison with an identical three-sound sequence standing alone or occurring in a larger item.[5]

(v) The following consonantal pairs with more than one feature difference match: v = p, t = l, t = n, h = k, h = g.

RECLASS was run on pairs of the inspected languages, with the phonetic similarity criteria above. The pair-wise comparisons had a different number of word matches in 100 words but all were "highly significant" ($p < 0.01$). Their exact significance levels are shown below (with accuracy up to four decimal places).

	Tagalog	Malayan	Fijian	Samoan	Hawaiian
Xokleng	0.0006	0.0001	0.0060	0.0033	0.0000
Kaingang	0.0004	0.0179	0.0014	0.0000	0.0000

It was experimented, among other, also with more constrained phonetic similarity criteria than Bender's "extended criteria method". For our purposes here, we do not need to enter into the details of these comparisons, but rather give just one example, serving to illustrate the

---

[5] This criterion does not figure in Bender's extended criteria method, but is included here since found useful in many language comparisons we made outside those reported in this book.

results of our program, running on data from Kaingang and Hawaiian, with the following stricter rules for counting a phonetic match between two words:

(i) $C^1V^1C^2$ in one language is accepted as corresponding to $C^3V^2C^4$ in another if C^1 is identical to C^3 and C^2 is identical to C^4, disregarding of the intervening vowels (= criterion (ii) above).

(ii) An item consisting of a CV alone is counted in comparison with an identical CV standing alone or occurring in a larger item. Vowel length and nasality are disregarded, and besides the vowel pair o = ɔ is considered as identical (cf. criterion (iii) above).

(iii) The following consonantal pairs are also considered as identical: r = l, k = ʔ. This criterion mimics common sound changes within the Austronesian family of languages.

Table 7.3. Kaingang and Hawaiian

Gloss	Kaingang	Hawaiian	Results
day	kurã	lā	
cut	kɨkɨm (pl.)	ʔoki	
near	kakã (or kakɔ)	kokoke	Actual Score: 10
shoot	pɛnũ	pana	Random Mean: 2.12
stick (wood)	ka	lāʔau	Actual Deviation: 7.88
stone	pɔ	pōhaku	Standard Deviation: 1.36
sun	rã	lā	Standard Score: 5.79
turn	wĩrĩn	wili	Significance: 0.0000
work (do, make)	han	hana	
woods (tree)	ka	ulu lāʔau	

As seen in Table 7.3, the program has found 10 matching words (=the actual score) in Kaingang and Hawaiian. If the association between the two languages were random, one could expect something like 2.12 matches (=the random mean), so the difference between actually observed matches and those to be expected by chance (=the actual deviation) is large, viz., 10–2.12 = 7. The standard deviation is low, viz., 1.36, which is again an advantageous situation. Finally, the standard score is large, viz., 5.79, recollecting that a standard score of 4.00 already yields a significance of 0.0000 up to the fourth decimal place. Thus, we have very strong reason to believe that the noted similarities are non-chance. Our second regime of evaluating statistical significance yields analogous results. Thus, it shows that in the random trials 108 languages have zero matches, 239 languages have one match, 295 languages have two matches, 209 three matches, 102 four matches, 35 five matches, 11 six matches, 1 seven matches, and none more than seven matches. Put differently, the probability that the found similarities between Kaingang and Hawaiian are purely chance are less than one in a thousand, according to the calculations by the second method.

7.3 A new problem: are the Kaingang and the Oceanic language families historically related?

The RECLASS program reveals significant similarities between languages of the Kaingang and the Austronesian language families regarding their kinship semantics and lexicons, and thus suggests a possible historical link (i.e. genealogical or diffusional relationship) between these families. This computationally generated hypothesis bears the distinct signs of a linguistic discovery, as described in Chapter 1 of the book. Thus, the hypothesis is novel, with no previous suggestions to this or similar effect in the linguistics literature. It is most unexpected both viewed in the context of current linguistic knowledge, and owing to the great geographical distance between the languages. And, finally, the hypothesis is important both with respect to its linguistic and extra-linguistic implications. In what follows, I try to test the hypothesis with standard, non-computational, linguistic means, exploring the grammatical structure and lexicons of the compared languages. The basic results were previously reported in Pericliev (2007, 2009).

7.3.1 Structural similarities

Some structural features of the Kaingang language family (for Xokleng, cf. Henry 1935, 1948, Urban 1985, Gakran 2005; for Kaingang cf. Wiesemann 1972, 1978, 1986) were inspected against a set of typically Austronesian features that have been proposed by Klamer (2002) as a heuristic for suggesting the affiliation of a language (i.e. whether it is Austronesian or not).[6] The Kaingang languages turned out to share Austronesian properties of both phonology and grammar.

Thus, like Austronesian languages, and especially their Oceanic branch, which are known to have lost the voicing contrast in obstruents and to have developed prenasalized consonants in opposition to plain

---

[6] Here, we can ignore the methodological problem of whether or not, or how, typological features may be used in historical linguistics (cf. the debate in Ross 2003 and Klamer 2003).

consonants, the Kaingang languages also do not have plain voiced obstruents, but contrast plain voiceless with prenasalized voiced consonants.

Many Austronesian languages prefer roots of CVCV type, and so do the Kaingang languages. Specifically, according to Henry (1948: 196), in Xokleng the CVCV pattern is prevalent and amounts to 35% of all root patterns in Xokleng (CV patterns being 14%, CVC 13%, CVCVC 12%, CVCCV 12%, CCV 5%, and CVCVCV 5%). As seen from these numbers, other typically Austronesian features of Xokleng are the "dropping" of final consonants (word-final consonants being present in only 25% of the patterns) and a dispreference for consonantal clusters (occurring in only 17% of the words). Besides, the possible final consonants and consonantal clusters are subjected to further restrictions we need not discuss here. The situation is similar in Kaingang.

Another, and related, phonological similarity is the insertion of paragogic vowels word-finally in both language families in order to open the syllable.

Similarly to many Austronesian languages, Xokleng forms emotional expressions by Verb + body part noun, in which the Experiencer of the emotion is the Possessor of the body part. For example, Xokleng's expression for "I am angry" literally means "My heart splits (in several places)" (Henry 1935: 213).

Like many Austronesian languages, Xokleng's numerals seem to behave like verbs in that they act like verbal predicates and take the same predicating particles as the verbs themselves (Henry 1948: 200, Henry 1935: 180). Xokleng, also similarly to many Austronesian languages, does not have a passive construction; it does have a subjectless construction that can be rendered with an English passive (Henry 1948: 199).

A distinction between alienable and inalienable possession is marked in the Kaingang family, as in all Macro-Ge languages (studied in Wiesemann 1986). Oceanic has three or more contrasting categories of possession. The Kaingang language makes a further distinction in that there is a third category of non-possessable items such as food (e.g. the word for corn falls into this category) (Wiesemann 1986: 373). This distinction between neutral and edible possession is widespread in Oceanic languages, and it appears in a few languages of eastern Indonesia.

Similarly to other Austronesian languages mainly in Eastern Indonesia, but also scattered elsewhere in Western and Eastern Austronesian languages (e.g. Malagasy, Manobo, Hawaiian, Batak, etc.),

Xokleng employs parallelism in narratives, myths, poems and songs, a verbal art form in which semantically synonymous pairs/triples etc. of words and phrases are used in parallel utterances. Urban (1986) has noted this feature of Xokleng and provides a more detailed discussion and examples.

It might be interesting to note that practically all Kaingang language family features I have been able to inspect from Klamer's list of about a dozen features turned out to be like those in Austronesian. These are the presence of prenasalized consonants, CVCV roots, paragogic vowels, verbs for emotional states expressed as V+body part, numerals acting like verbs, absence of passive constructions, alienable vs. inalienable nouns, and parallelism.

Additionally, we mention the following structural parallelisms between the language families.

Two other typically Austronesian features not mentioned by Klamer (2002), which are possessed by the Kaingang languages, are the affixing and reduplication as productive devices, and operating basically on verbs, and the fundamental verbal distinction in both Austronesian and the Kaingang languages between stative verbs and dynamic, or active, verbs.

Also, Austronesian contains a number of pockets of ergativity: some Polynesian languages (e.g. Tongan and Samoan), the Tamanic sub-group on Borneo, the South Suluwesi subgroup, Tagalok and other Philippine languages (Dixon 1994: 4). Most Macro-Ge languages are also (split) ergative (for a description of this aspect of Xokleng, cf. Urban 1985).

Finally, Austronesian languages typically draw a distinction between proper nouns (personal pronouns and names) and common nouns marked by articles. Similarly, in the Kaingang family third person pronouns may follow a noun to determine gender and number, especially when talking about humans (Wiesemann 1986: 377).

7.3.2 Lexical comparison: sound correspondences

In the following lexical comparisons, we focus on the Polynesian branch of the Austronesian language family, as it is geographically "nearest" to the Kaingang family. Our data for Xokleng comes from different sources (Gensch 1908; Henry 1935, 1948; Gakran 2005), and for Kaingang from the dictionary by Wiesemann (2002) and Wiesemann (1972). The data on cognate sets for Polynesian are based on Biggs and Clark (2006), Blust (1995), and *The Austronesian Basic Vocabulary Database*, but Tregear (1891), Williams (1957), Pukui and Erbert (1986), and Andrews (1865) are also consulted.

Table 7.4 shows the familiar sound correspondences (e.g., Biggs 1973, Tregear 1891) in the Polynesian languages Maori (New Zealand), and Hawaiian, alongside those that are known to hold for the Kaingang family (according to Wiesemann 1978).

Table 7.4. Sound correspondences between Xokleng, Kaingang, Maori, and Hawaiian

Nos.	Xok/Kai/Mao/Haw	Examples Nos.
1	p/p/p/p	23,24,25,39
2	t/t/t/k	31,32,36,39
3	k/k/t/k	1,2,5,26
4	k/k/k/ʔ	9,10,11,13,17,27
5	k/k/h/h	15,16,40
6	ð/Φ/t/k	33,34,35,40
7	h/h/(w)h/h	1,3,4,21
8	m/m/m/m	17,29,38
9	ŋ/ŋ/ŋ/n	11,12,24,36,37
10	w/w/w/w	28,30
11	l/r/r/l	1,2,6,7,8,9,15,16,18,19,22,38
12	a/ã/ā/ā	1,3,7,8,20,34,35
13	ɔ,a,ã/a,ã,ẽ/a/a	5,9,11,12,24,25,26,36,37,38,40
14	æ/a,ã/au,ao/au,ao	10,29,30
15	e/e/e/e	1,2,17,33
16	i,ẽ/i,ĩ/i/i	1,2,4,14,28,37
17	ũ/ũ/ū/ū	18,19
18	o,u,ẽ/o,ɔ,õ/ō/ō	6,13,27
19	u,o/u,o/u,o/u,o	4,9,15,16,17,21,22,36,40

NOTE: Abbreviations: Xok=Xokleng, Kai=Kaingang, Mao=Maori, Haw=Hawaiian.

The following similarity sets are illustrations of the sound correspondences. Each similarity set has a gloss, giving a general meaning, which may be further specified for some languages if somewhat different from gloss. The items in one language family that are similar to those of the other family are separated by equality "=". A dash "–" indicates a relatively clear word division in the Kaingang languages, segmenting stem from morphological endings (–m, –n, –r, –y, etc.). Brackets "()" enclose forms that are not part of the comparison (e.g. the verbal forms ke, he 'to say' in the Kaingang languages, which, when parts of larger verbs, simply indicate direct speech). A slash "/" stands for "or", and according to context may indicate a paragogic vowel at the end of a Kaingang word, or a doublet form. Note that a paragogic vowel in both Kaingang languages is the same or a more central vowel added after word final *r, v, y*; in Kaingang orthography, the paragogic vowel is not written, while in Xokleng an investigator like Henry (1935, 1948) and earlier linguists write these vowels and they may appear in my description below. Note also that a plus sign "+" after a Xokleng word below designates a word whose source is the early investigation by Gensch (1908), who does not make some phonological distinctions (e.g. central vs. non-central vowels) that are recognized today, which results in some indefiniteness in his description (in other respects pretty reliable). Finally, in the sequel, the Kaingang languages are written in their usual phonemic transcription, and the Austronesian languages in the way of their respective sources, with only minor and obvious changes (e.g. I use "?" in place of the more common apostrophe " ' ").

The following abbreviations are used for frequently cited languages and language groups:

PAn = Proto-Austronesian, PCEMP = Proto-Central-Eastern-Malayo-Polynesian, PCMP = Proto-Central-Malayo-Polynesian, PMP = Proto-Malayo-Polynesian, POc = Proto-Oceanic, Pn = Polynesian, PPn = Proto-Polynesian.

1. Be same or similar: Xokleng *halike*, Kaingang *hã ri ke* = Maori *whãrite*, Hawaiian *hãlike*.

2. Be same or similar: Xokleng *like*, Kaingang *ri ke* = Maori *rite*, Hawaiian *like*.

3. Prefix: Xokleng *ha–*, Kaingang *hã–* = Maori *whã–*, Hawaiian *hã–*.

4. Whistle: Xokleng *hui*, Kaingang *huɲ* = Maori *whio*, Hawaiian *hio*.

5. Near: Kaingang *kakã* (or *kakɔ*) = Maori *tata*, Hawaiian *kaka* 'fruits growing in clusters', Pn *tata* 'near'.

6. Ant/insect: Xokleng *lɔ* 'ant', Kaingang *ro* 'small bee' = Maori *rõ* 'stick insect', Hawaiian *lõ* 'species of bug' (Tongan *lo* and Samoan *loi* 'ant'), PPn *lõ* 'ant'.

7. Sun: Xokleng *la*, Kaingang *rã* = Maori *rã*, Hawaiian *lã.*

8. Day: Xokleng *la*, Kaingang *kurã* = Maori *rã*, Hawaiian *lã*.

9. Light/glow: Xokleng *kulaɲ* 'tomorrow, morning, early', Kaingang *kurã* = Maori *kura*, Hawaiian *ʔula.*

10. Stick: Xokleng *kɔ*, Kaingang *ka* = Maori *mã/kau* 'handle', POc *kayu* 'stick, wood', Fijian (Bau) *kau* 'tree, stick'.

11. Sick: Xokleng *kɔɲɔ* 'sick, pain, wound', Kaingang *kaɲa* 'sick, pain, wound' = Central-Eastern Pn *kaga* 'to place a curse on someone', Tuamotan *kaɲa* 'injure, illtreat'; Samoic-Outlier Polynesian *kago*,

Samoan *?ago/si* 'wasted away from sickness'; Fijian *gogo* 'weak, wasted away', Maori *ngongo* 'sick'.

12. Worm: Xokleng *(wai–)ŋɔ+* 'louse' (*kɔŋɔ* 'grub'), Kaingang *ŋa* 'louse, woodworm' (also *nuŋ?ə* 'worm-eaten, rotten, wasted away') = Pn *tuga* 'larva, maggot, organism causing internal decay', Maori *tunga* 'larva, worm-eaten, rotten (of timber)', Mangarevan *tuga* 'worm that devours sugar-cane'.

13. Penetrate: Xokleng *ko* = Maori *kō* 'wooden implement used for digging', Hawaiian *?ō*.

14. In, inside: Xokleng *ki*, Kaingang *ki* = Maori *ki*, Hawaiian *i*.

15. Cloth: Xokleng *kul/u*, Kaingang *kur/u* = Maori *huru* 'coarse hair', Hawaiian *hulu*.

16. Blanket: Xokleng *kul/u*, Kaingang *kur/u* = Hawaiian *huluhulu*.

17. Broth/food: Kaingang *kome* = Maori *kome*.

18. Shake (as dust from garment): Kaingang *rũ–m rũ–m* = Maori *rūrū*, Hawaiian *lūlū*.

19. Scatter: Kaingang *rũ–m (ke)* = Maori *rui*, Hawaiian *lū*.

20. Breathe (with difficulty): Kaingang *hã–m hã–m (ke)* = Maori *hāhā*, Hawaiian *hāhā*.

21. Blow: Kaingang *hu (he)* = Hawaiian *hu*.

22. Round/roll: Kaingang *ror* = Maori *(pi)rori*, Hawaiian *loli*.

23. Birth/origin: Xokleng *pɔ* = Maori *pū*.

24. Throw: Xokleng *pãŋ*, Kaingang *pẽŋ* = Maori *panga*, Hawaiian *pana*.

25. Hand/touch: Kaingang *pẽ* = Maori *pā*, Hawaiian *pā*.

26. Finish: Xokleng *kaŋ*, Kaingang *kã–n* = Hawaiian *kā*.

27. Dig: Kaingang *kõkõ–m* = Maori *kōkō*, Hawaiian *?ō?ō*.

28. Turn, reverse: Kaingang *wĩrĩ–n* = Maori *wiri* 'twist', Hawaiian *wili*.

29. Carry: Xokleng *mɔ*, Kaingang *ma* = Maori *mau*, Hawaiian *mao*.

30. Tree, forest: Xokleng *wæ+*, Kaingang *wã–ɲ* = Maori *wao*, Hawaiian *wao*.

31. The (def. art.): Xokleng *te*, = Maori *te*, Hawaiian *ke*.

32. Moist: Xokleng *tuy/u*, Kaingang *tuy* 'trickle intensely' = Maori *tōi*, Hawaiian *kōi* 'flow, spurt'.

33. Heart: Xokleng *ðe*, Kaingang *Φe* 'heart, chest, breast' = Maori *ate* 'liver, heart', *ateate* 'bosom', Tuamotan *ate* 'heart'.

34. Shell: Xokleng *kɔða* 'shell', *kɔðan* 'strip embira bark' (*kɔtĩ* 'smooth'), Kaingang *kuΦẽn* 'to peel, to shell', *kɨΦɛ* 'knife' = Maori *kota* 'cockle shell, anything to scrape or cut with', PPn **qota* 'dregs, residue'.

35. Wash clothes: Xokleng *ðaŋ*, Kaingang *Φã*, = Hawaiian *kā*, Samoan *tā*.

36. Rash (of skin): Kaingang *tuŋa* 'rash' = Rarotongan *tunga* 'scabbed, weevily; covered with sores', Tokelau *tunga* 'pimple', Pn *tunga* 'blemish, imperfection'.

37. Hand, arm: Xokleng *nẽŋa*, Kaingang *nĩŋɛ* (or *niŋã*) = Maori *ringa*, Fijian *liga–* 'hand, forearm', PMP **liŋa* 'hand, arm'. (*l ~ n* is a common alternation within Polynesian languages, e.g. *lima ~ nima* 'five, hand').

38. Ashes: Xokleng *mlã*, Kaingang *mrẽj* = Pukapuka *malamala*, Hawaiian *malamala* 'small piece of any substance broken from a larger', PPn **mala(mala)* 'chip, splinter, fragment'.

39. Pierce: Xokleng *pati* = Maori *pātia* 'spear', Penrhyn, Rarotongan, Tahitian *pātia* 'stab, thrust; spear, lance', Central-Eastern Pn *pā–tia* 'pierce'.

40. Stone: Xokleng *kaðu+* = Maori *whatu*, Hawaiian *haku*, Mangarevan *ʔatu*, Pn *fatu*.

As seen from the above list, the sounds (vowels and consonants) of each Kaingang-family wordform, with only a small number of exceptions, are totally predictable from the Polynesian-family wordforms, according to the correspondences from Table 7.4. More illustrations of the correspondences follow in the next section.

7.3.3 Lexical comparison: non-random lexical sets and additional levels of evidence

By a "non-random lexical set", I will understand a set of words sharing a similarity in meaning, form, or perhaps in some other way. Familiar examples based on shared meanings are lexical fields such as body parts, kinship terms or lower numerals, and the classical example of a non-random lexical set, formed on this basis, is the "basic vocabulary", whose elements (body parts, kinship terms, etc.) are themselves non-random word sets. There are also other non-random word sets, perhaps less commonly used in historical/comparative linguistics, which I will also compare below. Such comparisons provide an additional level of evidence over the traditional comparative method, and used complementarily to it, can lend further credibility to the comparisons, because a concentration of similarities within an antecedently fixed and limited (i.e. non-random) domain are generally less likely to be due to mere chance than the same number of matches in an open domain.

In the following, I slightly relax the strict conditions for counting a match used earlier, especially as regards vowels, and occasionally admit comparanda outside of the Polynesian family, for the following reasons. The first reason is methodological and has been nicely phrased by Campbell in the following manner:

> Where the intention is to call attention to a possible, but as yet unattested connection, one often casts a wide net in order to hold in as much potential evidence as possible. When the intention is to test a proposal that is already on the table, those forms admitted initially as possible evidence are submitted to more careful scrutiny. (Campbell 2004)

The second reason is empirical and has to do with the considerable presence of doublet forms involving vowels for the Kaingang family, not all of which may be registered in the sources I am using, and for which very strict sound matching criteria can turn out to be much too restrictive. For example,, as reported by Wiesemann (1972, 1978), in Kaingang there exist a number of free vowel alternations: *a* ~ *ə*, *ã* ~ *a, ã* ~ *ɛ, ã* ~ *ɔ, ɛ* ~ *e, ɔ* ~ *o* (e.g. *kãŋra* ~ *kãŋrə* 'picture', *kã* ~ *ka* 'tree', etc.).

7.3.3.1 Synonymous sets

If a single word from a set of synonyms in one language may resemble a word from a synonymous set in another language by pure chance, the event in which other words from both sets also formally resemble each other is much less likely to occur by chance. The higher the number of resembling words, the less likely the event, and hence the stronger the evidence for the existence of some link between the compared languages. By "synonyms" I understand both words with exactly coinciding and such with close meanings, and examples of both types are used as illustrations below.

(1) *Near*

Near1: Kaingang *kakã* (or *kakɔ*) = Maori *tata*, Hawaiian *kaka* 'fruits growing in clusters', Pn *tata* 'near'.
Near2: Xokleng *la*, Kaingang *rã* = Maori *rã*, Hawaiian *la* 'there, yonder'.

(2) *Rain*

Rain1: Xokleng *ugua*+ (? *ukua*) = Maori, Hawaiian *ua*, Rapanui, Rennell Is. (Solomons) *ʔua* (POc *quzan*).

Rain2: Xokleng *kuta* 'fall (rain)', Kaingang *kutẽ* 'fall (rain)', *ta kutẽ* 'rain' = Pwamai (New Caledonia) *kuta*, Jawe (New Caledonia) *kut*.

Rain3: Xokleng *tɔ*, Kaingang *ta* = Woleai (Micronesian) *uta*, Lau, Longgu (Solomon Islands) *uta*.

Rain4: Kaingang *kɔ (he)* 'drizzle' (also *ta kɔ*) = Maori *tō* 'fall (of rain)', Pn **tō* 'fall (of rain)'.

Rain5: Kaingang *kɔkɔ (he)* 'drizzle' = Maori *totō* 'to ooze, to trickle', Hawaiian *koko* 'reddish rain' (Andrews 1865).

(3) *Hit/Strike*

Hit/strike1: Kaingang *pẽ* 'hand, arm' = Hawaiian *pā*, Niue *pā* 'slap, strike, touch, clap'.

Hit/strike2: Xokleng *puke*, Kaingang *pɔ ke* = Niue *poki* 'slap'.

Hit/strike3: Kaingang *tã–ɲ* 'kill, beat to death' = Niue *tā* 'strike, kill, adze'.

Hit/strike4: Xokleng *tuŋge*, Kaingang *tag ke* = Niue *tuki* 'knock, pound, mash'.

(4) *Tree/Woods*

Tree/woods1: Xokleng *kɔ*, Kaingang *ka* = POc **kayu* 'stick, wood', Fijian (Bau) *kau*, Maori *mā/kau*, Namakir (Vanuato) *ka*.

Tree/woods2: Xokleng *kute*, Kaingang *kute* 'capão (flora), forming a type of flowers in southern Brazil, consisting of a group of tree vegetation' = POc **qutan* 'woods, forest', Mota *uta*.

Tree/woods3: Xokleng *wæ+*, Kaingang *wã–ɲ* = Maori *wao*, Hawaiian *wao*.

Tree/woods4: Xokleng *bekud+* = PAn **biŋkudu*, Paiwan *vukid* (Blust 1995).

(5) *Water*

Water1: Xokleng *ŋoy–waig+* 'river, stream', Kaingang *war* 'flood of water' = POc **waiʀ*, Maori *wai, awa* 'river, stream', Hawaiian *wai*.

Water2: Xokleng *ŋoy*, Kaingang *ŋoy* = Hawaiian *nō* 'seepage, to leak'.

Water3: Kaingang *kayã* 'salty' = Maori *tai*, Hawaiian *kai* 'salty water'.

Water4: Kaingang *wãya* 'mixture (with water)' = Fijian *vai–na* 'mixture with water'.

Water5: Kaingang *ŋunŋɔn* 'liquid' = Maori *ngongi*, Hawaiian *nono* 'oozing, seepage', Macassar *njonjo* 'liquid; to drip'.

Water6: Kaingang *ĕkɔ–r* 'sour water' = Maori *ehu* 'muddy', Hawaiian *ehu* 'dusty, disturbed'.

Water7: Kaingang *ku–pe* 'wash' (*ku–* prefix) = Vanua Lava (five dialects) *pe;* Mota *pei; pii* 'sprinkle water', *pia* 'foam from soap'.

Water8: Kaingang *me* 'liquid' = Mengen *me* 'water'.

Water9: Kaingang *run* 'carry, fetch water', *runya* 'vessel for water' = Maori *ranu–a* 'mix with liquid', Tongan *lanu* 'wash in fresh water', POc **danum* 'fresh water'.

Water10: Xokleng *ŋoy (be?)lele+* 'falling of water' = Maori *rere* 'waterfall' (Tregear 1891), Hawaiian *wai lele* 'waterfall'.

(6) *Breast/suck*

Breast/suck1: Xokleng *–kum(b)e+* 'female breast' = Maori *kōuma* 'breastbone' , Tuamotan *kōuma* 'chest, breast, bosom', PPn **uma.a* 'breast, chest'.

Breast/suck2: Kaingang *ũ–ɲ ũ–ɲ (he)* 'suck' = Maori, Hawaiian *ū* 'female breasts', Tongan *huhu* 'female breasts, to suck'.

(7) *Fire*

Fire1: Xokleng *pẽ,* Kaingang *pĩ* = POc **api*, Maori, Hawaiian *ahi*, Anuta *api*.

Fire2: Xokleng *akpunu+* 'burn', Kaingang *kaprũn* 'line of fire, much fire in the firewood' = Maori *kapura*.

Fire3: Xokleng *ðai–kɔlɔ* 'kindle fire' = Maori *toro* 'to burn, a flame, burning' (also Maori *kora* 'fire'), Tongan *tolo* 'to rub, to ignite'.

Fire4: Kaingang *pũn* 'burn', *pũr* 'burnt' = Proto-Central Pacific **pula* 'burn', Proto-Micronesian **pwula* 'burn', Rotuman *pula* 'burn', Hawaiian *pula* 'kindling', Waya (western Fiji) *bula–n* 'burn'.

Fire5: Kaingang *wãpũn* 'burn with big fire', *wãpũr* 'burnt to garbage' = Maori *māpura* 'fire'.

Fire6: Kaingang *kupũn* (=*hupũn*) 'to light up', *hupũr* 'illuminated with fire', *kupũr* 'burn in fire' = Central-Eastern Polynesian *kō–pura* 'flash', PPn **pula* 'shine', Maori *kōpura* 'flash, flicker, glance', Tahitian *opura/pura* 'to be flashing obscurely as fire', Tuamotan *kōpura/pura* 'to emit sparks, to glow or shine with unsteady light'.

Fire7: Kaingang *kɔm (ke)* 'light fire, light', *kɔm kɔm (ke)* 'to flash, to shine' = Tahitian *koma* 'spark', Maori, Tuamotan *koma*.

7.3.3.2 Polysemous/Homonymous sets

If a monosemous word in one language happens to resemble another monosemous word in another language by chance, the event in which a polysemous (or homonymous) word resembles a polysemous (or homonymous) word, is less likely to be merely coincidental, because it involves several meaning matches, rather than only one. The higher the number of meaning matches, and the more "unusual" the meanings of the polysemous/homonymous word, the less probable this event is, and hence the stronger the evidence for a non-chance link between the compared languages.

(1) In the following example, the compared forms have four meanings, the last two of which are "unusual" in that they seem quite divergent from the "basic meaning" of the form:

Sun: Xokleng *la*, Kaingang *rã* = Maori *rā*, Hawaiian *lā*.
Day: Xokleng *la* (Kaingang *kurã*) = Maori *rā*, Hawaiian *lā*.
Near: Xokleng *la*, Kaingang *rã* = Maori *rā*, Hawaiian *la* 'there, yonder'.
Below: Kaingang *rã* = Fijian (Bau) *e rā*, Fijian (Navosa) *ra*.

Besides, the Kaingang form *ra* 'hot' and Xokleng *lɔ* 'hot', apparently related to *rã* and *la*, respectively, also have the same correlative word *rā/lā* 'hot' in Polynesian.

(2) The following example exhibits three meanings, the last of which seems "unusual":

Cloth, clothes: Xokleng *kul/u*, Kaingang *kur/u* = Hawaiian *hulu* 'cloth; fur, wool'.
Blanket: Xokleng *kul/u*, Kaingang *kur/u* = Hawaiian *huluhulu*.
Colour: ? Xokleng *kul/u* = Paumotan *huru* 'colour', Hawaiian *hulu* 'colour, nature, kind'; regarding the meaning of Xokleng *kul/u* as 'colour', see below.

Compare also the different, but apparently related, Kaingang language family forms:

Hair: ? Xokleng *kren–kula–+* (= 'head'–*kula*) = Maori *huru* 'hair, coarse hair (properly, of the body, but sometimes used for the hair of the head'; cf. *uru*, the head; a single hair), Rarotongan *uro*; regarding the meaning of Xokleng *kula*, see below.

Fibre: Kaingang *kurẽ* (or *kurã*) 'internal fibre of taquara' = Hawaiian *pulu* 'coconut fibre', cf. *hulu-hulu* 'body hair, hair of eyelashes, fleece, fur, hairy', PAn **bulut* 'hairy filaments of certain plants, husk', Niue *pulu* 'fibre'.

(3) The following example shows the instrumental metonymy "tree–stick", which is typical for Oceanic languages, where the instrumental prefix *ka(i)–* has developed from **kayu* 'tree', cf. Lynch *et al.* (2002: 70):

Tree: Xokleng *kɔ,* Kaingang *ka* = POc **kayu* 'stick, wood', Fijian (Bau) *kau,* Maori *mā/kau* 'handle', Namakir (Vanuato) *ka.*
Stick: Xokleng *kɔ,* Kaingang *ka* = Fijian (Bau) *kau.*

7.3.3.3 Polysemous/homonymous and paronymous sets

By "paronyms", here I understand words in one language that are very close in form. Paronymous sets normally involve some derivational pattern. If the different meanings of a polysemous/homonymous word in one language are rendered by a paronymous set in another language, this would be an unlikely event, since normally we would expect a random set of words, rather than some derivational pattern, to do the job. The higher the number of meanings of the polysemous/homonymous word rendered by paronyms, the less likely the event, and hence the stronger the evidence for a non-chance link between the compared languages. Below are examples of paronymous sets in the Kaingang family that correspond to the different meanings of polyesemous/homonymous sets in Polynesian.

(1) The Kaingang language family paronymous set *{tã, (ð/Φ)ã, kã}* matches the Polynesian polysemous word *tā*:

Break (as wood): Kaingang *tã* = Hawaiian *kā* 'to split or break wood', Maori *tā* 'strike', Samoan *tā* 'to break firewood, to break up a dry tree', Fijian *tā* 'chop'.
Kill: Xokleng *taiɲ,* Kaingang *tã–ɲ* 'kill, beat to death' = Hawaiian *kā* 'murder', Rennell Is. (Solomons) *tā* 'hit, strike, cut, kill', Sikaiana (Solomons) *tā* 'kill, hit, kick', Luangiua (Ongtong-Java, Solomons) *kā* 'hit, kill'.
Wash clothes: Xokleng *ðag,* Kaingang *Φã* = Hawaiian *kā,* Samoan *tā.*
Beat (maize): Kaingang *Φãn* = Hawaiian *kā* 'to thrash out grain'.
Finish: Xokleng *kaŋ,* Kaingang *kã–n* = Hawaiian *kā.*

It is important to notice that the sound pattern of forming the paronymous set in Kaingang, viz. the alternation *t* ~ *ð/Φ* ~ *k,* coincides with the set of all the Kaingang sounds that correspond to Polynesian *t,* thus giving additional support to the three rules Nos. 2, 3, and 6 from Table 7.4. Notice also that the same alternation patterns are additionally observed within the Kaingang family itself, e.g.: Xokleng *kɔða* 'shell', *kɔðan* 'strip embira bark', but *kɔtĩ* 'smooth', Kaingang *ti* 'he/it';but *Φi* 'she', Xokleng *ti* 'he/it', but *ði* 'she'.

(2) The following example shows a correspondence between a paronymous set in Kaingang and a paronymous set in Maori and a homonymous set in Hawaiian.

Throw: Xokleng *pãŋ,* Kaingang *pẽŋ* = Maori *paŋa,* Hawaiian *pana.*
Shoot: Xokleng *pænũ* or *paŋ,* Kaingang *pɛnũ* = Maori *whana,* Hawaiian *pana,* PPn **fana* 'shoot with a bow'.
Bow/arrow: Xokleng *puɲ* = Hawaiian, Marquesan *pana* 'bow'.

7.3.3.4 Lexical fields

(1) *Body parts*

Head1: Xokleng *klẽ,* Kaingang *krĩ* = PPn **qulu,* Maori *uru,* East Futuna, Tongan, East Uvea *ʔulu* 'head'.
Head2: Xokleng *paʔi,* Kaingang *pãʔi* = Maori *u/poko,* Hawaiian *poʔo.*
Hand/arm1: Xokleng *nẽŋa,* Kaingang *nĩŋã* or *nĩɲɛ* = Maori *ringa* 'hand, arm', Fijian *liga* 'hand, forearm', PPn and PMP **linga* 'hand, arm'.
Hand/arm2: Kaingang *pẽ* = Maori, Hawaiian *pā* 'touch', Ra`ivavai *pā* 'to touch with'.
Leg/foot: Kaingang *wagwag* 'to limp' (*wag (ke)* 'to pass to the other side') = Maori *wae/wae,* Hawaiian *wawae.*
Eye: Xokleng *kɔna* 'eye, to look at', Kaingang *kanẽ* 'eye, to look at' = Maori *kana* 'stare wildly', Tuamotan *kana* 'stare', Central-Eastern Pn *kana* 'stare at' (PPn **konohi* 'eye', Maori, Penrhyn *kanohi* 'eye').
Breast: Xokleng *–kum(b)e+* 'female breast' = Maori *kōuma* 'breastplate', Tuamotan *kōuma* 'chest, breast, bosom' (cf. also Kaingang *ũ–ɲ ũ–ɲ (he)* 'suck' = Maori, Hawaiian *ū* 'female breasts').
Heart/liver: Xokleng *ðe,* Kaingang *Φe* 'chest, breast, heart' = Maori *ate* 'liver, heart', Hawaiian *ake* 'liver', Tuamotan *ate* 'heart'.

Chin: Xokleng *lɔ*, Kaingang *ra* 'jaw' = Maori *rae*, Hawaiian *lae* 'any projecting substance as a prominent forehead', Tongan *lae* 'forehead', Samoan *lae* 'beardless chin'.

Bone: Xokleng *koko+* 'bone, knuckle', *kuka*, Kaingang *kuka* = PAn **kukut* 'bone', **kuku* 'node, joint, knuckle', Hawaiian *kuʔe* 'joint, the nuckles'.

Mouth/lips: Xokleng *–kuðo* (from *–kuso+*) 'lips' = Fijian *gusu–na*, Samoan, Tongan, Nieue *ngutu*, PAn **ŋusu*.

(2) *Kinship terms*

Xokleng's kinship terminology is discussed by Henry (1941: 175–80) and Kaingang's by Wiesemann (1974). The comparisons below seem to show substantial similarity of Kaingang terms with Micronesian languages (viz. the terms for wife, husband, and mother). Note that we found the best match in kinship semantic patterns between Xokleng and the Micronesian languages Chuuk and Ulithian. The entry for 'elder sibling' is interesting, especially if the forms for 'younger siblings' could also be conceived as "similar". The entry for "family" is a remarkable resemblance both formally and semantically, and further allows us to tentatively explain the meaning of Xokleng *kɔɲŋəŋ* and Kaingang *kaɲŋəŋ* 'an Indian, a Kaingang', previously unexplained as far as I know, as meaning 'one of our family' by reference to the respective words for 'family', viz. *kɔi ka* and *kaɲkã*. The entry for 'child1' notes a similarity with a cognate set in some Solomonic languages, while those for 'father' and 'child2' show likeness with words in isolated New Guinea languages, for which no cognate sets are proposed in *The Austronesian Basic Vocabulary Database*.

Wife+woman: Xokleng *plũ*, Kaingang *prũ* = Proto-Chuukic **pʷpʷúlú* 'spouse', **pʷúlú–wa–* 'married', Satawalese *púlú–wa–(n)* 'his wife', Marshallese (Eastern Dialect) *pālee–*.

Husband+man: Xokleng *man* (or *mɛn*), Kaingang *mɛn* = Proto-Micronesian, Proto-Chuukic **mʷaane* 'man, male', Satawalese *mʷáán*, As, Minyaifuin (Gebe, New Guinea) *man* 'husband'.

Father: Xokleng *yug*, Kaingang *yɔg* = Kaulong (Au Village, New Guinea) *iyok*.

Mother: Xokleng *ɲɔ̃*, Kaingang *–nɔ̃* = PAn **t–ina*, POc, Proto-Micronesian **tina*, Samoan *tinā*, Mokelese (Micronesia) *ina–(a)* 'his mother', Mortlockese (Micronesia) *ina–*.

Child1: Xokleng *ŋɛ̃l/e*, Kaingang *ŋĩr* = Kwara'ae *ngela*, Lengo, Ghari *ŋgari*, Mbaungguu *ŋwɛle*, Fataleka *ŋwele* (all Solomonic).

Child2: Kaingang *kɔsin* = Sengseng (New Guinea) *po-kusan*.

Elder sibling: Xokleng *kake* 'relative', Kaingang *kãkɛ* (or *kãke*) 'elder brother', *kãke Φi* (*Φi* = female) 'elder sister' = PMP **kaka* 'elder sibling'. (Blust 1995 notes that there can be no doubt that in PMP **kaka* referred to elder siblings, while another word, **huaji*, to younger siblings; Kaingang's meaning correspondences to the latter term have the forms Xokleng *yawɨ*, Kaingang *yãwɨ* (*Φi*) 'younger brother/sister'.)

Family: Xokleng *kɔi ka (he)* 'relatives, people with the same body paint, family', Kaingang *kaŋkã* 'family, parents' = Pn *kāiga* 'kin, family, relative', Tuvalu (Ellice Is.) *kāiga* 'family, relative', East Futuna (Horne Is.) *kāiga* 'relative, family, parent', East Uvea (Wallis I.) *kāiga* 'parent, friend', Pileni (Solomons) *kaega* 'clan, family', Samoan *ʔāiga*. 'elementary family; family, lineage, kin, relatives', Tokelau *kāiga* 'kin, relative', Tongan *kāinga* 'relation, relative'.

(3) Numerals

Kaingang's numerals, according to Wiesemann, are *pir* 'one', *rɛŋre* (or *rɛŋrɛ*) 'two, second', *tãŋtũ* 'three', *wɛ̃ɲ–kãŋra* 'four', *[ʃĩko]* 'five'. Contemporary Xokleng has a base-two system, *pil* 'one', *lɛŋle* 'two', forming higher numerals by their combination: *lɛŋle to pil* 'three' *lɛŋle to lɛŋle* 'four', etc. (Greg Urban, personal communication). Henry (1948) lists *pil* 'one' and *lœŋle* 'two', as well as one word involving the number four, viz. *ðəipa* 'four-cornered', but says that the Xokleng have no "real numbers", presumably because e.g. *lɛŋle/rɛŋre* mean 'companion, friend, co-spouse (Xokleng), brother (Kaingang)'. An early investigation (Gensch 1908) lists what seems to be a quinary numeral system: *toktenúnlo+* 'one', *nunengláglo+* 'two', *lenglæmú+* 'twice', *umarikélko+* 'three', *umpétko+* 'four', *undupélemo+* 'five' (the accent denotes stress).

One: Xokleng *pil/i*, Kaingang *pir*, *pipir* 'few', *(wɛ̃ɲ) pãnpir* 'reunited', *pãnpin* 'group together long objects' = Maori *piri*, Hawaiian *pili* 'united, joining', Marquesan *piʔi* 'unite, kindred'. The Austronesian languages usually do not express quantity with the term, cf. however the related Tahitian *piti* with the same meaning 'to join, to unite with another' used as "two" in counting.

Two: Kaingang *rərə* 'fight by twos', *rən* 'grapple', *to rə* 'fight' (i.e. *rərə* probably *rə–rə* lit. 'grapple, fight + two') = Pn *rua* 'two', Tahitian *aro–rua* 'the second in a combat', or lit. 'to face, to turn towards + second'.

Xokleng's numerals given by Gensch look very interesting, even if not wholly understandable (to me). But a few speculations may not be out of place in accordance with my aim to "cast a wide net in order to hold in as much potential evidence as possible", which should subsequently be submitted to more careful scrutiny. Thus, first, these numerals seem like a continuation in counting after "two" of the other linguistic source(s), and the set undoubtedly shares the word for "two" with them. Secondly, they seem to contain some additional material over pure numerals roots, as witnessed e.g. by *nuneng–lǽglo+* 'two' vs. *lenglæ–mú+* 'twice'. Table 7.5 highlights the sequence overlaps between Xokleng and Austronesian numerals for three, four, and five, accompanied by some information from Kaingang.

Table 7.5. Sequence overlaps in the numerals for "three", "four", and "five"

	Xokleng (Gensch)	Xokleng (Henry)	Kaingang	Austronesian
three	umari**kél**ko			POc **to**lu**, PCEMP **təlu*
four	um**pét**ko	ðəi**pa** 'four-cornered'	ɸɨr 'corner' pɛnugnu 'quadrangle', pɛn 'angle, corner'	POc, PCEMP **[ə]**pat**, ****pat**i, ****pan**i
five	undu**pélemo**			POc **li**ma***

NOTE: Sequence overlaps are given in bold.

The highlighted Xokleng sequences, which are similar to those in Austronesian, seem to be supported by segmentation considerations. In all three words the initial *u–* seems the Xokleng (and Kaingang) pronominal *ũ*, and *–kɔ* is a predicating particle (Greg Urban, personal communication). Thus, we get respectively: for "three", *ũ–mari–kel –kɔ*, where *mari*, if guessed by its meaning in Kaingang, is an emphasis word meaning 'also, too'; for "four", *ũ–(m)pen–kɔ* (the Xokleng nasal *n* is changed to the homorganic stop *t* in this context, as described by Henry 1948), and besides in Xokleng apparently we have the segmentation *ðəi–pa* lit. 'corner–four', judging by the Kaingang word *ɸɨr* 'corner'; and, for "five", *ũ–ndu–pélemo*, where *ndu* is a postposition meaning 'after'. Making these assumptions, the comparisons are:

Three: Xokleng –*kel* = Hawaiian *kolu*, Maori *toru*, Proto-Micronesian *telu, Kisar *wo–kelu*, Kei *tel*, Yamdena, Selaru *tél* (all Maluku), Central Masela *wɔkɛl*, Emplawas *wokɛl*, Dawera Daweloor *'tɛl* (all Babar).

Four: Xokleng *pa* or *pen (? pɛn)* = Hawaiian *hā*, Maori *whā*, Anuta *pā*, Buru (Maluku) *pā*.

Five: Xokleng –*pelemo* = Hawaiian *pālima* 'five times, in fives, fivefold', Maori *rima,* Tungag *palpalimana*, Tiang *patlima* (both New Ireland).

7.3.3.5 Long words

Similarities in longer words are less likely to be coincidental than similarities in shorter words as is well-known in historical linguistics. Below are some examples:

Be same or similar: Xokleng *halike*, Kaingang *hã ri ke* = Maori *whārite*, Hawaiian *hālike*.

Smell, odour: Xokleng *(di?)kukræ+* 'stink', Kaingang *kɔkrã–ɲ* 'stink of rotten' (cf. also Kaingang *ka?i* 'smell', *kãhɔr/ɔ* 'odourless') = Maori *kakara*, Hawaiian *?a?ala* 'fragrant', PPn *kakalu 'cockroach', East Futuna (Horne Is.) *kakalu* 'that which smells bad', Maori *kekererū* 'stinkroach'.

Snow: Xokleng *kuklule+*, Kaingang *kukrir/i* = Maori *hukarere*.

Thunder: Xokleng *tɔ̃tɔ̃l*, Kaingang *(ta) tɔ̃ tɔ̃rɔ̃r (hɛ)* = PPn **(fa)titili*, Maori *(wha)titiri*, Hawaiian *(he)kili*, Samoan *(fãi)titili*, Tuamotan *(fa)tutiri*, Tahiti an (1773) *(pa)tiree* 'it thunders'.

Fish: Kaingang *kãkuɸər* 'small fish' = Maori *kō–kota* 'shellfish', Mangarevan *kokota* 'small shell-fish'.

7.3.3.6 Compound words

The comparison of "compound words" (in our context, words comprising more material than just a single stem) presents significant evidence when both the compounds themselves and their constituent parts match in the compared languages. Below I give several illustrations, including as component part a grammatical morpheme.

(1) Compare entries Nos. 1–3 from our list of similarity sets. These three entries illustrate similar compound words, e.g. Xokleng *halike*, Hawaiian *hālike*, etc., all having an identical meaning, viz. 'be same or similar'. These composite words comprise prefixes with identical form and function in present context, variously designated in the different languages: "emphatic" (Xokleng), "assertive" (Kaingang), and "causal"

(Polynesian) (from *$f\tilde{a}$), and stems (meaning 'be same or similar'), which are also formally similar, e.g. Xokleng Prefix: *ha* + Stem: *like*, Hawaiian Prefix: *hā* + Stem: *like*, etc. Such a coincidence of three compared entities, viz. a compound word as a whole and its two constituents, is so highly unlikely, as to be practically impossible to occur by mere chance.

(2) Henry (1935, 1948) lists for Xokleng *ŋaikaug* 'fear, be frightened', which comprises a prefix *ŋai–* (in other Xokleng sources written *wai–+* or *wã–*; Kaingang *wãŋ–* or *wẽŋ–*), a "reflexive" with general meaning, and a stem *kaug*. Henry draws attention to the fact that this prefix has a valency-decreasing function, writing that "Certain verbs that begin with *ŋai* omit it when they have direct objects" (Henry 1935: 204), giving, among others, examples with the verb 'fear, be frightened'. Compare

Frighten: Xokleng *ŋaikaug* = Hawaiian *makaʔu*, Maori *mataku*, PAn *ma-takut*.

Now, the stems seem related (cf. also Yamdena and Selaru (southeast Maluku) having *taut*, Kédang (Timor) *taug* or Puyuma (Formosa) *ma-kauð* 'fear, be frightened', where the middle consonant *k* is elided). Additionally, the Austronesian (Proto-Oceanic) prefix *ma–* is known to have a valency-decreasing function (Evans and Ross 2001), in that prefixing it to a verbal stem reduces the number of arguments this verb may have. As we see, Xokleng's prefix *ŋai–* behaves in exactly the same way, as actually does Kaingang's correlative. (Curiously, this same verb seems to be the common illustrative example of the phenomenon in both language families.)

(3) Compare the "long word" for fish above. The Polynesian *kō–kota* 'shellfish', is a compound word, comprising the prefix *kō* 'like, similar to' and the stem *kota* 'shell, scrapings'. The Kaingang *kãkuΦər* 'small fish' also seems to be a compound, viz. *kã–kuΦər*, as seen from its meaning equivalent *kuvər* in one of Kaingang's dialects (São Paulo) (Wiesemann 1978: 212). Its stem *kuΦər* then corresponds to Polynesian *kota* 'shell, scrapings' as evidenced by Kaingang *kuΦεn* 'to shell, to peel', Xokleng *kɔða* 'shell'. The Kaingang prefix *kã–* seems to be allomorphic to the preposed Kaingang particle *kɔm* 'similar to, parallel to', and hence also corresponding to the Polynesian prefix *kō* 'like, similar to'.

7.3.3.7 A compound word and a synonymous set

The next example also describes an event which would not normally be expected in random comparisons, so is of some interest. The constituent parts of the compound Polynesian word *pō-fatu* 'stone' (Maori *pō(w)hatu*, Mangarevan *pōʔatu*), in which the sequence *fatu* 'stone', seem to correspond to a synonymous set in the Kaingang family: Kaingang *pɔ* 'stone', and Xokleng *kaðu+* 'stone' (*kaðu+* from older *kasu+* given by Gensch, in which *s* apparently represents *ð*). Note that *kaðu* is "regular" in that it fully agrees with our sound correspondences in Table 7.4. It is interesting to note, whatever the exact implications, that the contemporary form for stone in Xokleng is *kɔði*, and it nicely matches Pre-Rotuman **hafu* 'stone' pronounced *[hɔθu]* (cf. also Xokleng *ðe*, Kaingang *Φe* 'heart', Pre-Rotuman **afe* 'liver', pronounced *[æθe]*, Biggs 1965: 188).

7.3.3.8 Predictions

The usual way of testing a scientific theory is to draw logical deductions from the theory and check whether these predictions of the theory fit the data or not. The more of these predictions are true, the more corroborated the theory is. A similar approach, of course, can be used in historical linguistics. In the following, this general mode of reasoning takes a specific form. I take a sequence of two words in Kaingang <W1 + W2>, whose meaning as a whole, as well as the meaning of one of the constituent words, W1, is known, but that of the other, W2, is not, though W2 can be reasonably reliably predicted from context. This prediction, then, under the assumption that the Kaingang and Austronesian families are related — somewhat anticipating the hypothesis that is put forward later — can be tested by seeing whether or not a correlative word in Austronesian exists with the appropriate predicted meaning. This reasoning mode mimics the real-life situation in which one tries to reconstruct the died-out meaning of a word in some language by reference to a related language that has, or might have, preserved this word meaning. A positive outcome of such a reconstruction constitutes positive evidence for the idea of the existence of a relationship among these languages. Additionally, it allows us to gain a better understanding of one of the languages by making the reconstruction.

(1) Kaingang *ka rigri* means 'small mosquito', *ka* in this context standing for 'mosquito'. The word *rigri*, however, is with unknown meaning and according to Wiesemann (personal communication) does not occur outside this word complex. Assuming a connection between

Kaingang and Austronesian/Polynesian, we can predict that if *ringri* designates 'small' — as it would follow from context — we could find a correlative in Austronesian. Indeed, the formally similar *riki* means 'small' in Austronesian.

(2) In the word complex Kaingang *ka pũr* 'black person, African', the word *pũr* 'burnt' = Proto-Central Pacific **pula* 'burn', Proto-Micronesian **pwula* 'burn', Rotuman *pula* 'burn', Hawaiian *pula* 'kindling', Waya (western Fiji) *bula-n* 'burn'. The unknown Kaingang meaning of *ka* in this context, probably 'person' as derived from context, seems to be confirmed by Hawaiian *ka* meaning 'the one who, the person in question'.

(3) In the early documentation of Xokleng by Gensch (1908), the form *kulu–* is prefixed in 7 words denoting colour, and we have the sequence *kulu* + <colour term> + *ma*, as exemplified in *kulukuprima+* 'white', *kuluklama+* 'yellow', etc. The form *ma* is known to be a predicating particle, but what does *kulu* mean in this context? It would be natural to suppose that *kulu* means more specifically 'colour', or more generally something related as e.g. 'a kind of', but no such use of the word is known e.g. to the investigator of Kaingang and Xokleng Ursula Wiesemann (personal communication). Assuming a relationship between Xokleng and Austronesian, we could expect to infer the actually unknown meaning of *kulu* from some corresponding word in Austronesian. Indeed, in a language like Hawaiian (cf. also Paumotan *huru* 'colour') one finds *hulu*, meaning — among other things — 'colour' ('species of colour', Andrews 1865) or 'a kind of', i.e. we have the "regular" correspondence:

Xokleng *kulu* = Hawaiian *hulu* (PAn **bulu*); cf. also Nos. 15, 16.

As additional piece of evidence for this conclusion, consider the "unusual" coinciding polysemy of *kulu/hulu* in Kaingang/Austronesian families, the forms in the two families sharing the meanings 'cloth, clothes, blanket, colour'.

(4) Gensch (1908) lists as entry and sub-entry in Xokleng

Xokleng *kulug–+* 'dark' (German *dunkel*)
Xokleng *kuru-loa+* lit. 'darker stuff' (German *dunkler Stoff*),

which have the same root *ku(l/r)u* for 'dark' (*l* and *r* freely alternating in Xokleng). The meaning of Xokleng *loa* does not occur elsewhere in Gensch (1908) and is unknown. The Xokleng form *loa* does not seem to be associated with its substantive literal translation *staff*, for if it were the case, then, first, it should have preceded the adjectival *kuru* 'dark' (Xokleng's word order being substantive + adj), and, secondly, it should, as an autonomous word, have been written separately from the adjectival form. Therefore, *loa* appears to be a sort of comparative degree, or intensifier, of the adjectival *kuru* 'dark'. This prediction is fully substantiated by the Polynesian particle *loa*, having two meanings: (i) 'long', and (ii) 'very, very much, exceedingly', a post-posed intensifier probably used in our context. I note that there is a full match also of the other Xokleng word in the complex; thus, Hawaiian *kulu* 'be late at night' (Pukui and Erbert 1986), 'first night in which the moon is dark or can't be seen' (Andrews 1865); cf. also PAn **kudem*, Nggela *kuro*.

Further evidence that we are on the right track is the word *halikelɔ* 'how long', listed several times by Henry (1935), in which *halike* means 'how' (Kaingang *hẽri ke* 'how'), and *–lɔ*, apparently related to the older form *loa+*, has to mean 'long', the first meaning of the identical Polynesian word. It is not clear whether in Xokleng *–lɔ/–loa+* are separate words or are only used in compounds (as it is the case e.g. in Kapingamarangi). Note that our argumentation here follows the idea of comparison of polysemous sets.

(5) For the word 'hair' in Xokleng, Gensch gives *kren–kula–ma+* (lit. = 'head'–*kula*–predicating particle), where the meaning of *kula* is unknown. Henry (1935) lists for 'hair' *klẽ kiki* lit. 'head feather'. Given also that a formally similar word in Kaingang, *kurẽ* (or *kurã*) has the similar meaning 'internal fibre of taquara', one could predict that the unknown meaning of *kula* is also feather or something similar. This prediction is corroborated by the complete match with PPn **kula* 'feather', Western Fijian (Navosa) *kula* 'feathers', as well as by the fact that a number of Austronesian languages (e.g. Sekar, Ujir, Yakan, Buru) form the words for 'hair' as the combination of 'head+feathers'.

7.3.3.9 Extra-linguistic data

There are several pieces of evidence, besides the linguistic evidence, that seem to make less incredible the idea of the existence of some linguistic link between the geographically distant Austronesian-speaking and Kaingang-speaking populations. First, genetically South America is the most diverse part of the world, and Central America is more similar to North America than to South America (Cavalli-Sforza *et al.* 1994: 339).

Secondly, and more specifically, the Macro-Ge people, in drawing a phylogenetic tree of 23 American tribes, grouped according to linguistic criteria (Cavalli-Sforza *et al.* 1994: 323–324), were found to be the worst outliers (with Macro-Tucanoans).

Thirdly, and most importantly, apart from these more circumstantial, even if quite suggestive, pieces of genetic evidence that (at least some parts) of South America do not fit into the scenario of exclusively North-South population movement — which is the prevalent current belief today — there emerged recently genetic work giving sound evidence for the predominantly South-East Asian and Oceanic origin of South American native populations. For example, Ribeiro *et al.* (2003), analysing the Macro-Ge-speaking Xikrin and the Tupi-speaking Parakanã (note that Tupi is believed to be related to Macro-Ge), found them to be genetically similar to Indonesians and South-East Asian populations, concluding that "These results corroborate the existence of genetic affinities between Brazilian Indians and South-east Asian and Oceanic populations", their investigation being intended to "further contribute to the theory of a predominantly Asiatic origin of the American natives" (p. 59). Ribeiro *et al.* (2003) cite other genetic sources making claims to the same effect.

And, finally, an argument from Xokleng's beliefs. According to Henry (1945: 127) "The Kaingang [i.e. the Xokleng] have a clear idea of a period long ago when a number of events happened: *their ancestors came out of the sea* and over the mountains to the west..." [italics mine]. This belief suggests sea migrations of the Xokleng, and does not seem to fit the current wisdom of north-south route of colonization of South America, at least as far as these tribes are concerned.

7.3.4 Towards an explanation

In this section, I showed parallels between the Kaingang and the Austronesian language families in grammar and kinship semantics, as well as presented a network of similarities in lexicon. In addition to this linguistic evidence, we noted some results in population genetics indicating affinities between Brazilian Indians and South-east Asian and Oceanic populations, as well as beliefs pertaining to the origin of the Xokleng people. The nature and scope of the presented linguistic parallels and extra-linguistic evidence seem to enforce the conclusion that these pieces of evidence, taken collectively, cannot be just random, a conclusion I have also reached by direct computation of probabilities of matches in basic vocabulary comparisons. There are much too many coincidences, and this requires an explanation. One plausible explanation is a historical (probably genetic) relationship between the Kaingang and the Austronesian language families, and specifically its Oceanic branch, the exact nature of which is presently unknown. If true, the hypothesis will have far-reaching consequences not only for linguistics, but for the study of human pre-history and migrations as well. However, caution should be exercised, and further studies are still required to get more definitive answers. Regarding the current classification of the Kaingang languages as members of the Ge family, it will be clear that if my hypothesis turns out to be true, then either this classification is not valid, or it is valid, and Ge is also somehow linked to Austronesian. At present I can only state these as two logical possibilities.

7.4 Conclusion

The discovery of entities that bear similarities which exceed chance is a recurrent problem of great importance in linguistics, and in science more generally, because such a discovery generates the new problem of explaining why these similarities exist. The computational complexity of this problem is substantial and increases with the increase in the number of the entities one needs to compare. The assessment of statistical significance, especially if conducted in an empirical manner, as with the permutation test, is also very costly and beyond human reach. In this chapter, I presented the RECLASS system, which carries out the general scientific task of detecting similarities and the meta-scientific task of assessing their plausibility, or significance, and illustrated it with one common linguistic application, viz. the testing of genetic classifications. RECLASS can alternatively operate with features or with wordlists. The discoveries of the system led to the formulation of a hypothesis of a long-range relationship between two geographically distant language families that bears the signs of a true discovery, as defined in the book, and we proceeded with standard, manual, linguistic testing, which corroborated to some extent the computationally generated hypothesis.

Chapter 8. Concluding Remarks

8.1 The cycle of machine-aided empirical discovery

What basic stages does the investigatory process in machine-aided empirical discovery pass through? Looking back at our illustrative examples in Chapters 2–7 may suggest some recurrent patterns of this process.

In all cases, we started the investigation with a problem. Some data were given to us in advance, and what was required in the problem was to explore computationally these data in some way or another. The computer programs we implemented modelled some basic and recurrent tasks of linguistic discovery. These included general scientific tasks (such as multiple concept discrimination in KINSHIP and MPD; the discovery of inductive generalizations in UNIVAUTO or MINTYP; or the discovery of feature/word similarities in RECLASS) and the accompanying meta-scientific tasks (such as the discovery of simplest and/or plausible solutions).

The data which served as input to the programs were generally represented in terms of the triple Object–Feature–Value. Thus, in the cases when we explored a set of languages (as e.g. in UNIVAUTO, MPD profiling languages, RECLASS), the languages were interpreted as the objects, and their properties as feature values (or words in RECLASS operating with wordlists). In distinctive feature analysis (MPD), the phonemes were interpreted as the objects, and their phonetic characteristics as feature values, while in profiling language disorders, the disorders were represented as the objects and language errors as feature values, etc.

Running our programs on these data yielded the discoveries of these programs. In just one of the presented illustrations, viz. UNIVAUTO's discoveries based on Greenberg's 30–language sample, these discoveries were verbalized and outputted as an article, i.e. in a form ready for publication. In all remaining illustrations, the programs discoveries were further interpreted, e.g. summarized, compared to other similar results, their weaknesses and strengths evaluated and so on. Further, computational machinery was built to facilitate the interpretation (for doing some statistics, etc.), but we did not pay much attention to this auxiliary, and less important, machinery. A most essential point in this investigation process was the *generation of new problems*, as a result of solving the original problem we started our inquiry with. Thus, KINSHIP found a flood of alternative componential models even after all generally accepted adequacy criteria were satisfied, which raised the new problem of how to choose among these alternative solutions. A similar situation held in the application of MPD to profiling languages in terms of their segment inventories: there turned out to be a multitude of alternative profiles one needed to choose among. Within the framework of the same application, once we found all profiles, the question arose of whether or not phonetic feature relatedness existed between the found profiles. Also, having a list of phonological universals, discovered by UNIVAUTO, a natural question cropped up as to whether there existed a reasonable generalization of all these isolated statements. Or, again, knowing that MINTYP always managed to find a minimal description in attempts to several different typologies, the new problem arose of whether this could be proved to be always true. Finally, having found statistically significant similarities in kinship semantics and lexicon between the geographically distant Kaingang and Oceanic language families, the new problem emerged of explaining why this was the case.

This brief review of the basic phases we have gone through in our illustrative examples reveals the cyclic nature of the investigatory process: we started with some original problem, built computational tools to solve this problem, but as a result of the application of these computational tools, we as a rule stumbled upon new problems, which we also had to solve. Our experience with applying the computational tools to diverse linguistic problems fully accords with the view of the philosopher Karl Popper to the effect that an investigation begins and ends with a problem, and the game of science is, in principle, without end.

8.2 Evaluating the computational systems

A common pragmatic criterion for evaluating machine discovery systems is the publication of their discoveries in the specialized domain literature. According to this criterion, the systems described here perform well: their outputs have found outlet in a number of linguistic publications we mentioned in the course of the book. Computer scientist Valdés-Pérez (1999) has alternatively characterized machine scientific discovery as the generation of novel, interesting, plausible, and intelligible knowledge, and has suggested that a successful system should ideally have all these capacities. A successful system should eventually lead to (linguistic) discoveries, which we defined similarly in Chapter 1 as findings which are true, novel, unexpected and important. Additionally, we have also mentioned as advantageous to discovery systems the features of portability and insightfulness, which were found to be common to other linguistic discovery systems that the author has been involved in (Pericliev 1999b, 2003). Below I describe the systems introduced in the book along these six dimensions. (Cf. also Colton, Bundy, and Walsh 2000 for an interesting similar discussion concerning basically systems in the domain of mathematics).

8.2.1 Novelty

UNIVAUTO has so far produced around 60 pages of text, covering about 250 new universals from the fields of word order and phonology. Some problems were found in the proposed word order universals in the classical article by Greenberg (1966a), a circumstance which has remained unnoticed by previous human researchers, and some of the problematic universals have been widely disseminated in the linguistic community (cf. e.g. the complete enumeration of Greenberg's ordering universals in *The Linguistics Encyclopedia*, London and New York, 1991).

Similarly, many novel phonological universals were found in the UPSID-451 database in comparison with Maddieson's (1984) findings, as well as some problems in these and other related proposals in the literature (lack of statistical significance and/or low level of validity and/or insufficiently diverse language support).

Inspecting two further word order databases from Greenberg (1966a) and Hawkins (1983), which are really small 24×4 tables, the MINTYP system also managed to find patterns that have escaped these authors, considered to be the authorities in the field in the textbook by Croft (1990: 57).

KINSHIP has performed componential analysis of a number of languages, generating novel solutions to many of them. The reanalysis of English, which was an object of much previous effort, led to the most economical model and the only one that manages to give a conjunctive definition of all kin terms in this terminological system.

RECLASS has generated several new hypotheses of a possible historical relationship between languages, one of which we tried to test in Chapter 7.

Three design properties of our systems enhance the chances of finding novel knowledge. The first is the systems' ability (exemplified specifically in UNIVAUTO) to explicitly check its own discoveries against those of a human agent exploring the same data. More generally, this strategy is not impractical in a linguistic discovery system on universals in view of the availability of universals archives, such as the *Konstanz Archive*,[1] which has collected and recorded in a convenient form much of what has ever been proposed in the linguistic literature. The second design property enhancing the discovery of novel knowledge — and possessed by all the systems described in the book — is the exhaustive search of a combinatorial space that the systems perform. Such comprehensive searches of combinatorial spaces, that are furthermore dense with solutions, are known to be very difficult, if not completely beyond the reach of a human investigator, a trite circumstance in computer science (but, unfortunately, not so in many domain sciences as linguistics). As a corollary of the exhaustive search, all the systems can make meta-scientific claims to the effect that "These are all objects of the studied type (relative to the database)". The third design property is the ability of the systems to handle diverse queries some of which may not have been seriously posed or pursued before (e.g. UNIVAUTO can handle different logical types of universals, varying the different plausibility constraints; KINSHIP can be used as a tool supplying answers to various questions regarding properties of kin terms and kin types contained in the databases explored, etc.).

8.2.2 Interestingness

The interestingness of our systems' findings are partly derived from the interestingness of the problems they automate. Indeed, linguistics has always considered the discovery or falsification of a universal an achievement, hence the interestingness of UNIVAUTO's findings. Modelling the Saussurian structural approach is fundamental in linguistics. Componential and distinctive feature analyses, the profiling of linguistic objects and similar problems handled by KINSHIP and MPD are also recognized as significant linguistic problems, and therefore their findings are of interest. The problem of finding economical accounts of a typology, the goal of MINTYP, is central in the discipline of linguistic typology. And, finally, RECLASS is designed to detect potential problems in genealogical language classification, the fundamental issue in historical linguistics, recognized from the very birth of our discipline.

Another major way in which we tried to increase the interestingness of our systems KINSHIP, MPD, UNIIVAUTO, and MINTYP are the guaranteed-simplest solutions they all generate. Indeed, in linguistics, as

---

[1] To be found at http://ling.uni-konstanz.de/pages/proj/sprachbau.htm.

in science more generally, simpler solutions are as a rule regarded as more interesting than the less simple ones.

Finally, some of our systems have additionally some more specific design traits that are intended to enhance the interestingness of their findings. For example, UNIVAUTO attempts to enhance the discovery of interesting universals by outputting only the stronger claims and discarding the weaker ones. Thus, if Universal 1 logically implies Universal 2, the first is retained and the second is ignored. For example, "All languages have stops" implies "If a language has a fricative it also has a stop" and the second claim must therefore be dismissed as a pseudo-universal. (Parenthetically, the latter claim has been actually made more than 60 years ago in a celebrated book by Jakobson 1941, and as far as I know, has not been refuted so far.)

8.2.3 Plausibility

The plausibility of posited universals has been a major concern for UNIVAUTO. Universals are inductive generalizations from an observed sample to all human languages and as such they need substantial corroboration. The system disposes with two principled mechanisms to this end. The first is the mechanism ensuring statistical plausibility, allowing the user to specify a significance threshold for the system's inferences. It is embodied in two diverse methods, the chi-square test and the permutation test, which can alternatively be used. The second plausibility mechanism pertains to the need for qualitatively different languages to provide support for a hypothetical universal for it to be outputted by the program. The specific measure of "typological diversity" of the supporting languages is chosen by the user of the system, by selecting the minimum number of language families and geographical areas to which the supporting languages must belong. The plausibility of (eventual) criticisms of a human agent's discoveries is even less problematic. Indeed, one can definitely (and not only plausibly) say when a proposition is false relative to a known database, and that is exactly what the system does.

The RECLASS program also essentially relies on the plausibility of its output. It employs assessment of statistical significance to determine the strength of feature value overlaps between languages or the similarities between words in their lexicons.

8.2.4 Intelligibility

With some discovery systems, the user/designer may encounter difficulties in interpreting the program's findings. With other systems, typically those that model previously defined domain-specific problems, and hence systems searching conventional problem spaces, the findings would as a rule be more intelligible. However, intelligibility is a matter of degree and UNIVAUTO seems unique in producing an understandable English text to describe its discoveries.

UNIVAUTO thus both states in English its discoveries (new universals+problems) and the supporting evidence that makes these discoveries plausible/valid. Additionally, it provides a general context into which it places these discoveries (in the introductory parts of the generated text), as well as a summary of the findings (in the conclusion part of the generated text). The readability and self-contained nature of the texts the system normally produces must not be overstated. Some users may prefer to use the output as a "skeleton article" to be subsequently enlarged and edited to fit further stylistic and linguistic needs.

The discoveries of KINSHIP, although involving no verbalization, are also perfectly legible in that the componential models the system generates are stated in the form used by linguists in their expositions. The profiling of classes performed by MPD is similarly understandable, as each profile states the necessary and sufficient conditions for discriminating every linguistic object from all other objects in the processed set. The output of RECLASS is also readily understandable in the sense that it is suggestive of the possible existence of a "historical relationship" (i.e. areal or genealogical relation between languages), but is only hypothetical, and hence requiring much further linguistic interpretation to get more definitive results regarding the plausibility of the computationally generated hypotheses.

8.2.5 Portability

Some discovery systems model general scientific problems (for induction, classification, explanation, etc.) and common meta-scientific problems (for ensuring simplicity, plausibility of output, etc.) and would therefore be readily portable to diverse problems in diverse scientific domains. The systems we described in this book are such systems.

UNIVAUTO mimics the general problem of discovery of (logic) patterns from data, and hence would be applicable not only to language universals discovery, where the objects described in the data are languages, but to any database describing any type of objects, be they linguistic or not. This however applies primarily to its discovery module. The text generation module, as it stands, is less flexible and most probably unportable to a domain outside of universals.

The MPD program handles multiple concept discrimination, which lies at the heart of the idea of linguistic system, a central notion in structural linguistics, and hence the system is applicable to a variety of domains and at all linguistic levels. We illustrated a number of applications, including such outside the realm of linguistics. MINTYP is applicable to any typology, and RECLASS, when operating with feature values, to any dataset, irrespectively of their subject matter.

The general mode of representation of the input to our programs in terms of Object–Feature–Value is another factor enhancing portability. Indeed, a large number of diverse problems may be represented in terms Object–Feature–Value, and some of these may involve in one way or another the processes computerized by our programs.

8.2.6 Insightfulness

The degree of formalization discovery programs require may result in our deeper understanding of the problem at issue, esp. if the sciences from which the problem is originally taken are not sufficiently formalized. Another source of insightfulness may be the outcomes of discovery programs, in the case when they make conspicuous some hitherto overlooked aspects or explicitly generate new problems. Some of these are worth mentioning here.

Exploring the 451 language database UPSID with UNIVAUTO for implicational universals has led to the formulation of a new problem, viz. the generalization of the 146 universals found. A phonological principle was induced to the effect that if Phoneme 1 implies Phoneme 2, then both phonemes share at least one feature and, besides, Phoneme 2 never has more features than Phoneme 1. The formulation of this new problem and its solution was made possible only after the system's discovery of all universals of this type valid in the database. The subsequent (machine-aided) representation of the phonemes in terms of their feature structure and their machine exploration highlighted this statistically significant pattern, holding in 94.5 per cent of all cases.

In the application of the MINTYP system to several linguistic typologies it was consistently found that a set of non-statistical universals existed that described all and only the actually attested types, whereas previous influential authors (Hawkins 1983), although strong proponents of exceptionless universals, had claimed them insufficient to do the job. This consistency of the system's results could not be chance of course, so that it was only a short step finding the explanation. Indeed, a linguistic typology is equivalent to a propositional function, and therefore, as known from propositional logic, for any propositional function there exists a propositional expression that generates it. As a corollary, for any linguistic typology there exists a set of non-statistical universals, describing all and only its attested types.

Additionally, MINTYP found alternative sets of (non-statistical) universals describing the same typology. This gave rise to the problem of choosing among alternatives, which was never recognized before. Since linguists have traditionally given preference to simpler descriptions, the problem shaped to "Find simplest solution(s)". This turned out not to be difficult, using a minimal set cover mechanism, that was previously implemented for our KINSHIP and MPD programs.

After implementing in KINSHIP all adequacy/simplicity criteria, requiring that a componential analysis should use the minimum number of overall features and the minimum number of components in kin term definitions, it was found that a huge number of alternatives were still possible, basically due to multiple kin term definitions, rather than overall features as was previously believed. This problem became conspicuous only after running KINSHIP on various datasets.

Analogously, only after profiling the world languages in terms of their segment inventories, it became obvious that there existed multiple profiles distinguishing many languages, and hence the new problems arose, first, of how to choose among alternatives, and secondly, of trying to find patterns among alternatives in terms of their feature structure.

In general, the major methodological insight emerged that *in an empirical, data-driven discovery there does not exist a unique description or summarization of the data*: many equally simple ones are possible, none of which is "better" than another, and we should further try to cope with the problem of how to choose among these "equally valid" solutions. In some cases, as in KINSHIP and MPD, we implemented intuitive further constraints that managed to reduce potential models to one or just a few. In other cases, as with the discovery of simplest accounts of a typology by MINTYP, all such accounts seemed reasonably "valid", and if we were to choose just one (as it is generally done in human approaches where alternatives usually remain unnoticed), we must admit that this would be done in a purely arbitrary fashion, unless of course we make a choice for some external (e.g. explanatory) reason. Our computational exploration of data brings forcibly to the fore the concerns, felt by structural linguists and wittily expressed by Fred Householder, of whether doing linguistics is finding "God' truth" or just "hocus-pocusing". This issue apparently deserves further attention, which we are not in a position to pay in this book.

Summing up the discussion in this section, our systems possess the capacities that characterize successful discovery systems, and generally can be assessed as doing linguistics well.

8.3 The future

How can we advance the discipline of machine-aided discovery? A natural research program to pursue would comprise the following steps:

1. Find and reduce an important linguistic problem to a task or a sequence of tasks (i.e. problems which are definite, well-formed, and solvable). In case, this cannot be done for the whole problem, find an approximation which is a substantial part of the original problem.
2. Write a computer program that automates the task.
3. Solve the original problem, using the computer program.
4. Go to step 1.

Step (3) is trivial and amounts to just running the program, and step (2) is technical and not addressed to a general linguist, so can be ignored here. The essential step is step (1), viz. how to find and reduce an important linguistic problem to tasks in our sense. We have already seen in Section 8.1 one possible origin of new problems, viz. the solution of other problems. This, however, is not the whole story, as there are other common potential sources.

Thus, first, one can start the search *inside linguistics* by looking for problems whose difficulty resides in the need for their computation, and having found a candidate (and eventually automated it), proceed with looking for analogous problems to the first. This was the process we have employed for most of the research reported in the book; e.g. having isolated and subsequently automated componential analysis of kinship terms, it was not difficult to uncover the analogous problem of distinctive feature analysis in phonology, and further analogies led to the other applications of MPD I have described in the book.

And, secondly, one can start the search *outside of linguistics*, from an already automated (or automatable) task, and ask: What linguistic problem(s) correspond(s) to this task or computer program? A well-known example following this route of reasoning is the transfer of biological phylogenetic programs to the linguistic problem of genetic language classification; another common example is the use of publicly available statistical packages for exploring different properties of language. Artificial Intelligence, and more specifically machine learning, also offer useful hints when one tries to extend the scope of application of some of the programs implemented in these fields.

The discovery of worthy linguistic problems and their logical analysis in order to reduce them to definite and automatable tasks is the most highly creative part of the above research program, as this process requires a number of traits on the part of the researcher, such as sound linguistic knowledge, imagination and logical thinking (as well as of course programming skills), which are rarely combined in a single person. We should draw the conclusion therefore that collaborative research in the field of machine-aided linguistic discovery, comprising scientists with different background, is highly commendable, practice which we actually observe in most current research in this direction. It is also advisable to build programs specially designed to generate research problems. We already saw that the RECLASS program, which was designed to detect potential problems in language classification, led to the quite unexpected hypothesis of the existence of a link between the geographically distant Kaingang and Oceanic language families.

The time seems ripe and we could expect major developments in the field, in which modern linguists (and other scientists, more generally) would be equipped with computational methods for "standard" scientific activities such as inducing laws, making classifications, discriminations, explanations, etc. Earlier scholars like Francis Bacon and Descartes believed that with the appropriate methods at hand even the most mediocre of us would be capable of solving the most difficult problems. This was a dream that would perhaps always remain a dream. Nevertheless, with the computer as a collaborator in our inquiries, we seem a bit closer to this dream.

Bibliography

Andrews, L. 1865. *A Dictionary of the Hawaiian Language, To which is Appended an English–Hawaiian Vocabulary and a Chronological Table of Remarkable Events.* Honolulu: Henry M. Whitney.

Assiter, A. 1984. Althusser and structuralism. *The British Journal of Sociology* 35: 272–296.

Atkinson, Q. and R. Gray. 2005. Curious parallels and curious connections — phylogenetic thinking in biology and historical Linguistics. *Systematic Biology* 54: 513–526.

Bacon, F. 1960[1620]. *The New Organon and Related Writings.* New York: Liberal Arts Press.

Batagelj, V., D. Kerzic and T. Pisanski. 1992. Automatic clustering of languages. *Computational Linguistics* 18: 339–343.

Bell, A. 1978. Language samples. In J. H. Greenberg (ed.) 1978b, vol. 1, 123–150.

Bender, M. 1969. Chance CVC correspondences in unrelated languages. *Language* 45: 519–531.

Beveridge, W. 1961. *The Art of Scientific Investigation.* London: William Heinemann Ltd. (4th edition)

Biggs, B. 1965. Direct and indirect inheritance in Rotuman. *Lingua* 14: 383–445.

Biggs, B. 1973. The languages of Polynesia. In T. Sebeok (ed.) 1973, vol. 8, 466–505.

Biggs, B. and R. Clark. 2006. *POLLEX: Comparative Polynesian Lexicon* (computer data base). University of Auckland.

Blevins, J. 2007. A long lost sister of Proto–Austronesian? Proto–Ongan, mother of Jarawa and Onge of the Andaman Islands. *Oceanic Linguistics* 46: 154–198.

Bloomfield, L. 1933. *Language.* New York: Holt.

Blust, R. 1995. *Austronesian Comparative Dictionary* (computer files). Manoa: University of Hawaii.

Botha, R. 1981. *The Conduct of Linguistic Inquiry: A Systematic Introduction to the Methodology of Generative Grammar.* The Hague: Mouton Publishers.

Bruner, J., J. Goodnow, and G. Austin. 1956. *A Study of Thinking.* New York: John Wiley.

Buchanan, B. G. and E. Feigenbaum. 1978. DENDRAL and Meta–DENDRAL: their applications dimension. *Artificial Intelligence* 11: 5–24.

Burling, R. 1964. Cognition and componential analysis: God's truth or hocus-pocus? *American Anthropologist* 66: 20–28.

Burnet, J., Lord Monboddo. 1774–1792. *Of the Origin and Progress of Language.* Edinburgh and London. (2nd edition)

Campbell, L. 2004. How to show languages are related: Methods for distant genetic relationship. In B. D. Joseph and R. D. Janda (eds), *The Handbook of Historical Linguistics*, 262–282. Oxford: Blackwell.

Campbell, L., T. Kaufman, and T. C. Smith–Stark. 1986. Mesoamerica as a linguistic area. *Language* 62: 530–570.

Cannon, G. 1968. The correspondence between Monboddo and Sir William Jones. *American Anthropologist* 70: 559–562.

Cannon, G. 1991. Jones's "Sprung from some common source". In S. Lamb and E. Mitchell (eds) 1991, 23–47.

Catford, I. 1977. A mountain of tongues: the languages of the Caucasus. *Annual Review of Anthropology* 6: 283–314.

Cavalli–Sforza, L., A. Menozzi, and A. Piazza. 1994. *The History and Geography of Human Genes.* Princeton, N.J.: Princeton University Press.

Chambers, J. K. and P. Trudgill. 1980. *Dialectology.* Cambridge: Cambridge University Press.

Cherry, C., M. Halle, and R. Jakobson. 1953. Toward the logical description of languages in their phonemic aspects. *Language* 29: 34–47.

Chomsky, N. 1957. *Syntactic Structures.* The Hague: Mouton.

Cloyd, E. L. 1969. Lord Monboddo, Sir William Jones, and Sanskrit. *American Anthropologist* 71: 1134–1135.

Colton, S., A. Bundy, and T. Walsh. 2000. On the notion of interestingness in automated mathematical discovery. *International Journal of Human–Computer Studies* 53: 351–376.

Comrie, B. 1981. *Typology and Universals: Syntax and Morphology.* Chicago: Chicago University Press.

Comrie, B. and G. Corbett (eds). 1993. *The Slavonic Languages.* London and New York: Routledge.

Covington, M. 1996. An algorithm to align words for historical comparison. *Computational Linguistics* 22: 481–496.

Covington, M. 1998. Alignment of multiple languages for historical comparison. *International Conference on Computational Linguistics, COLING98*, Montréal, 275–280.

Cowan, H. 1962. Statistical determination of linguistic relationships. *Studia Linguistica* 16: 57–96.

Croft, W. 1990. *Typology and Universals.* Cambridge: Cambridge University Press.

Crothers, J. 1978. Typology and universals of vowel systems. In J. H. Greenberg (ed.) 1978b, vol. 2, 93–152.

Daelemans, W., P. Berck, and S. Gillis. 1996. Unsupervised discovery of phonological categories through supervised learning of morphological rules. *International Conference on Computational Linguistics, COLING96*, Copenhagen, 95–100.

Dalby, D. 1970. Reflections on the classification of African languages, with special reference to the work of Sigismund Wilhelm Koelle and Malcolm Guthrie. *African Language Studies* 11: 147–171.

Dale, R., H. Moisl, and H. Somers (eds). 2000. *Handbook of Natural Language Processing*. New York: Marcel Dekker.

Derbyshire, D. and G. Pullum. 1981. Object–initial languages. *International Journal of American Linguistics* 47: 192–214.

Descartes, R. 1998[1619–1628]. *Regulae ad directionem ingenii/Rules for the Direction of the Natural Intelligence*. Rodopi Bv Editions. [Text, translated and commentated by G.Heffernan.]

Dixon R. M. W. 1994. *Ergativity*. Cambridge: Cambridge University Press.

Dobson, A. 1969. Lexicostatistical grouping. *Anthropological Linguistics* 11: 216–221.

Dolgopolski, A. 1986. A probabilistic hypothesis concerning the oldest relationships among the language families in northern Eurasia. In V. Shevoroshkin and T. Markey (eds), *Typology, Relationships and Time: A Collection of Papers on Language Change and Relationship*, 28–50. Ann Arbor: Karoma. (Russian original, 1964)

Dougherty, R. 1973. A survey of linguistic methods and arguments. *Foundations of Language* 10: 423–490.

Dryer, M. S. 1989. Large linguistic areas and language sampling. *Studies in Language* 13: 257–292.

Dryer, M. S. 1991. SVO languages and the OV:VO typology. *Journal of Linguistics* 27: 443–482.

Dryer, M. S. 1992. The Greenbergian word order correlations. *Language* 68: 81–138.

Dryer, M. S. 1995. Word order typology. In J. Jacobs, A. von Stechow, W. Sternefeld, and T. Vennemann (eds), *Syntax: An International Handbook of Contemporary Research*, 1050–1065. Berlin and New York: Walter de Gruyter.

Dryer, M. S. 1997. Why statistical universals are better than absolute universals. In K. Singer, R. Eggert, and G. Anderson (eds), *CLS 33: Papers from the Panels on Linguistic Ideologies in Contact, Universal Grammar, Parameters and Typology, The Perception of Speech and other Acoustic Signals*, 123–145. Chicago: The Chicago Linguistic Society.

Dryer, M. S. 2003. Significant and non–significant implicational universals. *Linguistic Typology* 7: 108–128.

Dunn, M., A. Terril, G. Reesink, R. A. Foley, and S. C. Levinson. 2005. Structural phylogenetics and the reconstruction of ancient language history. *Science* 309: 2072–2075.

Dyen, I., J. B. Kruskal, and P. Black. 1992. An Indoeuropean classification: a lexicostatistical experiment. *Trans. Am. Phil. Soc.* 82: 1–132.

Embleton, S. 1986. *Statistics in Historical Linguistics.* Bochum: Brockmeyer.

Embleton, S. 1991. Mathematical methods of genetic classification. In Lamb, S. and E. Mitchell (eds) 1991, 365–403.

Epling, P. J., J. Kirk, and J. P. Boyd. 1973. Genetic relations of Polynesian sibling terminologies. *American Anthropologist* 75: 1596–1625.

Evans, B. and M. Ross. 2001. The history of Proto–Oceanic **ma–. Oceanic Linguistics* 40: 269–290.

Ferguson, C. A. 1966. Assumptions about nasals: A sample study in phonological universals. In J. H. Greenberg (ed.) 1966c, 53–60.

Ferguson, C. A. 1974. Universals of nasality. *Working Papers on Languages Universals* 14: 1–16.

Ferguson, C. 1978. Historical background of universals research. In J. H. Greenberg (ed.) 1978b, 7–32.

Gakran, N. 2005. *Aspectos morfossintáticos da língua Laklãnõ (Xokléng).* Unicamp.

Gălăbov, I. 1986. Za proizhoda na grupa nazvanija ot bălgarskata narodna terminologija. *Izbrani trudove po ezikoznanie*, 472–483. Sofia: Nauka i izkustvo.

Gamkrelidze, T. V. 1978. On the correlation of stops and fricatives in a phonological system. In J. H. Greenberg (ed.) 1978b, vol. 2, 9–46.

Gelernter, H. 1983[1959]. Realization of a geometry–theorem proving machine. In J. Siekmann and G. Wrightson (eds), *Automation of Reasoning. Classical Papers on Computational Logic*, 99–122. Berlin/Heidelberg: Springer Verlag. (Originally published in 1959)

Gensch, H. 1908. Wörterverzeichnis der Bugres von Santa Catharina. *Zeitschrift für Ethnologie* 40: 744–759.

Gerov, N. 1897. *Rečnik na bălgarskii ezik*, vol. 2. Plovdiv.

Giere, R. (ed.). 1992. *Cognitive Models of Science. Minnesota Studies in the Philosophy of Science*, v. XV, Minneapolis: University of Minnesota Press.

Gleason, H. A. 1959. Counting and calculating for historical reconstruction. *Anthropological Linguistics* 1: 22–32.

Good, P. 1994. *Permutation Tests.* New York: Springer Verlag.

Goodenough, W. H. 1956. Componential analysis and the study of meaning. *Language* 32: 195–216.

Goodenough, W. H. 1964. Componential analysis of Könkämä Lapp kinship terminology. In W. H. Goodenough (ed.), *Explorations in Cultural Anthropology*, 221–238. New York: McGraw–Hill.

Goodenough, W. H. 1965. Yankee kinship terminology: a problem in componential analysis. In E. A. Hammel (ed.) 1965, 259–287.

Goodenough, W. H. 1967. Componential analysis. *Science* 156: 1203–1209.

Gordon, R. G., Jr. (ed.). 2005. *Ethnologue: Languages of the World.* Dallas, Tex.: SIL International. (15th edition)

Greenberg, J. H. 1949. The logical analysis of kinship. *Philosophy of Science* 16: 58–94.

Greenberg, J. H. 1954. A quantitative approach to the morphological typology of language. In R. F. Spencer (ed.), *Method and Perspective in Anthropology*, 192–220. Minneapolis: University of Minnesota Press.

Greenberg, J. H. 1959. Africa as a linguistic area. In W. R. Bascom and M. J. Herskovitz (eds), *Continuity and Change in African Cultures*, 15–27. Chicago: Chicago University Press.

Greenberg, J. H. 1963. *The Languages of Africa*. (Indiana University Research Center in Anthropology, Folklore, and Linguistics Publication 25; *International Journal of American Linguistics* 29: 1, Part II). Bloomington: Indiana University.

Greenberg, J. H. 1966a. Some universals of grammar with particular reference to the order of meaningful elements. In J. H. Greenberg (ed.) 1966c, 73–113.

Greenberg, J. H. 1966b. *Language Universals (with Special Reference to Feature Hierarchies)*. The Hague: Mouton & Co.

Greenberg, J. H. (ed.). 1966c. *Universals of Languages*. Cambridge, MA: MIT Press.

Greenberg, J. H. 1973. The typological method. In T. Sebeok (ed.) 1973, vol. 11, 149–194.

Greenberg, J. H. 1978a. Typology and cross–linguistic generalizations. In J. H. Greenberg (ed.) 1978b, vol. 1, 33–60.

Greenberg, J. H. (ed). 1978b. *Universals of Human Language*, vols. 1–4. Stanford: Stanford University Press.

Greenberg, J. H. 1980. Universals of kinship terminology. In J. Maquet (ed.), *On Linguistic Anthropology: Essays in Honor of Harry Hoijer*, 9–32. Malibu: Udena Publications.

Greenberg, J. H. 1984. Some areal characteristics of African languages. In I. Dihoff (ed.), *Current Approaches in African Linguistics*, 3–21. Dordrecht: Foris.

Greenberg, J. H. 1994. The influence of *WORD* and the Linguistic Circle of New York on my intellectual development. *Word* 45: 19–25.

Gregersen, E. A. 1972. Kongo–Saharan. *Journal of African Languages* 11: 69–89.

Guy, J. 1994. An Algorithms for identifying cognates in bilingual wordlists and its applicability to machine translation. *Journal of Quantitative Linguistics* 1: 35–42.

Hadamard, J. 1949. *Psychology of Invention in the Mathematical Field*. Princeton: Princeton University Press.

Halhed, N. 1776. *A Code of Gentoo Laws, or Ordinations of the Pundits*. London.

Hammel, E. A. (ed.). 1965. *Formal Semantic Analysis. American Anthropologist* 67, Part Two, Special Publication.

Hanson, N. 1958. *Patterns of Discovery*. Cambridge: Cambridge University Press.

Haspelmath, M., M. S. Dryer, D. Gil, and B. Comrie (eds). 2005. *The World Atlas of Language Structures*. (Book with interactive CD-ROM) Oxford: Oxford University Press. Available online at http://wals.info.

Hawkins, J. 1983. *Word Order Universals*. New York: Academic Press.

Hempel, C. 1965. *Aspects of Scientific Explanation*. New York: The Free Press.

Henderson, E. A. J. 1965. The topography of certain phonetic and morphological characteristics of South East Asian languages. *Lingua* 15: 400–434.

Henrici, A. 1973. Numerical classification of Bantu languages. *African Language Studies* 14: 82–104.

Henry, J. 1935. A Kaingang text. *International Journal of American Linguistics* 8: 172–218.

Henry, J. 1948. The Kaingang language. *International Journal of American Linguistics* 14: 194–204.

Hewson, J. 1974. Comparative reconstruction on the computer. In J. M. Anderson and C. Jones (eds), *Proceedings of the 1st International Conference on Historical Linguistics*, 191–197. Amsterdam: North Holland.

Hewson, J. 1989. Computer–aided research in comparative and historical linguistics. In I. Bátori, W. Lenders, and W. Putschke (eds), *Computational Linguistics "An International Handbook on Computer Oriented Language Research and Applications"*, 576–580. Berlin: Walter de Gruyter.

Hjelmslev, L. 1958. Dans quelle mesure les significations des mots peuvent–elles être considérées comme formant une structure? *Proceedings of the 8th International Congress of Linguists*, Oslo, 636–654.

Hockett, C. F. 1965. Sound change. *Language* 41: 185–204.

Hockett, C. F. 1966. The problem of universals in language. In J. H. Greenberg (ed.) 1966c, 1–29.

Holman, E., S. Wichmann, C. Brown, V. Velupillai, A. Müller, and D. Bakker. 2008. Explorations in automated language classification. *Folia Linguistica* 42: 331–354.

Holton, G. 1979. Einstein's model of construction of scientific theory. In P. Aichelburg and R. Sexl (eds), *Albert Einstein. His Influence on Physics, Philosophy and Politics*. Braunschweig/Wiesbaden: Vieweg.

Howard, I. 1971. On several concepts of universals. *Working Papers in Linguistics* 3–4: 243–248. Manoa: University of Hawaii.

Hurford, J. 1977. The significance of linguistic generalizations. *Language* 53: 574–620.

Hymes, D. 1964. Discussion of Burling's paper ("Cognition and componential analysis: God's truth or hocus-pocus?"). *American Anthropologist* 66: 116–119.

Jakobson, R. 1941. *Kindersprache, Aphasie, und allgemeine Lautgesetze.* Uppsala: Almqvist & Wilksell.

Jones, Sir William. 1807. *The Works of Sir William Jones*, vols. 1–13. London: Stockdale.

Keenan, E. 1978. The syntax of subject-final languages. In W. P. Lehmann (ed.), *Syntactic Typology*, 267-327. Austin: University of Texas Press.

Kessler, B. 2001. *The Significance of Word Lists.* Stanford: CSLI Publications.

Klamer, M. 2002. Typical features of Austronesian languages in Central/Eastern Indonesia. *Oceanic Linguistics* 41: 363–383.

Klamer, M. 2003. Rejoinder to Malcom Ross's squib. *Oceanic Linguistics* 42: 511–513.

Koerner, E. F. K. 1973. *Ferdinand de Saussure. Origin and Development of his Linguistic Thought in Western Studies of Language.* Brounschweig: Vieweg.

Koertge, N. 1980. Analysis as a method of discovery during the Scientific Revolution. In T. Nickles (ed.) 1980a, 139–157.

Kondrak, G. 2001. Identifying cognates by phonetic and semantic similarity. *The Second Meeting of the North American Chapter of the Association for Computational Linguistics, NAACL*, Pittsburg, 103–110.

Kroeber, A. L. 1909. Classificatory systems of relationship. *Journal of the Royal Anthropological Institute* 39: 77–84.

Kroeber, A. L. and C. D. Chrétien. 1937. Quantitative classification of Indo–European languages. *Language* 13: 83–105.

Kronenfeld, D. B. 1974. Sibling terminology: beyond Nerlove and Romney. *American Ethnologist* 30: 263–267.

Kronenfeld, D. B. 1976. Computer analysis of skewed kinship terminologies. *Language* 52: 891–918.

Kruskal, J. B., I. Dyen, and P. Black. 1973. Some results from the vocabulary method of reconstructing language trees. In I. Dyen (ed.), *Lexicostatistics in Genetic Linguistics*, 30–55. The Hague: Mouton.

Kulkarni, D. and H. Simon. 1988. The processes of scientific discovery: the strategy of experimentation. *Cognitive Science* 12: 139–175.

Labov, W. 1971. Methodology. In W. Dingwall (ed.), *A Survey of Linguistic Science*, 412–97. Maryland: University of Maryland.

Lakatos, I. 1971. *Proofs and Refutations. The Logic of Mathematical Discovery.* Cambridge: Cambridge University Press.

Lamb, S. and E. Mitchell (eds). 1991. *Sprung from Some Common Source: Investigations into the Prehistory of Languages.* Stanford: Stanford University Press.

Langley, P. 1998. The computer-aided discovery of scientific knowledge. *Proceedings of the First International Conference on Discovery Science*, Fukuoka, 25–39. Berlin: Springer.

Langley, P., H. Simon, G. Bradshaw, and J. Zytkow. 1987. *Scientific Discovery: Computational Explorations of the Creative Process*. Cambridge, MA, London, England: The MIT Press.

Laudan, L. 1980. Why was the logic of discovery abandoned? In T. Nickles 1980a (ed.), 173–183.

Laver, J. 1991. *Principles of Phonetics*. Cambridge: Cambridge University Press.

Leech, G. 1970. On the theory and practice of semantic testing. *Lingua* 24: 343–364.

Leech, G. 1974. *Semantics*. Harmondsworth: Pelican.

Lederberg, J. 1965. Signs of life: criterion–system of exobiology. *Nature* 207: 9–13.

Lehmann, W. P. 1967. *Reader in Nineteenth Century Historical Indo–European Linguistics*. Bloomington and London: Indiana University Press.

Li, H. and N. Abe. 1996. Learning dependencies between case frame slots. *International Conference on Computational Linguistics, COLING96*, Copenhagen, 10–15.

Lindblom, B. and Maddieson, I. 1988. Phonetic universals in consonant systems. In L. M. Hyman and C. N. Li (eds), *Language, Speech and Mind: Studies in Honor of Victoria A. Fromkin*, 62–80. New York: Routledge.

Lindsay, R., B. G. Buchanan, E. Feigenbaum, and J. Lederberg. 1980. *Applications of Artificial Intelligence for Organic Chemistry: The DENDRAL Project*. New York: McGraw Hill.

Lindsay, R., B. G. Buchanan, E. Feigenbaum, and J. Lederberg. 1993. DENDRAL: A Case study of the first expert system for scientific hypothesis formation. *Artificial Intelligence* 61: 209–261.

Lounsbury, F. G. 1956. A semantic analysis of the Pawnee kinship usage. *Language* 32: 158–194.

Lounsbury, F. G. 1964. The structural analysis of kinship semantics. In H. Lunt (ed.), *Proceedings of the 9th International Congress of Linguists*, Cambridge, MA, 1073–1090. The Hague: Mouton.

Lounsbury, F. G. 1965. Another view of the Trobriand kinship categories. In E. A. Hammel (ed.) 1965, 142–185.

Lowe, J. and M. Mazaudon. 1994. The reconstruction engine: a computer implementation of the comparative method. *Computational Linguistics* 20: 381–417.

Lynch, J., M. Ross, and T. Crowley. 2002. *The Oceanic Languages*. Richmond: Curzon Press.

Lyons, J. 1970. *Chomsky*. London: Fontana/Collins.

Lysek, C. 2000. Linguistic evidence suggests point of origin for Na–Dene. *Mammoth Trumpet*, vol. 15 no.1.

MacWhinney, B. 1995. *The CHILDES Project: Tools for Analyzing Talk*. New York: Lawrence Erlbaum.

MacWhinney, B., H. Feldman, K. Sacco, and R. E. Valdés-Pérez. 2000. Online measures of basic language skills in children with early focal brain lesions. *Brain and Language* 71: 400–431.

Maddieson, I. 1984. *Patterns of Sounds*. Cambridge: Cambridge University Press.

Maddieson, I. 1991. Testing the universality of phonological generalizations with a phonetically specified segment database: results and limitations. *Phonetica* 48: 193–206.

Maddieson, I. 1992. Phonemic systems. In W. Bright (Editor–in–Chief), *International Encyclopedia of Linguistics*, vol. 3, 193–194. Oxford: Oxford University Press.

Maddieson, I. 1999. In search of universals. *Proceedings of the 14th International Congress of Phonetic Sciences*, San Francisco, 2521–2528.

Maddieson, I. and K. Precoda. 1991. Updating UPSID. *UCLA Working Papers in Phonetics* 74: 104–114.

Malmkjær, K. (ed.). 1991. *The Linguistics Encyclopedia*. London and New York: Routledge.

Marinov, D. 1892. *Živa starina. Etnografsko (folklorno) izučavane na Vidinsko, Kulsko, Belogradčiško, Lomsko, Berkovsko, Orjahovsko i Vidinsko*. Russe.

Masica, C. 1976. *Defining a Linguistic Area: South Asia*. Chicago: Chicago University Press.

McClave, J. T. and F. H. Dietrich. 1988. *Statistics*. San Francisco: Dellen Publishing Company.

McGregor, W. 1996. Dyadic and polyadic kin terms in Gooniyandi. *Anthropological Linguistics* 38: 216–247.

McMahon, A. and R. McMahon. 2005. *Language Classification by Numbers*. Oxford: Oxford University Press.

Medawar, P. 1967. *The Art of the Soluble*. London: Methuen & Co., Ltd.

Mendelson, E. 1963. *Introduction to Mathematical Logic*. Princeton: D. Van Nostrand Company, Inc.

Mill, J. S. 1879. *A System of Logic Ratiocinative and Inductive*. London: Longmans Green.

Miller, J. 1973. A note on so–called "discovery procedures". *Foundations of Language* 10: 123–139.

Mladenov, S. 1929[1979]. *Geschihte der bulgarischen Sprache*. Berlin und Lepzig: Walter de Gruyter & Co. [translated in Bulgarian by Ivan Duridanov, 1979, *Istorija na bălgarskija ezik*. Sofia: Izdatelstvo na bălgarskata akademija na naukite.]

Murdock, G. P. 1949. *Social Structure*. New York: Macmillan.

Murdock, G. P. 1968. World sampling provinces. *Ethnology* 7: 305–326.

Murdock, G. P. 1970. Kin term patterns and their distribution. *Ethnology* 9: 165–207.

Nartey, J. N. A. 1979. A study in phonemic universals, especially concerning fricatives and stops. *UCLA Working Papers in Phonetics* 46.

Nerlove, S. and K. Romney. 1967. Sibling terminology and cross–sex behavior. *American Anthropologist* 69: 179–187.

Newell, A. and H. Simon. 1972. *Human Problem Solving.* Englewood Cliffs, N.J: Prentice Hall.

Nickles, T. (ed.). 1980a. *Scientific Discovery: Logic, and Rationality.* Dordrecht: Reidel.

Nickles, T. (ed.). 1980b. *Scientific Discovery: Case Studies.* Dordrecht: Reidel.

Nogle, L. 1974. *Method and Theory in Semantics and Cognition of Kinship Terminology.* The Hague & Paris: Mouton.

Noricks, J. S. 1987. Testing for cognitive validity: componential analysis and the question of extensions. *American Anthropologist* 89: 424–438.

Oakes, M. 2000. Computer estimation of vocabulary in protolanguage from word lists in four daughter languages. *Journal of Quantitative Linguistics* 7: 233–243.

Oswalt, R. 1970. The detection of remote linguistic relationships. *Computer Studies in the Humanities and Verbal Behavior* 3: 117–129.

Oswalt, R. 1991. A method for assessing distant linguistic relationships. In S. Lamb and E. Mitchell (eds) 1991, 389–404.

Pericliev, V. 1987. Are all sentences with constructional homonymity ambiguous? *Proceedings of the 14th International Congress of Linguists,* Berlin, 1032–1034.

Pericliev, V. 1990. On heuristic procedures in linguistics. *Studia Linguistica* 43: 59–69.

Pericliev, V. 1995. Empirical discovery in linguistics. *Working Notes of the Spring Symposium on Systematic Methods of Scientific Discovery.* Palo Alto, AAAI Technical Reports, 68–73.

Pericliev, V. 1999a. Further implicational universals in Greenberg's data (a computer–generated article). *Contrastive Linguistics* 24: 40–51.

Pericliev, V. 1999b. The prospects for machine discovery in linguistics. *Foundations of Science* 4: 463–482.

Pericliev, V. 2000. More statistical implicational universals in Greenberg's data (another computer–generated article). *Contrastive Linguistics* 25: 115–125.

Pericliev, V. 2002. Economy in formulating typological generalizations. *Linguistic Typology* 6: 49–68.

Pericliev, V. 2003. An Appraisal of UNIVAUTO – The first discovery program to generate a scientific article. *Proceedings of the 6th International Conference on Discovery Science,* Sapporo, 434–441. Lecture Notes in Artificial Intelligence. Berlin and New York: Springer.

Pericliev, V. 2004a. There is no correlation between the size of a community speaking a language and the size of the phonological inventory of that language. *Linguistic Typology* 8: 376–383.

Pericliev, V. 2004b. Universals, their violation and the notion of phonologically peculiar languages. *Journal of Universal Language* 5: 1–28.

Pericliev, V. 2007. The Kaingang (Brazil) seem linguistically related to Oceanic populations. *Journal of Universal Language* 8: 39–59.

Pericliev, V. 2008. Implicational phonological universals. *Folia Linguistica* 42: 195–225.

Pericliev, V. 2009. Kaingang and Austronesian — Similarities between geographically distant languages. In *Current Issues in Unity and Diversity of Languages, Collection of the Papers Selected from the CIL 18*, Seoul. Seoul: Linguistic Society of Korea.

Pericliev, V. and R. E. Valdés-Pérez. 1998a. Automatic componential analysis of kinship semantics with a proposed structural solution to the problem of multiple models. *Anthropological Linguistics* 40: 272–317.

Pericliev, V. and R. E. Valdés-Pérez. 1998b. A discovery system for componential analysis of kinship terminologies. In B. Caron (ed.), *Actes du 16è Congrès International des Linguistes* (Paris 20–25 juillet 1997). Oxford: Elsevier Sciences.

Poincaré, H. 1956. Mathematical creation. In J. Newman (ed.), *The World of Mathematics*, vols. 1–4, 2041–50. New York: Simon and Schuster.

Polya, G. 1957. *How To Solve It? A New Aspect of Mathematical Method*. New York: Doubleday Anchor Books, Doubleday & Company, Inc. (2nd edition)

Polya, G. 1965. *Mathematical Discovery*, vols. 1–2. New York and London: John Wiley and Sons.

Popper, K. 1961. *The Logic of Scientific Discovery*. New York: Science Editions.

Pukui, M. and S. Erbert. 1986. *Hawaiian–English, English–Hawaiian dictionary*. Hononulu: University of Hawaii Press.

Quine, W. V. O. 1965. *Mathematical Logic*. Cambridge: Harvard University Press.

Quinlan, J. R. 1986. Induction of decision trees. *Machine Learning* 1: 81–106.

Quinlan, J. R. 1993. *C4.5: Programs for Machine Learning*. San Francisco: Morgan Kaufmann.

Rea, J. 1973. The Romance data of the pilot studies for glottochronology. In T. Sebeok (ed.) 1973, vol. 11, 355–367.

Reiter, E., C. Mellish & J. Levine (1995). Automatic generation of technical documentation. *Applied Artificial Intelligence* 9: 259-287.

Ribeiro, D. M., M. S. Figueiredo, F. F. Costa, and M. F. Sonati. 2003. Haplotypes of α–globin gene regulatory element in two Brazilian native populations. *American Journal of Physical Anthropology* 121: 58–62.

Ringe, D., T. Warnow, A. Taylor, A. Michailov, and L. Levison. 1997. Computational cladistics and the position of Tocharian. In V. Mair (ed.), *The Bronze Age and Early Iron Age Peoples of Eastern Central Asia*, 391–414. Washington, DC: Institute for the Study of Man.

Ringe, D., T. Warnow, and A. Taylor. 2002. Indo–European and computational cladistics. *Trans. Phil. Soc.* 100: 59–129.

Robins, R. H. 1967. *A Short History of Linguistics*. London: Longman.

Romney, A. K. and R. G. D'Andrade. 1964. Cognitive aspects of English kin terms. *American Anthropologist* 66: 146–170.

Rose, M. D. and A. K. Romney. 1979. Cognitive pluralism or individual differences: A comparison of alternative models of American English kin terms. *American Ethnologist* 6: 752–762.

Rosenfelder, M. 2002. How likely are chance resemblances between languages. Available at http://www.zompist.com/chance.htm.

Ross, J. 1950. Philological probability problems. *Journal of the Royal Statistical Society, Series B* 12: 19–59.

Ross, M. 2003. Typology and language families: a comment on Klamer's "Typical features of Austronesian languages in Central/Eastern Indonesia". *Oceanic Linguistics* 42: 506–510.

Ruhlen, M. 1987. *A Guide to the World's Languages: Classification*. Stanford, CA: Stanford University Press.

Ruhlen, M. 1998. The origin of the Na–Dene. *Proceedings of the National Academy of Sciences* 95: 13994–6. Washington, DC.

Sampson, G. 1979. What was transformational grammar. *Lingua* 48: 355–378.

Sandfeld, Kr. 1930. Linguistique balkanique: problèmes et résultats. (Collection linguistique publiée par la Société Linguistique de Paris, 31.) Paris: Champion.

Sapir, E. 1921. *Language: An Introduction to the Study of Speech*. New York: Harcourt, Brace and World.

Saussure, F. de. 1996 [1916]. *Course in General Linguistics*. Edited by Charles Bally and Albert Sechehaye with the collaboration of Albert Riedlinger, translated and annotated by Roy Harris. Chicago and La Salle, Illinois: Open Court.

Schneider, D. M. 1965. American kin terms and terms for kinsmen: A Critique of Goodenough's "Componential analysis of Yankee Kinship Terminology". In E. A. Hammel (ed.). 1965, 288–306.

Sebeok, T. (ed.). 1973. *Current Trends in Linguistics*, vols. 1–11. The Hague: Mouton.

Sedlak, P. 1969. Typological considerations of vowel quality systems. *Stanford University Working Papers on Language Universals* 1: 1–40.

Selye, H. 1964. *From Dream to Discovery: On Being a Scientist*. New York: Arno Press, A NewYork Times Company.

Sheffler, H. and F. G. Lounsbury. 1971. *A Study of Structural Semantics: The Siriono Kinship System*. Englewood Cliffs, NJ: Prentice–Hall.

Shrager, P. and P. Langley (eds). 1990. *Computational Models of Scientific Discovery and Theory formation*. San Mateo, CA: Morgan Kaufmann Publishers, Inc.

Simon, H. 1977. *Models of Discovery*. Dordrecht: Reidel.

Stoeva, A. 1972. Njakoi semantični osobenosti pri rodninskite nazvanija. *Bălgariski ezik* 22: 73–76.

Swadesh, M. 1954. Perspectives and problems of Amerindian comparative linguistics. *Word* 10: 306–332.

Tanaka, H. 1996. Decision tree learning algorithm with structured attributes: Application to verbal case frame acquisition. *International Conference on Computational Linguistics, COLING96*, Copenhagen, 943–948.

Teeter, K. 1964. Descriptive linguistics in America: triviality vs. irrelevance. *Word* 20: 197–206.

Thagard, P. 1988. *Computational Philosophy of Science*. Cambridge, MA, London, England: A Bradford Book, the MIT Press.

Tomlin, R. 1986. *Basic Constituent Orders: Functional Principles*. London: Croom Helm.

Tregear, E. R. 1891. *Maori–Polynesian Comparative Dictionary*. Wellington, New Zealand: Lyon and Blair.

Trudgill, P. 2004a. Linguistic and social typology: the Austronesian migrations and phoneme inventories. *Linguistic Typology* 8: 305–320.

Trudgill, P. 2004b. Author's response: On the complexity of simplification. *Linguistic Typology* 8: 384-388.

Urban, G. 1985. Ergativity and accusativity in Shokleng (Gê). *International Journal of American Linguistics* 51: 164–187.

Urban, G. 1986. Semiotic functions of macro–parallelism in the Shokleng origin myth. In J. Sherzer and G. Urban (eds), *Native South American Discourse*, 15–57. Berlin: Mouton de Gruyter.

Valdés-Pérez, R. E. 1994. Conjecturing hidden entities via simplicity and conservation laws: machine discovery in chemistry. *Artificial Intelligence* 65: 247–280.

Valdés-Pérez, R. E. 1995. Generic tasks of scientific discovery. *Working Notes of the Spring Symposium on Systematic Methods of Scientific Discovery*. Palo Alto, AAAI Technical Reports, 23–28.

Valdés-Pérez, R. E. 1999. Principles of human–computer collaboration for knowledge discovery in science. *Artificial Intelligence* 107: 335–346.

Valdés-Pérez, R. E. and V. Pericliev. 1999. Computer enumeration of significant implicational universals of kinship terminology. *Cross–Cultural Research* 33: 162–174.

Valdés-Pérez, R. E., F. Pereira, and V. Pericliev. 2000. Concise, intelligible, and approximate profiling of multiple classes. *International Journal of Human–Computer Studies (Special Issue on Machine Discovery)* 53: 411–436.

Verner, K. 1875. Eine Ausnahme der ersten Lautverschiebung. *Zeitschrift für vergleichende Sprachforschung auf dem Gebieteder Indogermanischen Sprachen* 23.2: 97–130. [English translation in W. P. Lehmann 1967.]

Wallace, A. F. C. 1962. Culture and cognition. *Science* 135: 351–357.

Wallace, A. F. C. 1965. The problem of psychological validity of componential analyses. In E. A. Hammel (ed.) 1965, 231–248.

Wallace, A. F. C. and J. Atkins. 1960. The meaning of kinship terms. *American Anthropologist* 62: 58–80.

Werthheimer, M. 1959. *Productive Thinking.* New York: Harper and Row. (2nd ed.).

Wierzbicka, A. 1991. Kinship semantics: lexical universals as a key to psychological reality. *Anthropological Linguistics* 29: 131–156.

Wierzbicka, A. 1992. *Semantics, Culture and Cognition: Universal Human Concepts in Culture–Specific Configurations.* New York and Oxford: Oxford University Press.

Wiesemann, U. 1972. *Die phonologische und grammatische Struktur der Kaingáng–Sprache.* Janua Linguarum, series practica, 90. The Hague: Mouton.

Wiesemann, U. 1974. Time distinctions in Kaingáng. *Zeitschrift für Ethnologie* 99: 120–30.

Wiesemann, U. 1978. Os dialetos da língua kaingáng e o xokléng. *Arquivos de Anatomia e Antropologia* 3: 197–217.

Wiesemann, U. 1986. The pronoun systems of some Jê and Macro–Jê languages. In U. Wiesemann (ed.), *Pronominal Systems,* 359–380. Tübingen: Gunter Narr.

Wiesemann, U. 2002. *Dicionário Bilingüe Kaingang–Português.* Curitiba, Brazil: Editora Evangélica Esperança.

Williams, H. W. 1957. *A Dictionary of the Maori Language.* Wellington: Government Printer.

Wordick, F. J. 1973. Another view of American kinship. *American Anthropologist* 31: 1234–1256.

Xuang, X. and A. Fielder. 1996. Presenting machine-found proofs. *CADE13, Lecture Notes in Computer Science* 1104: 221–225.

Zeigarnik, A. V., R. E. Valdés–Pérez, and J. Pesenti. 2000. Comparative properties of transition metal catalysts inferred from activation energies of elementary steps of catalytic reactions. *Journal of Physical Chemistry* 104: 997–1008.

Index of subjects and authors

Index of languages

This index includes cited languages in the main body of the text, excluding their occurrence in the list of the 451 languages profiled in terms of their segment inventories, and given on pp. 115–122.

Lightning Source UK Ltd.
Milton Keynes UK
UKOW031510090613

211977UK00001B/30/P